Jefferson Davis: American Patriot

BOOKS BY HUDSON STRODE

THE STORY OF BERMUDA
THE PAGEANT OF CUBA
SOUTH BY THUNDERBIRD
FINLAND FOREVER
TIMELESS MEXICO
NOW IN MEXICO
SWEDEN: MODEL FOR A WORLD
DENMARK IS A LOVELY LAND
IMMORTAL LYRICS: *An Anthology of English Lyrics*
SPRING HARVEST: *An Anthology of Alabama Stories*

Jefferson Davis at 39, just after he became a United States Senator. The portrait was done by the British miniaturist Saunders and is owned by Mr. Davis's grandson Jefferson Hayes-Davis.

# JEFFERSON DAVIS

## AMERICAN PATRIOT

### 1808-1861

—●—

### BY HUDSON STRODE

—●—

Harcourt, Brace and Company

NEW YORK

© COPYRIGHT, 1955, BY
HUDSON STRODE

*All rights reserved, including
the right to reproduce this book
or portions thereof in any form.*

*first edition*

LIBRARY OF CONGRESS CATALOG CARD NUMBER: 55-5322

TYPOGRAPHY BY ROBERT JOSEPHY

PRINTED IN THE UNITED STATES OF AMERICA

To the memory of my mother-in-law
Marielou Armstrong Cory

# CONTENTS

| | | |
|---|---|---|
| Introduction | | ix |
| I | Heritage | 3 |
| II | Boyhood Education | 11 |
| III | A Soldier's Training | 32 |
| IV | Soldier in the Wild North | 50 |
| V | Trouble with Black Hawk | 63 |
| VI | First Love | 78 |
| VII | Marriage and Tragic Loss | 93 |
| VIII | Planter in Retirement | 106 |
| IX | End of Seclusion | 125 |
| X | The Young Congressman | 145 |
| XI | To the War with Mexico | 161 |
| XII | A Hero of Buena Vista | 175 |
| XIII | In the Senate | 194 |
| XIV | Father-in-Law in the White House | 215 |
| XV | Bitter Defeat and Happy Interlude | 230 |
| XVI | Secretary of War | 245 |
| XVII | Accomplishments in the War Office | 260 |
| XVIII | A "Strength and Solace" to President Pierce | 281 |
| XIX | "How Far Are You to Push Us?" | 296 |
| XX | Social Luster and Domestic Cares | 316 |
| XXI | The Democratic Party Splits Asunder | 336 |
| XXII | South Carolina Secedes | 360 |

|       |                           |     |
|-------|---------------------------|-----|
| XXIII | Farewell to the Capital   | 384 |
| XXIV  | The Man and the Hour Meet | 398 |
| XXV   | "If We Succeed"           | 408 |

Acknowledgments 429

Sources and Notes on Sources 436

Index 453

## ILLUSTRATIONS

Jefferson Davis at 39 *frontispiece*

*between pages 124 and 125*

Sarah Knox Taylor at 16

Joseph Emory Davis

Varina Howell at 18

Varina Davis about the time she became
  First Lady of the Confederacy

Jefferson Davis at the time of his second marriage

Jefferson Davis at about 49

# INTRODUCTION

IN THIS work I am hoping to reveal the truth about Jefferson Davis, "the most misunderstood man in history," as he was called by Landon Knight, his Ohio biographer. I have endeavored to combine biography and history in an acceptable synthesis, using care not to let the man become submerged in the milieu in which he lived. By making use of intimate private letters, never before printed, and of contemporary sources as well as public records, I hope to transport the reader to scenes, conditions, and events which made up the everyday life of this man who happens to occupy a unique place in world history. While touching on the interplay of historical forces, I have depicted those special events which serve to throw light on Jefferson Davis himself for, with Carlyle, I believe that this "discovery" should be the aim and endeavor of a biographer.

In my effort to penetrate to the core of the matter, I sought help from the direct descendants. I have been peculiarly fortunate in being given access to the large collection of family letters by Mr. Davis's grandson, Jefferson Hayes-Davis, a banker of Colorado Springs, who has heretofore declined to let anyone see them. Most of these documents had not been read since Mrs. Davis's death in 1906.

It was exciting to be the first to untie the hard knot of an age-soiled white ribbon about a packet, which included the love letters and bore this notation in Varina Davis's hand: "My dear

Husband's letters read for the last time May 26, 1890." It was moving to read a letter from the grief-crushed father to Winnie, the youngest daughter, at school in Germany, relating the death of Jefferson, Jr., the last of his four sons, who died at twenty-one of yellow fever in Memphis in 1878. In the envelope were four pressed miniature chrysanthemums—one red, one white, and two yellow—which the young man was holding when he died and which a kind lady had brought through the quarantine to console the father at Beauvoir.

The man became a real and vital human being as I read very personal letters between husband and wife; letters from Davis to his children, and inimitable, tender notes to his five-year-old grandson; scores of loving letters from sisters and brothers, nieces and nephews; from devoted brothers-in-law, his second father-in-law and mother-in-law; from numerous members of the Zachary Taylor family; from neighboring planters, Negroes and former slaves, fellow Congressmen, foreign ministers, admiring strangers. Certain penciled notes scribbled hurriedly when Davis was Secretary of War under President Franklin Pierce held revealing significance.

I was amazed to find, despite the ravages of war, with sackings and confiscations at Richmond and Brierfield, and numerous moves about two continents, that so many private family letters, besides those salvaged in public libraries and museums, had escaped destruction. The earliest extant letter of Jefferson Davis was written when he was sixteen and at college in Lexington, Kentucky, in August, 1824; the last, just before his death in 1889.

Seeking out other relatives who knew Jefferson Davis when they were children and who had heard their parents and grandparents talk of him, I found them unfailingly co-operative. From Newark, New York, to Pass Christian, Mississippi, they have entrusted precious private papers to me. I can say with profound gratitude that I have received the wholehearted assistance of the family.

# INTRODUCTION

My first desire to study the life of Jefferson Davis was conceived on an afternoon in late February, 1942. Sigrid Undset, the Norwegian novelist, was staying with us, and my wife and I took her to pay her respects to the three elderly sisters of the late General William Crawford Gorgas; they lived in one of the two houses on the University of Alabama campus that had escaped the torch of the invading Federals in 1864. When I presented the Nobel Prize winner to the white-haired ladies in the reception hall, she made a deep curtsy to each, for she had great esteem for their physician brother, who had routed yellow fever and made possible the Panama Canal.

During tea, the sisters pressed Madame Undset for details of her dramatic flight from her home at Lillehammer when, pursued by the Germans, she escaped over the snow-covered mountains into Sweden. Before she had quite finished, Miss Mamie, the eldest, interrupted, "I trust you buried your silver before you fled," and proudly brought forth some lovely bowls that had been saved when her family escaped from Richmond in 1865.

Miss Maria showed the visitor a lock of John C. Calhoun's hair framed under glass, a gift to their mother. Mrs. Palfrey, the most charming of the ladies, laid in her lap a large packet of letters from Jefferson Davis—some to their father, General Josias Gorgas, his chief of ordnance, later president of the University of Alabama, and as many to their mother. Madame Undset glanced thoughtfully at a few of the more intimate ones, commenting on their tender and affectionate endings. She had made a considerable study of the chief personalities of the War between the States, partly because her elder son Anders, whom the Nazis killed, revered Robert E. Lee as his favorite hero in all history.

"Of course," Sigrid Undset said, "in Europe we believe that the Southern states had every constitutional right to secede. But what has always seemed incomprehensible to me is the grudging attitude of the South, as well as the North, to Jefferson Davis. Lee's mistakes are completely forgiven; he is rightly glorified by both sides. But historians and biographers seem prone to magnify Davis's faults. Could anyone else have done so well, or held the

Confederacy together so long with so little? For all of his great generalship, I don't think Lee could have been successful as president of the Confederacy. Could Lincoln, with all his shrewdness? Why is Jefferson Davis not given his due?"

None of us had a wholly satisfying answer. I emphasized the commonly accepted theory that in its misery of defeat the South needed a scapegoat.

"But what was Jefferson Davis, the man, really like?" Madame Undset asked.

"He was noble!" the gentle Mrs. Palfrey spoke up with conviction. "A man of impeccable integrity, with a truly warm and generous heart."

"He was a splendid soldier," Miss Mamie affirmed, "though our domineering father sometimes got out of patience with him. In light of later facts, however, he admitted that most of the criticisms of Mr. Davis, including his own, had been unjust. His admiration increased with the postwar years, as did his affection. My mother always loved Mr. Davis."

"Then—why?" Madame Undset's question remained unanswered.

I promised her and myself to look further into the matter.

During the following years, however, being engaged in writing other books, I did only desultory reading on the subject. Though my wife's mother had spent four decades of her life in an effort to preserve and maintain the first White House of the Confederacy in Montgomery as a memorial to President Davis, whom she admired above all Southern figures, I had never been sufficiently warmed by the man's personality to write about him. A fortnight after my mother-in-law's death on June 3, 1951—coincidentally Jefferson Davis's birthday—on going through her scrapbooks and a suitcase of letters and various odds and ends about him, I came across a yellowed contemporary clipping giving a vivid account of his ironing at Fortress Monroe, where he was thrown to the stone floor and held down by four soldiers while a blacksmith riveted heavy shackles on his ankles. My indignation was aroused, and at that moment—at a quarter to four on the afternoon of June 17—I determined to seek the whole truth about the man and write his life in the light of what I discovered.

In my first researches, I ran across a significant review in *The Journal of Negro History* for April, 1924. (The work discussed was Dunbar Rowland's many-volumed *Jefferson Davis, Constitutionalist*.) I was struck by the similarity between the reviewer's query and Sigrid Undset's. "On reading these works," he wrote, "the historian will ask himself the question as to why the Southerners themselves have begrudgingly revered the memory of Jefferson Davis while making of Lee the hero of the South. . . . It is known, too, that Jefferson Davis came as near to representing the best in the South as did Robert E. Lee. Davis was an aristocrat of the benevolent order, considerate of the interests of the masses, and kind to his slaves."

When I went to Richmond to consult with the historian Douglas Southall Freeman, I was warned of the difficulties of the job and the prejudice a book on Jefferson Davis might encounter. With Lee, he said, he had had to face no such obstacle, for the North had "come to accept" General Lee as a national hero. Dr. Freeman gave me sage advice: "I hope you will approach your subject with complete detachment of spirit and without preconception. I need not tell you that we Southerners gain our audience in direct proportion to the fairness of our approach. They put up their guard against extreme statements; they cannot resist detachment." After my return home, he repeated and underscored, in a warm, generous note of encouragement, his caution against preconception: "I have the utmost faith in you and the enterprise you are pursuing, and I know you will never proceed from a thesis to a confirmation of it, but rather frame the thesis from the evidence."

I could say to him with complete honesty that I had no thesis. I was intent on discerning the mind and the heart of Jefferson Davis. The ax of truth and fair dealing was the only one I had to grind.

Of the prejudice Dr. Freeman mentioned, or rather apathy, I soon found aplenty among my Southern, as well as Northern, friends. Scarcely one out of a hundred among the countless persons I questioned had read a biography of Jefferson Davis, although there have been a baker's dozen of them, the last in 1937.

On finishing a second draft of the manuscript dealing with Mr. Davis's career up to secession, I sent it for critical comment to an erudite Swedish-born friend, a Harvard honor graduate and former director of the American-Swedish News Exchange, a man whose judgment I greatly value. "I am ashamed to tell you," he wrote, "that both my New England wife, who went to Smith, and I admitted this morning that so far all we had known about Jefferson Davis was that according to the war song, he was to be hanged to a sour apple tree.

"At the end of the week we had a call from some new neighbors, a couple who were both born in Massachusetts. When I told them I had been reading about Jefferson Davis for the first time in my life, the husband, who is an omnivorous reader, said, 'Didn't he have a bad record even before the rebellion?' Which, I fear, is a fairly typical impression, if any. Illogical as it seems now, I had been brought up to think that since the South was defeated, its leaders were not as able or as worthy of study and respect as those of the North. It must have been in the atmosphere I absorbed when I came to this country as a youth in 1900. I had always had a notion that there was something about Mr. Davis that was not right to talk about—only fit for discreet silence. I mention this to show what prejudice you have to overcome. The time is ripe for an eye-opener on Jefferson Davis. You have a tremendous opportunity to set the record straight. I think the American public will be relieved to read it."

Among the first I encountered who seemed to have some conception of the real Jefferson Davis was Raymond Massey, the noted portrayer of Abraham Lincoln. One night after a dramatic reading of *John Brown's Body* at the University of Alabama, I sat with him at a buffet supper at the president's mansion. When I told him that I was working on a biography of Jefferson Davis, he exclaimed, "My word! You really have undertaken something! A life of Lincoln is comparatively easy, for Lincoln was always an old man. But Davis was once young, handsome, dashing, even gay." I was surprised at his comment on Mr. Lincoln, but glad that one among thousands was aware of the brighter side of Mr. Davis's personality.

For many decades historians have been anatomizing Jefferson Davis to discover the cause of the Confederacy's death. As if some weakness, lack, or temperamental disproportion in one human being was more responsible for the debacle than the mighty odds favoring the opponents. While a biographer like Richmond's E. A. Pollard wrote in calculated malice, others, awed by the shadow of the Lincoln apotheosis, have felt impelled to damn Davis with faintest praise. It seems odd that two Northern biographers have in a certain measure had the most perceptive understanding of Mr. Davis's character: General Morris Schaff of Massachusetts and Landon Knight of Akron, Ohio.

In the introduction to his short biography a half-century ago, Mr. Knight wrote: "For four years Jefferson Davis was the central and most conspicuous figure in the greatest revolution of history. Prior to that time no statesman of his day left a deeper or more permanent impress upon legislation. His achievements alone as Secretary of War entitle him to rank as a benefactor of his country. But notwithstanding all this . . . of the living and of the dead, irrespective of whether they wore the blue or the gray, history has, with one exception, delivered . . . the verdict by which posterity will abide. The one exception is Jefferson Davis."

A general impression of Jefferson Davis—for those who hold any clear impression at all—still seems to be that though he was a man of fearless courage and integrity, which his bitterest enemies concede, he was not only a faulty politician, but a cold human being and an irascible, driven leader, who lacked the ability to steer the Confederacy to success. Discovering for myself the real Jefferson Davis, whom I too had once thought an austere doctrinaire, proved to be a stirring experience. I found him to be a warmhearted man who loved deeply, but one whose emotions were generally held in that composure and reserve which was a part, no doubt, of the pride of both his inheritance and training.

Though courage, probity, endurance, and inflexible pride were Davis family traits, great sympathy for the mistreated was one of his dominant characteristics. Jefferson Davis, I learned, understood how to "remember and respect the heart"; this was an instinct and a clarifying motive force throughout his life. It was because he had this master key in his hand that he could go anywhere, speak frankly, and be warmly received—among the Indians of Wisconsin Territory, into Maine, even into Faneuil Hall among Boston Abolitionists.

Great warmth of heart was a quality I had been surprised to discover—from relatives, from his own letters, from those of numerous Northern friends. Anna Farrar Goldsborough, who was "blood-kin" to Mrs. Davis, as well as a great-grandniece of Jefferson Davis, wrote me: "The memory is deep of the morning he called me to help him with his boots—he pulling on one strap, I on the other. The gentle pat of thanks on my small shoulder might have been an accolade from royal hands. . . . In my immediate family, which included members of her own blood, Aunt Varina was neither as loved nor as admired as Uncle Jeff, who was a hero, perhaps saint, in the eyes of those who venerated as well as adored him. He had the dimensions of a tragic figure, lonely, proud, noble in his suffering; in his unbending acceptance of defeat his was the silence of the martyr, the quiet endurance of fate by the stoic. My lawyer father, a stern, dominant man, kinsman to Aunt Varina, worshipped Uncle Jeff, whom he found to be the most noble man he ever knew."

"The strangest thing to me," writes Shelby Foote, who for years has been working on a history of the War between the States, "is how human and warm Davis turns out to be. . . . My admiration for him is virtually unbounded." In so many books, discounted or entirely passed over is the glowing testimony of President Franklin Pierce, Zachary Taylor, Iowa's General George

W. Jones, Boston's Caleb Cushing, Albert Sidney Johnston, Judah P. Benjamin, Mrs. Chestnut, and a host of other contemporaries. In *Destruction and Reconstruction,* which Henry Steele Commager, in his invaluable compilation *The Blue and the Gray,* pronounced "one of the most enchanting of all Civil War books," Lieutenant General Richard Taylor, only son of Zachary, gives such a vivid, heartfelt impression of Mr. Davis's amiability that one wonders how even a prejudiced historian could ignore it. In a single paragraph on page 24 the General speaks of his "affectionate reception" by the President, of Davis's "abundant kindness," his soothing of the feelings of certain disgruntled officers with "tenderness and delicacy of touch." "No wonder," Richard Taylor wrote, "that all who enjoy the friendship of Jefferson Davis love him as Jonathan did David."

Two days after I had finished this volume a stranger called on me, introducing himself as the Reverend Randolph Blackford, a Virginia-born Episcopal clergyman, now living in Talladega, Alabama. He told me that he had heard I was writing a life of Jefferson Davis and that since his parents had known him intimately, he wondered if he could be helpful. One of the visitor's great-grandfathers was James Maury Mason, Confederate emissary to England. His father, William Blackford, was for over three decades principal of the Episcopal High School at Alexandria. During his presidency Mr. Davis had often visited the Blackfords in Richmond and also after his release from Fortress Monroe. In his old age he had stayed with them at Alexandria and, under a campus tree, had made a speech to the assembled schoolboys. I asked the Reverend Blackford to give me in a word or a phrase the chief quality of the man, as he had gathered it from his parents and grandparents. With hardly a sign of reflection came the answer: "They always said he was such a lovable man."

When I asked the clergyman what his family considered an outstanding characteristic of Mr. Davis besides his "lovableness," he replied, "They said he always had a keen sense of humor."

"What in their opinion were his chief faults?"

"If there were faults, my family never mentioned one. My

father used to tell us boys at school, 'Mr. Davis was one of God's noblemen. Usually gentlemen are bred, but occasionally God himself makes a gentleman.' "

These flattering, second-hand opinions of a misunderstood man, so often maligned, did not in any sense affect what I had written. For they came, as I have said, after this volume was completed, and they have not resulted in any alteration of the text.

John Quincy Adams once spoke of Calhoun as "the most nationally-minded man in America." This expression might once have been used about Jefferson Davis, too, for as John Temple Graves recently wrote, "Like Calhoun, Davis was famously nation-minded before he was brought home by the centripetal force of Southern regional circumstances." Calhoun's brilliant young biographer Margaret Coit tells us that Calhoun believed "that the good of democracy was not equality but equity, not to press men down into a common mold, but to give them release to develop to the fullest limits of their natures." This was precisely the belief of Jefferson Davis, who received Calhoun's mantle of leadership. And, like Calhoun, he struggled to save the Union and its Federal principles as much as he tried to save the South.

Few Northerners understand that the South considered the withdrawal in 1861 analogous to that of 1776, except that the struggle for Southern independence was in no sense a rebellion, since by the Constitution its special form of government was a compact of states wherein each state reserved the right to secede from that compact whenever she felt her rights sufficiently infringed upon.

Jefferson Davis, the reluctant secessionist, explained his view of the causes of withdrawal thus: "It was not the passage of the 'Personal Liberty Laws,' it was not the circulation of incendiary documents, it was not the raid of John Brown, it was not the operation of unjust and unequal tariff laws that constituted the intolerable grievance. It was the systematic and persistent struggle to deprive the Southern States of equality in the Union, and generally to discriminate against the interests of their people, culminating in their exclusion from the Territories, the common property of the States, as well as by the infraction of their compact to promote domestic tranquility." And again in a succinct sentence he sums up the motive of the Southern people: "It was to escape from injury and strife within the Union; to find prosperity and peace out of it."

While Jefferson Davis has often been accused of a "lack of intellectual foresight," even by some admirers, up to 1861 there is no evidence in his career of such a flaw. For over a decade before secession he had urged the Southern states to industrialize, to become more self-sufficient, not merely because of the possible dread exigency of a separation, but for the health of Southern economy. Leaders like Robert Barnwell Rhett might offer to drink all the blood that would be shed as a result of secession, but never once did Jefferson Davis express conviction that the North would not coerce the South. Again and again, however, he expressed the *hope* that the North would abide by the Constitution and leave the South in peace. He believed, and openly affirmed in 1861, that the best way to forestall Northern invasion was to prepare as strong a defense as time, limited resources, and inferior numbers would permit. He felt that if the South exhibited enough resolution to arm itself against coercion, Northern public opinion might forestall a war, regardless of the attitude of the incoming Federal administration.

Partly because of the wealth of new material at my disposal, I have been impelled to divide this biography into two parts: *Jefferson Davis: American Patriot* (1808-1861) and *Jefferson Davis: Confederate President* (1861-1889). The first is devoted to Mr. Davis's early life and his career as an American patriot.

He came of patriot stock; his father had fought in the Revolutionary War, three older brothers had risked their lives in the War of 1812. Up to 1861 few indeed had taken more dynamic interest in the welfare and destiny of the United States than Jefferson Davis. For eleven years, from the age of sixteen to twenty-seven, he had been in the training and service of the

United States Army. On his return to soldiering during the war with Mexico he proved an outstanding hero. In the Senate he served notably as a statesman whose influence helped mold the destiny of his nation. As Secretary of War during Pierce's regime he gained a reputation second to none and at least equal to that of John C. Calhoun. In regard to territorial expansion, the Gadsden Purchase, the building of railroads, the increase in foreign trade, he was ever a forward-looking leader. Up to 1861 Davis's enormous contribution to the vitality of democracy was freely admitted and praised by the entire press. No living man at the time held so gloriously that combined record of conspicuous service on the battlefield and in statesmanship. When he departed from the Senate chamber forever in January, 1861, as Allen Tate said, he left it smaller. "It would never be the same again; he was the last of the Senate giants."

From the outset, both in research and writing, I have borne in mind something Goethe said in *Dichtung und Wahrheit:* "For the main point in biography is to present *the man* in all his relations to his time, and to show to what extent it may have opposed or prospered his development. What view of mankind and the world he has shaped from it, and how far he may himself be an external reflection of its spirit." Beyond this, I have endeavored to portray the man himself, truthfully, precisely, in such a variety of situations and intimate human relationships that he may stand self-revealed, and, I hope, no longer either misunderstood or begrudged. Now, reading over the completed text of volume one, I have the further and particular hope that those who do me the honor to read this book will feel enriched by acquaintance with a historical character as gifted and sensitive, as upright and valiant, as Jefferson Davis.

Hudson Strode

*Cherokee Road*
*Tuscaloosa, Alabama*
*June 3, 1955*

Jefferson Davis: American Patriot

# CHAPTER I

# HERITAGE

ON THE third day of a Kentucky June in 1808, the wife of Samuel Emory Davis presented her husband with a fifth son and tenth child. Although the four older male children had been given Biblical names, Samuel called this last boy Jefferson for the contemporary President of the United States, whom he staunchly admired. Since the eldest son, Joseph, then reading law at nearby Hopkinsville, was twenty-three, it seemed unlikely that Jane Davis would ever bear another child. Perhaps for this reason the baby Jefferson was given Finis for a middle name.

The birth took place in a pleasant four-room house built of logs. It was quite a good house for those pioneer days and peculiarly distinguished from comparable homes because it was the first in the district to have glass windows. In the mid-1790's settlers had come from miles around to gaze upon this luxury, which the Davises had brought all the way from Georgia when they settled in the promising Green River country.

Jefferson Davis's father had reached his eighteenth birthday in the historic year of 1776 when Thomas Jefferson wrote the Declaration of Independence. The Virginian's faith in democracy carried inspiring conviction far down into Samuel's native Georgia. His two half-brothers, Daniel and Isaac Williams, had already gone to the seacoast to offer their services in the cause of freedom. When his widowed mother sent him to take a supply of food and clothing to his older brothers, Samuel remained to fight with the revolutionary forces.

During the War for Independence he served under various commands in both Georgia and South Carolina. After three years' experience, young as he was, he formed his own company, and in December, 1779, helped defend Savannah from the British. At war's end the youthful captain returned to his home near Washington, Georgia, to find that his mother had died and that the house was wrecked. When the authorities gave him a tract of land near Augusta as a reward for his war services, Samuel moved to it and began to make a farm. Later he accepted the position of county clerk, which his education, though rude, enabled him to hold.

Samuel Davis's father Evan had been born in Philadelphia in 1702. By ancestry he was Welsh, Evan's father or grandfather having emigrated with two brothers in the seventeenth century. Exactly when "the three Davis brothers" did reach America or where they first settled is not known, so the identity of Jefferson Davis's great-grandfather has never been established.[1] He is generally presumed to have been John Davis, who first settled in New Castle County, Delaware, and whose brother David Davis became the father of Reverend Samuel Davies, an early president of Princeton.

According to the second most acceptable theory, the three Davis brothers were Sir Jonathan, Captain Dolan, and Nathaneal, who came to America from Kent, England. These three, of Welsh extraction, were reckoned gentlemen and possessed a coat of arms. The eldest, Sir Jonathan, settled in Hanover County, Virginia, where he had a large grant from the crown. The second brother, Captain Dolan, who moved to Philadelphia from St. Mary's, Maryland, is the reputed progenitor of Jefferson Davis.

Though it may never be known whether blue blood ran in Evan Davis's veins, he eventually came to Georgia, traditionally with a group of Welsh-stock Baptists. In middle age he married a widow, Lydia Emory Williams, who had also been born in Phila-

---

[1] See pp. 440-441.

delphia and who had two boys by her former marriage. In 1756, when he was fifty-four, Evan's only son was born and given the name of Samuel Emory after his wife's father. While no record throws light on Samuel's childhood, apparently he was fond of his half-brothers, for later he named a son of his own for Isaac, the younger, as he named his first daughter for his only sister Anna. The fact that Samuel was only nine when his father died doubtless accounts for his lack of detailed knowledge about his ancestors. But Evan had impressed it upon his son that he held equity in inherited property in the suburbs of Philadelphia, which he should one day claim.

During his revolutionary soldiering in South Carolina, Samuel had fallen in love with a bonny girl of Scotch-Irish ancestry named Jane Cook. According to tradition she was related to General Nathanael Greene, the Rhode Islander who finally drove the British from South Carolina. Her mother had been born Jennie Strahan in Scotland. As soon as Samuel was "established" and could support a wife, he set off on horseback to propose. Jane accepted his proposal and married him. "My father," wrote Jefferson Davis, "was unusually handsome, and the accomplished horseman his early life among 'the mounted men' of Georgia naturally made him."

According to Varina Davis and numerous descendants, Jane Davis retained her good looks, her remarkably fresh, fair complexion, and her brown hair, until her eighties. She is remembered for three special attributes: her "sprightly mind," her coolheaded bravery, and her passion for flowers. Wherever Jane went she carried flower seed and cuttings to make a garden.

On December 10, 1784, Jane gave birth to a boy. Named Joseph Emory, he was to be a supreme influence in Jefferson Davis's career. For about a decade following the birth of his first son, Samuel continued to cultivate his Georgia farm. But the sandy soil about Augusta was not as productive as he figured it should be for the amount of labor he and his two or three African slaves put into it. Hearing alluring reports of the fertility of Kentucky, which had been admitted to the Union in 1792, Samuel decided to sell his place and move to the promising land. By this time the number of children had increased to five. There were three more boys: Benjamin, Samuel, and Isaac; and a daughter, Anna, born in September, 1791, just before Isaac.

In 1793, with five children under nine—Anna was barely toddling and Isaac a babe in arms—the Davises bravely set forth for Kentucky. As typical of pioneers, their furniture and farm gear and Jane's spinning wheel were loaded on stout wagons. The older boys and the Negroes rode the extra horses and looked after the cattle. Samuel took along a supply of axes as well as several rifles and a large store of ammunition, for their chief sustenance would come from the game he killed.

Settling first in Merced County in the Blue Grass region, they moved after a short stay to Christian County [2] in the southwestern part of the state. It was a beautiful region with rich soil and magnificent forests, teeming with the wild luxuriance of untamed nature. The woods abounded with deer, bear, wild turkeys, and other game. The Davis land, comprising some six hundred acres, lay not far from the Tennessee border and a few miles east of Hopkinsville. Here Samuel built a double-barreled log house with a wide, roofed gallery or "dog-trot" between the two halves, each of which consisted of two square rooms with glass windows.[3]

It took energies of no ordinary kind to create a productive farm, but Samuel was strong and an indefatigable worker. He made small crops of wheat and corn, though his chief business was tobacco planting and the breeding of blooded horses, for which he acquired local fame. As the three eldest boys grew to proper size, they helped their father and the slaves with the farm work. Partly to piece out the income needed for the expanding family, partly in answer to a clamoring demand, Samuel later

---

[2] In 1819 Todd County was formed out of the eastern half of Christian. The Davis home place was some two hundred yards over the line in the part that became Todd.

[3] On the exact site of the house in which Jefferson Davis was born, the Bethel Baptist Church of Fairview was built in 1886. Today the church lies on the same side of U.S. Highway 68 as the handsome memorial obelisk, which rises 351 feet in Jefferson Davis Park, in Samuel's original tract.

turned a room of his house into a "Wayfarer's Rest," and hired a neighbor's girl to help.

At approximately two-year intervals, Jane Davis presented her husband with four Kentucky-born daughters, whose names strung together in the order of their birth sounded like a line of verse: Lucinda, Amanda, Matilda, and Mary. When Jefferson was born, Jane, past forty-five, was so ill that the care of the baby was entrusted to his sixteen-year-old sister Anna. The cradle Anna rocked him in was a sturdy, outsize one, large enough for a child of five, which stood by her bed in reach of her hand. But in the daytime it was taken into the warm kitchen that served as dining room.

While there was little trouble from Indians, occasionally escaped outlaws from Virginia or the Ohio Valley would terrorize the region. Since police protection was nonexistent, individuals who proved vicious or committed some outrage in the community would be pursued, investigated, and sentenced by Regulators, chosen from the most dependable settlers. Jane Davis once had a narrow escape from a felon, and her cool behavior in the crisis became a legend in the family.

After her strength had returned sufficiently for her to resume some care of the baby, Samuel and the boys went off one day with a posse to track down a desperado who had committed some horrifying crimes in the county. The older girls were at a rural school and Jane was alone in the kitchen with the two smallest ones and little Jefferson in his cradle. Suddenly the door was flung open and a villainous-looking fellow, armed with rifle and knives, demanded food. From vivid descriptions, as well as from his manner, Jane recognized him as the hunted criminal. Though trembling within, she pretended to take him for a weary traveler who had lost his way. Hospitably she invited the outlaw in, stirred up the fire, and set about to cook the best meal she could provide. During the process she kept him entertained with lively conversation, and fed him in installments as dishes were ready for serving. Before the famished man had consumed the last tasty morsel, the posse arrived, and took Jane's "prisoner" without a casualty. Jefferson was too young to remember the exciting event to which he was an unconscious eyewitness, but the recountal of his mother's courage in the face of danger was one of the first stories he heard.

Though Kentucky-born, Jefferson's memories began in Mississippi. Before the baby was two, his father decided to move again, this time to the deep South, where he heard fortunes were to be made in cotton. Selling his holdings to good advantage and most of his blooded horses, Samuel again packed his furniture and farm gear into wagons and started on an eight-hundred-mile journey. It took the travelers over eight weeks to reach St. Mary's Parish, Louisiana, where Samuel selected property on Bayou Teche for the new home. But a plague of malarial mosquitoes from the watery region made him realize his mistake. Within a year he moved across the Louisiana border to Wilkinson County, Mississippi. The farm he bought lay about a mile east of the county seat, Woodville, some twenty miles from the Mississippi River.

The site selected for the house was on high ground in a grove of poplars and romantic live oaks trailing long graceful strands of Spanish moss. On one side the land sloped gently to a spring of clear water. With the help of district carpenters and his own Negroes Samuel built a substantial and commodious frame house in the story-and-a-half style. The bricks were fired on the place and the cypress cut from Davis timber. Though two or three pretentious plantation homes had already been built near Woodville, it was quite a fine house for that part of the country in the year 1812. The large hall with huge double doors was plastered. The rooms were paneled in cypress. A wide veranda extended entirely across the front with windows from floor to ceiling opening into the parlor and the master bedroom. The handsome hardware came from England, with the British royal coat of arms embossed on the sturdy locks. In those days of armoires Samuel built in useful cupboards and a medicine closet. For a touch of elegance the parlor had its mantel of black Italian marble with Ionic columns.

While the house was being finished, Jane laid out a flower garden and walks bordered with shrubs. She planted hedges of Prairie Queen roses to divide the orchard and garden. At first the place was called "Poplar Grove," but later when the roses flourished Jane called it "Rosemont," as it is known today.

At fifty-six Samuel Davis considered himself permanently settled; nearing retirement age he was starting a new life as cotton planter. Just as he got his first crop seeded, the War of 1812 began. Though he had special need of his sons' help on the new farm, the Revolutionary veteran was glad when Benjamin and Samuel, Jr., volunteered. Little Jeff saw his three oldest brothers, including Joseph, who was practicing law in Natchez, go off to war. Isaac, who was in his early teens, remained with the home guards. It was Isaac who taught Jeff to fish and ride a horse, and, in time, to shoot. Jeff's beloved sister Anna continued to mother him; he still slept in her room in his rocker-crib [4] close to her bed. His second sister, Lucinda, a tall, quiet girl, who loved gardens and verse, shared in the mothering and read poetry to him. In the late summer of 1813, just before he started to school, Jefferson heard the grisly tale of the massacre at Fort Mims over in Alabama Territory, where Chief Weatherford and his Creek Indians slaughtered four hundred whites, leaving "a heap of ruins, ghastly with human bodies."

Jefferson grew into a handsome boy with gold hair and large blue eyes that were to turn blue-gray in middle age. His body was well formed; his constitution sturdy. He had a quick, bright mind and winning smile, for by disposition he was warm and happy-hearted. Not only because he was the baby did he receive an abundance of attention and affection, but because his natural charm attracted it. Though he was admittedly the family favorite, he was not spoiled. Neither Samuel nor Jane would have endured a spoiled child.

[4] This crib-on-rockers may be seen today in the basement of Confederate Memorial Hall in New Orleans. All of Anna's own children and grandchildren slept in it, for the sake of sentiment, according to the testimony of Anna's granddaughter, Miss Anna Davis Smith.

Little Jeff began to note that his father was "a man of wonderful physical activity" and became aware of his "unusually grave and stoical character." His mother had outwardly a warmer and more facile nature than his father, but she too had something of the stoic in her make-up. Rigid self-control and a strong sense of duty were dominant traits in Jane's nature as well as Samuel's. From his parents Jefferson inherited that inflexible composure he was later to reveal. Though sometimes stern, Samuel was never harsh; he would express his disapproval by quiet withdrawal into courteous coldness. There is no record in the Davis family of a case of physical punishment.

Life had not been easy for Samuel Davis. With a wife and ten children to bring up, it was hard to get ahead. While reasonably prosperous, he could never afford more than a dozen slaves, and unlike the aristocratic planters Samuel worked in the fields with his Negroes. However, in Wilkinson County his integrity and good judgment were soon recognized and he became a man of influence. Never an ardent churchgoer, he was yet a religious man; early in his life he had joined the Baptist church, and he had confidence in God's kind intentions, His merciful love and just decisions.

Like the rest of the family, Samuel had a strong belief in the potentialities of his youngest son. The advantages he himself had missed he craved for little Jefferson. In the sparsely peopled community, tutelage of any kind was hard to come by, and he was concerned, because Jefferson had to make a start, like any other child, in a backwoods school.

# CHAPTER II

# BOYHOOD EDUCATION

WHEN he was five Jefferson Davis's education began in a typical log-cabin school about a mile from his house. To reach it, he and his youngest sister, Mary, two years his senior, had to walk through a dense wood. Because he was male, Jeff carried the lunch basket and considered himself her protector. Both his father and his brother Joseph had impressed upon the little fellow their conviction that cowardice is the most contemptible of bad qualities.

An incident which reveals Jeff's early training in bravery concerns an itinerant chairmender, who was accustomed to take his work home stacked upside down on his head. Since the man became dangerous when he got drunk, the district children were warned to avoid him. One day as Jeff and his sister were threading a particularly gloomy part of the wood, they saw coming directly toward them through the high underbrush what they took to be the bogy, with upturned chair legs bobbing above his head. Jeff seized Mary's hand and said resolutely, "We will not run." As the dreaded figure came nearer the frightened children stood their ground. But the chair legs turned out to be the branching antlers of a handsome buck. The animal came up quite close, sniffed, stared in perplexity at the wide-eyed tots, and then trotted off into the woods.

After two years Samuel Davis was thoroughly dissatisfied with Jefferson's rudimentary instruction. Determined that his promising son should have a first-rate education, he made a drastic decision. He would send him back to Kentucky to a boys' school near Springfield, run by Dominican friars. It took considerable breadth of view for the Baptist Samuel to risk his son's exposure to Catholic influence in his most susceptible years. Besides, the boy was extremely young to be taken from his mother. And as yet no steamboats plied the Mississippi, no stagecoaches coursed the woods. A traveler went from Natchez to Kentucky by horse or on his own feet. Little Jeff would have to go on horseback.

Doubtless the father's resolution was strengthened by the fact that Major Hinds, a friend of Joseph, was about to set out for Kentucky. Joseph, who had resumed his law practice in Natchez after his return from the war, was a stout advocate of Samuel's plan and assisted materially in its execution. For Joseph believed strongly in the boy's potentialities, as did all the brothers and sisters. To Joseph the problem was perhaps more complex than one of mere schooling, for he feared that the character of this beautiful and highly intelligent child might be weakened by the oversolicitude of a middle-aged mother and adoring elder sisters.

Major Hinds was delighted to take the seven-year-old Jeff along as a companion for his own seven-year-old son, Howell. In the Hinds party, besides the Major and his lady, were a sister-in-law, a niece, a Negro maidservant, and a Negro manservant in charge of the pack mules, loaded with supplies and equipment for camping out. To make a seven-hundred-mile journey on horseback through Indian territory where scarcely a white settlement existed was a hazardous adventure for an adult. But the child was excited at the prospect of traveling through the Wilderness mounted on his own pony. Although the Fort Mims massacre had occurred only two years before, he himself had no fear of Indians. And in northern Mississippi the Indians were mostly Choctaws, a tribe friendly to the white man. But Jane Davis could not bring herself to consent. To avoid a painful scene, Samuel did not let her know when the expedition was leaving. The little boy departed without even a good-by kiss from his mother.

The journey to Kentucky took several weeks. Jeff was particularly impressed by the number of unshaved men who were making the trip on foot. In flatboats they had floated down the Ohio and the Mississippi to New Orleans to sell their wares and now were returning cross country by their own power. Jeff liked the campfires and sleeping out under the stars wrapped in blankets. Deer bounded through the forest. Wild turkeys roosted on the tree branches. The Major's rifle provided all the game they could eat, and sometimes in north Mississippi it protected the party from panthers. Jeff enjoyed the stops at the four rest places, which broke the monotony of days in the saddle. These "stands," or "stations" as they were called, were log houses where the weary could pause for a few days and the sick could remain until they got well or died. The first three were run by white men married to squaws, and the fourth, at the Tennessee River crossing, was owned by a Chickasaw half-breed.

The climax of the adventure came at Nashville, where the party was received by Andrew Jackson, hero of the day. As commander of the battalion of Mississippi dragoons, Major Hinds had fought beside the General through the magnificent engagement of New Orleans the previous January. Jackson had returned only a few months before from the battlefield to his estate, called the "Hermitage." The mansion that was to become famous was yet a dream. In 1815 the commodious dwelling was built of logs.

Jeff had heard much about the tough Tennessee warrior from his soldier brothers, so he was acutely interested in the nation's idol. Affectionately called "Old Hickory," Andrew Jackson was still in his forties. Altogether Jeff found the General "very gentle and considerate." He noted that he punctiliously said grace before meals, and, as he later wrote, he was impressed by Andrew Jackson's "unaffected and well-bred courtesy." Not once during his stay did he hear the General, so notorious for vivid profanity, curse. While encouraging Jeff and Howell and his adopted son Andrew, Jr., to contests of running and jumping and pony races, he discouraged them from wrestling. "To allow hands to be put on another," he said, "might lead to a fight."

In Jeff's eyes, Rachel Jackson, about whom such a national

scandal was to be unleashed, was "amiable and affectionate," though her education did seem "deficient." Rachel and the General made the Hinds party so welcome that they remained a fortnight. This visit with Andrew Jackson, when Jefferson Davis was a lad of seven, was doubtless the most memorable of his life. As he confessed in old age, it inspired a reverence and affection for the democrat that ever remained with him.

Intimate contact with the military hero may have had some subtle influence in shaping the boy's ideals and aspirations; the following two years in a Catholic school certainly had considerable effect on young Jeff, especially in imponderables. The school was connected with a Dominican church, which owned large estates, with productive fields, cattle and sheep, a flour mill, and African slaves to do the heavy work. While its friars were individually vowed to poverty, the order, through gifts and prudent management, was already well-to-do, although the Dominicans had arrived in Kentucky only in 1806.

When Jeff entered St. Thomas the great majority of the pupils were from Catholic families. Within a few months he was the sole Protestant, as well as the smallest boy in school. Because he was so young, old Father Angier had put a little bed for him in his own room, and looked after him with the tenderness of a near relative.

Besides being instructed in English and Latin grammar, Jeff learned from the British-born friars to speak well, to be careful of both his enunciation and pronunciation. And as he witnessed the fruits of service and self-abnegation practiced by the Dominicans, he acquired enduring respect for discipline and authority as instilled by the Catholic faith. But he did not become a Catholic, for the priests were scrupulously careful not to convert him. Perhaps of significance in fixing later opinions was the sight of slaves working on the church farms, and he heard no doubts voiced about the morality of the institution of Negro slavery.

Jeff got into serious trouble just once. When some of the older pupils planned a prank, he was persuaded to be a minor accomplice. He agreed that after Father Angier was asleep, he would blow out the light that always burned before a holy image. This he did. It was the signal for the conspirators to throw into the room quantities of stolen cabbages, squashes, potatoes, and cold biscuits. The uproar roused the monks. When a lamp was finally lighted, the older boys were in their bunks feigning sleep. Jeff was the only wakeful one. Like inquisitors the churchmen surrounded him and questioned him in turns. He insisted he did not know much and what little he did know he would not tell. Because of his adamant refusal to inform, the friars judged he must be whipped. The old man with whom he roomed was consigned to administer the chastisement.

Father Angier escorted Jeff up to the punishment room in the attic and strapped him face-down on the cot. But because he loved the boy, the priest found it hard to strike the first blow. He promised to spare Jeff if he would tell him even the least thing he knew about the commotion. Jeff confessed, "I know who blew out the light."

"Yes?" the priest said eagerly, bending down to unstrap him.

"I did."

The old man was considerably taken aback, but he let the boy off. Then he gave him such a gentle lecture that Jeff cried. It was more effective than ten whippings; he never again got into mischief at St. Thomas.

During his stay among the Dominicans, Protestant Jeff, sensitive and impressionable, remarked the consolations of the confessional to his fellows, as well as their confirmations and first communions. One evening, he sought Father Wilson, the school's head, to tell him he had decided to become a Catholic. The priest was in his room eating his simple meal. The good man smiled indulgently at the boy's intended profession of faith. He suggested that for the time being he had better partake of some nourishing Catholic food, and offered him a biscuit and some cheese. After this incident, Jefferson Davis never felt inclined to join any church until he was past fifty and President of the Confederacy, when he was confirmed an Episcopalian.

While Jefferson was receiving as good tutelage as any boy in America could get in 1815-16, another lad, seven months younger, named Abraham Lincoln, was growing up lanky and wild, without benefit of any schooling whatever on a Hardin County creek bank thirty miles west of St. Thomas. During Jeff's second year at the school, the Lincolns moved north to Indiana, the father selling his cabin and clearing "for twenty dollars in cash and ten kegs of whisky," a medium of exchange in pioneer days. As Jefferson Davis was being educated into the Southern aristocracy, Abraham Lincoln in the school of hard knocks was being seasoned to play a decisive role in the politics that eventually destroyed that aristocracy.

Near the close of Jeff's second year at St. Thomas, Jane Davis demanded that her boy be brought home. This time he would go by water. During his residence with the Dominicans a remarkable thing had happened: three large boats propelled by steam-driven paddle wheels had been put into operation on the Mississippi River and came up the Ohio to Louisville and Cincinnati. Their names reflected their revolutionary means of propulsion: *Volcano, Vesuvius,* and *Aetna.*

A young Mississippian named Charles Green, who had been acting as Jeff's guardian while studying law at Transylvania University, came to the school to fetch him. Jeff took an affectionate, manly farewell of the good priests, who had given him lessons in character and deportment which were to sustain him through life. At Louisville he boarded the *Aetna* with a far keener sense of adventure than when he had mounted his pony for the long overland journey two years before. For Jefferson, just turned nine, was among the first American citizens to travel on a river boat propelled by steam, an invention that seemed at the time as miraculous as the flying machine would almost a century later. In the slow trip down the Ohio and the Mississippi, the keen-eyed boy had a rare opportunity to see the interior of his country. The scenery along the clear Ohio, which Audubon called *La Belle Rivière,* was very appealing. The boat would tie up at settlements for traffic, and Jeff would observe the roustabouts at work. He remarked the villages of Evansville, Indiana, and Henderson, Kentucky, only a few miles apart. At Fort Massacre, the Ohio was over a mile wide and afforded him a magnificent view of some fourteen miles.

On the Illinois side of the river the boat passed Cave-in-Rock, the rendezvous of notorious felons like Samuel Mason and Micajah Harpe, who headed gangs of river pirates and murderers. Their stories were related to passengers when the ships passed the rock, and Jefferson must have recalled the cool courage of his mother when confronted with the desperado in her Kentucky kitchen. Certainly he learned that outlaws formed another segment of his country's population, as did derelict squatters in buckskin pantaloons, stained with grease and blood. He could see that the Indians who came to the riverbanks to sell haunches of venison for the *Aetna*'s provisions were a cleaner lot than many of the white men, and they had a special air of independence and dignity. Jefferson never ceased to be interested when the steamboat stopped to take on fuel wood and salty old Captain de Hart ostentatiously used his brass spyglass and bellowed orders into his speaking trumpet.

What Jefferson felt when he saw the transparent Ohio merge into the muddy current of the vast Mississippi near Cairo, Illinois, we do not know. But at this spot on November 17, 1820, three years later, John James Audubon, who made the trip from Cincinnati to Natchez by flatboat, wrote in his diary a sentiment that suggests the subsequent career of Davis himself. "The meeting of the two streams reminds me a little of the gentle youth who Comes in the World, spotless he presents himself, he is gradually drawn in to thousands of Difficulties that make him wish to keep apart, but at last he is over done, mixed, and lost in the Vortex."

The clear Ohio kept out of the mud-dark current as long as it could by hugging the Kentucky banks, and then after several miles its clearness was reduced to a mere strip and at last completely merged with the yellow brown. The *Aetna* moved faster now in the down current, which ran about four miles an hour.

Though heat from the sun-reflecting water made the summer atmosphere extremely hot and sultry, the bird life was fascinating with white-headed eagles, blue cranes, and flocks of purple grackles.

Sometime after the miserable-looking settlement at New Madrid, Missouri, they passed encampments of Indians near Chickasaw Bluffs. Below the mouth of Wolf River the boat stopped at a Tennessee village called Memphis, where Jefferson was to reside six decades later. Then came glimpses of Arkansas cypress swamps and of Osage Indians. The farther south they steamed, the more lush was the vegetation, with bull rushes and tall canes and green briers entangling the trees. But the Yazoo River that rose in north Mississippi emerged clear between willows just above Vicksburg. And then twenty miles below Vicksburg the boat began to round the huge jutting peninsula called Palmyra, which caused the great river to serpentine twenty miles from its direct course. By the time the Mississippi reached Palmyra it had gathered waters from territory that would in the future form thirty-three states of the Union. On the south side of the peninsula lay the wild, silt-rich land out of which Jefferson was one day to carve his own plantation, "Brierfield."

As the boat came in sight of Natchez Bluffs and the familiar magnolias and mists of Spanish moss, Jeff could see that sawmills had been built over ditches cut back inland from the river and running into the interior, so that in flood time timbers could be floated to the river for transport.

Natchez, where his brother Joseph lived, was a town of approximately 2,000 inhabitants in 1817. Its growing wealth was attested to by a flourishing bank and two printing offices, as well as the first magnificent mansions, like that of Mr. Postlewaits, which were to make the town a show place. The river was crowded with various craft: flatboats, broadhorns, skiffs, and canoes jostled crudely lashed-together rafts that had come from as far away as western Virginia. Natchez Under-the-Hill, where the steamboat *Aetna* tied up, was a mass of warehouses, grog shops, and rotting derelict boats. The town proper, which stood two hundred feet above the bluff and was reached by an oblique carriage road, had some form and pattern, for regularly spaced trees marked off the streets. Besides two domed public buildings and two steepled churches, there was a frame theater, a public reading room, and a really good hotel, the Natchez, built in Spanish style with patio and piazzas.

Isaac had come up from Woodville to fetch Jefferson home. When he and Joseph met their little brother they were surprised to find how much he had grown. They must also have been well pleased with the boy's progress and development. At nine he had had experiences of travel that few adults could match. From British-born instructors, he had acquired the beginnings of a first-rate liberal education, which overcame provincialism and gave him an air of assurance.

With his keen instinct for observation and his remarkable gift of memory, Jefferson would not need later to read historians on America's heroic age, for he himself had been a witness and a participant. Few New England men of letters and few statesmen besides Andrew Jackson were to have such a broad variety of experience as Jefferson Davis had before he was ten. He had glimpsed a land spacious, compelling, and almost empty. He had felt the impact of the crude makings of a great nation. He had rubbed shoulders with deck hands, adventurers, squatters, Indians. He had observed valor and indominitable faith along with shiftlessness. He had seen the mighty need for roads. He had acquired a background for surveying his country's inordinate possibilities. And in time he was to use all his patriotic devotion to advance the nation's destiny.

Wondering if Jeff's mother would recognize him immediately because of his increased inches, Isaac and he planned a little joke to test her. As they approached Rosemont, Jeff dismounted and walked alone up to the house. He found his mother sitting expectantly on the veranda. Pretending to be a stranger, he called out to ask if she had seen any stray horses about. Jane Davis replied that she had not, but that she saw a stray boy, and rushed down the steps to gather him in her arms.

When Jeff went to greet his father, he found him working in the fields with his Negroes. Taken by surprise, Samuel, who always sought to repress deep feelings, hugged the boy with unrestrained affection and embarrassed him by kissing him again and again.

Hardly before the remains of the ceremonious fatted calf had been consumed as cold cuts, the subject of Jefferson's next schooling became paramount in family councils. At length a boys' boarding school at Washington in nearby Adams County was decided upon, partly because it was only a few miles from Natchez and Brother Joseph. Not that the independent Jefferson needed any special looking after, for he was shortly off on a new pony to West Feliciana Parish in Louisiana to see his sister Anna. The twenty-five-mile ride was nothing remarkable for such a seasoned young horseman.

Anna had married a planter named Luther Smith, who inherited the plantation called Locust Grove near St. Francisville. Smith's grandfather, an Episcopal minister, had originally moved to this Spanish territory because his Tory principles had kept him loyal to the British crown. Feliciana was already considered the most aristocratic parish in the state and was shortly reckoned the wealthiest after New Orleans. Bayou Sara, the river port of St. Francisville, was doing a flourishing business, and all about were rising plantation homes like Waverly, Rose Down, Rosedale, Afton Villa, Oak Grove, Beech Wood. Here had settled scions of cultured, blue-blooded families: Percys, Barrows, Bowdens, Sterlings, Pirries, McGehees. Audubon, the ornithologist, was to come to the bird-rich parish and live first in one plantation house and then another as tutor, dancing master, and portrait painter, while he filled his portfolio with incomparable paintings of birds. At Beech Wood in 1822 he was to make his best self-portrait, at thirty-seven.

It was a particularly happy reunion for Jefferson and Anna in her new estate, for he loved her like a mother. And his second brother, Benjamin, now a Louisiana physician thirty-one years old, brought his young wife over to Locust Grove to meet the baby brother.

In late September, Jefferson entered the chosen boys' school with the high-sounding name of Jefferson College.[1] The principal, James McAllister, who was considered "a man of great learning" by the community, taught the more advanced pupils, while his Scotch assistant instructed the smaller boys with an authoritative cane as well as textbooks.

Jefferson spent autumn week ends in Natchez with Joseph, who was busy drafting the constitution of Mississippi, about to be admitted to the Union as a state. The event was celebrated on December 10, 1817, which coincidentally or designedly fell precisely on Joseph's thirty-third birthday. Serving importantly as a member of the first constitutional convention was Joseph's last public office. He refused to go further in a public career, for he had determined to become a cotton planter. Already he was looking about for suitable land at low cost.

When the brand-new Academy of Wilkinson County opened its doors in Woodville the next year, Jeff was brought back to study at home. The principal was a scholarly Bostonian named John A. Shaw. Jefferson admired him because he was "quiet and just," and, according to his own testimony, he learned more from Mr. Shaw in the time he was with him than he ever learned from anyone else.

In his own quiet and just way, Samuel Davis taught his son a most effective lesson. One day at the academy a task of memory was assigned to Jeff which he felt was beyond his ability. Forthrightly, he told the teacher he could not master so much. But the man refused to lessen the assignment. On the following day, when Jeff had not memorized the whole selection, the teacher prepared to punish him. Young Jeff's sense of fairness rose in revolt. Picking up his books, he walked out, went straight home, and explained the situation to his father. Samuel Davis deliberated. "It's up to you," he said soberly, "to elect whether you will

---

[1] Jefferson College functions today as a boys' military school. The author visited it in November, 1954.

work with head or hands. My son cannot be an idler. I need more cotton pickers and will give you employment."

Roused extra early the next morning, Jeff went to the fields carrying his enormous sack. Pluckily he picked cotton all day long with the Negroes. For a second hot day he sweated with them in the sun-beaten fields. After this day's picking had been weighed, he came to his father and confessed that he had changed his mind. Samuel Davis listened gravely. Then he spoke casually of the disadvantages under which a gentle-bred man suffered when becoming a laborer. He agreed with his son that he was wise to give education another trial.

Chastened by the experience, Jeff returned to school prepared to endure anything. When he took his usual seat, the instructor made no comment whatever on his absence. He always suspected that his father had had a private conference with the principal. In any case Jeff was never known thereafter to complain of hard lessons. He became more diligent in his pursuit of knowledge. By the time he reached his thirteenth birthday in June, 1821, he was considered ready for a university.

Transylvania University at Lexington, Kentucky, was selected, because in 1821 this institution (founded in 1780) was regarded as superior to any west of Princeton, and its students came from leading Southern families. Joseph could well afford to pay Jeff's expenses at Transylvania, for his law practice and banking interests at Natchez had proved so lucrative that in May, 1818, he had bought a large tract of rich cotton land on Palmyra Peninsula between Natchez and Vicksburg. Annual expenses at Transylvania were reckoned at somewhere between $112 and $130, though this amount did not allow for clothes and pocket change. A year's tuition cost only $30, plus $5 admission fee. For boys who lived in the dormitory board and lodging could be had for $1.50 a week. The better-off students, however, lived in more comfort with private families, where board, lodging, fuel, light, and laundry ran $2.50 a week.

At the time Jefferson entered Transylvania, it was situated on fourteen acres in the highest and most attractive section of Lexington. The student body numbered 383, variously enrolled in colleges of medicine, law, and theology, as well as in the regular classical course. Transylvania's faculty had been most carefully selected and included not only New Englanders educated at Harvard and Yale, but instructors from France, Scotland, and Ireland.

Jefferson was deeply impressed by the president, Horace Holley, who was a Yale graduate and an ordained Unitarian minister. But by some parents he was considered too unorthodox because he did not believe in an incarnate Devil. He also went to the theater, attended horse races, and acted now and then as a race-track judge. He could see no harm in occasional dancing and card playing in his own home. Holley's enemies, who complained that he exalted morality and Christianity too much above creed and dogma, often questioned him on doctrine. Calmly insisting that he was no sectarian, he once said boldly, "I belong to no set of prejudices or obstinate and silly peculiarities, and for this very good reason, that I have tried them all and found them nonsense by experience. . . . My religion is the love of God and man; my creed, the Gospel." Jeff imbibed religious tolerance from Horace Holley, and his own attitude toward religion in later years was strikingly in accord with the President's views.

The breadth of Holley's tolerance was somewhat counterbalanced by the piety of the orthodox Reverend Mr. Bishop, a Scotsman who taught sacred and profane history, and took the Bible literally. But Jeff became quite fond of Mr. Bishop. And he admired the pronunciation of the professor of Latin and Greek, who was a graduate of Trinity College, Dublin. Jeff was at his best in the subjects these two men taught, but he also learned "a little of algebra, geometry, trigonometry, surveying, and natural philosophy." At Transylvania, as Allen Tate has noted, "he formed the habit of omnivorous reading." Because he was so devoted to reading, only rarely did he engage in sports.

In Lexington Jeff boarded with Postmaster Joseph Ficklin and his wife in their brick house on a corner of East High Street and

South Limestone. Mrs. Ficklin delighted in making him comfortable and happy. She liked both his dignity and his fun-loving nature. Years later when he visited Lexington with his wife shortly before he became Secretary of War, the aged Mrs. Ficklin remarked to Varina Davis, "Jeff is the same dear boy he was when he was sixteen."

At the close of his third college year, because of his good grades and his popularity, Jeff was appointed junior orator. At commencement on June 14, 1824, just after his sixteenth birthday, he delivered his first speech, before an audience composed of faculty, students, and townfolks. The chosen subject was "Friendship," a concept that remained a heartening force throughout his long and troubled life. A contemporary declared "he had a peculiarly sweet voice and a convincing way of asserting himself." The Lexington *Monitor* reported, "Davis on 'Friendship' made friends of his hearers."

Jeff from his first year had many warm friends among townspeople in Lexington. That he was well-liked by fellow students is attested by written comments. His schoolmate George W. Jones of Iowa, who became a United States Senator, wrote glowingly that "young Davis was considered by the faculty and his fellow-students as the first scholar, ahead of all his classes, and the bravest and handsomest of all the college boys. . . . Always gay and buoyant in spirits . . . he had the innate refinement and gentleness that distinguished him through life." Another classmate, Judge Peters of Kentucky, wrote, "He was a good student . . . amiable, prudent . . . and beloved by teachers and students."

Jeff had even won "the favorable regard" of the great Henry Clay, whose son Henry, Jr., was a friend whom he often visited at "Ashland," the Clay estate about a mile and a half from Lexington. But the individual who particularly attracted Jeff's imagination was an older student from east Kentucky named Albert Sidney Johnston, five years his senior and two classes ahead of him. Johnston had been enrolled at Transylvania in 1818-19, but he had remained only for a session because he felt a restlessness to join the navy. He had been persuaded, however, to spend the winter with his wealthy half-brother, Josias Stoddard Johnston, in Louisiana. In 1820 on his return to Transylvania, he buckled down to his studies, made an impressive record, and accepted an appointment to the United States Military Academy in 1822. From early boyhood, Sidney Johnston was an acknowledged leader among his comrades because of his integrity, energy, and fearlessness. With an ardent and enthusiastic temperament counterbalanced by a remarkable self-control, there was a natural nobility about him and "a kind of loftiness of soul" that made him a figure framed for personal hero worship. In Sidney Johnston, young Jefferson found his ideal of manliness.

Only one thing marred the happiness of Jeff's first two years at Transylvania—a letter from his father, which he received just after the close of his second year. It was not Samuel Davis's deficiency in syntax that disturbed him, but the turmoil of mind and heart expressed between the lines, as well as directly. At sixty-five Samuel Davis regarded himself as a failure. Planters around him had become far richer than he; some of them owned ten times as many slaves. His affluent son Joseph was prominent in Natchez society and had acquired a large plantation. In desperation Samuel had undertaken a futile trip to Philadelphia to recover some valuable property once belonging to his grandfather.

Philadelphia June 25 1823

My dear Son Jefferson

I have a few minutes past taken your letter out of the Post Office which has afforded me inexpressible satisfaction it being the only information which I have received since I left the Mississippi Country 'tho I have wrote often and from various places. my Journey has been unpleasant and expensive I have been delayed of necessity about seven Weeks only arrived here last Thursday noon in bad health and continue much the same I have left James [2] & my horses at a little Village called Harford in Maryland seventy two miles from here from there I came in Mail Stages to Wilmington where I took I took [sic] passage in a Steam

---

[2] The Negro James Pemberton later became Jefferson Davis's devoted body servant and then overseer.

boat to this place which is the most beautiful City I ever saw the place where my father drew his first breath & the place if I had applied some thirty years ago I might now have been immensely rich but I fear all is lost here by the lapse of time yet I shall continue to search everything to the extent before I leave here which will likely be late in Aug or early in Sept as such you can write me again before I leave here. I am much pleased to find that you are at College perhaps on my return Voyage I may come thro Kentucky if so I shall call and see you but if otherways I know where you are and shall frequently write to you while my hand can hold a pen let me be where I may which is very uncertain I had frequently applyed at this Post Office got Nothing before your letter and got that broke open which had been done by a man of my name. Whenever I leave here or before I shall write you that you that [sic] may not send any thing to be broken open after I am gone if any discovery should be made favorable to my interest I shall be sure to let you know in due time & should I never return or see you any more your fathers pra [sic] I have notifyed you where I have left your boy James he is in the care of a Davis Malsby in the Village aforenamed I have also Written the same to David Bradford [3]— Remember the short lessons of instruction offered you before our parting Use every possible means to acquire useful knowledge as knowledge is power, the want of which has brought mischief and misery on your father in old age— That you may be happy & shine in society when your father is beyond the reach of harm is the most ardent wish of his heart—

      Adieu my Son Jefferson
       your father
       Saml Davis

The letter made such an impression on Jefferson that more than thirty years later, when he came across it in the presence of his wife, he was so moved he could not read it but had to leave the room quickly.

[3] David Bradford was Samuel Davis's lawyer son-in-law, who had married his third daughter, Amanda.

The youth was doubtless distressed by the odd humility that caused Samuel Davis to write "father" in lower case and "Son" with a capital, particularly since he had always seemed to his children so wise, just, and bracing. He must have been struck by his father's repeated injunction to "use every possible means to acquire useful knowledge as knowledge is power." For, as it turned out, Jefferson Davis impressed people all his life with the scope of his information on an amazing variety of subjects. And he was assuredly touched by his old father's heartfelt wish that he "shine in society." In later years, although Jefferson cared little enough for what is called society, whenever he did appear in any drawing room he shone effortlessly.

Young Jeff had passed his examinations for the senior class with honors when he learned he had been appointed a cadet at the United States Military Academy. His father had used his influence with Congressman Rankin of "the lower district of Mississippi" to secure his son's appointment. Joseph urged him to accept. Because of the slowness of mails in the first quarter of the nineteenth century, Jeff did not receive the document forwarded from Natchez until some weeks later. The commission had been made out on March 11, 1824, by John C. Calhoun, Secretary of War, and signed by President Monroe. Although the honor was greatly sought in 1824, when there were only 250 cadets and about thirty applications for every appointment, Jeff was in no sense elated. He had been anticipating his senior year at Transylvania with all its special privileges and attractions, and he was hoping after graduation to study law at the new University of Virginia, which had been founded only five years before by the man for whom he was named. Joseph had apparently intended sending his brother to "Mr. Jefferson's College" at Charlottesville, but now he was pouring all his spare cash into his plantation in Warren County, where he was building a mansion. Before Jeff replied to the Secretary of War, he had some correspondence with Joseph on the subject and his brother promised that if he were not satisfied with West Point after one year he would send him to Virginia.

Finally on July 7, 1824, Jeff reluctantly accepted the commission with no waste of words and with no hint of either pleasurable anticipation or gratitude:

The commission of cadet granted the undersigned March 11th, and remitted to Natchez, on account of my absence, was forwarded here. I accept it.

Am not able to go before Sept. for reasons I will explain to the Superintendent on my arrival.

Yours & c<br>Jefferson Davis

The curt coolness of his reply to official Washington was in marked contrast to the deep emotion of a letter written three weeks later to his sister-in-law, Susannah, wife of Isaac. On the Fourth of July, three days before he accepted the commission, his father had died at Isaac's house in his sixty-eighth year. Susannah had sent him the sad news. It came as a peculiarly crushing blow to the youth so far from loved ones, for he was still grieving for his youngest sister and childhood playmate, Mary, who had died only two months before on May 2, at eighteen.

His reply dated from Lexington, August 2, 1824,[4] reveals much of the heart and the mind and deep feeling of the young Jefferson. A few of his sentences seem uncommonly formal and mature for a lad who had just reached sixteen. At the same time, some of his sentiments suggest the influence of the contemporary Romantic poets. (Byron, whose poems were in high favor with young and old, had died in Greece the preceding April.) In addition, for the first recorded instance, Jefferson Davis gives evidence of a tinge of melancholy that was a part of his highly sensitized nature and which he struggled to keep hidden from the world.

Dear Sister:

It is gratifying to hear from a friend, especially one whom I had not heard from so long as yourself; but the intelligence con-

---

[4] Written on extra-heavy stationery this is the earliest extant letter of Jefferson Davis. It is an especially treasured possession of his grandson, Jefferson Hayes-Davis, of Colorado Springs.

tained in yours was more than sufficient to mar the satisfaction of hearing from any one. You must imagine, I cannot describe, the shock my feelings sustained at the sad intelligence. In my father I lost a parent ever dear to me, but rendered more so (if possible) by the disasters that attended his declining years. When I saw him last he told me that we would probably never see each other again. Yet I still hoped to meet him once more; Heaven has refused my wish. This is the second time I have been doomed to receive the heart-rending intelligence of the death of a friend.[5] God only knows whether or not it will be the last. If all the dear friends of my childhood are to be torn from me I care not how soon I follow.

I leave in a short time for West Point, State of New York, where it will always give me pleasure to hear from you. Kiss the children for Uncle Jeff. Present me affectionately to brother Isaac; tell him I would be happy to hear from him; and to yourself the sincere regard of

Your brother,<br>Jefferson

Jefferson had not seen his father during the last three years. So he could remember him as a man of "wonderful physical activity" and particularly as an accomplished horseman. The very last time he had seen him, his father, at sixty-four, was "about to mount a tall and restless horse, so that it was difficult for him to put his foot in the stirrup. But suddenly he vaulted from the ground into the saddle without any assistance." It was better, he may have reflected, to have the last visual remembrance of his father in a moment of strength than to recall him harrowed by ill-health, frustration, and the despair indicated in the Philadelphia letter.

Affairs had gone worse with Samuel Davis after his disappointing and expensive journey to Philadelphia. In consequence of liability for offering security for his son-in-law Robert Davis, he

---

[5] His sister Mary, who had married a South Carolinian named Robert Davis when she was sixteen, left two baby girls. Her grave may be seen in the family cemetery at Rosemont, close to that of her mother, Jane Davis.

had to sell his plantation to Joseph. He also gave him a bill of sale for the six Negro slaves he had left. In late June of 1824 he had some misunderstanding with Samuel, Jr., the only son who had remained at Woodville to help him with the farm. While the fields were in crop the frustrated father left with his Negroes for Vicksburg. There he bought a flatboat for them and himself and drifted back down the river to Joseph's plantation near Palmyra, managed by Isaac, while the owner was practicing law in Natchez and in Greenville. On the journey Samuel "took the fever" and died six days after landing.[6]

In late August Jefferson began making preparations for the trip to West Point. As yet he had no interest in a military career. Certainly he had no conception that the appointment to the Academy would hold such significance in his life. And he could not have dreamed his acceptance would play an ultimate part in the nation's destiny. He was conscious only of a lack of enthusiasm. It was almost as if his guiding angel were warning him that what seemed so fair and free might prove a gift of bitter consequence.

Jefferson's grief over the death of his unhappy father made him acutely aware that he had spent six of his sixteen years away from parents and home. And now he was going still farther away to live among other strangers. There was one bright hope in his heart: that Albert Sidney Johnston, who had been two years at West Point, would accept him as a real friend.

With sorely mingled emotions Jefferson bade farewell to his college friends at Transylvania and to his friends among the citizens of Lexington, which had become like a second home. He was particularly loathe to say good-by to the Ficklins, who had treated him more like a favorite son than a boarder. He told them he hoped he would not be entirely forgotten.

In the early spring of 1825, during his first year at the Academy, Jefferson was highly gratified to learn that he was indeed

[6] Samuel Davis's last troubled weeks are explained in a letter of William Stamps, brother-in-law of Jefferson Davis. (Jefferson Hayes-Davis Collection of family letters in Colorado Springs.) Samuel Davis was buried on Joseph's plantation "Hurricane." Within recent years his remains were moved to "Beauvoir" on the Mississippi coast, the last home of Jefferson Davis.

remembered by his elders in Lexington. At a George Washington birthday dinner at Monsieur Giron's Confectionary Shop, members of the Union Philosophical Society, which included such distinguished citizens as President Holley, Robert J. Breckinridge, Theodore W. Clay, and Judge Bledsoe, drank toasts to the Constitution, to Greek independence, and to the health of several individuals, among them the faraway Jefferson. It was W. B. Reed who composed and proposed the following toast, as printed in the Kentucky *Reporter*, March 7, 1825: "To the health and prosperity of Jefferson Davis, late a student at Transylvania University, now a cadet at West Point. May he become the pride of our country and the idol of our army."

# CHAPTER III

## A SOLDIER'S TRAINING

WHEN Jefferson Davis passed through New York on his journey to the Military Academy at the end of August, 1824, it was a metropolis of 200,000. Whatever impression the city may have made on him is not recorded, but he never in his life cared much for cities. The trip up the Hudson to West Point was no special experience to Jeff, who had been brought up not far from the Mississippi and had traveled on the great river by steamboat since he was nine.

The Academy, established in 1802, was only six years older than young Davis himself. Physically it was completely unimpressive in the raw plainness of its stone and stucco buildings. West Point was merely a straggling village with little to recommend it, except its fine situation on the Hudson bluffs. A makeshift hotel called Gridley's provided lodging for arriving cadets, who were accommodated three in a bed, until admitted to the Academy and assigned quarters in the South Barracks.

Jeff found he had arrived too late for the new term. All the other candidates had been examined and were now engaged in their studies. But, fortunately, Captain Ethan Allen Hitchcock, a member of the staff, who had known Joseph Davis while recruiting in Natchez, pleaded in his behalf for a special examination, though it was against the rules. As it so happened, a cadet named Washington had just returned from a long sick leave in Europe and was still in the process of being examined on the work he had missed. Permission was granted Davis to appear before the staff. Captain Hitchcock told him that he would be examined forthwith, particularly in arithmetic. Jeff's heart sank: he confessed it was a subject he had never taken at Transylvania, although he knew algebra and geometry. The alarmed captain quickly fetched an arithmetic book and told him to study fractions as fast as he could.

Jeff had barely commenced when he was called before the examining board. The professor of mathematics, Charles Davis, asked him how, the three terms of a direct proportion being given, he would put the fourth. He answered that "the proportion was that the fourth should bear to the third the relation that the second did to the first." The examiner, believing him to have considerably more knowledge than he did, shortly turned him over to the French professor, who was so delighted to find that the sixteen-year-old candidate could read Greek, that he took up the rest of the examination period discussing with him the construction of Greek sentences. After this unorthodox and sketchy examination, Jefferson Davis was passed as qualified for entrance into the Academy. "Since that time," he wrote later, "I have never believed that an examination formed a very conclusive rule of decision upon the qualifications of a person subjected to its test."

Davis was assigned to a room eleven feet square and occupied by two other cadets. Out of their government pay of $16 a month with a monthly subsistence allowance of $12, the cadets had to buy their own plain furniture: table, straight chair, mattress, washstand with pitcher, small mirror, basin, slop pail. Every room was required to have a broom and scrub brush and a bucket for fetching water from the pump or "when that failed, from the spring near the cavalry stables."[1] Each boy in turn was room orderly for a week. One of his Saturday evening jobs was to scrub the floor thoroughly, so that the room would be turned over spotless to the sequent orderly on Sunday morning. In winter the rooms were heated by log fires and the only bath was a tub placed before the hearth. During the warm months, under strict super-

[1] In 1826 a water system was introduced.

vision, the boys bathed in the Hudson. The clothes Jeff had to buy immediately included, among many items: four pairs of white trousers, a gray uniform, blue fatigue jacket and trousers, and a military cap with glistening black leather bill.

When Davis entered the Academy, the able superintendent was Brevet Lieutenant Colonel Sylvanus Thayer of the engineers. He was only thirty-nine, good looking, a gentleman, and always faultlessly groomed. But he was not popular, because he was considered unapproachable and an uncommonly strict disciplinarian. The boys claimed he had them spied upon. Major William J. Worth, the commandant, also good looking and a superb horseman, was not popular either. Though he was a year younger than Thayer, the boys called him "Old Hant," because he would appear like a ghost in their quarters when least expected.

At dawn, reveille aroused the sleeping cadets from their narrow mattresses on the floor (no bedsteads were permitted). According to a routine, Jeff rose, dressed quickly, answered roll call, made his quarters tidy for inspection that came half an hour after reveille. "From the boom of the sun-rise gun until breakfast at seven," he studied mathematics like all the new men. Thirty minutes were allowed for breakfast. Jeff sat on a rough wooden bench at a bare table bearing iron and tin utensils. General conversation in the mess hall was frowned upon. After an interval the boys fell in on the parade ground for their march to mathematics classes in the building called the Academy. From eight to eleven the new students worked before blackboards in the classroom. Then they were sent back to their rooms to study until noon. Dinner was at one. From the time they finished their midday meal until two o'clock the cadets could relax and indulge in what brief recreation they chose. At two o'clock, lines were formed again, and first-year men marched back to the Academy for two hours of French under Claudius Bérard, a man of taste as well as learning, who used his own text in French grammar. The hours between four and sundown were given over to military drill. After supper the cadets returned to their quarters for study until final roll call at half-past nine. All lights were out by ten.

With nine hours devoted to recitation and two to four hours to drill and military exercises, depending on the season, it was a regime that proved too rugged for many boys. But Jeff, who was younger than his classmates, seemed to bear up extremely well. While there was continual grousing about the poor food, we have no evidence of complaint from Cadet Davis. The steward of the mess hall, who furnished board for ten dollars a month, worked on this principle: "Give young men plenty of first-rate bread and potatoes, and they will require little meat and never complain." According to Jeff's classmate Albert E. Church in *Personal Reminiscences of the Military Academy from 1824 to 1831*, "when the carver at the head of the table asked a cadet what part of the roast or boiled beef he preferred, he always answered 'a big bit anywhere.'" Apparently Jeff thrived on the coarse fare, for the word "robust" is often used about him by contemporaries.

A few of the regulations, however, seemed to him unnecessarily puritanical. The rules forbade playing card games, using tobacco in any form, or imbibing an alcoholic beverage. Jeff learned he could not keep in his room a cooking utensil, a novel, or a dramatic play. He could subscribe to only one "approved" magazine. The Academy library was open two hours a week, on Saturday afternoon, for those who wished to withdraw books. Since Jeff had a passion for reading, he must have come to welcome winter days of downpour when bad weather made drilling unfeasible and no special study was assigned to consume the hours ordained for drill.

Though a cadet might possess a musical instrument if he chose, he was not allowed to play upon it except during the recreation period. Like all the students, however, Jeff had his regular dancing lessons from Papanti, later a celebrated dancing master in Boston for nearly half a century.

Sometimes after taps the cadets would make toast with bread and butter sneaked from the mess table, and on rare occasions they could even roast a turkey over the wood fire in their rooms.

Now and again, when they were supposed to be asleep, they would slip out to a nearby place called George's and eat buckwheat cakes.

Perhaps the factor that had brought Jeff the greatest joy in his first session at the Academy and reconciled him to giving up his senior year among friends at Lexington was the presence on the campus of Albert Sidney Johnston. Sidney, as Davis always called him, was now twenty-one and stood six feet one inch in height. He had a superb physique; his back was straight as a rifle barrel; his shoulders, broad and square; his chest, almost massive. The clear red and white complexion came from his Scotch forebears. His brown hair had a natural wave that was somewhat unruly. The nose was slightly irregular, the cheekbones rather high. His sculptured chin was considered both "delicate and handsome." But his most impressive features were the noble forehead and blue-gray eyes, which had "a kind of magnetic power over men." Because of his striking appearance, his energy, and trustworthy character, he was a leader at West Point, as he had been at Transylvania.

Young Davis was immediately accepted in Johnston's "set." The name "set," as he later wrote, is "well understood by those who have been ground in the same Academy mill." And William Preston Johnston says his father formed with Jefferson Davis "a fast friendship that grew and strengthened, and knew neither decay or end." Sidney's most intimate friend within the set, however, was his roommate Leonidas Polk. This idealistic, dreamy-eyed, large-headed youth from Tennessee was to become the Episcopal bishop of Louisiana and a fighting general in the Confederate Army.

As boy and youth, Davis sought the company of those older and wiser than he. Among the cadets who particularly impressed young Jefferson in his first year was Alexander D. Bache, who stood at the top of the first or graduating class. This great-grandson of Benjamin Franklin had inherited some of his ancestor's genius. "He had the power of demonstration," Davis wrote, "beyond that of any man I ever heard." But Bache was not cut out for soldiering. Instead he became a college president, and later, superintendent of the United States Coast Survey Service.

Another man who impressed him even more was the cadet who held first place in the class to which Sidney Johnston belonged. His name was William H. C. Bartlett, and he too was a close friend of Johnston and Polk. He had arrived so poorly prepared that during his first year he had to use a dictionary constantly to find out the meanings of words in textbooks, and an English grammar to teach him how to construct his sentences in demonstration. Yet so remarkable was his native intellect that he stood number one from his first year to his last. Davis admired him for overcoming the lack of early advantages, and for his extreme modesty and his "solid merit and exemption from pretensions." Later Bartlett became professor of natural and experimental philosophy at the Academy and an author of books on the study of the physical universe.

"Sidney Johnston valued one feature of cadet-life very much," Davis once told Johnston's son William Preston, "the opportunity to select one's own acquaintance from congeniality of tastes, which was denied to the officer in barracks." Like Johnston, Cadet Davis, though courteous to all, was decidedly eclectic in his friendships.

In the spring of Jeff's first year, on March 17, 1825, according to Academy custom, the names of the cadets entering the following summer were read out at chapel. If Jefferson Davis heard the name of Robert Edward Lee, there was no particular reason to note it, unless mention was also made that Lee was a Virginian and the son of that noted Revolutionary general Lighthorse Harry Lee, whom all schoolboys of the day remembered for his eulogy of Washington as "first in war, first in peace, and first in the hearts of his countrymen."

When the new term began, three other Virginians besides Lee arrived with proper credentials. Two of these subsequently dropped out, but the third, named Joseph Eggleston Johnston, was to graduate with his compatriot. Both R. E. Lee and Joseph

E. Johnston were a year and several months older than Jefferson Davis, though in a class behind him. These two Virginians were to play contrasting roles in the climactic years of Jefferson Davis's career. The noble Lee was to cast glory on the Davis administration and to prove a friend, ever loyal, co-operative, consoling, and admiring. Joseph E. Johnston, on the other hand, was to cause Davis most painful irritations and disappointments during the progress of the war, and to libel him maliciously when they were both past seventy-five.

When Cadet Davis first met Cadet Lee, this eighteen-year-old Virginian was already notably handsome and distinguished by his breeding and dignified manners. Soon it was said, according to a fellow cadet, that Lee's "personal appearance surpassed in manly beauty that of any cadet in the corps." And before Davis was graduated, Lee's sculptural good looks, his carriage, and his "beautiful and symmetrical limbs," which "looked as though they had come from the turning laths," earned him the sobriquet: "Marble Model."

Johnston, like Lee, was of aristocratic antecedents. But where Lee was the essence of modesty, Johnston had an inclination to strut. Dr. Freeman likens him to a gamecock. Because of his attitude and his good opinion of himself, the cadets nicknamed him the "Colonel." Yet there is no record of his unpopularity at the Academy; and apparently no natural antipathy existed between Johnston and Davis.[2]

The year Lee and J. E. Johnston entered the Academy, Albert Sidney Johnston was in the graduating class, Leonidas Polk was a second classman, and Jefferson Davis, a third classman. Here under one roof, in 1825-26, were gathered five of the future leading figures of the Confederacy.[3] Besides Lee, the two Johnstons, and Polk, there were other cadets during Davis's years at the

---

[2] The gossip that Cadets Davis and J. E. Johnston had a fist fight over the favors of a barmaid has no foundation in fact.

[3] A sixth, who was destined to a fame almost as great as Lee's, was then a mere baby in Clarksburg, Virginia. Thomas Jonathan Jackson had been born the year Davis came to West Point, and he was to become a cadet in 1842, when Davis was a cotton planter in Warren County, Mississippi.

Academy who were to become Confederate generals. Among them were his classmate, Thomas Drayton; Gabriel Raines, '27; Albert Blanchard, '29; and John B. Magruder, a tall, elegant young man with an odd lisp, class of '30. In Davis's last year entered L. B. Northrop, whom he was to make commissary general of the Confederate forces. A very good friend of Davis was Henry Clay, Jr., whom he had known in Lexington and who was to die in the war with Mexico. Of the West Pointers who were to fight with the North, Davis liked best of all Kentucky-born Robert Anderson, whose unhappy destiny it would be to command Fort Sumter.

Near the close of his first year at the Academy, Jeff was cheered by a visit from his brother Joseph, who had taken the place of his father. When William Burr Howell, a Natchez friend, was advised to go north for the health of his baby son, Joseph decided to accompany the Howells and to see his young brother at West Point. This Howell, while on leave as a naval officer, had come fortune hunting to Natchez from New Jersey, where his father was governor. Joseph Davis, prominent and well-to-do attorney, had liked the personable, very tall young man, taken him under his wing, and sponsored him in Natchez society. Howell soon courted and won Margaret Kempe, an heiress, to whom Joseph was attached. At their wedding, Joseph had been a groomsman and they had named for him their first-born.

The party, which included Joseph Davis, the three Howells, and little Joe's nurse, traveled first by carriage, with two extra horses on a lead rope. They drove through the Wilderness to a landing on the Ohio River, where they boarded a boat going northeast to Brownsville. There they took the stagecoach, and were pleasantly surprised to find as fellow passengers two noted Englishmen: George Cruikshank, the caricaturist, and Robert Owen, the socialist founder of New Harmony. The Mississippians greatly enjoyed the company of the Britishers, particularly that of the genial, bright-eyed painter, who delighted in dandling the baby. And Joseph was impressed by the socialist theories of Owen.

After a few days of rest and sight-seeing in New York, Joseph and the Howells took the river boat for West Point. As the boat landed, "a robust, red-cheeked young man of seventeen" came dashing down to the landing stage and caught his brother in his arms. Young Mrs. Howell was immediately struck by the cadet's "beautiful blue eyes and strong, graceful figure." She little dreamed, however, that this young fellow with "the open, bright expression" would one day be her son-in-law. Jeff was to remember his mother-in-law's "exceeding beauty and changing color," as he first saw her on the Hudson River boat.

There is no record of what the Davis brothers talked about, but doubtless the subject of money came up, for Jeff had begun sending his mother a monthly amount from his small savings, as soon as furniture and clothes had been paid for. Twice Jane Davis had returned the money, but finding that she hurt his feelings, she was constrained to keep the monthly tributes, realizing how much pleasure it gave him to be able to assist her with the first real money he had ever earned. Most likely Joseph tried to persuade him that such a sacrifice on his part was unnecessary. But according to Varina Davis's *Memoir,* Jeff continued to send a small sum home every month. Dodd regards this gesture of helping his mother as "a touching testimonial of the sacrifices" which his family had made for him.

The visitors remained only a few hours at West Point, but during most of the stay, as Mrs. Howell remembered, "Jeff sat very close to his brother with his hand slipped through his arm."

Unless a cadet was meeting relatives or had some other good excuse, he was strictly forbidden to loiter about the public wharf, or to enter a public house like North's or Benny Havens's, where liquor was served. Havens set up his establishment during Jeff's first term and remained a West Point institution until he died in his ninetieth year. In time the cadets made up a drinking song about Benny, which continued to be sung long after his death in 1877. One of the numerous stanzas goes:

*To our comrades who have fallen, one cup before we go,
They poured their life blood freely out pro bono publico;
No marble points the stranger to where they rest below
They lie neglected far away from Benny Havens, Oh!*

The chorus runs:

*Oh! Benny Havens, Oh! Oh! Benny Havens, Oh!
So we all sing reminiscences of Benny Havens, Oh!*

Jefferson Davis had sharper remembrances of Havens's place than most cadets, for he was in the first lot ever to be court-martialed for drinking at the forbidden place. During the summer encampment, on the last Sunday in July, 1825, when a cloudburst flooded the floorless tent of Davis and some others, he and four companions stole off to seek shelter and incidentally to have some fun. They found both at Benny Havens's. While they were warming themselves with consoling drinks and generally rejoicing, Captain Hitchcock appeared. To him, as he was to testify, some of the young men "had a certain wildness of countenance which is produced often times by the use of ardent spirits." On August 25, 1825, Cadet Davis was commanded to appear before a military court. He was accused of breaking regulations: first, by going out of bounds on July 31, 1825; second, by being seen in a "public house or place where spirituous liquors are sold kept by one Benjamin Havens at or near Buttermilk Falls and distant about two miles from West Point"; and third, that he did himself "drink spirituous and intoxicatious liquors."

At the trial Captain Hitchcock reported that when discovered at Benny Havens's Cadet Davis "exhibited extreme embarrassment . . . [which] might have proceeded from being found in the circumstances I stated . . . but a part of it I attributed to the use of spirituous liquors." "Old Hitch," as he was called by the boys, was the officer who had kindly assisted Jeff in getting a special examination and he may have been trying to make it easy for the youth. Before the military tribunal young Davis defended himself with dignity and spirit. He protested that the prohibition against going to Havens's place had not been "officially" promulgated and consequently was "something less than law." He asserted that malt liquors, cider, and porter, he did not understand to be spirituous. Then he ended his brief, manly defense with an implied plea for clemency. "It is better," he affirmed with oratorical effect, "a hundred guilty should escape than one righteous person be condemned."

On September 3, 1825, however, the court found him guilty and sentenced him to dismissal. It was a tragic moment for young Jeff. But his agony of spirit was short-lived. Because of his bearing before the tribunal, as well as his previous good record, the court "respectfully recommended the remission of the sentence." By an order of the Secretary of War, signed by "Alex. McComb, Major General, Inspector of the Military Academy," Cadet Davis was pardoned and returned to duty. One other cadet, Hays, was pardoned, but three young men found guilty of similar charges were forthwith dismissed. Thus, when he was seventeen, the military career of Jefferson Davis almost came to an end.

Once again during his West Point career the temptation of diversion from the Spartan austerities of the Academy system not only endangered his commission but very nearly cost him his life. As his wife wrote of the occurrence sixty-odd years later: "Mr. Davis came near escaping all the anguish and turmoil of his life by a fall." He and his friend Cadet Emile Lassere had slipped off to Havens's one evening for a "little frolic," when someone brought the word that one of the instructors was coming. Jeff and Lassere skedaddled. In avoiding the main road and taking a short cut back to barracks along the river, Jeff slipped and plunged sixty feet down the bluff to the river bank. The force of his fall was luckily broken by a stunted tree which he clutched in his descent. The horror-struck Lassere, creeping to the edge of the rocky cliff, peered down and yelled in a mournful voice, "Jeff, are you dead?" Though seriously injured and in great pain, Davis had a strong desire to laugh. Unable to speak, with the breath knocked out of him, he made a faint sign of life by waggling the one hand he could move. Both hands were dreadfully lacerated by the tree branches, but the tree had saved his life. However, he lay ill in the Academy infirmary a long time and "for a while he was expected to die."

A third time during his West Point period a party almost proved his undoing. At Christmas in 1826 a few of the Southern boys thought it would be a special treat to introduce some of their Northern friends to eggnog. Though the record is not clear, Cadet Davis seems to have been one of the hosts. Robert E. Lee and Joseph E. Johnston were among the Southerners who were invited, but they declined.

In the dark of early Christmas morning, young Davis was going about issuing invitations when he was tipped off that Hitchcock was on the prowl. He rushed to No. 5 North Barracks, where the eggnog was being prepared, and gave the warning: "Put away the grog, boys, Old Hitch is coming." While he was speaking Captain Hitchcock entered the room. He promptly sent Davis to his quarters under arrest. "Fortunately for him," Dr. Fleming says, "he went to sleep and did not get into the riot that followed." Nineteen of the cadets, however, who remained at the party, defied the officials and "drove them out of the room with stove wood." One officer was chased all the way to his quarters with a drawn sword. Jeff's roommate, Walter Guion of Mississippi, got a pistol and attempted to shoot Captain Hitchcock. The cadets threw missiles through the halls, broke windows, tore out the railings of staircases. The rioting lasted about an hour and a half. Altogether, according to Albert E. Church in his *Memoir*, "it was one of the most violent outbreaks ever known" at West Point.

The rioters were court-martialed and dismissed. Because Davis steadfastly refused to answer questions about his roommate, he was kept in confinement for many weeks. "This conduct," says William Dodd, "as well as his general demeanor, made him popular with his fellows, a relationship which he prized more highly than the esteem of the authorities."

By all odds the most influential instructor at the Academy in Jeff's day was the chaplain, Charles McIlvaine, who eventually became Episcopal bishop of Ohio. Still in his twenties, he was "tall and majestic in bearing." In the pulpit he was as eloquent as he was pious, and he possessed an extraordinary power of voice "like that of some stage star." Though he carefully composed his hour-long sermons, he would often pause and burst forth in "an unpremeditated grand tide of oratory" and sometimes preach for two hours.

In the 1820's the cadets cared little for religion, few even belonged to a church, and many were outright skeptics. But McIlvaine won their interest as well as their respect. Leonidas Polk confessed that he was the first cadet to kneel in chapel. Jefferson Davis and Albert Sidney Johnston were among the first to follow his example. Largely because of McIlvaine, Leonidas Polk entered the ministry. And perhaps it was the chaplain's early influence on Jefferson Davis that eventually led him to become an Episcopalian.

Besides ministering to the spiritual needs of the Academy, McIlvaine taught history and geography, and gave a course in moral and political philosophy. Jeff did his best work in this last course, which included a survey of American constitutional law.

Biographers have claimed that it was at the United States Military Academy that Jefferson Davis and Robert E. Lee acquired their confirmed belief in State Rights, because the textbook used for constitutional law was *On the Constitution* by Judge Rawle of Pennsylvania, who upheld the doctrine of the constitutionality of secession. A significant paragraph is often pointed out:

"If a faction should attempt to subvert the government of a State for the purpose of destroying its republican form, the national power of the Union could be called forth to subdue it. Yet it is not to be understood that its interposition would be justifiable if a State should determine to retire from the Union. . . . The secession of a State from the Union depends on the will of the people of such a State."

But Davis himself is authority that the Rawle text, which he knew well, had ceased to be used the very year he took the course, and that his required text was Kent's *Commentaries.*

During Davis's period at West Point the other cadets were often stirred by news of the struggle of the South American countries for freedom from Spain. Sidney Johnston was approached by agents of revolutionary governments with tempting offers. The lure of potential fame and fortune in the continent of the dashing Bolívar was romantically compared by him and his friends with routine duty in the United States Army. But in the end Johnston prudently declined, though not many years hence he offered his services to the Republic of Texas when it tried to throw off the yoke of Mexico. In the meantime he applied himself to his studies.

In Jeff's second year, he was proud to see his friend Sidney made adjutant of the corps, the position of top distinction, and one that Robert Lee was to have when he became a first classman. Though Johnston ranked second in his class, he was made adjutant because William Bartlett, who ranked first, had small inclination for the responsibilities that went with the honor. When final examinations came around, Jeff, to his amazement, saw Sidney drop down to eighth place and almost lose his commission.

In mathematics Johnston was ranking third in his class and he had studied so faithfully for the final that there were only two problems in the entire course he could not solve. By ill chance one of those two very propositions was given him to demonstrate. He had to confess to the professor his unpreparedness and beg for another. Then "by a coincidence not included in his doctrine of chances," he was given the only other problem he could not solve. Dismayed, as well as chagrined, he was sent back to his seat. The ominous look on the examiner's face told him he was in danger of losing his commission.

When he got to his room, in considerable perturbation, he

wrote a full explanation to the commissioners, frankly stating the facts and virtually challenging them to give him the stiffest examination possible. After some debate, in which Commandant Worth interceded for him, the authorities decided to give him a last trial. The difficult and rigorous examination to which he was submitted proved his claim of general proficiency. But because of the irregularity of his mathematics examination and his utter lack of talent for drawing, Albert Sidney Johnston was in the final year ranked eighth instead of second. Since his own peculiarly fortunate experience on entering West Point, Jefferson Davis had never had much confidence in the testing power of examinations, and after Johnston's extraordinary bad luck with questions he was confirmed in his doubts.

When Cadet Davis himself was graduated on July 12, 1828, he stood only twenty-third in a class of thirty-three. Why Jefferson Davis, whose intelligence was uncommonly keen, did not win a higher rating, is unexplained. He had done extremely well at Transylvania. Perhaps his youth was partly responsible. At graduation he had barely turned twenty, whereas Lee, for instance, was six months beyond twenty-two. Probably his absorbing habit of reading interfered with his formal study. In any case, he had no natural bent for or little interest in mathematics, the most important subject at the Academy. And his record in deportment was not calculated to raise his standing. Jeff's high spirits, fun-loving nature, and independent temperament did not make for a perfect record in conduct like that of the exemplary Robert E. Lee, who got not one black mark in four years. In fact, Davis rated 120 demerits his "plebe" year, 70 his second, and 137 his third, the period of the "riot." A total of 200 would have meant automatic dismissal.[4]

[4] At the end of his first year Davis stood barely in top half of his class, 32 among 69 members; in June, 1826, he ranked 29 in a class of 49, twenty cadets having been dropped. After the annual examinations in 1827, Davis stood 29 in a class of 37. During his four years of study he received his highest grades in rhetoric and moral philosophy, French and drawing. Even in his senior year he was well down in the lower half of the student body in conduct, ranking 163 among the 207 students. These figures are taken from a letter of March 12, 1907, to Dr. W. L. Fleming from Capt. F. W. Coe, Adjutant at the Military Academy.

It is barely possible that his standing was affected by grudging instructors. One of his teachers, presumed to be Lieutenant Kinsley, had found the young Mississippian antipathetic at sight. Jeff heartily returned the lack of cordiality. From his authoritative point of advantage the professor would overtly try to humiliate him and confuse him in recitation. With his proud manner the young man stood his ground and refused to be cowed by the rostrum taunts. "There was never a recitation which did not witness a duel of eyes and words between them," writes Mrs. Davis. One day in a lecture the professor spoke on presence of mind as one of the cardinal qualities essential in a young soldier. Then looking balefully and pointedly at Jeff he said he did not doubt "there were many, who, in an emergency, would be confused and unstrung, not from cowardice, but from the mediocre nature of their minds." Unblinkingly the youth took the intended insult, but silently vowed to get even if opportunity arose.

Some days later, while the Academy building was filled with cadets in a class held in the magazine of explosives, students were being instructed in the process of making "fire-balls," a kind of primitive hand grenade. The fuse of one of the balls became ignited. Cadet Davis, who saw it first, calmly called to his enemy instructor: "What shall we do, sir? This fire-ball is ignited."

The professor immediately barked a command: "Run for your lives!" and flew for his. Before the tumultuous exodus became a stampede, Davis picked up the grenade and tossed it out a window. Later, General Thomas Drayton, a fellow cadet, wrote of the incident: "Jeff, by his presence of mind, saved many lives and also the building from being demolished."

Many years afterward when asked if he had not taken a great risk, Davis replied, "No, I was very quick, and felt sure I had time to 'try' him." Mrs. Davis says her husband never changed his adverse opinion of the professor; "for all his life, he was horrified by one who would oppress the weak or an inferior in a defenceless position."

Like the rest of his class, Jefferson Davis was graduated with the brevet of second lieutenant. He was commissioned to report after a furlough to Jefferson Barracks near St. Louis on the Mississippi River. It was a congenial assignment, for several of his friends were stationed there, among them Sidney Johnston.

At the time of his graduation there was little in his Academy record to foretell that Jefferson Davis was destined to play an extraordinary role in American history. But in his personality he was outstanding. By now he had gained his full height, approximately five feet eleven.[5] He was handsome of face, with chiseled features and an excellent bone structure. A fellow cadet, General Crafts J. Wright, recorded from memory: "Jefferson Davis was distinguished in the corps for his manly bearing, his hightoned and lofty character. His figure was very soldierly and rather robust; his step springy, resembling the tread of an Indian brave on the warpath." "The West Pointer of Southern origin in almost perfect type" is Dodd's summation of Cadet Davis at graduation.

What had four years at the United States Military Academy done for him in shaping his character? "Now such was the inborn nature of Jefferson Davis," writes General Morris Schaff of Massachusetts, himself a cadet after Davis's time, "that while all the virtues of West Point, education, honor, frankness, truthfulness, and good manners found a native soil to grow in, still in it, too, were already germinated seed of a certain reserve and dignity that found the air congenial and had flourished by the time he graduated into a distinctively aristocratic bearing that clung to him to the end; and much to his serious disadvantage in his presidential life." "The result of his four years at West Point," argues Schaff with shrewd perception, "instead of inculcating the pliancy and assumed cordiality of the politician, was to develop a personality of the reverse order."

Schaff here hits upon a prime source of Davis's failure to please

[5] Dodd says, "He was now over six feet." One who knew him at Ft. Gibson in Arkansas when he was about twenty-seven says he was "just under six feet." Most commentators and contemporaries speak of him as tall, or remark that because of his erect carriage he seemed taller than he was.

a lesser breed of men during his term as President of the Confederacy. Pliancy and the *assumed* cordiality of the politician Davis certainly lacked in the political arena; they were attributes for which he had no regard. But it is likely that he would have lacked those qualities if he had never set foot on the Academy's drill field; for sincerity and steadfastness to principle were deeply ingrained in his nature. Perhaps the discipline instilled at the Academy was the greatest boon Jefferson Davis derived from his West Point training. It helped to give him a sovereign self-control when in later years he was all but overwhelmed by uttermost tragedy.

# CHAPTER IV

## SOLDIER IN THE WILD NORTH

AFTER his graduation from the Military Academy, Brevet Lieutenant Davis was granted a three months' furlough before reporting for duty at Jefferson Barracks in Missouri. While at Rosemont he became better acquainted with James Pemberton, the servant his father had given him shortly before he died. It had been Samuel Davis's custom to give each of his children a favorite slave when he or she left home, but since Jeff could not take James to West Point, he had remained as a house boy at his mother's place. When they were both youngsters, James had chosen the youngest Davis for his master as surely as Jefferson had chosen him. The Negro was of "a dark griffe color," for he had a strain of Indian blood. Already he had acquired gentlemanly manners and soon he was imitating his young master in diction.

Jeff spent some weeks with his brother Joseph at the plantation which he had bought in 1818. Isaac and his family had moved to a farm of their own after a cyclone had destroyed his house, wrecked the improvements he had made, killed one of his little boys, and made him a cripple. He and Susannah could not endure the unhappy associations. Though still connected with law firms in Natchez and Greenville, Joseph had given up his active practice to devote his entire energies to cotton planting and stock breeding, and he was making a notable success. At the plantation Jeff met Joseph's new wife, the eighteen-year-old Elizabeth van

Bentheysen, whom he had married the year before in New Orleans. She came of a good Dutch family from New York, where most of her relatives resided. A young woman of extraordinary amiability, she was somewhat frail looking and hardly pretty. Her mother, however, who had borne twelve children, was considered strikingly beautiful, with a mass of natural curls that remained golden into middle age. To support her younger children when she was left a widow, Mrs. van Bentheysen kept a kind of boarding house for gentlefolk in New Orleans, where Joseph was a guest when he met Eliza. Jefferson found that the gentle Eliza was proving a devoted young stepmother to Joseph's three daughters by a former union, and they in turn loved her, as numerous extant letters about "dearest Mamá" reveal. Jeff was charmed by his nieces—Florida, Caroline, and Mary—who had been tenderly reared by his sister Lucinda. All three were pretty, and the youngest was a beauty.[1] Now they had a governess, but Joseph planned to send them, as he and his father had Jefferson, to a Catholic school: the Ursuline College in New Orleans.

After four years of West Point dormitory living, the seductive plantation routine, with so much family love, made it hard for the young soldier to say good-by. When he took the northbound river boat for St. Louis, it was comforting to have with him James Pemberton, who, as his body servant in the ensuing years in the wild North country, was to prove a blessing beyond all reckoning.

Lieutenant Davis found Jefferson Barracks beautifully situated on a bluff nine miles south of St. Louis, surrounded by groves of oaks and hickories, with no undergrowth to interrupt a horseback ride in three directions. Jeff was happy that Sidney Johnston had been made adjutant by General Henry Atkinson, who was in command. It was an agreeable place in which to begin active duty, particularly since the commander's Louisville-born wife

[1] A very fine portrait of Mary, presumably by Rembrandt Peale, hangs in the reception hall at the home of her granddaughter, Mrs. Mary Lucy O'Kelley, at Pass Christian, Mississippi. The three girls married in their teens: Florida became Mrs. McCaleb; Caroline married a Leonard of Norfolk, Virginia; and Mary became the wife of Dr. Charles Mitchell.

made the barracks "a delightful home for young officers serving their apprenticeship in arms." St. Louis was near enough for Jeff to mingle in its hospitable society. Although only a rough town of some 5,000 inhabitants in 1828, it was gay and pleasure-loving, with the old French flavor still dominant. At a dance given by the Chouteaus in St. Louis, Johnston had met his wife, Henrietta Preston, whose sister was married to the governor of Missouri.

From the congenial routine of Jefferson Barracks, Lieutenant Davis was all too quickly transferred to the northern outpost of Fort Crawford, hard by Prairie du Chien, a trading post on the Wisconsin River near its confluence with the Mississippi. The fort had been built and garrisoned for the protection of white settlers from hostile Indians. As early as 1766, Prairie du Chien was described as "a great mart, where tribes from the most remote branches of the Mississippi annually assemble, bringing with them furs to dispose of to traders." It was in these northern wilds that John Jacob Astor, the immigrant fur trader from Waldorf, Germany, laid the foundations of the Astor fortune.

When Lieutenant Davis, arrayed in his best uniform, reported to regimental headquarters with all the proud formality of a West Pointer, he found only a major in temporary command, and that officer not in his office. The Lieutenant finally discovered Major Bennett Riley seated at a table in the commissary concentrating on a game of solitaire. To his smart salute, the Major responded with a vague nod, waved him casually to a chair, and intently continued his game. After some minutes he paused to look at the new lieutenant: "Young man, do you play solitaire?" he asked. "Finest game in the world! You may cheat as much as you please and have nobody detect it."

This reception was far from what the eager young officer fresh from the Military Academy had expected. But it gave him quick understanding of the difference between the strict decorum of West Point and the casualness of camp life on a rude frontier.

Lieutenant Davis's first assignment was about as tough as any tenderfoot not yet twenty-one could have faced. He was ordered to procure proper timber to strengthen and enlarge Fort Crawford, which was sagging in disrepair. Since the surrounding prairies were virtually treeless, he was advised to go far north to seek a virgin forest with a plenitude of red cedars, hackmatack, and other durable woods, as well as pine. In his new role of lumberman, in which he had never had the slightest experience, Jefferson ascended the rivers with a detachment of men in an open boat. He was accompanied by two *voyageurs,* French Canadians whose profession it was to act as guides when they were not trapping fur-bearing animals.

As they made their way upstream, a large party of Indians hailed them and said they "wanted a trade in tobacco." In all innocence, Lieutenant Davis told his men to row over to the bank to barter. But the *voyageurs,* versed in the subtleties of savages, perceived on arrival that for all their ostentatious friendliness, the Indians' intentions were evil. They warned the officer of impending danger.

Desiring to avoid trouble, Lieutenant Davis gave orders to push away at once and to make the fastest speed possible upstream. The foiled Indians rushed to their canoes and pursued them, whooping with fury. Jeff knew well enough that if they were captured, they might be put to torture before being scalped. In desperate plight, as the seasoned rowers in the light canoes gained on them, he hit upon the idea of making a sail out of a blanket, for luckily the wind was in the right direction. Though the breeze was so strong the boat almost overturned in the rough water, the sail device worked, and after a breathtaking chase, the white men made their escape.

About ten miles from the mouth of the Menomonie River and some 175 miles above Fort Crawford, Lieutenant Davis set up his lumber camp. The region was in its pristine splendor, with deer, elk, and black bear in abundance. Here in this primeval northern forest, according to dubious testimony of a lumberman's magazine, under the command of the young Mississippian, "the white man's axe was first heard in the pine forests of Wisconsin."

When the trees were felled, they were cut into logs, dragged to the bank, heaved into the river, fastened together in rafts, and floated downstream to the Chippewa, thence to the Mississippi, and finally salvaged at Prairie du Chien on the Wisconsin. The rugged assignment was made exciting by the potential menace of savages. Once, when the soldiers were working near the river bank, a sentinel gave the alarm and the party barely had time to hide before a flotilla of canoes, full of Indians striped with war paint and chanting war songs, came along. One canoe landed, and a suspicious brave walked within twelve feet of Jeff's hiding place.

In the fall of 1829, after this severe trial of the young man's hardihood and ability, Lieutenant Davis was sent on a scouting mission that paid an unexpected dividend. About fifty miles from Fort Crawford one black, cold night, accompanied by a sergeant, he rode up to a log cabin at Sinsinawa Mound, and called out to inquire for a Mr. Jones. When the owner of the cabin said he answered to the name of George Jones, the Lieutenant asked shelter for the night. The men were welcome to share his buffalo robes in the house, Jones replied, and they could corral their horses with his on the prairie.

Before he dismounted, Lieutenant Davis asked his host if he had ever attended Transylvania University and if he remembered a boy named Jeff Davis.

"Of course, I do!"

"Well, I'm Jeff."

The amazed Jones pulled him from his horse, embraced him heartily, and led him into the cabin. They talked away the rest of the night and kept on talking for days. This George Wallace Jones, afterward a general and United States Senator from Iowa, was one of Jefferson Davis's most loyal and devoted friends throughout his long life.

Late in the year, Davis was transferred to Fort Winnebago, which had been built on Lake Winnebago to command the portage some two miles from the junctions of the Wisconsin and Fox rivers. It was John Jacob Astor who in 1828 had persuaded the Government to establish an agency and build a defensive structure at this strategic spot, and to furnish teams of oxen for transporting canoes from one river to the other.

At Fort Winnebago, where he found several West Pointers, Jeff took a keen interest in both the neighborhood pioneers, with their salty, picturesque speech, and the different types of Indians who were continually turning up from vast distances to trade at the sutler's store, already the largest in the Northwest. He learned the difference between Sacs and Foxes, Winnebagos and Kickapoos, Sioux and Comanches. The stamina of the half-breed mail runners never ceased to astound him. With heavy sacks of mail some could cover forty miles a day by pausing to rest five minutes every five miles. He became fond of an orphan Indian boy, who was called Tochonegra, the Otter, because of his skill in diving after fish. From the prow of his canoe "he would hurl his spear at a fish and then dive into the water and seize the injured prey with his hands." The Lieutenant admired the boy's pluck and independence and he enjoyed buying him raisins and other treats at the sutler's.

Though Jeff instinctively liked the Indians for certain admirable traits, he also marveled at the courage and fortitude of the pioneers, who, because of some discontent back home or some compelling roseate dream, had left behind all the so-called creature comforts. With their wives and little ones, daring men had begun new lives in cabins of green logs hastily thrown together, small protection against the terrible sub-zero weather. Babies had been known to freeze to death in cribs a few feet away from their parents. The incredible toil in clearing land, planting and working a crop with indifferent farm tools, was made the harder by unpredictable Indian malignancy. Many a pioneer did his first plowing with a rifle lashed to the plow beam. Hostile Indians had devilish ways of harassing settlers. Cabins might be set afire in the dead of a freezing night. Savages would sometimes steal a farmer's horses and cattle, leaving the poor fellow without means of livelihood. Occasionally a child would be snatched from the yard where he was playing, and more rarely a mother and all her little ones would be carried off captive. Lieutenant Davis was once sent to rescue a kidnaped boy and found him ragged, dirty, darkly sunburned, but quite content with the red men.

When he visited the pioneers in their cabins, Jeff was struck by their homely inventiveness, "the variety of things they could do and he could not." "Sustained effort, danger, and the habit of living alone with nature," he later told a friend, "had developed in them a thousand radical virtues."

At Fort Winnebago neighboring pioneers often shared in the camp diversions, and from miles around would bring their wives and daughters to the "gumbo balls." The name came from the refreshments, which consisted of bowls of hot gumbo served with copious bread. The young lieutenant, who had been taught at West Point by Boston's top dancing master, enjoyed stepping it to frontier fiddle tunes like "The Moon It Is Rizin', Jinnie, Come Away."

Other diversions, besides dancing, ranged from amateur theatricals and moonlight sleigh rides on the frozen lake to the cruel sport of wolf baiting and betting on horse fights. Stallion ponies were trained in a log arena, and when a fight was on, the spectators stood outside around the walls, their eyes riveted to chinks. The Indians would wildly shout encouragement to the horse they had bet on, and under the frenetic excitement they would sometimes raise their wagers to their last blanket. When a horse was finally driven into his corner by his adversary and refused to come out, the referee declared the bout ended.

But card games were the most popular of all soldier pastimes; both officers and men played cards for long successions of idle hours. Lieutenant Davis, like Captain W. S. Harney, the fort commander, had no interest in cards or gambling of any kind. Harney's hobby was his garden; he took pride in the flowers and fresh vegetables he grew. Jeff's spare hours were mostly given to reading. Though it is not known what he read in that far-flung region, "the fact is," as Dodd says, "that he was a student and won the reputation of being chary of losing time from his books." For relaxation other than reading and dancing, Jeff delighted in riding "crazy horses." Several times he barely escaped being killed, but he seemed to have absolutely no fear and invariably conquered his mount.

Jeff's routine of camp life at Winnebago was interrupted now and again by punitive expeditions on the Comanches and other hostile tribes. He was sent, too, on various reconnaissances. He and a file of soldiers under him, according to his own testimony, were perhaps the first white men who ever passed over the country between the Portage and the village of Chicago. Along the way they lived like the natives on corn and wild rice, fish and waterfowl. At another time, as William Preston Johnston was told, "with only two men, he passed from Rock Island to Chicago without molestation and with only a single threatening demonstration from the Indians he met."

Once, however, on a scouting trip, he and his soldiers were confronted by a large party of surly Indians. When the Lieutenant asked the way, a brave stationed himself directly in front of his path and pointed a direction Davis knew could not be right. Having developed something of a sixth sense concerning Indian deceit, he suddenly spurred his horse [2] directly toward the brave, seized him by the scalp lock as he dashed by, dragged him a distance, and let him drop violently to the ground. The action was so quick, so surprising, that the Indians fell back in dismay, while the white men passed through their midst unharmed.

In 1831 Lieutenant Davis was recalled to Fort Crawford and sent up to Yellow River to construct a sawmill in the forest. He straightway set about making friends with the neighboring Indians. His responsive amiability and dignified authority pleased them so much that he was "adopted by a chief within the sacred bonds of brotherhood." Because of his youth, they affectionately called him "Little Chief."

[2] Davis's horse was named Red Bird after the noted Indian warrior whose capture in 1827 gave settlers enough sense of security to move in about the lead mines of Galena, Illinois. Albert Sidney Johnston considered Red Bird "one of the noblest and most dignified specimens of manhood" he ever saw. The chief died in prison.

In this primeval region far from supplies, Jeff's work was extremely arduous and beset with difficulties. He had never had experience with a sawmill, and the winter turned out to be one of the worst the North had ever known. It snowed steadily until the flat ground was more than three feet deep in snow, and then came periodic freezing rains. Even down in central Illinois, where there was at least a modicum of civilized comforts, the winter was almost unbearable. For half a century afterward the season was remembered in the Northwest as "the winter of the deep snow."

Young Davis had never concerned himself with care of his health. Though he possessed a highly sensitive nervous system, he had been remarkably well all his life. Now heedless of health hazards and the admonitions of James Pemberton, he often got soaked to the skin while directing the sawmill construction. At last he came down with a virulent case of pneumonia.

Without benefit of physician and with only the rudest camp fare for diet, Jeff lay at the verge of death. Except for the vigilant ministrations of his body servant, he probably would have died. It was the heartening devotion of James Pemberton that kept the breath of life in him. Delegating much authority to James, he entrusted him with his weapons, his money, his reports. Through the colored man, during his semidelirious illness, the Lieutenant tried to direct the construction work. When he began to convalesce, he had lost so much weight and was so weak that James would pick the tall young man up in his arms like a child. Sometimes he would carry his master to the window to glimpse the thrilling beauty of the whitened landscape.[3]

When the sawmill was at last completed and operating to his satisfaction, Lieutenant Davis returned to Fort Crawford to superintend expansive enlargements. Almost immediately he faced

---

[3] After this near-fatal illness in the far North, Jefferson Davis was susceptible to colds and grippe; occasionally the colds would be accompanied by agonizing seizures of facial neuralgia, which would render him literally blind with pain. Later, at critical hours in history, sometimes when momentous decisions had to be made, he was all but incapacitated by neuralgic anguish. The glare from the northern snow, Varina Davis writes, permanently weakened his eyes.

a different kind of crisis. Because of his fresh color, his virtual lack of beard, and his gay laugh, Jeff at twenty-three looked nearer nineteen. When he took charge of the building project, a pugnacious, powerfully built soldier boasted that he would thrash "that baby-faced lieutenant" if he attempted to boss him. The bruiser's threat was promptly communicated to the Lieutenant.

Next morning when Jeff told the soldier to put a piece of dressed scantling in a certain place in the construction, the man deliberately picked up a rough plank instead. The Lieutenant patiently explained. With a sneering laugh the soldier threw down the rough plank and then ostentatiously stooped to pick up another one just as rough. All the workers stopped still, intent on what would happen. Quick as a flash, Jeff seized a stout stick of wood lying at his feet and struck the man down before he could raise his plank. Then he proceeded to beat him until the bully yelled for mercy. The soldiers, amazed at this swift turning of the tables by the pluck and authority of the young officer, gave him a rousing shout of approval. Dropping his cudgel, Davis said quietly, "This has been a fight between man and man and I shall not notice it officially." From that day he never had disciplinary trouble.

Before the construction job had been completed, Second Lieutenant Davis was sent with First Lieutenant Abercrombie on a mission requiring uncommon tact and firm resolution. It was their duty to remove, "at bayonet point if necessary," squatters who had staked out claims and built cabins around the lead mines near Dubuque, Iowa. Though the Government was negotiating with the Indians for the region and a treaty was in the process of being made, the land still belonged to the red men and they, too, were in ugly mood.

A few weeks before, Lieutenant Wilson had been sent with a small detachment to effect the removal, but he had failed to budge a single frontiersman. Now Abercrombie and Davis were commanded to execute Government orders. With fifty soldiers they reached Dubuque in severe winter weather and found themselves facing some four hundred squatters and miners heavily armed. Because Davis had previously known some of them when on brief duty at Dubuque, Abercrombie let him handle the situation. Lieutenant Davis approached the men in a most conciliatory manner. A rangy red-headed fellow, their chosen spokesman, informed him that if he knew what was good for him he would take his soldiers away and "leave honest men alone."

Realizing that the squatters were determined on armed resistance, Lieutenant Davis urged the redhead aside for a man-to-man talk. He assured him that it was only a matter of a short time before all their claims would be fully established. He made clear that the Government had first to dispose of the Indian claims peaceably by treaty. Then he addressed the sullen crowd, making his first extemporaneous speech in public. Taking no notice of their heckling insults, he soon had them all listening attentively. Later he and Abercrombie visited individual families in cabins and explained the lack of any power on their part to modify or long delay execution of the orders from Washington. Lieutenant Davis expressed sincere sympathy about their having to move in the cold weather and offered to furnish some wagons for their convenience. But he reiterated that go they must. Abercrombie gave them some time to think the matter over and to prepare for the removal.

In the meantime Jeff spent some days with his Transylvania schoolmate George Jones, who lived not far from Dubuque. Jones's two little boys took a great fancy to the young Southerner, who, the father says, would "hold them on his lap as if they were his own."

When he returned to the lead-mine region, Jeff found a score of the miners, including the redhead, in a one-room log saloon. His orderly warned him not to go in, for he had been told the men intended to kill him. Brushing aside the warning with a confident smile, Davis promptly entered, and after cheerfully passing the time of day, ordered drinks for everybody. "My friends," he said, "I am sure you have thought over my proposition and are going to drink to my success. So I treat you all."

The next day an office was set up and the various claims with detailed descriptions of each piece of property were registered. The men were assured the claims would be legally theirs the day the treaty with the Indians was concluded. One frail woman was allowed to remain in her cabin, but everybody else departed.

Lieutenant Davis had proved himself an able diplomat. Not a drop of blood had been shed, not a blow struck. And at the conclusion of the treaty, the squatters returned to their houses and repossessed their claims.

Brevet Colonel Zachary Taylor had been observing young Davis's conduct and abilities with special interest even before he took temporary command at Fort Crawford because of the illness of Colonel Willoughby Morgan. In 1832 he made Davis his aide.

Though the Colonel's father, Richard Taylor, was a pioneer in Kentucky, Zachary was Virginia-born (in Orange County), and brought to Louisville in a saddlebag when he was eight weeks old. On both sides his family were gentry, and he himself married a Maryland blue blood, Margaret Mackall Smith. But his education had been extremely sketchy, and at twenty-four, he had entered the army with a commission of first lieutenant.

Now at forty-seven, the same age as Jefferson's brother Joseph, Zachary Taylor was chafing because he had not yet been promoted to a full colonelcy, though he had been a brevet colonel for thirteen years. He had good cause to be disgruntled, because he had done heroic service in the War of 1812, and to every post he had been sent he had brought conspicuous benefits. On his army pay he could hardly have supported his family in adequate style if he had not possessed farms which brought him an income. As Jeff learned, by inclination Zachary Taylor was as much a farmer as he was a soldier. Besides his inherited acres in Kentucky, he had bought a plantation in West Feliciana Parish, Louisiana, where Jeff's eldest sister lived, and more recently, land in Wilkinson County, Mississippi, Jeff's own home county.

With much in common, the two men got on splendidly together

for some time. Lieutenant Davis was punctilious in the performance of his duties, and though he was a voracious reader, he also found time to be an attractive asset in post society. While he did not care much for drinking, he would take his shot of whisky now and again, and he was always in evidence at the dances.

One story, not authenticated and decidedly suspect, which appeared in Nehemiah Matson's *Memories of Shaubena* in 1878, tells how Jefferson Davis almost got into serious trouble at a celebration dance following an Indian wedding, which he attended with Colonel Taylor and Captain Tom Smith.

The Lieutenant became attracted by a beautiful young half-breed and took her for his partner in nearly every set. "He would do many remarkable things, sometimes changing the order of the dance to suit his fancy. When quadrilles were danced, he would change into a waltz, so he could have his arms around the waist of the young squaw; then again, freeing himself from her, he would dance with all his might, causing his tall form to jerk and wiggle as it swayed to and fro; sometimes jumping up and down in quick succession, and yelling at the top of his voice, in imitation of the Indians at the door." According to the story, Colonel Taylor sat on the sidelines and "almost split his sides with laughter."

The young woman, misinterpreting the laughter, felt that she was being mocked, and so informed her burly Indian brother standing at the door. Bleary-eyed with grog, the Indian pulled out a long scalping knife and approached Davis, who warningly drew his pistol. Women screamed. The music stopped. Colonel Taylor sprang between the two and halted what might have been a mortal combat. Though the story, not published until forty years after the alleged event, may be completely without foundation, it bears on the tradition that as a young man Jefferson Davis was something of a gay blade, as well as a correct officer with scholarly inclinations.

# CHAPTER V

# TROUBLE WITH BLACK HAWK

WHEN Jefferson Davis first came to Fort Crawford early in 1829, many Sacs and Foxes were still living in their traditional villages. He had heard exciting stories about Black Hawk, the remarkable Sac leader, who was considered a terror by other Indian tribes, for by his own account the number of men he had slain "staggered credulity." Once, in the War of 1812, when an ally of the British, Black Hawk had caught Zachary Taylor's soldiers in a defenseless position and routed them with British cannon.

Black Hawk, now past sixty, had been born in 1767 at the Sac village on Rock River in western Illinois, where his father was the tribal medicine man. He was thirty-nine when five Indian leaders signed a momentous treaty at St. Louis with General William Henry Harrison by which they ceded to the Government "upwards of 51,000,000 acres,"[1] lying mostly in what is now western Illinois and Wisconsin. The Indians had been allowed to retain their hunting and fishing rights until the land should be needed by white men and put up for sale. But because of the soil's remarkable fertility near the mouth of Rock River and because of the potential protection of Fort Armstrong, which had been built on Rock Island in the Mississippi not many miles from

---

[1] For this vast territory the United States paid in goods the value of $2,234.50 and pledged an annuity of $1,000. Black Hawk declared that the Indians were drunk when they signed away millions of acres for a pittance, and he always maintained that this treaty was the origin of all the troubles between his people and the Americans.

Black Hawk's own village, squatters were pushing closer and closer to the Indian settlements.

In 1829, at the urgency of President Andrew Jackson, Congress decided the time had come to survey the lands of western Illinois and open them for sale. At the Government's request, Keokuk, the eloquent and conciliatory chief of the Sacs, of whom his relative Black Hawk was extremely jealous, removed his people to the west side of the Mississippi. But when Black Hawk was told that his own village was included in the survey, in smoldering rage he refused to budge. The Sacs became a nation divided; those who sided with the dynamic Black Hawk became known as the British Band, because of the old Indian's pro-British sympathies.

Davis knew that blood was bad on both sides in the spring of 1831 when the Indians returned from their winter hunt to plant corn and found "the whites prepared to resist them and Black Hawk's own wickiup occupied." The old warrior, Davis felt, had a right to be indignant. The settlers had burned some of the Indian lodges, destroyed fences, beaten squaws, and even plowed up the burial ground of Black Hawk's ancestors. They had brought whisky into the Indian villages, made his people drunk, and cheated them out of horses, guns, and traps. The furious brave began making his own wily depredations on the squatters' property and livestock. Openly he entered one settler's cabin, seized a barrel of whisky, broke in the head, and poured the demoralizing liquor on the ground. At this overt hostile action a group of pioneers sent an urgent petition to Governor Reynolds of Illinois requesting militia to oust the Indians from their own homes. Although the garrisons at Fort Armstrong and Fort Crawford were there to protect the settlers, for political reasons Reynolds called for volunteers.

The Governor made a special request of Colonel James Strode [2] of Galena to organize all Jo Daviess County for action. Strode,

---

[2] James M. Strode was the great-grandfather of the author of this biography. For some years he lived in Chicago and then went to England, where he lived until his death. His four Virginia-born sons remained in America.

a lawyer from Virginia, who had come to Galena because of prospective fortune in the lead mines, was then a candidate for state senator (and later elected). Calling the miners and settlers together on the old racecourse by the river, he explained the critical situation and asked for volunteers. Influenced by his political opponent, they disputed his command. Then Strode ill-advisedly declared martial law. The men became surly, and he was powerless to act.

Lieutenant Davis was dispatched posthaste to Strode's relief. When he arrived in Galena on Saturday with a small detachment of regulars, he found the citizens in dark and muttering mood. Once before he had handled a more difficult situation when he persuaded miners to abandon their homes in mid-winter. Now with increased understanding and with his ingratiating personality, the young lieutenant smoothed the ruffled tempers. On Monday he organized the volunteer regiment and shortly turned it over to the blundering Colonel Strode.

Then Lieutenant Davis returned to Dixon's Ferry, Illinois, which because of its strategic situation on Rock River often became a kind of casual army headquarters. The Lieutenant was a warm friend of John Dixon, the ferryman, who kept a "house of entertainment" in otherwise uninhabited country. Often when scouting he had stopped at this rambling ninety-foot-long log house, with a middle section of two stories, which served as store, bank, post office, and inn. Dixon was perhaps the most popular man in the Northwest. Indians had implicit confidence in "Father Dixon," and entrusted their money to his keeping.

Besides Indians, fur traders, miners, mail carriers, and itinerant preachers who traveled the trail passing Dixon's Ferry, "men destined to a place in history messed and traded" with John Dixon. In the year of 1832, Frank Stevens records in *The Black Hawk War*, "among the men who enjoyed Dixon's hospitality were Col. James M. Strode, the then noted but erratic criminal lawyer of Galena, Illinois; Lieutenant Colonel Zachary Taylor, who afterwards became President of the United States, and General Winfield Scott, who wanted to be; Lieutenant Jefferson

Davis, who was President of the Southern Confederacy; and Captain Abraham Lincoln, who dissolved it. We find them all associated with the old trail and eating and lodging with mine host Dixon, singly and together. There were besides Lieutenant Albert Sidney Johnston and Lieutenant Robert Anderson, the fateful commander of Ft. Sumter." "Dixon," says Stevens, who was born at Dixon's Ferry, "often laughingly spoke of the fact that while he often sold them bills of goods, Lieutenant Davis and Lieutenant Anderson were always cash customers."

Jefferson Davis sometimes fished and hunted squirrels near Dixon's Ferry. Occasionally he was accompanied by Lieutenant Robert Anderson, West Point friend from Kentucky, three years his senior, "a shy young man with great trusting brown eyes, pink cheeks, and thin lips that twisted up towards the left."

Shortly after Davis had helped Strode organize militia at Galena, a large troop of mounted volunteers from Beardstown, Illinois, marched on Black Hawk's village. Warned by Federal officers from Fort Armstrong, Black Hawk escaped with his entire band across the Mississippi in the night during a terrific rainstorm. Finding the village empty, the volunteers gave vent to their displeasure by burning it to ashes. On June 30, along with nine chiefs, the bitter Black Hawk was finally induced to sign a new treaty by which he promised to stay on the hunting grounds west of the Mississippi.

Back at Fort Crawford, Davis heard that Black Hawk was in no wise content. And according to rumors at the end of 1831, the Indian leader had dispatched a lieutenant to solicit British aid in Canada and sent runners as far south as the Gulf of Mexico, urging Indians to rally round him in a confederacy that would crush the white intruders.

But on the surface everything was peaceful in the Northwest when Jefferson Davis left on furlough on March 24, 1832, "to attend to some private matters" in Mississippi. Since he had had no leave in three and a half years, he had a great deal of vacation time coming to him. He had been at his mother's place hardly a month when news drifted down to Woodville that in defiance of treaties, Black Hawk on April 6 had crossed to the east bank of the Mississippi near the mouth of the Iowa. "His band," according to Albert Sidney Johnston's *Journal* of April 10, "consisted of four or five hundred well-appointed horsemen, besides men and boys employed in transporting the canoes, capable of bearing arms, making an active and efficient force of between five and six hundred: the whole—men, women and children—amounting to above two thousand souls. . . ."[3] The ultimate intentions of Black Hawk were unknown." In his autobiography Black Hawk claims he was merely going "to make corn."

Encumbered by squaws, children, and old folks, it hardly seemed to Jeff down in Mississippi that Black Hawk's intention was to fight. But in Illinois news spread that Black Hawk had raised the British flag and was hunting trouble. Settlers within three hundred miles were alerted. On April 16, as Jeff learned much later, Governor Reynolds of Illinois issued an appeal to the militia of the northwestern section of the state. Until April 24, however, General Henry Atkinson, in command of all Federal troops in the Northwest, was sending emissaries to Black Hawk to urge him to return to Iowa. On the twenty-sixth Black Hawk sent a final answer: "his heart was bad," he said, and he was determined not to turn back. With all of his impedimenta he moved northeast and disappeared in the forests.

In answer to Governor Reynolds's urgent call to arms, thirteen hundred horsemen and three hundred foot soldiers volunteered for thirty days' service. They reached Rock Island on May 7, the day Zachary Taylor assumed command of the First Infantry at Fort Armstrong. Among them was a homely, good-natured captain of militia from Sangamon County. His name was Abraham Lincoln. "Being out of a job," this gawky young man of twenty-three, who stood six feet four and a half inches tall, had volunteered on April 21. Five days later by a large majority he had been chosen captain of a company of sixty-eight volunteers. Though he understood nothing of military discipline and had to

[3] Most estimates give one thousand as the maximum number of persons who were in Black Hawk's band.

borrow a horse on which to go to war, the men picked the lanky fellow in blue jeans to lead them because they liked him. He knew how to josh and to keep them amused with salty anecdotes. They admired his extraordinary physical prowess, his athletic skill in wrestling, jumping, and foot racing. Absorbing as much about drilling tactics as he could in five days, Lincoln had set off at the head of his motley company.

The militia were an independent lot, their ranks well seasoned with roughneck no-goods who had little respect for authority. But in his droll, down-to-earth way, Lincoln could manage his gang. Within a fortnight, however, he had got himself into trouble by disobeying Colonel Taylor's Order of April 30 forbidding the unnecessary firing of arms. On the march to the Yellow Banks, after crossing Henderson River with great inconvenience, by way of celebration, his men indulged in wanton shooting. The action promptly brought upon the captain's head a minor disgrace. He was reprimanded "by being compelled to wear a wooden sword." [4]

Thereafter Lincoln was cautious, and his men never again fired a gun in playful exuberance. But on the night of May 9 a volunteer from another company persuaded some of Lincoln's men to break into officers' quarters with a tomahawk and steal four bucketfuls of whisky. The next morning when the order came to march some of Lincoln's command were too drunk to proceed. Though he was blameless in this affair, the captain received a sharper reprimand and was again sentenced to wear the ignominious wooden sword for two days.[5]

On May 14, just before Lincoln's company arrived at Dixon's Ferry, eager Illinois volunteers under Major Stillman's command, who had joined up partly for "the sport of killing Indians," had advanced thirty miles beyond Dixon's when they saw approaching three Indians bearing a white flag. In his autobiography,

[4] Carl Sandburg says Captain Lincoln himself "against orders, shot off a pistol inside the camp; he was arrested, his sword taken away, and he was held in custody one day."

[5] According to Sandburg: "A court-martial ordered Captain Lincoln to carry a wooden sword two days."

Black Hawk claims he sent them to request a conference with General Atkinson, so that they might come to a peaceable solution and avoid bloodshed. But Stillman's advance men seized the Indians as prisoners. When his emissaries did not return, Black Hawk sent five young men to reconnoiter. These scouts were met by forty white men at full gallop, who pursued them and killed two. The volunteers at their first kill had become as jubilant as fox hunters. Excitedly the whole force of more than two hundred and fifty dashed forward and were met by a detachment of Black Hawk's braves.

At the first volley from the Sacs, the white troops retreated "in the utmost confusion and consternation." Black Hawk was utterly astounded when the Illinois militia turned tail and fled. The volunteers began what Albert Sidney Johnston called "a disgraceful flight." Some two hundred and sixty Americans were chased back thirty-odd miles to base by less than fifty Indians. From three o'clock to daylight on the morning of May 15 the straggling volunteers arrived at Dixon's Ferry in the grip of mass panic, breathing out Falstaffian exaggerations of their desperate fight against two thousand ferocious redskins. Instead of desiring to wreak vengeance, many volunteers clamored to be discharged. "Injun fighting" was not at all the sport they had expected. Stillman's men had thrown away all their equipment, their rifles and saddlebags, which the Indians salvaged to good advantage. Some sneaked off in desertion, their excuse being they had to go home to plant their crops.

On July 10, after two re-enlistments of a few weeks each, Abraham Lincoln's war service ended.[6] He was never involved in any fighting, for after that engagement, which became known in history as Stillman's Run, the Americans had not been able to find Black Hawk's band. Lincoln was mustered out of the army more than a fortnight before the first of the only two real fights occurred. Having lost his horse, he was forced to walk home most

---

[6] The often-repeated story that Jefferson Davis swore Abraham Lincoln into service is apocryphal. But at one of Lincoln's re-enlistments Lieutenant Robert Anderson did administer the oath.

of the way. But he was tireless on the march and rallied his fatigued companions with a flow of anecdotes.

For two months Black Hawk had successfully eluded the white soldiers; his band was seemingly swallowed up in the forests somewhere between Dixon's Ferry and Fort Winnebago. Word came that they were now here, now there. And suddenly the Indians would strike at isolated farms, appropriate the provisions, and sometimes kill the settlers. By July, Black Hawk's people were suffering terribly from lack of food in the region of Four Lakes, where Madison, Wisconsin, now stands. They gnawed on bark, sucked juices from tree roots, and in desperation ate their leanest ponies. Many old people and children dropped and died from the exhaustion of long marches. Meanwhile hundreds of volunteers, whose enlistments had expired, had gone back to their homes.

During "this kind of warfare that could hardly be called a war," Jefferson Davis in lower Mississippi was having a struggle within himself. He had become somewhat disillusioned about army life on the Northwest frontier. He felt the Indians had been unjustly treated, that Black Hawk had bitter reasons for grievance. Besides, considering Zachary Taylor's own discontent over his slow promotions, he could see little brightness in an officer's future. His imagination had recently been stirred by a new invention—a train that ran on tracks with an engine propelled by steam. One railroad, sixteen miles in length, from Honesdale to Carbondale, Pennsylvania, had been experimented with in 1829, the locomotive imported from England. The following year the first regular railway built in the United States had started operation in South Carolina. Jefferson felt that this new invention would have a mighty influence on social and industrial conditions. He envisioned land hitherto valueless because of its distance from civilization suddenly acquiring great potential value, and isolated settlements marketing their farm products in the towns located on waterways. He thought he himself might like to be connected with a railroad, and perhaps he knew of a prospective company where he could be employed. From Woodville he wrote his brother Joseph to sound out his opinion.

Joseph answered him briefly, addressing the letter to J. F. Davis, Esq., Woodville, Mississippi.

Hurricane<br>July 9, 1832 [7]

My dear Brother

I am fearful you may allow my opinion to influence your conduct in a matter that deeply concerns your future life— No one can judge for another and the worst of all reasons is that such a one *said so*. In determining upon a plan of life we should look to the end and take not the shortest route but the surest. . . .

Of this RailRoad I have no high opinion and, as you know, have always regarded it as a failure sooner or later. I had therefore rather have Com$^r$ Engineer under the authority of the Gov than be in the employ of a small Comy.

Say to my mother I hope to see her this summer.

Your Brother

It seems strange that Joseph, who was an advanced thinker— he even favored woman's suffrage, affirming it was only right and just that a woman who paid taxes should vote—did not foresee the railroad's future as did his young brother. His letter apparently squashed Jefferson's thought of resigning his commission. But on what date Lieutenant Davis left Mississippi to return to duty is not known or exactly when he arrived. He must have rejoined his regiment by July 21, the day Black Hawk's people were at last overtaken at Wisconsin Heights, a crossing of the Wisconsin River some twenty miles below Fort Winnebago. According to Charles Aldrich in an article, "Jefferson Davis and Black Hawk," in *The Midland Monthly,* Davis gave him the following vivid account of an engagement that certainly sounds as if it were that of Wisconsin Heights.

[7] The date of this letter proves conclusively that Jefferson Davis was still in Mississippi on July 9, though his biographers seem to believe he was then with the First Infantry in Illinois. They assign varied dates for his return. This letter is in the possession of Jefferson Hayes-Davis of Colorado Springs.

"We were one day pursuing the Indians, when we came close to the Wisconsin River. Reaching the river bank the Indians made so determined a stand and fought with such desperation that they held us in check. During this time the squaws tore bark from the trees and made little shallops, in which they floated their papooses and other impedimenta . . . across to an island; also swimming over their ponies. As soon as this was accomplished, half of the warriors plunged in and swam across, each holding his gun in one hand, and swimming with the other. As soon as they reached the opposite bank, they opened fire upon us under cover of which the other half slipped down the bank and swam in like manner. This was the most brilliant exhibition of military tactics that I ever witnessed, a feat of the most consummate management and bravery, in the face of an enemy of greatly superior numbers. . . . I have never read of anything that could be compared with it. Had it been performed by white men, it would have been immortalized as one of the most splendid achievements in military history." [8]

In any case, the half-starved Indians, though defeated, made a gallant defense at Wisconsin Heights, the first real engagement of the so-called war. Now Black Hawk, determining to recross the Mississippi and avoid further trouble, headed west by a devious route. He found he could expect no mercy from the whites, for when he sent a large raft full of women and children down the Wisconsin to Fort Crawford to ask permission to cross the Mississippi, they were all killed on arrival.

On July 27 General Atkinson dispatched nine hundred of the best mounted volunteers to join the regulars in intercepting the fugitive enemy. Then he ordered the steamboat *Warrior* up the Mississippi to prevent their escape. On Wednesday, August 1, Black Hawk and his famished band reached the Mississippi at a point two miles below the mouth of a little river called Bad Axe. Here Black Hawk began the slow process of sending his

[8] Cyrenus Cole says in *I Am a Man, The Indian Black Hawk*, "Jefferson Davis awarded Black Hawk the reputation he craved."

people across the Mississippi in the only three canoes available. Near the mouth of Bad Axe the captain of the *Warrior* discovered a band of Indians about a hoisted white flag. Black Hawk called out that he wanted to surrender. Captain Throckmorton, "affecting to believe that an ambush was intended," shot a six-pounder crashing into their midst, and then followed with rounds of cannister and musket fire. Leaving their dead, the Indians beat a hasty retreat. Along the bottoms at the foot of a bluff, three hundred militiamen under General Henry charged the trapped Indians, who fell back, shooting from tree to tree. The whites fought furiously with bayonets as the enemy tried to escape. Some Indians leaped into the river; others sought shelter on an island lush with willows. The soldiers kept up a relentless fire, dropping squaws along with braves. "It was not a battle," writes Cyrenus Cole, "it was massacre of red men, women and children in rags, by white soldiers, some of them in uniform."

The slaughter was virtually completed when Zachary Taylor arrived in hot haste. Eager to see the Black Hawk menace stilled forever, Taylor led his men breast-deep into the water across a slough to an island, beat about the willows, and finished off the last lurking brave.

After three hours of bloody carnage near the mouth of Bad Axe, one hundred and fifty Indians lay dead. Many others were drowned. A miserable lot of forty-odd starving, wounded Indians, mostly women and children, were taken prisoners. The Battle of Bad Axe, which occurred on August 2, 1832, crushed forever the power of Black Hawk and his cohorts. But with his son, the Thunder, the leader himself escaped. Lieutenant Davis was dispatched with a small detachment of regulars to bring Black Hawk back dead or alive.

Jefferson Davis now comes again definitely into the chronicles, though in the Army Records, a Return of the First Regiment of Infantry for the month of August, 1832, says that "Jeff. F. Davis joined his company from leave on August 18." The date August

18 is probably that on which he reached headquarters at Fort Crawford, where records were kept. Since Colonel Taylor and the staff were in the field after mid-July, there was small opportunity to note properly Davis's return until the First Infantry got back to headquarters.

Hearing that the old warrior was hiding on an island in the Wisconsin above Prairie du Chien, Lieutenant Davis went to explore. Black Hawk had vanished. In the meantime two Winnebago chiefs, Chaeter and One-eyed Decori, former friends of the Sac, had been stalking Black Hawk because of the Government's promise of concessions for their tribe. For some days he eluded the Winnebagos too; but one evening, as he entered a wigwam near the river, they spied him. When they confronted their victim, Black Hawk "saw at once his fate was sealed. He silently held out his hands for the accustomed cord."

Shortly afterward, when Lieutenant Davis met the Winnebagos bearing a white flag, he found Black Hawk and his son captive. He brought them all down to Fort Crawford on August 18, and it was then his return from furlough was officially noted.

At Fort Crawford, Lieutenant Davis found Colonel Taylor still thoroughly disgusted with the foolishness of the volunteers under Stillman, who he considered had precipitated an unnecessary war. Taylor doubtless spoke much in the same vein to Davis as he did to his friend Quartermaster General Thomas Jesup to whom he wrote on December 4, 1832, that "that disgraceful affair of Stillman ought not to have occurred. . . . That attack made on the Indians brought on the war. Had the regular troops overtaken them, at any rate in conjunction with the militia in the field before any blood had been shed, they would have been removed back to the west side of the Mississippi without there being a gun fired." In fact, the Colonel looked upon the whole campaign as "a tissue of blunders, miserably managed from start to finish"—and so did Lieutenant Davis.

At eleven o'clock on the morning of August 27, 1832, Davis saw Black Hawk brought in before Colonel Taylor and General

Street, the Indian agent. The old Indian, lean and sinewy, was dressed in a resplendent suit of white deerskins, which Winnebago squaws had made for him. Because he kept the hair of his head plucked except for the long scalp lock, his forehead seemed extraordinarily high. A prominent Roman nose gave his face distinction. His eyebrows were as scant as Mona Lisa's, and perhaps for this reason his restless black eyes were the more arresting.

It was a moment of dramatic tension when One-eyed Decori, the Winnebago, began to speak. "My father," he said, "we deliver these men into your hands. . . . If they are to be hurt, we do not wish to see it. Wait until we are gone before it is done."

General Street replied: "My children, I am well pleased that you have taken Black Hawk. . . . I shall now deliver these men to the chief of warriors here." He indicated Colonel Taylor, who said: "The great chief of the warriors [now Winfield Scott] told me to take the prisoners and send them to Rock Island. I will take them and keep them safe. . . . The great chief of the warriors will use them in such a manner as shall be ordered by your great father, the President."

When the confrontation was ended, Lieutenant Davis was put in charge of Black Hawk and about forty other prisoners. He led them on board the steamboat *Winnebago* to deliver them to General Scott, who had recently arrived at Fort Armstrong to replace General Atkinson. By the time the boat reached Rock Island, however, the Asiatic cholera, which had struck the Northwest in early August, was raging with such virulence that Scott ordered Davis to take the prisoners on down to Jefferson Barracks below St. Louis.[9]

As Lieutenant Davis proceeded down the river with his famous prisoner of war, he treated the Indian with "all the consideration and courtesy due a fallen warlord." The twenty-four-year-old

---

[9] It had first been decided that Lieutenant Robert Anderson would have charge of captive Indians, but that amiable officer had himself been hospitalized with the cholera. Albert Sidney Johnston, too, had contracted the plague, and suffered as much agony from the empiric treatment as from the painful disease. Hot as the season was, he was, he wrote, "wrapped on the floor in heavy blankets, drenched with vinegar and salt, and made to drink brandy with cayenne pepper."

lieutenant and the battle-scarred warrior, old enough to be his grandfather, took each other's measure. Davis knew that Black Hawk could be both treacherous and cruel, but there was about him a fierce pride and dignity that came close to nobility. In his autobiography,[10] Black Hawk expressed his appreciation of Lieutenant Davis: "We started for Jefferson Barracks in a steamboat under the charge of a young war chief who treated us all with much kindness. He is a good and brave young chief with whose conduct I was very much pleased. . . . On our way down we called at Galena and remained a short time. The people crowded to the boat to see us, but the war chief would not permit them to enter the apartment where we were—knowing, from what his feelings would have been if he had been placed in a similar situation, that we did not wish a gaping crowd around us."

During the river journey two of the Indian prisoners were seized with cholera. Lieutenant Davis was moved by their suffering, which was painful to see, and did all he could to alleviate their agony. Faced as he was with the probable spread of the contagion, he granted their request to be put ashore so that they could go to the happy hunting grounds together. The boat drew up to the bank and the contaminated men were taken off. His heart ached, Davis later told his wife, when he saw the Indian who was suffering least supporting the head of his dying friend.

At Jefferson Barracks, Lieutenant Davis delivered his prisoners to General Atkinson, who released most of them on pledges of allegiance and future good behavior. Atkinson ordered Black Hawk confined to barracks and fettered him with ball and chain. The old Indian was deeply mortified. "If I had taken him prisoner on the field of battle," he said in his autobiography, "I would not have wounded his feelings so much, knowing that a brave war chief would prefer death to dishonour."

From Jefferson Barracks, Black Hawk was transferred to Fortress Monroe in Virginia, where three decades later Jefferson

[10] Black Hawk's "Autobiography" was dictated in October, 1833, to Antoine Le Claire, who translated it phrase by phrase to J. D. Patterson, who wrote it down in English.

Davis, the President of the fallen Confederacy, was displayed to jeering crowds and then shackled with ankle irons to make his humiliation the more galling.

Lieutenant Davis had reached Jefferson Barracks even more disillusioned by the inefficiency with which the war had been prosecuted. He felt as Sidney Johnston did, that the so-called war might have been "averted by foresight and a little timely generosity on the part of the Government." The fight had cost $3,000,000 and the lives of some two hundred whites, including the settlers who had been butchered in revenge. It had taken some four thousand whites under arms to defeat five hundred Indians encumbered by their families. "A dishonorable chapter in the history of the border," is Reuben Twaites's verdict in his monograph *The Black Hawk War*. Jefferson Davis always felt that the white men had won small glory in the uneven conflict. Later when questioned about the little war which momentarily had stirred the nation, he would say frankly: "The real heroes were Black Hawk and his savages."

When Black Hawk's autobiography came out at the end of 1833, Lieutenant Davis was surprised to find it tactfully dedicated to "Brigadier General H. Atkinson," the good man who had sadly bungled the war and who had put Black Hawk in chains. The close of the dedication, with its noble simplicity and restraint, he was to recall with poignant irony in 1865.

The path to glory is rough, and many gloomy hours obscure it. May the Great Spirit shed light on yours—and that you may never experience the humility that the power of the American Government has reduced me to, is the wish of him who, in his native forests, was once as proud and bold as yourself.

Black Hawk

10th Moon 1833

## CHAPTER VI

## FIRST LOVE

ON HIS return to Fort Crawford, Lieutenant Davis was a frequent caller at the Zachary Taylor home. During his absence the Taylors had moved into the commandant's log-and-frame house, which was later remodeled with a pleasant little glassed-in veranda. Near the end of the Black Hawk trouble, Mrs. Taylor had arrived from Louisville, bringing with her two black servants, her two small children, and an older daughter, Sarah Knox, who immediately attracted Lieutenant Davis.

Sarah Knox had been born on March 6, 1814, at Vincennes, Indiana, when her father was stationed there. At eighteen she was in the bloom of her girlish loveliness. According to relatives, she was "very beautiful, slight, with wavy brown hair and clear gray eyes, very lovely and lovable, and a young woman of decided spirit." The favorable description is borne out in the only known extant portrait of her which hangs in the Louisiana Historical Museum in New Orleans. Here at sixteen she is obviously "lovely and lovable," though pretty rather than beautiful. The large eyes are trusting, innocent, and yet intelligent. The mouth is small and prettily modeled; the nose, slightly tiptilted. Her wavy brown hair is parted in the middle and divided into four graceful curls, which hang to her bosom. The pink dress is daintily and sparingly trimmed in white lace. Over her left forearm and wrist is draped a filmy scarf; her right hand rests lightly on a table beside a book of embossed leather decorated in gold. There is something suggesting the Venetian school in the artist's conception, though the quality the unknown painter evidently saw in her might be called "adorable," and adorable was presumably what young Jefferson found her.[1] Born on the same day as Elizabeth Barrett Browning, eight years later, Sarah Knox possessed that special appealing quality women native to the sign of Pisces are reputed to have, a quality which supposedly frames them to be adored by their husbands.

Jefferson learned that Knox had spent comparatively little time with her father. She had lived at her grandfather Richard Taylor's estate "Springfield" near Louisville, while receiving her early education at Thomas Elliott's school nearby. Later she had attended the Pickett School in Cincinnati. During Colonel Taylor's long furlough in 1831 she had joined her parents in their town house in Louisville. There she took special dancing lessons from the elite's fashionable dancing master, a black man known as Professor Patrick. According to the boast of relatives, she became "the best dancer in Kentucky," and always had a string of beaux in attendance.

Apparently almost as soon as he met Sarah Knox, Jefferson plunged into an ardent, if discreet courtship. All the Taylors liked him, including the servants. The little girl Betty and Dick,[2] the only boy, became his lifelong friends. But when he spoke to his chief of the hope of marrying his daughter some day, he found that Colonel Taylor frowned on the union. The Colonel had vowed that his two remaining daughters would never marry soldiers. His eldest daughter, Ann, who had married Dr. Robert Wood, an army surgeon, had recently borne a baby in most primitive surroundings at remote Fort Snelling in Minnesota. He was too painfully aware of the wretched life his own wife had

---

[1] In a letter to the editor of *American History Magazine*, Posey S. Wilson says Sarah Knox had "her father's fine hazel eyes," and he adds, she had also his forehead "which, though indicating strength and courage, moral and physical in a man, was not particularly becoming in a woman." Wilson's description, however, is not based on remembrance; Sarah Knox had been a bridesmaid at his parents' wedding.

[2] Richard Taylor became a general in the Confederate Army.

led, moving from frontier post to frontier post, with few amenities, and suffering tortures of anxiety when he was absent fighting.

Jefferson realized there was considerable truth in the Colonel's contention about the trials of army wives. Besides, since he had no private means, a second lieutenant's pay was barely enough to keep a single man and his body servant. But he had not the slightest intention of giving up Sarah Knox. Biding his time, he continued to court her. Parental objection to the match only made the attachment stronger.

Relations between Colonel Taylor and the Lieutenant remained cordial enough on the surface until one day when an insignificant court-martial was held. Colonel Taylor, Major Thomas Smith, Lieutenant Davis, and an anonymous, recently arrived lieutenant composed the court. The new officer asked to be excused from wearing his full-dress uniform, as was required by army regulations, since it had been left behind at Jefferson Barracks. Colonel Taylor, who was a stickler for army etiquette though notoriously casual enough in his own dress, voted no. Smith, with whom Taylor was on bad terms, said yes. To the Colonel's astonishment and rage, Jefferson Davis also voted aye. Later he was reputed to have declared with vehemence that no man who sided against him with Tom Smith should ever marry his daughter. Jefferson Davis, who came to realize his own propensity for speaking in too positive a tone when he believed he was right, said fifty-odd years later (April 25, 1879), "I was right as to the principle, but impolitic in the manner of asserting it."

Whether the story as it has come down is true or not, Colonel Taylor shortly refused to allow Lieutenant Davis to call at his home and forbade Sarah Knox to see him. She did not obey the parental injunction. Not only did the young lovers meet at garrison social functions, but they contrived ways to meet in private. Captain and Mrs. McRee, who lived in a commodious tent, would invite the young couple to their place and then discreetly disappear. Mary Street, daughter of the Indian Agent, General Street, was in the same situation as Sarah Knox; for her father disapproved of her sweetheart, Lieutenant George Wilson. So the girls, who were intimate friends, arranged to have Wilson call at the Taylors' while Mary was there, and Davis call at the Streets' while Sarah Knox was a visitor. Knox contrived a still better way. She would take Betty and Dick on long walks far from the fort, and then when Jefferson appeared, as if by chance, the children would be sent off to play by themselves. These clandestine meetings added romantic spice to the courtship. But it was hard for both Davis and Taylor to bear the strained atmosphere between them, and the Colonel sought to have the Lieutenant transferred to another command.

In that exciting year of 1832, in which he met his first love, Jefferson faced another decision: whether he should obey a Federal command or be true to what he regarded as the sacred constitutional principle of liberty and State Rights.

South Carolina was seriously threatening to "nullify" what the South considered an unjust tariff decreed to protect New England industries. The matter had been brewing since the year of Jefferson's graduation from West Point, 1828, when John C. Calhoun had expounded his theory of nullification. As presented in his famous "Exposition," the South Carolinian argued that: (1) the tariff was ruinous to the South; (2) "protection" for privately owned industry was unconstitutional; (3) when an act was both unconstitutional and injurious, any state had a constitutional right peacefully to nullify the law within her borders until Congress should appeal to the states and be sustained by a vote of three-fourths of them.

Though President Andrew Jackson was supposed to disapprove of the tariff, at the Jefferson Day banquet in Washington in 1830, he had significantly proposed the toast: "Our Federal Union: it must be preserved." And he had taken occasion several times after that night to declare openly he would meet nullification with force. In the fall of 1832 when South Carolina called for a state convention to adopt an Ordinance of Nullification, President Jackson promptly increased the Federal garrison at Charleston's Fort Moultrie.

On November 24, 1832, by a majority of 136 to 26, South Carolina declared the tariff laws void in the state and promised armed resistance if the Federal Government should try to enforce them. Jackson warned the South Carolinians that the laws would be enforced by bayonets, if necessary. But, at the same time, he urged Congress to make a further revision of the tariff.

Jefferson Davis had been brought up on the Jeffersonian principle of State Rights, and, though he could not bring himself to agree with Calhoun's nullification as the right solution of the tariff controversy, he determined to resign his army commission if ordered to march against South Carolina to enforce execution of the laws. For months the tension in Washington and Charleston was discussed in the far-off northern military posts. Rumors circulated that the regiment to which Davis belonged would be among those sent to subdue South Carolina. "By education, by association, and by preference," he later wrote, "I was a soldier, then regarding that profession as my vocation in life. Yet, looking the issue squarely in the face, I chose the alternative of abandoning my profession rather than be employed in the subjugation or coercion of a State of the Union. . . . The compromise of 1833 prevented the threatened calamity, and the sorrowful issue was deferred until a day more drear, which forced upon me the determination of the question of State Sovereignty or Federal supremacy—of independence or submission to usurpation."

In that same spring of 1833, when bloodshed had been avoided in South Carolina and Lieutenant Davis had not had to resign his commission, he accepted a promotion to a first lieutenancy in a newly created regiment of dragoons under the command of Colonel Henry Dodge. Bidding Sarah Knox a lover's farewell, he went to Kentucky on recruiting duty. While in Lexington, where he had spent three happy school years, cholera suddenly swept through the gay town. Most of his old friends fled. Lieutenant Davis remained at his post, looking after his recruits' welfare and becoming involved in caring for the town's helpless sick. Fearless for his own person, he was continually exposed to contamination.

Once when he came across an aged Negro and a white man lying dead in an isolated cabin, he helped fashion two rude coffins, and then directed the burial.

After gathering still more recruits in Louisville, where Sarah Knox's kinfolk and friends entertained him, Lieutenant Davis returned to Fort Crawford and resumed his semisecret courtship of the girl he loved. The months of May and summer were among the happiest Jefferson was to know. In these alien northern latitudes the season was peculiarly beneficent, fruitful, and lovely. Rains came in goodly proportion and wrought an almost tropical luxuriance of vegetation. The wild rose thickets were massed with white blossoms. Wild grapes, cherries, and plums swelled in copious abundance. Bee trees oozed golden honey. A plenitude of deer, duck, geese, and turkeys made the area about Prairie du Chien a happy hunting ground. For Jefferson Davis it was not only a time of maturing love, but it was a devoutly welcome respite after the strenuous past four years and the recent traffic with cholera.

Again Knox asked her father for permission to marry Lieutenant Davis. The old soldier remained obstinate. Disappointed, but undaunted, Knox and Jeff became secretly engaged, and delayed plans for their marriage until some more opportune time. At the end of the idyllic summer, the Lieutenant left with Dodge's dragoons for unsettled western Arkansas and the region to become known as Indian Territory. When he boarded the steamboat, like any young man in love, he carried away a flower Knox had given him as a keepsake and reminder. It was a wild pansy known sentimentally by the name "heartsease."

After he arrived at Jefferson Barracks, where he was on brief duty before proceeding to Arkansas, Jeff continued to hope, and seemed inclined to believe that Colonel Taylor might relent. An enlightening comment on the affair is given by Charles Anderson,[3]

[3] Anderson's material is in the form of a seventeen-page unpublished manuscript article in the Trist Wood Collection of Taylor papers. Trist Wood was the great-grandson of Zachary Taylor. When he died in 1952, the collection was inherited by John A. Kelly of the German Department of Haverford College, Penn-

who had been a playmate of Sarah Knox, a classmate at Mr. Elliott's school, and later one of her youthful beaux who went to visit her when she was in school in Cincinnati. At this time, nineteen-year-old Anderson, youngest brother of Robert, who was to command the Federal forces at Charleston in 1860-61, was visiting his cousin, the wife of General Atkinson. Anderson wrote:

"As to Lieut Davis, although never intimate with him myself, I knew him well as a friend of my brother Robert and whom I continually met in society or on the parade. And on one occasion —the 'Infair' given to Lieut Alexander and my Cousin Nannie (nee Bullitt) upon their marriage—at the instance of my cousin Mary Atkinson and because my usual room at Headquarters was wanted for her Louisville visitors, he invited me to room with him during that short occasion, at his quarters just across the Parade. . . . I knew him therefore quite well, that is, as a green youngster of nineteen just entering into society might be supposed to know an established and admired grown-up gentleman of the 'Beau Monde.'

". . . Whilst so rooming with Lieut Davis, I went over to Headquarters, as was my daytime custom. I was sitting in the parlour with Genl Atkinson. I can even recall the very newspaper article of the *National Intelligencer* which I was then reading. (It was McDuffie's speech against the 'Removal of the Deposits.') Lieut Col. Kearney of the 1st dragoons . . . entered the parlour. He said he came to see Genl. Atkinson on a delicate business. I got up to leave but they both insisted on my remaining and I therefore resumed my seat. What was my surprise to learn, that the purpose of this visit was to enlist Genl. Atkinson in persuading

---

sylvania, by whose courtesy this article is used. From Kuttawa, Kentucky, June 5, 1893, Anderson sent the article to Mrs. Davis in New York, who in turn sent it to Zachary Taylor's youngest daughter Betty, who set it aside.

As a boy Charles Anderson, who later became lieutenant governor of Ohio, lived at "Soldier's Retreat" near Zachary Taylor's father's home "Springfield." His distinguished father, Colonel Richard Clough Anderson, a native of Hanover County, Virginia, had been Government surveyor for Kentucky and Ohio. "Soldier's Retreat" was famous for its hospitality—in the same year, President Monroe and Andrew Jackson were house guests. Though Southern by birth, the Andersons opposed secession and took the Union side in the war.

Col Taylor (his special friend and next in command) to assent to the marriage of his daughter (my early playmate and best friend) to Lieut Jeff Davis, my then bedfellow! I do not propose here to publish that whole coloquy. But, there is one item of it so pertinent to this case that I feel in honor bound to declare it. The General asked Col Kearney 'What is Col Taylor's objection to this match?' Col Kearney replied, 'He says—he will be damned if another daughter of his shall marry into the Army;—that he himself knows enough of family-life of Army Officers; that he scarcely knows his own children or they him;—etc, etc. *He makes no other objection whatever to Lieut Davis—*' [4] And, then followed this remarkable statement by Col Kearney and quickly and fully assented to by Genl Atkinson, viz: 'And, you know Genl that Mr. Davis is one of the brightest and most promising officers in the whole Army.' . . . What made this opinion so 'remarkable' to me was: that it was not then (I confess my blunder) my own estimate of Lieut Davis. For, whilst I did think him one of the most humorous, witty, and captivating gentlemen whom I had ever met, I did not think he showed to me any signs of such sober abilities, as these wiser heads had so cordially accorded him. I am only giving, now, my then, 'impressions,' not his actual powers or character. For, his intermediate Life has most abundantly proved, that even they were underestimating his worth. But one reflection often still presses itself on me;—what a change of manners must have occurred in him, from that joyous and sportful humorist of *my* impressions—into the sober, grave, philosopher-thinker and statesman of his after developed character?"

By odd irony it is Robert Anderson's brother who furnishes this most vivid and apparently accurate impression of Jefferson Davis at twenty-five. "Witty," "sportful," "captivating," he seemed to the youth of nineteen, while his superior officers admired him for his sober abilities and considered him one of the army's most promising men. It is strange that Anderson did not reflect that a prime reason for Davis's change from a "joyous humorist" to a

---

[4] The italics are Anderson's.

"grave philosopher-thinker" was the death of his bride, Anderson's own childhood sweetheart.

When he got into Arkansas, Jefferson saw at once that this wild territory was no fit place for any woman, let alone a bride and his beloved Knox. Conditions of soldier life were cruder there than they had been in cold Wisconsin. Long marches through uninhabited terrain were tedious and grueling. The soldiers suffered gruesome privations; food supplies were unpredictable. For a fortnight once, Lieutenant Davis himself had absolutely nothing to eat but tough buffalo meat, out of which the resourceful James Pemberton tried vainly to make a tasty soup. At another time "cold flour was the only food." The mortality among the men was exceptionally high, and Lieutenant Davis had the added burden of bolstering morale, besides the duties of adjutant to which he was appointed shortly after his arrival in Arkansas.

His chief solace was the letters he received from Sarah Knox and from various members of his family, including nieces and brothers-in-law, some gay, some sad, but all breathing deep affection and tender regard for his welfare. Florida, Joseph's eldest daughter, whose "eyes were so bad she could scarcely see the keys on the piano," would begin a letter thus: "Once more, my dearest Uncle, I enter on my long cherished employment—writing to you." Because she was only nine years younger than Jefferson she generally signed herself, "Your sister Florida." At eighteen, this niece, who spoke of herself as "the very type of all obscurity," oddly but feelingly advised her beloved uncle: "Cherish ambition, cherish pride, and run from excitement to excitement. It will prevent that ever-preying upon melancholy, it will blunt your sensibilities and cause you to be unmarred—armoured—amidst all afflictions."

From his brother-in-law Judge Bradford, Jefferson received a letter referring to the death of "Sister Matilda Vaughan" on March 16.

West Feliciana, June 18, 1834

To Lieut. Jefferson F. Davis
Fort Gibson, Arkansas
Dear Brother—
... Mother is greatly affected by grief and wishes to see you above all things and to hear from you frequently if you cannot come to see her before another summer.

Amanda is about to lay in, and I hope to have to open this letter to inform you you have a young namesake in my family, which might occur before the closing of the mail. . . .[5]

I have little time for scientific or literary reading. I have a volume of Jacotal's *Enseignment Universal* with which I am greatly taken—

Mother says Jim's wife is in good health—

Your affectionate Brother<br>David Bradford

Though absence may have made the lovers' hearts grow fonder, it also brought misgivings, as is revealed in a longish letter Jeff wrote to Sarah Knox on December 16, 1834.[6] It is a somewhat strange letter, which was confiscated among other papers by Private Spillman Willis of the Thirty-third Illinois Regiment while stationed in New Orleans, and sold to the Libby Prison Company of Chicago during the War between the States.

'Tis strange how superstitions sometimes affect us, but stranger still what aids chance sometimes bring to support our superstitions. Dreams, my dear Sarah, we will agree, are our weakest thoughts, and yet by my dreams I have been lately almost crazed, for they were of you, and the sleeping imagination painted you

---

[5] The baby turned out to be a girl, but in September, 1838, a boy was born and christened Jefferson Davis Bradford. He entered the United States Military Academy on July 1, 1856, and became a colonel in the Confederate Army.

[6] Most unfortunately all of Knox's letters to Jefferson Davis have been lost. Professor John A. Kelly of Haverford College wrote the author on June 6, 1954: "In Trist Wood's papers I found mention of a lost suitcase full of Davis letters and papers that had been in the possession of the Taylor family."

not as I felt you, not such as I could live and see you, for you seemed a sacrifice to your parents' desire, the bride of a wretch that your pride and sense equally compelled you to despise. A creature here, telling the news of the day in St. Louis, said you were about to be married to a Doctor McLarin, a poor devil, who served with the battalion of rangers. Possibly you may have seen him. But last night the vision was changed. You were at the house of an uncle in Kentucky. Captain McCree [sic] was walking with you. When I met you he left you and you told me of your father and of yourself, almost the same that I have read in your letter tonight. Kind, dear letter; I have kissed it often and it has driven away mad notions from my brain.

Sarah, whatever I may be hereafter, neglected by you I should have been worse than nothing, and if the few good qualities I possess shall, under your smiles yield fruit, it shall be yours, as the grain is the husbandman's. . . . Your own answer is the most gratifying to me; is that which I should have expected from you, for you are the first with whom I ever sought to cast my fortune, so you are the last from whom I would expect desertion. When I wrote to you I supposed you did not intend soon to return to Kentucky. I approve entirely of your preference to a meeting elsewhere than at Prairie du Chien, and your desire to avoid any embarrassments which might widen the breach made already cannot be greater than my own. Did I know when you would be at St. Louis I could meet you there. At all events, we will meet in Kentucky. Shall we not soon meet, Sarah, to part no more? . . .

Do you remember the heart's-Ease [sic] you gave me? It is as bright as ever. . . . How very gravely you ask leave to ask me a question. My dear girl, I have no secrets from you. You have a right to ask me any question without apology. Miss Bullitt did not give me a guard for a watch, but if she had do you suppose I would have given it to Captain McCree [sic]? But I'll tell you what she did give me—a most beautiful and lengthy lecture on my and your dreams once upon an evening at a fair in Louisville. . . .

. . . I hope you find in the society of the Prairie enough to amuse, if not to please. The griefs over which we weep are not those to be dreaded; it is the little pains, the constant falling of the drops of care, which wear away the heart.

Since I wrote you we abandoned the position in the Creek nation and are constructing quarters at Fort Gibson. My lines, like the beggar's day, are dwindling to the shortest span.

Write to me immediately, my dear Sarah, my betrothed; no formality between us. *Adieu ma chère, très chère amie.*

Jeff

Written somewhat in the romantic style current in the 1830's, the letter clearly reveals how the young man was tormented by the possibility, however vague and ill-supported, that he might lose his sweetheart. And, more, it shows how deeply he desires her to share in whatever he may accomplish.

Not only was Jeff unhappy over his long separation from Sarah Knox and fearful of losing her, but he was concerned more and more about his ability to provide properly for a wife. Now, as he was approaching his twenty-seventh birthday and his seventh year of army service, he realized that he had been unable to accumulate anything from his meager lieutenant's pay. While not extravagant or self-indulgent, he believed that the dignity of a United States officer called for expert tailoring and the finest quality of made-to-order boots. And he had had the expense of his body servant, James Pemberton. The probability of quick army promotion was less encouraging than ever. Cadets recently graduating from West Point found there were few vacant posts to divide among them; in fact as Ganoe states in his *History of the United States Army* one hundred and seventeen army officers resigned in 1836.

A few days after writing the December, 1834, letter to Sarah Knox, an unpleasant experience with a martinet occurred which may have entered into Jefferson's debate with himself about resigning from the army.

At reveille on Christmas Eve morning, rain was pouring dismally on the dragoon camp near Fort Gibson, so Lieutenant Davis did not leave his quarters to answer roll call. He had been susceptible to colds ever since his near-fatal case of pneumonia from exposure in Wisconsin. Upon being sent for by Major

Mason, his immediate commanding officer, to explain his absence, Lieutenant Davis answered, "Because I was not out of my tent, and the regulations require when it rains the rolls shall be called in quarters by chiefs of squads." Davis was entirely within his rights, but Major Mason shouted, "You know it is my order that all officers of this command attend the reveille roll-call in their respective companies." Then, according to Mason's report to the headquarters, Lieutenant Davis "did in a highly disrespectful, insubordinate and contemptuous manner, abruptly turn on his heel and walk off, saying at the same time 'Hum!'"

Major Mason ordered him back, told him to consider himself under arrest, and to go to his quarters. Lieutenant Davis stared him straight in the face. Major Mason repeated the order. Then, according to the Major, Davis said contemptuously, "Now are you done with me?" Not until the Major had peremptorily repeated his command for the third time did the Lieutenant go to his quarters, where he spent Christmas Day under arrest, and many days following. In March at a general court-martial held in Memphis, he was arraigned and accused by his superior officer of "conduct subversive of good order and military discipline."

The accused pleaded "not guilty." His self-defense reveals that talent for eloquent argument which later undid many of his opponents and won him special renown in the United States Senate. As a young man he could use long and involved sentences and not lose his way, as his summation of his own case quoted in part shows.

"The origin of the charge under which I am arraigned was absence from the company parade at Reveille roll call on the 24th of Dec, 1834. I have shown by Private Decons, the orderly who came for me, that I had risen and left my sleeping apartment when he was sent to me by Maj. Mason immediately after Reveille; I have shown by Assistant Surgeon Porter that my health was broken at that time, that exposure in the discharge of my mornings' duties had been injurious; and by Lieutenant Northrop I have shown that the weather on that morning was bad; further it has appeared by the evidence of Major Mason, that I had in a previous winter suffered from the influence of this climate & feared a like result from the present winter; and therefore had a right to expect from my commander, a care similar to that by which he attempted to account for not noticing the absence of Lieutenant Izard from the Reveille roll call of the same morning, but when differently treated, and called on to account for my absence from Reveille, I preferred to defend my course by the General Army Regulations rather than to give an individual explanation, for reasons shown by the evidence of Captain Perkins and Lieutenant Bowman, on the harshness of Major Mason's manner to subordinates, and the wounding reception he gave officer's explanations of conduct which he (Major Mason) deemed censurable. And how was the defence I offered for my conduct received? . . . without any attention being paid to the distinction between good and bad weather, I am answered 'it is my order that all officers attend reveille.' I have shown by Captain Perkins that no such order existed, and when the witness for the prosecution was questioned as to the order he spoke of, it shrinks in his own hand to an individual requirement of me, though he could not say that I ever had been absent from a reveille roll call before whilst on company duty. . . .

"On the day when I learn that the caprice of a commander can increase or decrease the obligations of my commission, can magnify or diminish the quantum of military offence contained in military acts, I shall cease to consider myself a freeman and no longer feel proud of my sword. . . .

"If an officer shown to be harsh and disregardful of the feelings of others, irritable and forgetful. . . . If such an officer can with the jaundiced eye of passion see in simple questions, and facings about, contemptuous and disrespectful conduct, there can be little security for his subordinates in his official intercourse. The next point in the prosecution was for looking at my accuser, when angrily addressing me . . . can it be required of a Gentleman, is it part of the character of a soldier to humble himself beneath the haughty tone, or quail before the anger of any man? . . .

"I felt that an examination into the charges would wipe away the discredit which belonged to my arrest. The humble and narrow reputation which a subaltern can acquire by years of the most rigid performance of his duty, is little worth in the wide world of Fame, but yet is something to himself. If I have complied with the first part of the 11th paragraph of the 2nd Article General Army Regulations, and my commander has shown a disregard to last part of the same paragraph, then have I by my arrest and charges been injured, and I look to the court for redress."

Lieutenant Davis, the accused, had turned accuser. In the eyes of the court he had made the Major seem of small caliber. But he was speaking in defense of all soldiers who might be discriminated against or persecuted by some small-minded or jealous superior. For Davis never failed to be stirred to indignation by injustice. On March 15, 1835, the military court acquitted him and ordered him to resume his sword.

After this unpleasant trial, with his love for Sarah Knox a constant ache in his heart and with his problems of properly maintaining a wife unsolved, Jefferson requested a brief furlough to talk over everything with his brother Joseph.

# CHAPTER VII

# MARRIAGE AND TRAGIC LOSS

WHEN Jefferson arrived at Hurricane and bared his heart to his brother, he found Joseph had changed his mind about an army career since his July, 1832, letter. Now he confessed he could not see much future for an army officer, since so many West Point graduates in the past two years were without assignments. Besides, he argued, the United States was an isolated nation, far removed from European quarrels. He felt that the Americans were eager to develop the resources of their new country and to steer clear from entanglements with Europe. Their remoteness made it possible for them to stick to such a policy. Jeff was convinced that if he stayed in the army there would be few opportunities for him except in fighting Indians, with whom he had a certain sympathy. His recent experiences in the Northwest had taught him that there were many disillusions and few rewards in that kind of army life.

Joseph himself had not hesitated to abandon a lucrative career as lawyer when he saw what wealth cotton planting could bring. The Davis plantation in Warren County lay on what was then a peninsula [1] about thirty miles by water south of Vicksburg. Altogether the peninsula contained some 11,000 acres, of which Joseph then owned about 6,900. The peninsula became known to river boat captains as "Davis Bend," though Joseph's estate was

---

[1] Today it is a huge island encircled by the river. It was detached from the mainland some time after Grant captured Vicksburg.

called the "Hurricane" after that disastrous cyclone of 1827, in which one of Isaac Davis's sons was killed and Isaac himself suffered a broken leg.

When Joseph bought the property that was incorporated into Hurricane, it was composed mostly of wild land, but partially of several small farms, which original settlers had cleared. With the help of Isaac, Joseph had consolidated various forty-acre farms, cleared much new land, and brought a tract of some 5,000 acres under profitable production. Joseph told Jefferson that if he wanted to become a planter he would give him some 1,800 acres of uncleared land and lend him the money to buy the needed slaves. Though Jeff had never farmed, he felt he could learn with Joseph as mentor. And he was greatly tempted by the richness of his brother's library, which was reputed to be the finest private library in the state; for Joseph, who had never had the advantage of a college education, was a voracious reader.

It cost Jefferson some pain, however, to throw over an army officer's career. But above all else he desired Sarah Knox. To provide a respectable living for her, he determined to become a planter. He wrote her his intentions; she spoke with her father. But even with the prospect of Jefferson's becoming a private citizen, for some unexplained reason the Colonel still would not approve the match.

It is possible that Zachary Taylor dreaded the Delta climate with its miasmas and mists that were believed to breed malaria. He had pertinent reason to be fearful, for in 1820 when his wife and four daughters were living at Bayou Sara, Louisiana, all of them went down with the "bilious fever," as he called the disease. The two youngest girls died. His wife came very close to death. The probability of losing her "nearly unmanned" him, as he wrote to Quartermaster General Thomas Jesup on September 5, 1820. For Taylor was a truly devoted husband. In his apprehensive letter he averred, "I am confident the feminine virtues never did concentrate in a higher degree in the bosom of any woman than in hers." Mrs. Taylor eventually recovered, and so did Ann and

Sarah Knox, who was six years old at the time.[2] But the haunting fear of the fever remained with him.

When Knox begged her father's blessing the last time, she pointed out that she had been engaged for almost two years and that he had found no fault in Lieutenant Davis's character or conduct. "Some day," she insisted, "you will see his rare qualities as I do." Then she declared with Taylor-like determination that she would marry Jefferson Davis, with or without parental consent. Her decision was a rash one for the times. Even young men in the 1830's hesitated to marry in the face of a father's strong disapproval.

Knox wrote Jeff that she would meet him at her Aunt Elizabeth's home "Beechland," three miles from Louisville. This widowed aunt was her father's eldest sister, who had married a cousin, John Gibson Taylor. Though Zachary Taylor would not give Knox his blessing, he gave her a generous sum for her trousseau. Captain McRee arranged for her steamship passage from St. Louis and she bade her mother and father a tearful farewell. It was the last time they saw her.

Lieutenant Davis sent in his resignation from the army to take effect on June 30, 1835. Arriving in Louisville some time before the fifteenth, he persuaded Knox to have the wedding almost immediately—on June 17, 1835—and in the early afternoon so that the couple could catch the New Orleans river boat that left at four o'clock. Invitations were sent by hand to relatives and a few close friends. So there was no romantic elopement, despite many erroneous and fantastic stories that have been told, including one depicting the wedding as performed at night by a priest in the middle of the Mississippi River.

In a letter to Major H. T. Stanton on August 20, 1879, Richard H. Taylor, Zachary's nephew, wrote: "In order to correct the many silly stories about the first marriage of Jefferson Davis, I will give you the facts: In the first place, they never ran off: Mr. Davis married Miss Sarah Knox Taylor at the residence of her father's sister near Louisville and *with her father's consent.*" And

---

[2] Betty and Dick were not yet born.

according to Fall Taylor, in a letter to Trist Wood, Zachary's great-grandson (June 10, 1893): "Gen'l Taylor wrote to his sister to ask that the young couple should be married in that house, as he was in the, then, far Northwest and could not attend the wedding." He got his information from "Cousin Ann Edwards," [3] Mrs. Gibson Taylor's daughter, who was ill upstairs in the house when the wedding was performed. Obviously, from family testimony of eyewitnesses, the impression is definite that Zachary Taylor finally assented to Sarah Knox's union with Jefferson Davis, but he did not give the faintest indication that the match was pleasing to him. In fact, his displeasure is obvious from a touching letter Knox wrote to her mother on the morning of her wedding day.

Louisville, June 17, 1835

You will be surprised, no doubt, my dear mother, to hear of my being married so soon. When I wrote to you last I had no idea of leaving here before fall; but hearing the part of the country to which I am going is quite healthy I have concluded to go down this summer and will leave here this afternoon at 4 o'clock; will be married as you advised in my bonnet and traveling dress. I am very much gratified that sister Ann is here. At this time having one member of the family present, I shall not feel so entirely destitute of friends. But you, my dearest mother, I know, will still retain some feelings of affection for a child who has been so unfortunate as to form a connection without the sanction of her parents, but who will always feel the deepest affection for them whatever may be their feelings toward her. Say to my dear father I have received his kind and affectionate letter, and thank him for the liberal supply of money sent me. Sister will tell you all that you will wish to know about me. I will write as soon as I get down and as often as my mother may wish to hear from me;

[3] A sprightly, remarkable old lady of 81 in 1893, Ann Taylor Edwards was twenty-three at the time of the marriage. Her two younger sisters, Mrs. Randall and Miss Margaret Taylor of Annapolis, attended the wedding and remembered it clearly.

and do, my kind ma, write. I shall feel so much disappointed and mortified if you do not. I send a bonnet by sister, the best I could get. I tried to get you some cherries to preserve, but could not. Sally has kindly offered to make your preserves this summer. Farewell, my dear mother; give my best love to pa and Dick. Believe me always your affectionate daughter.

                                                        Knox

All of Knox's relatives who were in convenient traveling distance gathered at Beechland for the wedding. Besides Mrs. John Gibson Taylor, the hostess, and her family, two of Zachary's brothers, Hancock, from Springfield, and Joseph, from Woodford, came with their families, and also Mrs. Gray, another sister of the Colonel. Knox's elder sister, Ann, had arrived from the Northwest with her husband, Dr. Robert Wood. Nicholas Taylor, Knox's young first cousin, was asked to serve as Jefferson's best man.

But even with so many of the bride's kin on hand to witness the ceremony, the troubled course of the couple's love ran into an unexpected snag at the last hour. The wedding guests were gathered, when Lieutenant Davis, elegantly dressed in black broadcloth with a flowered silk waistcoat, drove up to Beechland in ill-concealed agitation. He took Mrs. Gibson Taylor and Hancock Taylor aside and told them an extraordinary story.

On Jefferson Street in Louisville, as he was driving out to his wedding, he had been hailed by Pendleton Pope, the county clerk, who had issued the license. Pope asked to see the paper again, and Jeff, sitting in the buggy, handed it down. To his consternation the man declared it invalid. "I am informed," Pope stated coolly without reading it, "that the young lady is not of age and that her father is intensely antagonistic to the marriage." Then he tore the license to bits, dropped the pieces in the street, and walked away. Dreading a public scandal, the indignant young bridegroom restrained his fury and drove as fast as he could to consult with Knox's family.

Mrs. Gibson Taylor assured him that from the tone of Zachary's last letter she felt sure the Colonel's consent could now be secured in writing—but it might take weeks before an answer could be returned from Fort Crawford. While the wondering guests and the shaken bride waited, Hancock Taylor drove back into Louisville with Jeff to force the issue of the license. When Pope was located, he finally agreed to issue a new license if Hancock Taylor would swear under oath that his niece was of age. Hancock knew that in the family records kept by his brother the date of Knox's birth was recorded as March 6, 1814. She was now three months past her twenty-first birthday.

In the marriage register of the county court the clerk duly recorded: "June 17, 1835, Jefferson Davis to Sarah Knox Taylor, daughter of Colonel Zachariah Taylor and of lawful age, as proved by the oath of Hancock Taylor." It may well have crossed Jeff's mind that Zachary Taylor was the instrument of this last climactic attempt to prevent his marriage. But by way of apology for his highhanded behavior, Pope explained that he had recently been threatened with a damage suit by an enraged father because he had issued a license for a young woman who was a minor.

According to Charles Anderson's version of the contretemps, the "prudent Pope . . . against such risk—demanded bonded or other safe security," and Hancock Taylor "gladly went with the ex-Lieut. upon his bond . . . and—so—the orderly marriage took place. . . ." "But," he added, "that small *faux-pas* stirred up that whole primitive community with a 'scandal in High Life.'"

At reckless speed, the bride's uncle and the bridegroom drove back through the afternoon heat to the agitated bride and the murmuring wedding guests.

Whether the tense delay or the lack of parental blessing was responsible, there was little joy in the parlor when the couple at last stood before the Reverend Mr. Ashe, rector of Louisville's Christ Episcopal Church. During the ceremony the bride's eyes were filled with tears, and some of the other ladies openly wept. The young children, observing that the Lieutenant stood erect and dry-eyed, "thought it very strange, and took a dislike to him, deciding he must be heartless." [4]

When the ceremony was concluded and the guests had moved across the hall to the dining room to eat wedding cake and toast the couple with wine, there was still a strange tension in the atmosphere. Later, it was recalled by family members that a queer foreboding seemed to grip the celebrants and some audibly expressed their feeling they would never see Sarah Knox again.

As their steamboat made its slow way down to Vicksburg, the young couple had every reason to expect an enriching life of exceptional happiness. The state of an established Southern planter before 1860 was an enviable one. He had the leisure in which to be a gentleman, much like the lord of an English manor. His lady could indulge herself in the art of gracious living. With all the responsibilities and *noblesse oblige* that such a situation entailed for master and mistress, there was yet time for reading, hunting, entertaining, and for travel. It was an unflurried existence, in which life might be savored.

Sarah Knox was peculiarly fitted to be both helpmate and chatelaine. By nature, sympathetic, amiable, and charming, she was also lively and energetic. She had been taught the wifely virtues by her blue-blooded mother, who was a born homemaker, delighting in such domestic activities as handling cream, making cheese, preserving fruits, rearing children, and pleasing menfolk. And having been brought up with devoted slaves as household servants, Knox could understand the needs and appreciate the loyalties of Negroes.

Of course, both Jefferson and Knox were aware they were not headed for any inherited plantation home furnished with heirlooms. They were going to be the guests of Joseph Davis until Jeff had cleared some acres, planted his first crop, and built a

[4] Testimony of Mrs. Magill Robinson, daughter of Hancock Taylor on August 27, 1907. She was eleven years old at the time of the marriage, and still residing in Louisville at eighty-three, the only living witness to Jefferson Davis's first marriage.

house for his bride. But there was no hurry, no urgency. For Hurricane was commodious and maintained an abundance of trained servants. Relatives and friends were always welcome and the presence of Jeff and his bride greatly desired. Joseph, who was only sixteen days younger than Knox's father, was eager to have his favorite brother close, to discuss all he had been reading these late years, while accumulating a fortune. Knox would be company for Eliza, Joe's frail young wife. The bride would have time aplenty to become accustomed to Delta plantation life before assuming responsibilities herself. Although in a sense she and Jeff would be pioneering, carving out a home for themselves in a wilderness, they were to do it gradually, from a base marked by luxurious comfort.

Except for the obstinate disapproval of the bride's father, which they both trusted would soon dissolve, there was everything to point to a rarely blessed union, for they were deeply in love. A long boat trip was not at all undesirable for a honeymoon. It had its own characteristic diversions. The steamers carried freight, as well as passengers, and sometimes they would spend a day or two tied up at Cairo, Memphis, and smaller river towns, unloading and loading. The passengers would go ashore to see what was to be seen, present letters of introduction, or visit old friends. There was a mild kind of kaleidoscopic variety to river travel, which both Knox and Jeff enjoyed.

On June 30, 1835, less than a fortnight after his marriage, and about the time they reached their destination, Lieutenant Davis's resignation from the army became effective. He had served seven years, more than the term considered requisite to repay the Government for education at West Point. But if Jefferson had not fallen in love with Knox Taylor, it may be doubted that he would have given up a profession which in so many aspects he found congenial to his temperament. Though scholarly in his tastes, he had the bearing and the qualifications of a man born to command. He had proved himself peculiarly adept in dangerous crises. He had not balked at undertaking direction of such unfamiliar jobs as timber-cutting and sawmill building. He had earned a reputation both for diplomacy and fearlessness.

Now Jefferson was entering an entirely different career—that of Southern planter. The land he was to transform into productive fields was virgin, overgrown with gigantic trees and rank with cane and briers. The initial task had elements of the Herculean, but Jeff had the needed will and the persistence.

The house that was to be Knox's temporary home was more elegant than any in which she had lived. It was huge, with two main stories and a third story that alone could house a dozen guests with their body servants. While Hurricane House had dignity and solidity, the surrounding galleries did not give it the grace of some of the mansions in Natchez. But it had bathrooms with running water, for Joseph had brought from Cincinnati mechanics who understood rudimentary plumbing. They had constructed an enormous tank in the attic, into which the Negroes pumped water early each morning.[5] Adjoining the main house and connected by a pergola was an annex containing the dining room and a large sitting room on the lower floor and a study and music room on the second floor. Joseph's books were shelved in the annex sitting room, in his office, and in the cottage library in the garden, a replica of a Greek temple with square Doric columns on all four sides.[6]

Before the house, which stood on a rise of ground facing the Mississippi, extended no groomed park in the English fashion, but the native forest trees had been thinned to make finer specimens, and avenues cut that gave vistas of the river. Here and there, along with magnolias and camellias, had been set out exotic trees and flowering shrubs from foreign lands. (Later, to improve the grounds Joseph brought over an English landscape

---

[5] These details were gathered from Mrs. Mary Lucy O'Kelley of Pass Christian, Joseph Davis's only surviving great-granddaughter, whose mother Lise lived with him until his death.

[6] When the Federal troops burned Hurricane they also burned all but a few of the books; but they spared the columned library itself and for some years Joseph's granddaughter Lise Mitchell Hamer made her home there with her husband and children.

gardener, who created between the casual park and the river a curving band of green meadow three miles long, which was kept cropped like turf.) Behind the house the rose garden, which was in late bloom, merged into the orchards now ripe with peaches. To one side stood an array of stout stables and barns, the cotton gin and blacksmith shop, and conglomerations of cribs and outbuildings. Farther away still spread the hamlet of clustering Negro cabins, gleaming with whitewash and each provided with vegetable garden and chicken run.

Governor John Anthony Quitman, who had come down from New York in the 1820's, told how a guest was treated when visiting a gentleman's plantation: "Your coffee in the morning before sunrise, little stews and soporifics at night, and warm foot baths if you have a cold. Bouquets of fresh flowers and mint juleps sent to your room. A horse and saddle at your disposal. Everything free and easy and cheerful and cordial." Quitman, often a guest at Hurricane, was captivated by the gracious quality of Southern life, and bought a plantation on Davis Bend, as well as building a splendid mansion at Natchez.

To Knox, who had spent so many of her years in frontier army posts, Hurricane had aspects of an Eden. Her only apprehension was of the miasma that sometimes rose in the evening and hung about until morning, for it was supposed to carry the contagion of malaria. Jefferson, too, mistrusted the fog from the fens, and he urged his bride to remain indoors until the sun had dissolved the mists.

Almost immediately the bridegroom plunged into the work of clearing some of the acreage on the south of the peninsula which Joseph had assigned to him. It was harder and more expensive business than he had expected. Clearing Mississippi bottom land cost many times the price of the acres themselves. The impenetrable walls of cane and briers had to be burned, trees felled, ditches made, and the wet heavy land broken.

At daybreak Jeff would rise from his wife's side, and as soon as he had had coffee and a light breakfast, he and James Pemberton would mount their horses and start out to direct the slaves Joseph had sold him on credit. At noon the brothers would meet at Hurricane to talk over the work of the morning. Then they would have one o'clock dinner with Knox and Eliza and whatever relatives were in residence. After a "resting spell" or siesta they would start out again. Though he had competent overseers, Joseph kept an eye on everything himself, so he and Jeff would ride to this field and that, then around the barns and the gins until late afternoon.

Knox seemed to delight in Hurricane's daily routine and had no yearning for town life. Eliza, who was the personification of amiability and sweet nature, made her feel more than accepted. Davis kin came in quantities to welcome her. Everything was going harmoniously on August 11, when Knox wrote her last extant letter to her mother at Fort Crawford.

Dearest Mother:

I have just received your affectionate letter forwarded to me from Louisville; you may readily imagine the pleasure it afforded me to hear from you. . . . How often, my dear Mother, I wish I could look in upon you. I imagine so often I can see you moving about attending to your domestic concerns—down in the cellar skimming milk or going to feed the chickens. . . . Tell Dick I have a beautiful colt, prettier than his I expect. Mr. Davis sends his best respects to you. . . . My love to Pa and Dick. . . . Remember me most affectionately to Sister and the Doc [Dr. Wood]. Kiss the children. . . . Do not make yourself uneasy about me; the country is quite healthy.[7]

Before her mother could have received the letter with the reassuring last line, Knox was stricken with malaria, one day after Jeff had developed the disease. When the bride and groom did not respond to such treatment as the nearest physician prescribed,

[7] The letters of Sarah Knox Davis to Mrs. Taylor remained for years in the Trist Wood Collection, New Orleans.

it was decided the change of a river trip might prove beneficial.[8] They went by boat to Bayou Sara to stay with Jeff's eldest sister, Anna, Mrs. Luther Smith, who lived nearby at Locust Grove in West Feliciana Parish. Jefferson hoped their recovery would be speeded by the higher ground of Locust Grove. As they disembarked at Bayou Sara, Knox must have had forebodings, for it was here in 1820 that two of her little sisters had died of the fever, while her mother and her sister Ann and she herself had been quite ill.

Both Jefferson and Knox became alarmingly worse after their arrival at the plantation and were put to bed in different rooms. Anna devoted herself tirelessly to nursing, and a sister-in-law, widow of Dr. Benjamin Davis, came to assist. At first Jefferson was thought to be the more dangerously ill of the two. Then Knox's fever rose so high she became delirious. The bride's critical condition was kept from the husband, who was forbidden by the doctor to leave his bed. But on September 15, hearing Knox burst into eerie singing—the song was "Fairy Bells," something connected with their courtship—he got up and staggered fever-ridden into her room. She did not recognize him. He saw that she was dying. There was nothing he could do for her except hold her in his arms, until, like the Lady of Shalott "singing, in her song, she died."

Brokenhearted, the young husband was led back to his own bed. To his critical condition was added the complication of a searing grief and a troubled conscience. If he had not persisted in marrying her against her father's objection, if he had not brought her to the Delta, Knox would have been alive. Now, she who had been his wife for less than three months was dead at twenty-one. The physician and the family feared Jeff would die too. Weak as he was, however, he insisted that the funeral service be held in his sickroom. Knox was buried in the Smiths' family

[8] This is the version in a manuscript collection in the Evans Memorial Library, Aberdeen, Mississippi. It bears out the testimony of one of the old slaves, who said Sarah Knox was taken from Hurricane "on a litter." The family is divided on the subject, though Varina Davis wrote that the couple was stricken after arrival at Locust Grove.

cemetery in the southwest corner not far from Jefferson's brother Benjamin and Luther Smith, Anna's husband.[9]

For a day or two Jeff's life hung in the balance. But under Anna's tender ministrations he began to recover. The convalescence was slow. It was more than a month before he was able to return to Hurricane. It was eight years before he overcame his grief.

[9] The house in which Sarah Knox died still stands, though in moldering condition with part of the roof caved in; the cattle's winter hay is stored in one end of the drawing room. Some two hundred yards away, beyond a high wall of aged japonicas, lies the cemetery. Knox's brick-covered grave is surmounted by a chaste marble tomb with four rounded columns supporting the top slab which bears the simple inscription:

Sarah Knox Davis
Wife of Jefferson Davis
Died Sept. 15, 1835
age 21

# CHAPTER VIII

## PLANTER IN RETIREMENT

WITH the loss of his first love, the inspiration and cause of the new-planned life, Jefferson Davis's world had collapsed about him. The shock of his beloved's death changed Jefferson's nature, and in fact his whole life. Learning to bear his grief brought a stoicism to his character that was later to be translated by those who did not understand or like him into disdainful coolness. On his return to the plantation, still shaky from the burning fevers which had sapped his vitality, he could not rally. Knox was so intimately associated with sights and objects about Hurricane that he was poignantly and constantly reminded of her absence. Physically he was too weak to direct the land clearance, which might have relieved his mind of the pressing sorrow.

Deeply concerned at his young brother's debility and emotional dejection, Joseph counseled a complete change of scene and a prolonged rest. So, late in October Jefferson sailed from New Orleans for Havana with his faithful James Pemberton to look after him. He sailed literally, for there were as yet no ocean-going steamboats. The voyage in the blue tropical waters, which took almost three weeks, he found peaceful and soothing. His only excitement was a daily bath on deck—a douche of salt water James poured over him from a bucket.

Knowing no one in Cuba and not caring for society, he wandered about the picturesque old streets of Havana and out among the suburban plantations with no other companion than his Negro friend. He visited Mantanzas and other ports and outlying towns. In Havana he enjoyed watching the Spanish garrison on parade. Shortly, he got out his sketchbook, which he had scarcely touched since his West Point days, and began sketching scenes and details that struck his fancy. Suspicious authorities, who sensed his military associations because of his soldierly bearing despite his abnormal thinness, accused him of being an American army officer spy. He was warned never again to approach the Spanish fortifications. Thereafter, whenever he ventured out he was closely followed and his every movement noted. No longer could he divert himself with sketching.

Under the hostile surveillance Havana lost its charm and Jefferson became restless. One day, learning that a ship was about to sail for New York, on the spur of the moment he booked passage. But the big city held little interest for him. He went down to Washington to see his onetime Transylvania schoolmate, George Wallace Jones, who was then the last delegate to Congress from Michigan Territory. Jones, who by his own confession loved the younger man dearly, was as delighted to have Jeff turn up in the national capital as he had been to give him lodging one black winter night in his cabin on the lone prairie.

Jefferson received a warm welcome in the Congressional "mess," Dawson's Boarding House, near East Capital Street, where his host lived along with the powerful Thomas H. Benton, Senator from Missouri, and his colleague, Dr. Lewis Linn, Senator William Allen from Ohio, the noted John H. Crittenden of Kentucky, and a bright, modest Representative from New Hampshire named Franklin Pierce. Jones and his friends made the days pleasant for the young widower. With his betters and elders he saw Washington, witnessed Congressional sessions, but he felt in no mood for social functions. Promising to return for a future visit, Jefferson left for Mississippi to resume work on his plantation.

As soon as he got to Hurricane he wrote to his mother to let her know of his return and to ask her to come and visit him. Jane Davis was living with her daughter Lucinda, who was married to

William Stamps; their home was close to her own place, Rosemont, which she continued to farm. She replied on April 8, 1836. It seems a somewhat formal letter for a mother to a son who recently had undergone a crushing loss and who had just returned home after six months of travel. But Jane Davis had something of the Spartan in her and an extraordinary mastery over her emotions. Independent in spirit, she was always careful never to be a burden to her children or let them think they were bound by duty to look after her.

April 8, 1836

My dear Son

I received your kind letter by the girls and your kind favor was joyfully accepted by your Mother. I am very anxious to see you indeed—and hope I shall have that pleasure before long or as soon as you find it convenient. My Children [1] are gone to school. When they return I shall bring them to see you, as they are desirous of so doing, and spend sometime with you.

I have planted a small crop of corn and have a fine stock of cattle. I have Charles employed in cutting cord wood.

As regards your kind offer we will arrange it when I visit in the fall. This summer I intend spending most of my time with my daughters Anne and Amanda. Mr. Stamps and Lucinda are as kind to me as Children could be. . . . As to my own health it is as good as I could expect at my time of life. I must conclude this short letter with the sincere love of your affectionate Mother

Jane Davis

In the summer of 1836 in Warren County, Mississippi, Jefferson Davis really began to put down roots. His allegiance to one

[1] This is the only extant letter from Jefferson Davis's mother that the author has been able to discover. The handwriting is that of a person of intelligence and education, and it is a youngish hand, though Jane was now seventy-four. The letter is in the possession of her great-grandson Jefferson Hayes-Davis of Colorado Springs. The children referred to are Hugh Davis, son of her daughter Lucinda, whose first husband was a Davis, but no relation; and Isaac Davis Stamps, son of Lucinda by her second husband, William Stamps. The boys were away at boarding school. Isaac, Jefferson's favorite nephew, was killed at Gettysburg.

state had never before been localized. He had spent only eight of his twenty-eight years on Mississippi soil. Born in Kentucky and returning there for some primary education and for college, half of his first sixteen years had been passed in his native state. The next four years he spent in West Point, New York, at the Military Academy. The five years sequent kept him on the edges of the unsettled Northwest, mostly in Wisconsin. The last two years of his army service were passed in Arkansas and Indian Territory. Having now enjoyed some weeks in the national capital, Jefferson had come back to Mississippi with an exceptional knowledge of his country as a whole. In no sense could he be called a provincial.

For the next seven years Jefferson Davis remained a recluse on Davis Bend. Except for another brief visit with his friend George Jones in Washington in 1838, he rarely left the peninsula, and then only on business or family necessity. The most consoling and stimulating factor in Jefferson's new way of life was the interest and devotion of his eldest brother. Joseph, who had no son of his own, was still more like a proud father than a brother. Now he obviously took a fresh zest in living by having at hand for daily conversation an attractive young man with the mental caliber of Jefferson.

In 1836 Joseph, at fifty-one, was strikingly handsome. In a portrait painted when he was in his late thirties by Raphael West, he faintly resembles a stronger Shelley. It is a fine face with a high broad forehead and a sensitive chiseled mouth. The open, sparkling gray eyes are his most striking feature. The whole conception is characterized by innate elegance and aristocratic bearing. In 1884, on sending to Joseph's granddaughter Lize a photograph of the painting, Jefferson wrote: "He was my *beau ideal* when I was a boy, and my love for him is to me yet a sentiment than which I have none more sacred." Joseph had been successful in everything he attempted: lawyer, banker, planter. "Between 1810 and 1840," says William Dodd, "Joseph Davis built up a fortune from practically nothing to an estate approaching a million dollars in value." Contemporary sources claim he was one of the five wealthiest men in Mississippi. Besides Hurricane he eventually owned several other plantations in Mississippi and property in Arkansas, Louisiana, and Kentucky. A generous-hearted fellow, Joseph was said to give away plantations to relatives as he gave away horses to friends.

According to Reuben Davis (no relation) in his *Recollections of Mississippi:* "Joseph Davis was the admitted arbiter of every question of honor . . . and his decision was final." At that time when gentlemen were continually challenging each other to duels, to be a successful arbiter and prevent the duels from taking place was no small accomplishment. Reuben Davis goes on to say: "He was a great lawyer and debater, and his wealth was the honorable accumulation of his professional gains. . . ." The noted orator-attorney, Seargent Prentiss, said he would rather have anyone oppose him in the courtroom than Joe Davis. His intellect was so keen that he could go straight to the heart of a matter and pick the flaws in an opponent's argument with uncanny precision. Though Joseph had no taste for public office with its turmoils, politicians and statesmen were ever seeking his advice and influence. Devoting himself to study and reflection, his mind was a vast storehouse of information which rendered him a fascinating conversationalist as well as a formidable lawyer.

A eulogy published in Vicksburg at the time of his death declared Joseph "simple, modest and retiring in his manner, but elegant at the same time." If his background did not entitle him to be called an aristocrat, he looked every inch one. Though he enjoyed the good things of life and spent his money freely, he was extremely practical and expert in management. His fault was one common to many able heads of families: he believed strongly in his own opinion. When he gave good advice he was displeased when it was disregarded. For this reason several of his relatives did not get on so well with Joseph; but he never tried to force his opinions on his youngest brother. In Jefferson he recognized an intelligence as fine if not finer than his own and respected it, despite the twenty-three-year disparity in ages.

Perhaps no pair of mutually admiring brothers more greatly

relished after-dinner talks in the library than Joseph and Jefferson. Both possessed extraordinary versatility of interests. Both had a gift for logic. And, as Varina Davis writes, "intercourse with his brother Joseph was well calculated to improve and enlarge the mind of the younger brother." For almost three decades Joseph had been a student of governmental law. He was an authority on the formative years of the United States Government. There was nothing about the Constitution or *The Federalist* he did not know. He subscribed to the London *Times* and various other British periodicals, as well as to the *National Intelligencer*, and Richmond, Charleston, and New Orleans newspapers.

In Joseph's spreading library, Jefferson made a serious study of books like Adam Smith's *Wealth of Nations* and *Elliot's Debates*. He read John Locke, and the writings of the Virginian for whom he was named. Though the brothers had endless discussions, apparently they did not argue, for they were in remarkable accord. Both were staunchly State Rights Jeffersonian Democrats. They regarded the Constitution as a sacred compact, "not to be tampered with or evaded without the sacrifice of honor and good faith."

In one special characteristic Jefferson was deemed a spiritual son of his brother: "he could hardly comprehend anyone's differing from him in political policy after hearing the reasons on which his opinion was based." In such an attitude there was a special kind of strength, but it carried a minus as well as a plus.

While Jefferson reveled in Joseph's talk and Joseph's books in the evenings, by day he was diligent in the pursuit of agriculture. He carefully remarked his brother's methods of slave management and agronomic techniques. In Natchez with Joseph and James Pemberton to advise him, he had bought ten carefully selected slaves. He had put his faithful body servant in charge of them. Pemberton, with a shrewd understanding of both the black man's and the white man's psychology, was indispensable. But even more so was Joseph, who was noted throughout Mississippi for his model plantation. Strange as it seems, the democratic plutocrat Joseph had been influenced by the utopian philosophy of the socialist Robert Owen, whose *A New View of Society* he had read before meeting him on the stagecoach in 1824.

As Joseph's Negroes testified both before and after the War between the States, they were most kindly treated. No overseer was ever given the right to punish them. The Negroes enjoyed a kind of self-rule devised by Joseph, in which the older or more settled ones acted as the jury for offenders. Though the Negroes themselves set the penalty, the master reserved the right to pardon or mitigate the severity of the sentence, which Jefferson noted he did more than often. Joseph would preside on the front veranda in a rocking chair, while the black jurors sat on the front steps and the accused stood on the ground before them.

The slaves were encouraged to be thrifty, resourceful, and inventive. They could raise their own vegetables and produce their own eggs to supplement their weekly rations. Eggs bought by the big house were paid for at market prices, though they could also be sold in any market. When a slave could do better at some other employment than daily labor, he was allowed to do so, paying for the worth of regular field service out of his earnings. One of the slaves ran a variety shop, and sometimes he would buy the entire fruit crop from the Davis estates to sell and ship. Joseph chose his favorites among the Negroes for advancement according to their qualities and aptitudes. Any individual talent that revealed itself was nurtured.

Jefferson was particularly impressed by a responsible and gifted Negro named Benjamin Thornton Montgomery, whose father, John, had been born a slave in Loudon County, Virginia. John had been taught to write by his master's young son, who would pass on daily to the little black boy the knowledge imbibed from his tutor by tracing letters with a stick in the river-shore sands. As a youth John had been brought to Natchez, where Joseph Davis purchased him. His bent was carpentry; he became expert in building. Then he took up civil engineering, devising his own instruments. He had a knack for measuring ditches and making levees and in estimating their cost before the work was begun.

John passed on his knowledge of reading and writing to his son Ben Montgomery, who had acquired a little library of his own by the time Jefferson came to Hurricane. Later, when Ben's two boys, Isaiah and Thornton, were of sufficient age, Jefferson sent a clever man he owned named George Stewart over to Hurricane to tutor the Montgomery boys. At ten Isaiah had gone as far as long division in arithmetic and read a great deal in history. And at ten he was taken to live in Hurricane House and set to work filing papers and letters in Joe Davis's office. At night he slept on a soft pallet in the master's big downstairs bedroom next to the office. One of his duties was to meet the passenger boats that plied the Mississippi and get the mails; on the way home he would improve his education by reading the newspapers.

As the Montgomery boys grew up they helped Joseph with his large correspondence, business and political. Because his word had significance in state politics, he frequently needed four or five copies of a long letter or a manuscript article. In those days before typewriters the Montgomerys did the copying for him, and thus they came to have considerable knowledge of what was going on in the world. As the aged Isaiah on a trip to Boston in 1907 told an interviewer from the *Transcript:* "We just barely had an idea of what slave life was." Jefferson often heard neighboring planters twit Joseph about his indulgence with his Negroes. And later, when hoopskirts became the fashion, they joked, "Now the Davis brothers will have to widen their cotton rows to make room for the lady pickers' hoops."

Jefferson Davis inherited his attitude to slavery, as he had inherited much of political ideology, from his father Samuel, who had been a follower of Thomas Jefferson since 1776. And Dodd says that "Thomas Jefferson favored the institution of slavery in 1820," and that "Chief Justice Marshall defended it, as he would any other form of property." Born and reared among happy blacks, Jefferson had also known the satisfied slaves employed by the Dominican friars at St. Thomas. He was convinced that servitude was a necessary steppingstone to the Negro's eventual freedom and "measurable perfectibility." He firmly believed that the Negroes brought from Africa were benefited by their contact with white civilization and Christianity. He was convinced that as the instrument of supplying cotton to the textile industry, which meant better employment in England and in the Continent, as well as in New England, the Negro made a real contribution to world prosperity. Blacks bred in the blistering African climate were adapted for work in the Southern cotton fields, which few Anglo-Saxon white men could stand.

Jefferson also believed that the only hope for improvement in the condition of the Negro lay in the slow process of fitting him for economic competition with his white superiors. He felt that sudden emancipation would destroy a race that was not fitted for that competition. He sought earnestly to advance the Negro, but, like Abraham Lincoln, he did not believe the black man would become the white man's equal in the United States.[2]

And though Davis knew there were, as in all countries and among all races, individual instances of cruel treatment, he was satisfied that between no employer and laboring class had such kindly and regardful feelings subsisted. "It was under black huntsmen," as he later told Dr. Craven when in prison, "the young whites took their first lessons in field sports. They fished, shot and hunted together, eating the same bread . . . sleeping under the same tree with their Negro guides. . . . Early associations of service, affection, and support were powerful." Jefferson Davis regarded Southern planters like his brother and himself as provid-

[2] In Lincoln's *Collected Works*, published for the Abraham Lincoln Association of Springfield, Illinois, Vol. V, pages 370-375, appears Lincoln's "Address on Colonization to a Deputation of Negroes." On August 14, 1862, in trying to persuade some free colored leaders to start a movement for the Negroes to leave the United States and colonize, with governmental assistance, in Central America, he said among other things: "You and we are different races. We have between us a broader difference than exists between almost any other races. . . . I think your race suffers very greatly, many of them by living among us, while ours suffers from your presence. . . . Even when you cease to be slaves, you are yet far removed from being placed on an equality with the white race . . . on this broad continent, not a single man of your race is made the equal of a single man of ours."

Beveridge in his biography of Lincoln further discusses his attitude to the Negro.

ing a beneficial tutelage for a childlike race unprepared as yet to take care of itself in a white man's world.

In the early spring of 1838, after almost two years on Davis Bend, Jefferson returned to Washington to pay the promised visit to Congressman Jones. This time, according to his host, "Lieutenant Davis soon won the high esteem and respect of the foremost men in the national Capital." Franklin Pierce, especially, found Jefferson *simpatico,* and took him to call on President Martin van Buren. The President invited him for breakfast at the White House. Jefferson noted immediately Van Buren's refined taste, particularly in the bowls and vases of roses throughout the drawing rooms, which were altogether less elegant in their furnishings than he had expected. He found Van Buren "soigné and astute," a delightful conversationalist, with "perfect breeding" and a "graceful deference of manner." Each noticed the discriminating dress of the other. In the middle of a serious conversation after breakfast, the President broke off and looking closely at the New Orleans shoes on Jeff's narrow, high-arched feet, said, "Where did you get your shoes, may I ask? I had a pair like that made in France, but I have never seen that stitch since." Jefferson was flattered, for if he had a vanity it was his well-shod feet.

In late March of 1838 another of those strange accidents which seemed fated to Jefferson almost took his life. He was invited to an evening party given by the Secretary of War, Joel Poinsett, the South Carolinian who, as United States Minister, discovered the flower in Mexico which he introduced to the United States as the poinsettia. Jeff went along with his friends Jones, Crittenden, Allen, and Dr. Linn. Jones and Linn left the party early, but Crittenden urged Davis and Senator Allen to remain and return later with him. After Jones and Linn had gone to bed, they heard Allen calling out in distress. As Jones tells the story: "Davis was bleeding profusely from a deep cut in his head, and the blood was streaming down over his face and upon his white tie, shirtfront and white waistcoat. Mr. Allen, who had been drinking champagne freely, was somewhat intoxicated, and missing the bridge (Mr. Allen being supposed to be familiar with the road) Davis had followed him and they had both fallen into the Tiber, a small rocky stream which they had to cross. Davis, who was perfectly sober, had endeavored to save himself and had pitched head foremost into the creek and cut his head badly."

Jefferson was on the verge of fainting from loss of blood when Dr. Linn got him to bed and applied restoratives. In the morning Jones found him unconscious and rushed to call Dr. Linn. "After several hours of hard work," says Jones, "we restored him to consciousness. Dr. Linn remarked that he would have been dead had I been five minutes later in reaching him."

On April 14 Jefferson had written to his friend, Joseph's brother-in-law, William van Bentheysen of New York. But before a reply reached him Jeff was sufficiently recovered to start overland for Mississippi. After he arrived at Hurricane he received a letter from Van Bentheysen dated New York, April 18, 1838.[3]

I started for Washington on Wednesday (11th) accompanied by my wife—and lo when we arrived in Washington *friend Jeff* had gone—I set myself to work to find you out—commenced by introducing myself to your friend *Jones*, who by the way appears to be a very fine fellow——from him I learned that you had left for Philadelphia the Thursday previous to proceed via Pittsburg for home—this was a damper—being obliged to spend the day "a la Havana"—Mrs. V. and I made the best use of our time in visiting the various places worth seeing before 5 P.M. Started for Baltimore—remained in B. over night and next morning took flight for Philadelphia in hopes of overtaking the *fugitive*—but alas nothing so sure as disappointment again—friend Jeff had the start of us by several days and not being able to find out positively which way he had gone we gave up the pursuit. . . . We came home on Monday a little tired and a little chagrined that we had missed you. . . .

[3] This letter from Joseph Davis's brother-in-law, written on quality stationery in a sophisticated hand, conclusively proves 1838 to be the year of Jefferson's near-fatal accident in Washington.

We were much startled to hear of your serious accident in Washington. . . .

Write to me and let me know how your health is— Give my love to brother Joseph, Eliza and the rest.

Believe me with<br>Sincere regards<br>Your friend<br>W van Bentheysen

The society of Washington and the few months' association with prominent men of the day had relieved the troubling grief of Jefferson's mind. But though he had been introduced under the happiest circumstances and received everywhere with warm cordiality, he was in no sense enamored of life in the national capital. In its glitter he had discerned something antipathetical. He felt much better attuned to the seasonal rhythms of a planter's life than to the show, the intrigue, the who's-in-who's-out of politics. On February 9, 1839, a year after his diverting visit, in a consoling letter to his friend George Jones, who was temporarily pushed aside in his political career, he could write: "The happiness you will find in the midst of your amiable family will greatly exceed all you could have hoped for at Washington, that hotbed of heartlessness and home of the world's worldly."

That summer of 1838, after his spring visit to Washington, Jefferson was left alone at Hurricane as his own housekeeper, as well as manager of Brierfield, for Joseph took his wife first to Hot Springs, Arkansas, for the benefits of the baths, and then to Louisville. His daughter Florida, Mrs. McCaleb, to whom he had given the plantation called Diamond Place, had gone with them. From her Jeff received a loving letter written on July 18, 1838. She wrote partly in French. Her father had been ill. She beguiled the time by reading and playing the guitar. "I hope, dear Uncle Jeff, to see you with Mr. McCaleb in Louisville. Be sure not to disappoint me. I feel as much alone as if I were in the deserts of Arabia. . . . Give my love to Mr. McCaleb." In a postscript she added: "Mamá, ma chère mamá desires me to ask how you succeed in housekeeping. Papá is anxious for your health."

Occasionally Jeff received a long, fascinating letter from Mary, Joseph's youngest daughter, who had married Dr. Charles Mitchell, now pursuing graduate medical studies in Paris. Joseph had provided sufficient funds for the young couple to have an apartment in one of the best sections of the city, and they had been going to many distinguished parties. Mary wrote that she had been surprised to see "elegantly dressed Negresses accompanied by white Frenchmen on the boulevards," and she wondered how the roses she had planted for Uncle Jeff were faring.

Though Jefferson was more than comfortable and even pampered in his brother's house, he wanted his own home, as he and Knox had planned, on the property they had together named "Brierfield." Following his own architectural design and with James Pemberton to supervise the Negroes, in the fall of 1838 he built a one-story house in a splendid grove of oaks. Designed for coolness in summer, the bedrooms opened out on a surrounding gallery of paved bricks encased in latticework. Jefferson was particularly proud of the six-foot-wide outer doors, because of the maximum amount of cool air admitted, though when a door was opened "it looked as if a whole side of the house had disappeared, Japanese-fashion."

It was not difficult for Jefferson to adjust himself to bachelor housekeeping since his dietary requirements were always extremely simple. Cornbread was his favorite staple fare. But he began his dinner with soup, a never-failing ritual at Hurricane, for Joseph maintained that "a gentleman always begins his dinner with soup." So his indifferent cook served well enough. Though the absence of Knox was continually in his consciousness, the life of a contemplative had a certain attraction for him. He had his devoted James Pemberton to look after him, advise or chat with him. James was the perfect servingman, both respectful and attentive, and his master always invited him to sit when they discussed business. At the close of a discussion of the day's farm activities, Jeff invariably gave his friend a good cigar. With books borrowed from Joseph and new books ordered for his own increasing library, Jefferson could beguile the rainy spells when plantation work halted. He devoured the English classics, prose and poetry. Shakespeare was ever fresh to him. He liked the romantics, Byron and Burns. Agreeing with the popular taste of the time, he enjoyed Sir Walter Scott's historical novels. He found the neoclassicists cold, however, and he had no enthusiasm for the Puritan Milton. Though making no regular practice of attending any church, Jefferson read deeply in the Scriptures.[4] In an article in the New York *Herald* after his death his youngest daughter, Winnie, declared that she had never met a clergyman who knew the Bible better than her father.

Jefferson Davis took profound interest in the welfare and contentment of his Negroes, who lived in neat cabins to the right and left of Brierfield House beyond groups of fig trees. He provided for their wedding feasts and wakes. He had a dentist from Vicksburg come periodically to care for their teeth. His corncribs were without locks, so that the Negroes could take what grain they required for their chickens. A day nursery provided for the little children of working mothers. Jefferson knew by name all the black children, who adored him and who would line up morning and evening to wave and call to "Marse Jeff" when he rode past the quarters. A quality which Varina Davis points out revealed itself at this reclusive period of his life: he could not bear for anyone to be inimical to him. If somehow one of his Negroes became annoyed with him, he was never satisfied until he had got back into the slave's good graces.

In the work hours Jefferson was absorbed in making a success of his new profession. He was what was known as a "careful planter." The conscientiousness and devotion he had displayed in his military service he brought to husbandry. By 1843, he had become moderately well-to-do. The only wormwood in his lot was that Knox was not beside him to share in the realization of their young dreams.

[4] When Joseph brought an Episcopal clergyman to live at Hurricane some years later, Jefferson attended the morning services for the white people or sometimes the afternoon services for the colored.

So Jefferson continued his self-imposed exile, enlarging the cultivated area and, going somewhat counter to the tendency of the times, diversifying his crops. During the hot months he also supervised his brother's vaster holdings; for Joseph continued to take Eliza to Northern resorts for her health. The main event of Jefferson's summers was the semiweekly arrival of the river boats bringing mail and ice and goods ordered from New Orleans. In gratitude for favors Jefferson would send the captain gifts of flowers and fruits for the passengers' delectation. In the long evenings, when not at Hurricane, he had for company, besides James Pemberton and the English poets, Congressmen whose speeches had been delivered in Washington "only yesterday," that is, within a month.

Though Jefferson seemed contented with his monastic home life, Joseph and the rest of the Davises were disturbed about his prolonged withdrawal from society. They were convinced that Jeff had been a widower long enough and needed a wife. And Joseph felt that Jeff's abilities were being wasted on the alluvial Delta silt. He hoped he would emerge from his asceticism and serve his state in some public function.

From the remote purlieus of Brierfield the young planter had continued to take a fervent but detached interest in political questions. He knew all that was going on and had his decided opinions, though his consuming concern was for the job at hand: becoming a successful planter. In writing to his Iowa friend George Jones in 1839, he revealed something of his state of mind and heart:

"As the head of the democratic party I wish him [Van Buren] success, but he has sowed indecision, a plant not suited to the deep furrows ploughed by his predecessors. You perceive that when I write of politics I am not of my element and naturally slip back to seeding and ploughing about which I hope to talk with you all next summer.

"It gave me much pleasure to hear that I was not forgotten by Dr. Linn and Mr. Allen. I esteem them both and I *love* the

Doctor. . . . My health is better than when we parted and I hope to visit Sinsinawa next summer looking something less pale and yellow than when we met last winter."

In a letter of July 24, 1840, to Senator William Allen of Ohio, thanking him for a copy of a speech he had delivered in Congress, he showed he was conversant with the important speeches of the hour. In praising Allen's printed words, which he considered an excellent "English sample of the Demosthenes style," he was critical of John C. Calhoun, whose politics he admired greatly. "I recollect you saw in Mr. Calhoun's speech on the independent Treasury an especial likeness to the Grecian orator. I thought he was too sententious. . . ."

After writing at some length on the matter of an independent Treasury, he came to personal affairs:

"I am living as retired as a man on the great thoroughfare of the Mississippi can be, and just now the little society hereabout has been driven away by the presence of the summer's heat and the fear of the summer's disease.

"Our staple, cotton, is distressingly low and I fear likely to remain so until there is a diminished production of it, an event which the embarrassed condition of cotton planters in this section will not allow them to consider. If our Yankee friends and their coadjutors should get up a scheme for bounties to particular branches of industry I think the cotton growers may come in with the old plea of the manufacturers 'not able at present to progress without it.'"

Here Jefferson Davis touched significantly on agricultural subsidy, which did not become really effective until almost a century later, when Franklin D. Roosevelt inaugurated the New Deal.

Some months after his thirty-fifth birthday, in the fall of 1843, Jefferson took an active part in politics for the first time in his life. Within one week of Election Day the Democrats of Warren County, becoming dissatisfied with their candidate for the Mississippi legislature, withdrew him and persuaded the widower to run. The Whigs were so in the majority in the district that they had felt strong enough to run two Whig candidates.

In the Vicksburg *Sentinel* of November 1, 1843, appeared the first printed news of Jefferson Davis's entry into politics. According to the paper, he received the unanimous nomination of the party. In commenting, the editor wrote with a flourishing pen: "Mr. Davis is a sterling Democrat, a man of unsullied private character, talents of a high order, extensive political information, and judging from his remarks before the convention, a fine public speaker. There may be some in the country to whom Mr. Davis from the secluded privacy in which he has lived, is unknown, to these we repeat, Mr. Davis is what we have stated *a man, every inch a man.*"

The election was to take place the Monday following the sudden switch in candidates. An odd excitement swept the district with the announcement. The confident Whigs became apprehensive and hastily withdrew one of their candidates, virtually guaranteeing the defeat of the young squire of Brierfield. But the Whigs were taking no chances. They called on the famous Seargent S. Prentiss, the most popular orator of the state, to meet the newcomer in public debate at Vicksburg on Election Day.

A stand was set up for the debaters at the foot of the courthouse stairs, which the voters had to pass to get to the ballot room. In alternate quarter-hour periods the political opponents argued their side. Prentiss, a little man with a lame leg and a magnificent head, had an extraordinary skill "for analysis and logical induction." But Jefferson Davis gave a fine account of himself against Mississippi's number-one speaker. The excitement was considerable as the debate continued for the better part of the day. Of course, Davis lost the election, though by a much smaller majority than anyone anticipated. Never again was he to run for the state legislature. But the Democrats had their eye on him as a shining new champion of the cause of State Rights.

It is a sad commentary that when any striking man rises on the political scene, no matter how pure his motives, how impeccable his integrity, the malice of both known and unknown enemies will sometimes gnaw at his reputation. Few good men have had to contend more with false accusations and insinuated calumny than Jefferson Davis. Lurking in the background of his very first campaign of 1843 was an issue destined to crop out years later in unscrupulous attempts to link with it the name of Davis. It was called the "Act of Repudiation." Speculators who had swarmed into Mississippi on the wave of cotton prosperity in the 1830's had urged the issuance of some $7,000,000 worth of bonds by the Planters' Bank and the Union Bank. With dubious legality the state had sanctioned and guaranteed such a bond issue. Then came the financial panic of 1837, during Van Buren's first year in office. In the early '40's when bondholders failed to receive their interest and banks themselves began to fail, the Democratic governor of Mississippi urged the legislature to pass an Act of Repudiation. With the Whigs in control, the legislature honorably refused to do so and insisted the debt must be acknowledged. But at the next session when the Democrats had a large majority of legislators the act was passed. The Democrats thereafter became known as the party of repudiation.

While a staunch Democrat himself, Jefferson Davis, like many others of his party, did not agree with the Democratic majority on the repudiation issue. He declared openly that the obligations of the state should be met and the validity of the debt determined by the courts. Thus in the campaign debate with the Whig Seargent Prentiss the burning theme of repudiation was not a point of controversy; it was not even mentioned, because it was one on which they were in agreement.

Since Jefferson Davis never in his life sat in the Mississippi legislature and since this was the first and only time he was candidate for the office of state representative, later allegations that attributed to him any part in the enactment of repudiation were completely without foundation. However, during the War between the States, the charge of being a leading repudiator was to be brought out against him in London by Robert J. Walker, an agent of the Federal Government. A onetime powerful United

States Senator from Mississippi and a Democrat strongly in favor of repudiation, the Northern-born Walker had turned coat expediently in 1861. Becoming a radical Republican, he was sent to England to discredit the Confederacy. Knowing thoroughly the true facts, the former "Wizard of Mississippi politics" unscrupulously tried to fasten some of the blame of repudiation on Jefferson Davis. "Even after the war, the slander was cast in his teeth" by his long-time enemy Winfield Scott, and later by the rash young Theodore Roosevelt, out of careless malice. The vindication of history, however, has been complete, and back in the 1840's the true facts were, of course, well known.

In referring to this early period of Davis's career, the New Orleans *Times Democrat* later said conclusively: "Not only was it Mr. Davis's first appearance in the political arena as a candidate for the legislature, subsequent to the repudiation of the bonds, but, he never at any time, before or afterwards, held any civil office—legislative, executive, or judicial—in the State government. Furthermore, his supposed sympathy with the advocates of the payment of the debt by the State was actually (although ineffectually) employed among the repudiators as an objection to his election to Congress in 1845." Because of his antirepudiation stand, many Whigs were to cast their votes for Davis in that election.

Joseph was very proud of his pupil-brother and urged him to let the Democrats advance him to political eminence. Jefferson's appearance on the local political scene in the fall of 1843 marked the end of his seven years' seclusion. In the perfervid words of Thomas Dixon, his searching investigator and admirer seven decades later: "He stepped forth to take his place in the world of action—the best equipped, most thoroughly trained, most perfectly poised man who had ever entered the arena of American politics." Within two years he had taken his seat in the United States House of Representatives.

Sarah Knox Taylor, daughter of Zachary Taylor and first wife of Jefferson Davis, at sixteen. Louisiana Historical Museum, New Orleans

Joseph Emory Davis, eldest brother of Jefferson Davis, at 39. The portrait was painted in 1824 in New York by Raphael West and is owned by Jefferson Hayes-Davis.

*Above left:* Varina Howell at 18, the time of her marriage to Jefferson Davis; *above right:* Varina at about the time she became First Lady of the Confederacy, from a painting owned by her great-granddaughter Mrs. Gerald Bennett (born Varina Margaret Webb) of Colorado Springs; *below:* Jefferson Davis at the time of his second marriage, painted by John Henry Byrd, from the L. W. Ramsey Collection, by courtesy of Craddock Goins

Jefferson Davis at about 49, during his last term in the United States Senate. From a painting owned by his great-grandson Joel Webb of Colorado Springs, and never before reproduced

# CHAPTER IX

## END OF SECLUSION

THE SECLUSION of Jefferson Davis was broken not only because of his emergence into political limelight, but because he met a girl named Varina Anne Howell. She was the seventeen-year-old daughter of Joseph's friends the William Burr Howells of Natchez. Joseph had persuaded them to let her come to Hurricane for an extensive Christmas house party, which in the South sometimes lasted for months. Chaperoned by her devoted tutor, Judge George Winchester, a close family friend, Varina traveled upriver by the steamboat *Magnolia*, then known as a "floating palace" and surpassing any Southern hotel in its cuisine and lush decorations. The two disembarked ten miles north of Hurricane at Diamond Place, the plantation Joseph had given his eldest daughter Florida McCaleb. Varina was to pay a brief visit here and then be fetched to Hurricane.

One morning while Varina was admiring December blossoms in the McCaleb garden, a handsome man rode up and brought her a message. Joseph Davis was expecting her on the morrow and sending his niece, Mary Bradford, and a groom with an extra saddle horse, as well as a carriage to transport the luggage. The messenger was Jefferson Davis, who was en route to Vicksburg to a political caucus concerning the next year's presidential nominee. He tarried no more than half an hour, but long enough for Varina to notice how much joy his mere presence gave to his relatives and the servants.

What Jefferson thought of the tall, vivacious girl with the heavy-lidded dark eyes is not known. But in their brief meeting he certainly made a deep impression on Varina. She noted that he rode with more grace than any man she had ever seen and "gave the impression of being incapable of being unseated or fatigued." She remarked, too, that he was handsome, well-proportioned, and as active as a boy. While she found him almost gallant in his courteous manner, she sensed a reserve in his rather aloof charm that was like a challenge. That night, in a letter to her mother, the seventeen-year-old miss set down her first impressions of the man whose brilliant yet tragic destiny she was to share. Her letter reveals her instinctively keen perceptions when only a girl.[1]

"To-day Uncle Joe sent, by his younger brother . . . an urgent invitation to me to go at once to 'The Hurricane.' I do not know whether this Mr. Jefferson Davis is young or old. He looks both at times; but I believe he is old, for from what I hear he is only two years younger than you are. He impresses me as a remarkable kind of man, but of uncertain temper, and has a way of taking for granted that everybody agrees with him when he expresses an opinion, which offends me; yet he is most agreeable and has a peculiarly sweet voice and a winning manner of asserting himself. The fact is, he is the kind of person I should expect to rescue one from a mad dog at any risk, but to insist upon a stoical indifference to the fright afterward. I do not think I shall ever like him as I do his brother Joe. Would you believe it, he is refined and cultivated, and yet he is a Democrat!"

Varina had been brought up to take it for granted that people of cultivation and refinement were Whigs and Episcopalians or possibly Presbyterians. She took the usual Southern pride in family. Her maternal grandmother, a magnificent old lady, had been a Grahame of Virginia and an heiress, who had married an Irish

[1] In the Jefferson Hayes-Davis Collection are vivid, entertaining letters from Varina at the age of twelve while she was in boarding school in Philadelphia. As remarkable in lack of punctuation as Gertrude Stein's at the height of her fame, the childish letters indicate an original and independent mind.

gentleman of means named James Kempe. Her father's father, Delaware-born Richard Howell, had been a major in the Revolutionary War and a distinguished governor of New Jersey, eight times re-elected successively. His mother was Keziah Burr, a Quaker cousin of Aaron Burr. Varina was puzzled because the Davises expressed no claim to high-bred lineage and yet she had never known anyone more aristocratic in appearance and manner than Uncle Joe and this younger brother. Though neither of them were church members, she knew that their father had been a Baptist, and that was more shocking to a Howell than being a Democrat.

The next day Varina learned something of Jefferson Davis's history from Mary Bradford, a favorite niece of both brothers, as they rode through the December woods to Hurricane. Behind the girls came the groom on horseback and the carriage bringing the new dresses Varina's mother had provided for her first house party. While there is no direct evidence that Joseph had matchmaking intentions when he urged Varina's presence at Hurricane, he was apparently gratified to watch Jefferson's interest in her grow after his return from Vicksburg.

Varina would often find occasion to steal away from the young folks and join the brothers in the library where they discussed serious matters. Jefferson was intrigued by the girl's quick mind, her independence of thought, her ability to translate Latin at sight with clarity and grace. Although she had had only two seasons at Madame Greenland's school in Philadelphia, her education, he found, was far superior to that of most women of the day. The stimulator of her pursuit of learning was Judge Winchester, originally from Salem, Massachusetts, who had taught her for twelve years gratuitously, because she was apt and earnest and took joy in pleasing him. The Judge was her ideal of manhood, she told Jefferson, and she called him "Great-heart." He had never treated her as a child, but as a discriminating adult, with a good mind and a gift of humor. Jefferson discovered that at seventeen Varina was not only well grounded in Latin and English classics, but was desirous of learning more of governmental principles. He was amused at her intense Whig allegiance in this Democratic household, but pleased that she would listen with keen awareness to any side of an argument. Despite her high-spirited nature, she could be a perfect listener.

After the first week Joseph and the other members of the house party contrived to leave the widower and Varina largely to themselves. In the white music room with its cream and rose furnishings, they would sit together before an open fire of hickory logs and converse for hours on a variety of subjects ranging from the structure of Latin odes to current world affairs. At first Jefferson seemed attracted more to the girl's qualities of mind and conversation than to her physical charms. Varina gave the impression of beauty, though she did not have clear-cut features. A decided brunette, she had a rich, healthy coloring. Her knowing dark eyes were enormous and the full lips bespoke her delight in laughter. Her lustrous black hair, which she wore parted in the middle according to the fashion, was brought down low to conceal the ears and gathered in a widespread bun high on the back of her head. At seventeen Varina's figure was willowy, and her carriage had grace as well as poise. For her part, the girl was flattered that the handsome man of thirty-five paid marked attention to a seventeen-year-old. The coolness of his charm continued to excite her interest, as well as the fact that everybody on the entire peninsula seemed "to bow down to the younger brother."

In the mornings Jefferson and Varina rode together about the plantation. For her he had carefully chosen a dark bay, while his mount was a white Arabian. In the Hurricane stables there were thirty stalls of high-bred horses. With special pride Jefferson exhibited Black Oliver, a Canadian stallion that had sired many of the "then renowned Davis pacers." Another favorite of his was Highland Henry, a large red bay that glinted like gilt in the sun. He warned her against Gray Medley, a horse of untrustworthy temper, which had mortally injured a groom. Since Jefferson had come to Davis Bend no horse bred at Hurricane had been sold, but many were presented as gifts to nieces and nephews and to visiting friends who took a fancy to this or that mount. Varina was impressed by the solicitude of both brothers for their horses and the affectionate tones in which they spoke to them.

On one of their rides Jefferson took Varina to see his own house at Brierfield and to meet James Pemberton and some of his other black friends. The Negroes were delighted with the girl in the dark blue riding habit and mighty pleased about Marse Jeff's new interest. Although Jefferson was a master at concealing his feelings, Joseph had reason to believe that his brother was "courting." And noticing their pleasure in each other's company, he felt assured that this might be a good match for Jeff.

Toward the end of January Jefferson proposed. They became secretly engaged. In February Varina returned home to tell her mother she had fallen in love. Jefferson was eager to present himself in Natchez to ask the Howells in the proper old-fashioned form for her hand. But Varina restrained him. Her mother seems to have had some doubts about the union. Perhaps it was because Jefferson was a widower and almost eighteen years older. While she was very fond of Joseph and remembered the boyish cadet at West Point most pleasantly, Mrs. Howell wanted Varina to wait, to be sure this was not just a young girl's infatuation for an older, more sophisticated man. Judge Winchester, however, spoke stoutly in behalf of Varina's choice, and in the Howell household the gentle Judge was regarded as an oracle of wisdom.[2]

The delay in hearing favorable news from Natchez filled Jefferson with concern. On March 8, 1844, he wrote from Hurricane.

My own dearest Varina

I cannot express to you my gratitude for your kind letter; when the "Concordia" put out the letters . . . one from you . . . came to dispel my gloomy apprehensions.

I am truly obliged by the defence put in for me by my friend the Judge. . . . He would have a poor opinion, I doubt not, of

---

[2] Some of the relatives believe the Howells were delighted and that they had expected what would happen when Varina went to Hurricane. Mr. Howell had run through most of his wife's money and there were already nine children. Perhaps Varina did not want Jefferson to think she could be too easily won.

any man who having an opportunity to know you would not love you. . . .

But why shall I not come to see you? In addition to the desire I have to be with you every day and all day, it seems to me but proper and necessary to justify my wish to marry you, if you had not forbidden me I should have answered your letter in person and let me ask you to reconsider your position. . . .

Since you left I have found the house particularly dull. I believe everybody thinks of you, as soon as they see me, or . . . when I enter any of the rooms in which we were together. . . .

If I have time I will write this better i.e. with less scratching. Pray don't read at night, nor punish your angel eyes by keeping a light in your chamber all night. In all things be careful of your health. Otherwise what pain shall I not suffer to know that you are sick, suffering, or that I can not be with you.

Bon soir, ma chère ange, Je suis notre

Jeffers Davis [3]

Almost by the next boat Varina wrote that she had won her mother's consent. But when her letter arrived Jefferson was absent from home because of a family calamity. When he returned considerably perturbed, Varina's letter was awaiting him. He wrote her at once, and entrusted the letter to Eliza's brother William van Bentheysen, who was presently leaving for Natchez, to deliver to her in person.

Hurricane<br>March 15, 1844

My dearest, my own one,

I have just returned from the performance of a most painful and melancholy duty. My Brother-in-law was assassinated day before yesterday—I went out to his late residence yesterday and returned today bringing with me my sister and her children.

[3] This letter, like the majority of intimate personal letters quoted in this biography, is in the possession of a grandson, Jefferson Hayes-Davis of Colorado Springs. The writer found it in a bundle tied with white ribbon, and in Varina's handwriting a note that these letters from her dear husband were last read on May 26, 1890.

In such gloom nothing could give me pleasure unless it were a part of you. Your letter, all that I could have of you, was waiting my arrival, and deeply do I thank you for it.

It had been my intention, if you did not further interdict me, to have gone down tonight by the "Concordia" to be seen of you, not to see you, because I do that notwithstanding the space that divides us: but your own heart will tell you of reasons enough to prevent my going away under the existing circumstances.

Two things in your letter are very gratifying to me, that your mother has ceased from opposing the course of your love, and that *you are in good health*. . . . I entreat you take care of my wife. . . .

You were equally wrong to blame and scold me for having neglected to write to you and then when you went to the other extreme and concluded I must have small-pox, as I had not written. If after the unlimited declarations I have made to you of my love I could neglect you—

I will ask Wm V. Bentheysen to deliver this to you—

Adieu, au revoir, ma chère, très chère, plus très chère Varina. Dieu te benisse. I commenced with no expectation of being able to write one page. I have nearly filled three with I know not what and haven't time to examine—

Ever and entirely I am your<br>Jeffers Davis

To My Varina

The sister referred to was Amanda, whose husband, Judge David Bradford, was ambushed and killed on the highroad as he returned home on horseback from court at Washington, Mississippi. The assassin was angered because a lawsuit had been decided against him. Jefferson was particularly fond of this much older brother-in-law, who wrote him affectionate letters and who had named his third son for him.

After getting his widowed sister and her seven children installed in Hurricane, he arranged his affairs at Brierfield and within a fortnight presented himself at the Howell home, which was coincidentally called "The Briers" because of the masses of

Cherokee roses that abounded on the ninety-eight-acre estate half a mile south of Natchez. The house itself stood on a high bluff about two hundred yards from the Mississippi. It had been built for Judge Perkins by the noted architect Levi Weeks in 1812, the same year Samuel Davis had built Rosemont. In style, too, it was story-and-a-half construction, so popular before 1820, though its floor space was almost twice that of Rosemont. A charming house, painted white, it sat high above the ground, with a wide veranda extending the length of the façade and with four graceful dormer windows breaking the high slanting roof. A large hall, two parlors, and two bedrooms comprised the front part of the first floor. The striking feature was the back drawing room which ran the entire length of the house, with its back wall formed entirely of floor-to-ceiling windows. The upstairs was reached by concealed staircases at either end of the drawing room. There were four smallish bedrooms and one huge room about sixty by twenty-four, which could be used as a ballroom or a dormitory for an overflow of house guests. The Howells had been given the place by Mrs. Kempe in 1826, two years before Varina's birth.[4]

Varina's parents were immediately drawn to their future son-in-law, whom they had seen when he was a red-cheeked cadet of sixteen. The numerous little Howells took to him, for Jefferson had an instinctive, sympathetic understanding of children. The forceful and elegant old grandmother, Margaret Louisa Kempe, was impressed by his bearing and his conversation and amazed to find such superior qualities in a Democrat. After the first face-to-face appraisal, the Howells gave their wholehearted consent. The betrothal was celebrated privately. For an engagement ring Jefferson gave Varina a pale emerald surrounded by diamonds.

But no date for the wedding was set, and the romance of courtship was interrupted, because Jefferson found himself im-

---

[4] Today the owner, Mrs. William Wall, formerly of New Orleans, has furnished the house handsomely and made improvements in the spreading garden. The concealing walls of the staircases have been removed and graceful, unobtrusive banisters add to the unusual charm of the back drawing room.

mediately thrust further into politics. He was chosen a delegate to the Democratic state convention that was to name its candidate for President. Although Warren County instructed him to favor Martin van Buren for re-election, he took occasion to dilate upon the superior qualifications of John C. Calhoun, the man he had come to admire above all others in American statesmanship. He pointed out that because of Calhoun's stand on free trade, the annexation of Texas, honest and efficient administration in Washington, and defensive measures for Southern harbors, the South Carolinian was really the ideal candidate. He moved that if Van Buren was not nominated, Calhoun should be considered Mississippi's second choice.

Davis made such a fine impression on the assemblage that he was given precedence as elector-at-large and urged to take an active part in the coming canvass. On March 25, 1844, a week after he had left Varina, he wrote to President van Buren asking him three questions that he felt sure would be brought up by the opposing Whigs. They concerned Van Buren's attitude to Texas annexation, the constitutional power of Congress over slavery in the District of Columbia, and the tariff of 1828.

On the same day he wrote an appeal for guidance to his friend Senator Allen of Ohio.

" 'The sick man knows the physician's step,' but I assure you that if breaking a long silence to ask a favor of you expose me to the suspicion of remembering you only because of my trouble, the fact is nevertheless quite otherwise. I am one of the Presidential 'electors' for the State of Mississippi and though I doubt not the democratic character of our people, I fear false statements and false issues in the approaching canvass and expect the Whigs to make great exertions.

"I wish you to aid me with my statements which can be made available against the charge of *defalcation* and extravagances under Mr. van Buren's administration, against the present Tariff as productive of revenue, against the U.S. Bank. . . .

"I have mingled but little in politics and you perceive by this letter have an arsenal poorly supplied for a campaign. Labor is expected of me and I am willing to render it. I believe much depends on this presidential election, and that every man who loves the Union and the Constitution as it is should be active."

There is no record of what the replies to these letters were. But when Van Buren came out against the annexation of Texas, it cost him the Democratic nomination, which went, not to Calhoun, but to James Knox Polk of Tennessee.

Because of his spontaneous eloquence, Davis was now sent by the Democrats to speak in all the counties of the state in an effort to defeat Henry Clay, the Whig candidate. Everywhere he proved popular. A tireless worker, he campaigned energetically for the election of Polk and Dallas. Since in those days the only railway in Mississippi was the short line between Vicksburg and Jackson, he had to travel by private carriage or horseback, staying in the homes of gentlemen along the route. In between long rides he would dash to Natchez to visit the girl he was to marry. About these long, strenuous rides Varina wrote, "His mind dominated his body in so great a degree that he was able to endure almost what he pleased."

At the same time Jefferson's first oratorical opponent, Seargent Prentiss, was speaking eloquently on Henry Clay's behalf. Varina, who had been brought up to believe in the abilities and virtues of Clay, the Whig, had a disturbing time trying to reconcile herself to her fiancé's views. Yet when her Whig friends criticized Jefferson Davis she would defend him vehemently; and to girl intimates she would say, "Oh, he is so noble, so highminded, and good." She worked herself up into such a nervous tension about her sweetheart's political position in the community that she was put to bed with a wasting fever.

Was she troubled by other thoughts as well? Was she jealous of the first wife who had been Jefferson's ideal and who was still so dear in his memory? Did she suspect she would always play a second role to her future husband's political interests? Varina had latent qualities of both passion and possessiveness, as well as a worldly sense that demanded approbation both for her lover and herself. In any case, her illness was prolonged. During the summer the absent Jefferson would write her notes about his political activities and subscribe them as from her husband in the manner of one dated June 22, 1844:

Farewell, my own love, and again I pray you take care of yourself—

A Dieu au recrire<br>Votre mari<br>Jeffe Davis

After Polk's election in November, 1844, Jefferson could attend to his neglected plantation affairs and envision changes to be made in preparation for the coming of Brierfield's young mistress. Now that the Democrats had won, even the Natchez Whigs, to Varina's delight, were singing the praises of the admirable Mr. Davis. But she was still so weak from her breakdown that the family feared the marriage would have to be postponed indefinitely. Varina, however, thought otherwise and wrote to ask Jefferson if Uncle Joe would come to the wedding. On November 22, he replied.

Dearest Varina

Brother Joe answered to your inquiry that he thought it probable he would attend at the ceremony of our union, but that he had not previously thought of it.

Should your Mother be willing to write Brother Joe & Eliza on the subject I would be glad if she would do so. . . .

Farewell, my own sweet Wife,

Ever yours,<br>Jeffer Davis

But still no nuptial date could be set. From a strange, brief letter of December 11, 1844, written on the steamboat *Ambassador*, something seems to have gone amiss with the engagement.

Dear Varina

I am on my way to New Orleans and thence my course is not quite certain, probably to the bayous South west of the city.

Brother Joe, who will probably see you, can tell you all that I could write beyond what you know as well as myself.

May God grant you a speedy restoration to health. . . .

With my kind remembrances to your parents, I am as ever yours

Jefferson Davis

It is hardly a missive a man would send his fiancée, unless he were upset or annoyed. Was Jefferson going off on a new business venture? His intention seems vague and his manner somewhat impatient. He gives her no address to which she may write him. How did this odd formal note, without any lover-like overtones, affect the girl? Whatever the events or reasons that prompted the note, the course of their love was certainly not running smooth.

But in early February, 1845, when Jefferson went to Natchez to see her, Varina suddenly revived. She became so much like her high-spirited self that the marriage was scheduled almost immediately, for February 26, the time early spring comes to the region, with blossoming bulbs and fruit trees.

On his way down the river to his second wedding Jefferson Davis unexpectedly met his first father-in-law on shipboard. He had not seen Zachary Taylor since his military service at Prairie du Chien. The General was proceeding to guard the disputed border in south Texas, a prelude to war with Mexico. It was a moving meeting, for the two had not communicated since the death of Sarah Knox. But Jefferson knew that General Taylor and his wife had not long since called on his sister Anna Smith at Locust Grove and asked to see the place "where their dear one was buried." The two men, who shared a common grief, forgave each other and became more than reconciled. A mutual admiration, which was to flower in the coming war, was reborn there in the middle of the Mississippi. Nothing could have been calculated to bring back more sharply a surge of sad memory about Jefferson's first love than this chance meeting with Knox's father the day before his second marriage.

As befitted the union of a widower and a girl just recovered from a prolonged illness, the wedding did not take place in the church, but in the first parlor of The Briers. With the Reverend David Page, Rector of Trinity Episcopal Church, officiating, the couple was married in the presence of family members and intimate friends, who remained for a wedding breakfast, spread in the great room upstairs. Varina's unusual bridal jewelry was inherited from her Grandmother Kempe: a necklace, brooch, earrings, and a bracelet fashioned of large white sapphires cut in rectangles and set in palest gold. In the necklace there were nine stones, five in the bracelet and the brooch, and three in each of the pendant earrings. Though not of great cost, the pieces were exquisitely wrought and strikingly beautiful.[5]

The circumstances of a quiet home wedding with the Episcopal ceremony, followed by a wedding breakfast, must have reminded Jefferson sharply of his first marriage. But this time the consent of the bride's parents had finally been offered with love and enthusiasm.

Again after the wedding, Jefferson and his bride boarded a river boat and went downstream to Bayou Sara, the place that had filled Zachary Taylor with such horror. From here they drove to visit Jeff's sister, Mrs. Luther Smith, at Locust Grove, where Sarah Knox had died. If Varina thought it strange that her honeymoon should have begun where the first wife passed away, she was careful to conceal hurt or resentment in her *Memoir*. But she never ceased to be a little jealous of her husband's attachment to the memory of his first love. Outwardly the girl behaved beautifully under the mixed emotions of the situation. Perhaps she felt that it might help exorcise the ghost of her rival if together she and her husband looked down upon the

---

[5] For four generations the descendants of Varina have been married in these jewels; in 1951 the Indiana bride of her great-great-grandson Gerald Bennett, Jr., wore them at her wedding. They are preserved in a Parisian jeweler's box. In September, 1953, the author was shown the jewels by a great-granddaughter, Mrs. Varina Webb Bennett, in the vault of the First National Bank of Colorado Springs. Another case contains the emerald engagement ring, and diamond brooches given Mrs. Davis by Confederate admirers after the war, and various other jeweled keepsakes.

marble and earth that covered the mortal body. The bride and groom carried flowers to the family burying plot. Placing them gently on the grave of Sarah Knox, they stood for a while side by side, each alone in his own contemplation.

From Locust Grove Jefferson took his bride to Woodville to present her to his mother and his two sisters who lived there. The sisters were much like their brother, Varina thought: "spirited, intelligent women, with a wonderful inborn dignity." Although Jane Davis was now eighty-three and confined to a chair, Varina found her "still fair to look upon. Her eyes were bright . . . her complexion clear and white as a child." Only two years before, on January 27, 1843, the Episcopal Bishop of Louisiana, Leonidas Polk, Jeff's West Point schoolmate, had confirmed Jane Davis at a private ceremony in her own home.[6]

After the dutiful family visits, the couple went to New Orleans for the real honeymoon. They stayed at the St. Charles, then the South's most fashionable hotel and the favorite rendezvous of well-to-do newlyweds. With the now sparkling Varina, who proved to have a gift for attracting interesting and prominent persons, Jefferson began to enjoy again the world of society. Supremely happy, they remained in New Orleans for more than a month.

On their return to the plantation Varina delighted in her first attempt at housekeeping. She took a sincere interest in the Negroes and she won them immediately. The strange terrain beyond the cultivated acres fascinated her with its vistas of sloughs, thick with lemon-colored water lilies and glorified by blue and white cranes and thousands of migrating wild geese. She liked the funny house Jeff had designed, though she teased him about

---

[6] While no biographer has mentioned Jane Davis's church affiliations, except to suppose she was a Baptist like her husband, she attended the Episcopal church in Woodville. Bishop Green wrote in his diary that Mrs. Davis "was confirmed May 23, 1843." He is slightly in error. On a trip to Woodville in November, 1954, the author discovered the following entry in Vol. 1, page 19, "Record and Parish Register," St. Paul's Episcopal Church:

Confirmations
January 27, 1843. Mrs. Jane Davis (in private)
By the Right Rev. Leonidas Polk, D.D.

the enormous fireplaces "looking as though they had been built in Queen Elizabeth's time to roast a sheep whole." Neighbors from miles around called and they returned the calls, and almost every evening the couple rode over to Hurricane to dine with Joseph and Eliza. Joseph enjoyed his role of lord of the manor with a table of twenty or so. Besides his wife and the three Mitchell grandchildren and Amanda and her seven Bradfords, there were a niece and a nephew of Eliza and generally one or two of her Van Bentheysen brothers with their families, and occasional house guests.

At first, Varina paid Eliza infinite little attentions, because she was always unusually warm and kindly disposed to frail or ill persons. Joseph enjoyed her bright and witty conversation, and she was eager to draw from his superior store of knowledge. But she began to sense that her "dear old Uncle Joe" loved his youngest brother better than anything else in the world. Varina, who was extremely possessive by nature, found the Davises a close-knit clan with a strong sense of family devotion. It was hard for her to share Jefferson to the extent they expected. According to family testimony, she and Joseph became secretly jealous of each other's influence. Soon Joseph, who though the soul of benevolence had always been the dominating force in the Davis family and everything else in his orbit, discovered that the independent young Varina had her own decided ideas and tastes, and deferred only to her husband. The man whom she had thought "she could never like as well as Uncle Joe" became the center and the very reason of her existence. In her feminine way she felt more fiercely possessive toward him than did Joseph, who throughout the years had built up an assumption of devoted possessiveness.

Despite any little concealed frictions, the first months of marriage passed happily. Brierfield prospered as a plantation. Varina reveled in her role of chatelaine. Two of her brothers came for visits: William Francis and then Joe Davis, whom Jefferson had first seen in baby clothes when a cadet at West Point. He had given William a pony to be used by the other Howell boys as they came to Brierfield. On September 18 Joe wrote to Bill enthusiastically: "Your Pony is one of the greatest." But he was disgusted with the dog that had gone with him duck shooting: ". . . a no-account dog named Merit. . . . He is the most trifling dog I ever saw. He knows nothing about hunting, and as for bringing in ducks, he is hardly equal to old Dash, and you know he won't go in the water at all. I shot two with Mr. Davis's rifle this morning, and had to go in for them myself. As soon as he saw what I wanted he ran." Jefferson enjoyed having the youths about, and for the next twenty years there were few months in which one or more of the eleven Howell children were not staying with the Davises.

In the midst of their new-found happiness Jefferson was persuaded to let his name be put up for the United States House of Representatives. At the meeting of the Democratic nominating committee, he was chosen without a contest. Not only was he a popular candidate, but, as Dodd says, he "commanded a powerful social 'backing' in some of the Whig counties." He made a vigorous campaign.

Never sparing himself on a canvass, Jefferson would ride for long hours under the scorching summer sun. On October 4, when he arrived in Woodville to spend an extra day with his mother before his scheduled speech in his boyhood town, he was shocked to find her laid out for burial. She had died the day before. The Episcopal minister was on his way to read the service. Jefferson saw his mother buried in the family cemetery a few yards from the house, close by her youngest daughter, Mary. He learned he had been named an executor of her will [7] along with his nephew Hugh Davis, son of his sister Lucinda Stamps by her first marriage. Jane had left her eleven slaves and all of her "stock and furniture" to her orphan granddaughters Jane L. and Ellen M. Davis, whose mother, Mary, had died at eighteen. After

[7] At Rosemont the author was given a copy of Jane Davis's will by Miss Louise R. Johnson, who, with her brother, is the present owner of the place. The will was dated May 20, 1839, and may be found in Will Book No. 2, Chancery Clerk's Office, Woodville, Mississippi. It was recorded and probated on February 12, 1846.

the funeral, in his grief, Jeff rode through the night forty-odd miles to Natchez to tell Varina the sad news. He spent an hour with her and then, taking a fresh horse, he returned to Woodville to keep his appointment to speak, because people had driven in from miles about to hear him. He could not bear to disappoint friends. But it may have been a fault rather than a virtue that he so cavalierly disregarded his own physical well-being.

Jefferson won the election, and straightway began training James Pemberton to manage Brierfield during his absence in Washington. Before Varina had become accustomed to being mistress of a plantation, she was to be whisked away to the national capital as a Congressman's wife. She was yet six months under twenty, while Jefferson was now thirty-seven.

Proud and happy for her husband, Varina was excited about the prospect of sophisticated Washington. But she was to find the reverse side of the medal peculiarly unattractive. Of the darker aspects of public service she later wrote: "Then I began to know the bitterness of being a politician's wife and that it meant long absences, pecuniary depletion from ruinous absenteeism, illness from exposure, misconceptions, defamation of character; everything which darkens the sunlight and contracts the happy sphere of home."

While they were packing, word came that the great John C. Calhoun was to speak in Vicksburg. Jefferson Davis, his ardent disciple, who put the same strict construction on the Constitution and State Rights, was asked to introduce him in a half-hour speech. In the midst of closing up the house, Jefferson dictated a speech to his wife. When he had revised it, Varina made a fair copy in her best hand. Then they drove to Vicksburg, whence they would begin the Washington journey by water.

Calhoun's boat from Memphis was so late in arriving that the large assemblage was exhausted by the time he appeared on the stage with Jefferson Davis and the committee. Varina, still inwardly clinging to her Whig ideals, had steeled herself not to be impressed by the nation's foremost Democrat. "But," she writes, "when Mr. Calhoun, with head erect, cast his eagle eyes over the crowd, I felt like rising up to do homage to a king."

As Jefferson Davis rose to give the welcome speech, Varina gazed at her lap, for he had asked her not to look at him while he was speaking. Because it was the first time she had heard her husband address an assembly, both of them were nervous. At the beginning he had difficulty in remembering the speech she had copied so carefully for the benefit of the reporters. After a few minutes he abandoned it completely and gave an excellent new speech, the words following easily and logically. "He spoke fast, the thoughts crowded each other closely. A certain magnetism of manner and the exceeding beauty and charm of his voice moved the multitude." After that day, she claims, no speech was ever written for delivery (though some were written for the press)—only dates and names were jotted down on a few inches of paper.

It was a great evening for the Vicksburg audience, as well as for the young wife. Calhoun, without a single appeal to the emotions, and with no music in his voice, enthralled his hearers, though his unexciting theme was the duty of a citizen to the state. After the speech, the statesman paid special attention to young Mrs. Davis, who found his manner so paternal and sympathetic that she confessed to him her apprehension and sorrow at the coming separation from her mother. The friendship born between them that night lasted until Calhoun's death.

The next day the Davises, with their nineteen-year-old niece Mary Jane Bradford as companion to Varina, took the steamboat for Ohio. They were to go as far as possible by water and then take a stagecoach. In the Ohio River narrows floating ice impeded their progress; and finally the ice closed about the boat in viselike embrace. For an entire week they were stuck fast, vainly praying for a thaw to release them. During the waiting the Davis party became acquainted with the pilot's wife, who could not understand what the gentleman was "takin' them delicate, puny-lookin' gals through all that cold fur." In order to draw her out, Mr. Davis evaded her searching questions as to who they were or where they were going. At last, red-faced with indignation, the woman burst out, "My name's McGruggy an' I ain't ashamed of it, and I don't see but what I'm good enough for that man to tell me whar he is goin'. Besides, Davis ain't no aristocratic name, is it?"

The ice of personal relations was thus broken in a good laugh. At parting Mrs. McGruggy gave Varina a few apricot seed, which she later sent to Brierfield to be planted and which for nine years bore fruit.

After the Davises had endured a week's icebound incarceration in the middle of the Ohio, a steaming little boat squirmed up to their rescue. The passengers were transferred to it. Puffing valiantly all night, it reached the south bank by morning. Here, together with old Colonel Robert N. Roberts, United States Representative from South Mississippi, the Davis party was provided with a horse-drawn sled. In the freezing weather, perched precariously on their trunks, they started forth on a sidewise slanting road that ran halfway up the mountain. The frozen snow had made the road extremely treacherous. When they had traveled about a quarter of the distance to Wheeling, West Virginia, the sled suddenly slipped over the edge. Down a twenty-foot embankment plunged the two Congressmen and the two young ladies, their trunks and bags tumbling pell-mell after them.

Colonel Roberts landed against a tree with such force that he broke a rib. Varina received contusions about the head from a piece of baggage. But at last the sled was righted and, with pain added to the great discomfort, they traveled all day. At nightfall the battered party reached Cresap's Hotel on the Ohio. The hostess recalled the visit of Varina's parents and Joseph Davis twenty years before, when they went to New York the year before Varina was born.

By the time they reached Wheeling, Colonel Roberts was in intense pain, but he determined to go on. The stage route from here ran over the Allegheny Mountains and this journey was more harrowing than the open sled ride. The way was steep, rough, and twisting. Often the passengers were hurled to the roof of the coach. When the old vehicle would slip to the edge of yawning precipices, the girls could not restrain exclamations of terror. Again and again Jefferson and the other men, except for Colonel Roberts, would leap from the stage into deep snow to chock the wheels, while the driver turned his team across the road to hold the stage back. Though Jefferson suffered severely from frozen feet, he did not complain. To minimize the miseries of the journey and rally the girls' spirits he would gaily sing "We'll Tough It Out till Morning."

At last, after three weeks en route from Vicksburg, the Davises made their unimpressive entry into Washington. Black and blue, chilled to the bone, and almost delirious with fatigue, they arrived at the National Hotel on Pennsylvania Avenue, where President Polk had stopped for his inauguration. Varina recalled that her tutor, Judge Winchester, had told her one day while reading "Childe Harold," that there was nothing conceived in the whole realm of fiction that equaled reality and that she must train herself to be ready for any condition life might present. This experience of violent travel, which she had struggled to endure with stoicism to win the admiration of her husband, was like a strange shadow cast before tragic events as yet far distant.

# CHAPTER X

# THE YOUNG CONGRESSMAN

ON DECEMBER 8, 1845, at the age of thirty-seven, Jefferson Davis was sworn in as a member of the Twenty-ninth Congress of the United States. His political position was considered somewhat remarkable in that he had virtually sprung straight from plantation and library into the House of Representatives, for he had never held any kind of civil office in his own state. But the New York *World* may have been justified in a later opinion which characterized him then as "the best-equipped man intellectually, of his age, perhaps, in the country."

After her husband had taken his seat in Congress, the nineteen-year-old Varina began to feel more at ease. At first, shaken from the journey, she had been overawed by the sophistication and smartness of some of the hotel's guests. She who had always had a good opinion of herself confessed that she felt a bit "countrified." It was by no means because of the city itself, however, for Washington resembled more a sprawling town than a nation's capital. In 1845 the white population was under 30,000; the number of slaves was around 2,000; and there were approximately 8,000 free Negroes. Only two streets were paved, and most of the sidewalks were made of gravel and ashes. Pennsylvania Avenue was roughly laid with big cobblestones. On its northern side a walk of bricks extended from Capitol Hill for a mile; this was the city's only promenade, and in fair weather it was crowded with the elite. Houses were spaced helter-skelter; pretentious mansions sometimes neighbored rude cabins. Back yards were crowded with cowsheds, pigsties, chicken runs, and privies. Except for Pennsylvania Avenue, no street was lighted at night.

One of the first things Jefferson Davis noticed was that the wings of the Capitol had not yet been begun and the old wooden dome of the central portion cried out for replacement by one in marble. The War Department was housed in an inadequate two-story brick building. Saloons were prevalent, but so were churches. Of the thirty-odd churches in Washington five were Episcopalian. Varina was to ally herself with the Church of the Epiphany. Though her husband was not a communicant he would often attend services with her and he contributed to that church's building fund.

The capital's streets looked best under a winter snowfall, which the Davises soon saw. Then the jarring cobbles of Pennsylvania Avenue were transformed into white smoothness and the thoroughfare became festive with jingling horse-drawn sleighs, full of fashionable folk.

Within a fortnight the Davises left the expensive hotel for rooms down the avenue. As was customary, they joined a nearby "Congressional mess," a boardinghouse in which men of similar political convictions and congenial tastes lived and took their meals together. At the boardinghouses there was always a predominance of men, for in those days of difficult travel a majority of the Congressmen left their wives and families at home. In 1846 only five Senators and four Representatives maintained houses.

Relieved of housekeeping duties, Varina could devote many hours a day to helping her husband with research and correspondence; together they franked all the documents sent to his constituents. Thus, in a way, she was both private secretary and amanuensis in that time before the typewriter. In her spare hours she attended House sessions and shrewdly noted the qualities of the men who spoke. She went, too, to the Senate to look upon the more famous. She knew the leading Senators by reputation, for when hardly more than a child, she had read aloud to her father their speeches in the *National Intelligencer*. She listened amazed to the exciting verbal duels between the leonine Thomas H. Benton of Missouri and her girlhood idol Henry Clay.

In manner and appearance the most extraordinary of all the Senators was Sam Houston, newly arrived from Texas. By his height of six feet four and his remarkable dress, he would have been conspicuous in any assembly. His waistcoats were sensational: one of flaming scarlet cloth, another of cougar skin. He carried himself with formal grandeur. On being presented to a lady, he would make a waist-deep bow and say in deep bass, "Lady, I salute you!" While other Senators orated, Houston whittled. For hours each day he would fashion little wooden hearts, about the size of a quarter. He carried them in a snakeskin pouch to offer to ladies who pleased his fancy, saying, "Lady, let me give you my heart."

Davis and Houston had met in the Arkansas wilderness at a sutler's store when Houston was on his way to fame in Texas. He told Varina that after talking a short while to her husband, he had said: "The future United States Senator salutes the future President." Later, when Texas was an independent republic, before its entry into the Union, Houston, as its President, had wanted Davis to be his secretary of war. Still later, when he fought against secession, he turned against the Mississippian.

During his first months in Washington Jefferson Davis was so engrossed in official duties that his bride enjoyed few diversions besides occasional routine receptions. The Representative often worked until two o'clock in the morning. But men of parts began to call. For, as Gamaliel Bradford said, Washington recognized the young Mississippian "as a scholar and a thinker." Varina was proud to remark that her husband attracted "the stronger and more polished minds of the time."

Davis frequently visited John C. Calhoun at his lodging. As he later wrote, he found Calhoun's conversation "both instructive and peculiarly attractive. . . . As a Senator he was the model of courtesy; he listened attentively to each one who spoke, neither reading nor writing when in his seat. . . . Wide as his knowledge, great as was his wisdom reaching toward prophetic limits, his opinions were but little derived from books or conversation. Dates he gathered on every hand, but his ideas were the elaboration of his brain, as much his own, as is the honey not of the leaf, but of the bag of the bee."

Davis was careful never to tarry late in the evening, for the South Carolinian made a habit of retiring early. He would rise at dawn and attend to his correspondence before the diplomatic world had taken breakfast. In their hours for going to bed and getting up, Davis and Calhoun were as dissimilar as were the admiring friends Byron and Shelley; for Davis, like Byron, found it difficult to go to sleep before midnight, while Calhoun, like Shelley, rose with the lark. However, as Margaret Coit says in her excellent biography of the Senator: "Calhoun and Davis resembled each other, not only in appearance, but in character, nerves, temperament, and intensity of purpose." And she points out that these planter-scholars found the life of the intellect richer and more meaningful than that of the exterior world.

Jefferson noticed that his girl-wife was instinctively attracted to men of distinction, like the Russian minister, Bodisco, and that witty and charming bachelor James Buchanan, then Secretary of State. She was an attentive listener, alert and sympathetic, when gentlemen talked of state affairs; and when occasion arose she could be a sprightly conversationalist. Young as she was, Varina herself seemed far more interested in ideas and statesmanship than in social chatter or women's talk.

It was a tense and critical time in American history. War with Great Britain over Oregon seemed as threatening as trouble with Mexico. Davis's friend Senator Allen from Ohio had created national excitement by introducing resolutions calling for a formal notification to England that the partnership signed in 1818 was dissolved. As William Dodd points out, this "practically meant war, because reoccupation was supposed to follow this 'notification.'" John C. Calhoun, despite ill-health, was induced to return to the Senate because of the imminent danger of war.

To Calhoun war was "a terrible evil to be justified only by the rights and honor of his country."

On February 6, 1846, Jefferson Davis delivered as his first important speech one on the charged Oregon question. Unlike many hot-air orators who were appealing only to the emotions, the Mississippian sifted the historical facts. He spoke of the visits of Spanish navigators to the port of Nootka Sound before the arrival in 1788 of a nondescript British fur trader named Meares. He touched on the Hudson's Bay Company and the Nootka Convention between England and Spain. He urged caution and coolness. "I hope, sir," he said, "the day is far distant when measures of peace or war will be prompted by sectional or class interests. War, sir, is a dread alternative and should be the last resort." This was the same opinion he later expressed over and over again before the commencement of the War for Southern Independence.

Davis deprecated the cry of "the whole of Oregon or none, now or never" and the recent campaign slogan "54° 40' or fight." He did not want to divide the territory of Oregon, for he would preserve it for the eventual extension of the Union. But he strongly emphasized avoidance of war with Britain. With a soldier's understanding, he pleaded for better defenses and a preparation for possible hostilities, instead of jingoistic slogans.

As to the dispute with Mexico, Davis justified "Southern haste in regard to Texas as contrasted with delay in Oregon," because the Texas case was much farther advanced and more intimately identified with American interests. Texas had been admitted into the Union on December 29, 1845, with the Rio Grande designated as her southern boundary. Mexico was claiming that the Nueces was the proper boundary. Davis reminded Congress that in case of war either with Mexico or England, the South was the exposed portion of the Union; for nothing had been done by the Government adequate for the South's protection. "Who are those that arraign the South," he asked, "imputing to us motives of sectional aggrandizement? Generally, the same who resisted Texas annexation, and most eagerly press on the immediate occupation of the whole of Oregon. The source is worthy of suspicion. These are the men whose constitutional scruples resisted the admission of a country gratuitously offered to us, but now look forward to gaining Canada by conquest. These are the same who claim a weight to balance Texas, while they attack others as governed by sectional considerations."

Speaking as a Southerner, he said with fervor, "It is as the representative of a high spirited and patriotic people that I am called on to resist this war clamor. . . . From sire to son has descended our federated creed, opposed to the idea of sectional conflict for private advantage and favoring the wider expansion of our Union. If envy and jealousy and sectional strife are eating like rust into the bonds which our fathers expected to bind us, they come from causes which our Southern atmosphere has never furnished. . . ."

In this his maiden speech Jefferson Davis revealed his deep attachment to the Union as well as to the Constitution. The chamber was obviously impressed by the strength and reasonableness and persuasion of this new Representative whose beautifully modulated voice had both power and a peculiar sweetness.

For Varina, who had sat enthralled as she watched the reaction on the floor and in the galleries, there was an outstandingly memorable incident. She saw old ex-President John Quincy Adams rise on his short legs and come to sit close to the young speaker in order to catch every syllable. Noting the alert, fixed interest of the bald-headed statesman, whose large mouth was so wont to express ostentatious disdain, Varina was very proud of her husband. And when Davis sat down, Adams crossed over to some friends and remarked, "That young man, gentlemen, is no ordinary man. Mind me, he will make his mark yet. He will go far."

The potent influence of Calhoun in the Senate and the speeches Jefferson Davis and others made in the House brought about a reduction of the demands on Great Britain and took the menacing ultimatum out of the resolutions of Senator Allen.

In his next public utterance, made on March 16, 1846, Davis spoke stoutly against "log-rolling." He had discovered that Representatives from Illinois and Michigan were in collusion to procure funds for special localities with little consideration to national benefit. "I have been surprised and have regretted," he said, "to hear gentlemen treat the question of appropriation as though it were a division of Treasury spoil between the different sections of the Union. . . ." When challenged about his support of appropriations for his own state's benefit, he replied firmly that he would ask for nothing which could not be justified in the minds of men living most remote from the locality. "I feel, sir," he declared, "that I am incapable of sectional distinction upon such subjects. I abhor and reject all interested combinations." The high tone and force of his remarks made another splendid impression. Here was obviously a politician of integrity who cherished ideals in a time when even a man of conspicuous probity like Daniel Webster was not above suspicion.

In fact, Senator Webster was definitely accused by the aged Representative Charles Jared Ingersoll of filching the sum of $5,460 from a special fund of secret-service money while Secretary of State in 1840. Though ex-President Adams declared that Mr. Webster had had no opportunity to defraud the Government, the yeas demanding an investigation outnumbered the nays 136 to 28.

Along with three Northern Congressmen, Jefferson Davis was put on a committee to examine charges which might lead to impeachment, to call witnesses and demand all correspondence if needed. Ex-President Tyler himself was summoned before the committee in behalf of Mr. Webster. Davis, who was the latter's opponent on numerous points of policy, was secretly urged by some Northern Democrats not to lift a finger to "whitewash" the Massachusetts Whig, since Webster was regarded as a likely candidate for the presidency. Indignant, he refused to make "a partisan report." The minority report, which he did draw up, was finally accepted by the committee with certain emendations. It was so worded as to remove the stain from Webster's reputation.

The Senator from Massachusetts appreciated the forthright manner in which the Mississippian had defended him and made a formal call to thank him. Then both Mr. and Mrs. Webster called upon Mrs. Davis and later invited her to visit them at their home in Marshfield.

At the Congressional mess, or boardinghouse, which the Davises had chosen so as to be with their good Iowa friend George Jones, two other Mississippi representatives and their wives also lived. But Mississippi's impressively handsome Senator Jesse Speight lived some blocks away. Speight was no respecter of persons; he would even call the great Henry Clay and old General Cass over to his seat when he desired to speak with them. Two or three times, at odd hours and when nothing particularly important was in question, he summoned Jefferson Davis to his home. One snowy morning before breakfast a note was brought up to Mr. Davis. He read: "Come over. Speight." Seizing a pen he replied with consummate curtness: "Can't. Davis." Though they both laughed over the exchange when they met, the Senator never again made any highhanded demands on the younger man.

Jefferson Davis was much interested in the nation's first "Exposition," which was held in Washington during his term as Representative. He took Varina to see this kind of magnified county fair set up on C Street near the edge of the Capitol grounds. Here agricultural and manufactured products from the various states were displayed. Of one special "attraction" that was like a trifling prologue to the mechanical age, Varina wrote: "The crowd was constant about a certain stand, and my husband made a place for me to see the wonderful thing on it. It was a small box, and through a slot on the top was slowly pushed two narrow edges of cloth, and sewed a pretty good seam." While they were watching the demonstration, ex-President Tyler wandered up behind them to view this magical contraption called a "sewing Jenney."

As the tall thin gentleman stumbled over a loose plank, Davis caught and steadied him. After Varina was presented, Tyler took

Davis's proffered arm and they walked off, making way through the throng for her and talking of the outrageous charge of misappropriation against Daniel Webster. Tyler led them to a shed in which one of the cows from "Sherwood Forest," his Virginia plantation, was stalled. The attendant was asked to milk her into a large tin cup. When the cup was full of "unpleasantly warm but rich milk," it was presented to Mr. Davis. The three strolled out into the Capitol grounds and sat on a bench, passing the tin loving cup from lip to lip. As they took turns in sipping, the men "talked above" Varina, and she was bored. After an hour, when the cup was quite empty, Tyler turned to her and said with all his winning charm, "Have I spoiled your morning, Madam, with my dull talk?" Before she could voice a wistful complaint, her husband quickly interposed: "Oh, no, my little wife is trying to be a statesman." They all laughed, and shortly Tyler made a courtly adieu.[1]

When Varina got home, she immediately wrote her father about the sewing machine and said, "Who do you think drank out of the same tin cup with us today? Why, ex-President Tyler, and he is not the man the *National Intelligencer* made him out at all. He is not handsome, but he looks like a very fine gentleman, and I am sure was not afraid to meet the question of the tariff." In another letter she wrote about another and stranger mechanical invention: "We went down today to see Mr. Morse's machine make the wires talk and to repeat messages from one town to another. There are small wires stretched from Baltimore to this place, and they are brought into the windows of a house on the Avenue. Inside of a little stall a man sits and sends messages and receives the answer. I think it is a trick, but paid my two-bits to get a message 'that it was a fine day.'"[2]

Gradually Jefferson Davis and his wife began to indulge in

---

[1] Varina did not see Tyler again until sixteen years later when he came with his wife to visit the Davises at Richmond. Two years after that, Varina's sister married his grandson.

[2] By July, 1837, Morse had created a telegraphic instrument. In 1843 Congress granted him means to construct an experimental line between Washington and Baltimore.

the social life of the capital. He had renewed his friendship with Senator Dodge, under whom he had served as a lieutenant in the West. They went often to parties given by Dallas Bache, Daniel Webster's great-grandson, who had been a brilliant classmate of Davis at West Point and who now headed the Coastal Survey. They spent delightful evenings at the home of Robert H. Walker, then Secretary of the Treasury, and here at one party Davis found his wife deep in conversation with Charles Ingersoll and Vice-President George Dallas, discussing the relative merits of Virgil and Dante, Wordsworth and Byron. Although Davis opposed him in his censure of Webster, old Mr. Ingersoll came several times to call on the young couple. At one gay, intimate supper which Dallas Bache gave at the Coast Survey headquarters, he served Rhine wine, which he had learned to relish in Germany while living with Alexander Humboldt. Under the exhilaration of the drink, Davis became the life of the party and sang with gusto Indian songs he had learned in Wisconsin. His wife had rarely seen him gayer and more unrestrained.

On May 7, the Davises celebrated Varina's twentieth birthday quietly, for Jefferson's mind was gravely disturbed by the Mexican situation. He wondered if Mexico would actually fight for the disputed stretch of land between the Nueces and the Rio Grande. General Zachary Taylor's "Army of Observation" had remained encamped on the beaches of Corpus Christi from August, 1845, to March, 1846, while President Polk's attempts to settle differences through diplomatic channels met with repeated failures. On March 8, 1846, according to instructions from Secretary of War Marcy, Taylor marched from Corpus Christi to the bank of the Rio Grande opposite Matamoros and began to erect fortifications. The General had started out with a meager force of 1,500 regulars, which had been gradually swelled by volunteers to an aggregate of 4,000.

On Saturday, April 25, learning that a large body of Mexican regulars had crossed the Rio Grande farther west, Taylor sent a small detachment of dragoons to see what was going on. In disputed territory the Americans were ambushed; eleven were killed and the rest captured by Mexican cavalry. General Taylor immediately informed Washington that "hostilities may now be considered as commenced." On May 11, President Polk announced to Congress that Mexico had passed the boundary of the United States and "shed American blood upon the American soil. . . . War exists," he declared, "and exists by the Act of Mexico." [3] Straightway Davis in the House and Calhoun in the Senate reminded the Executive that while the President could declare a state of hostilities, it was the right of Congress only to declare war.

(But the war had actually begun, and Jefferson Davis was now faced with another upheaval in his personal life. Though he had been in Congress less than six months and married only fifteen, he believed it his patriotic duty to offer his services. In a letter to the Vicksburg *Sentinel* he expressed a willingness to command a regiment of Warren County volunteers: "My education and former practice would I think, enable me to be of service to Mississippians who take the field. If they wish it, I will join them as soon as possible, wherever they may be.")

In the interval of waiting, details of two battles on May 8 and 9 were received in Washington. At Palo Alto and Resaca de la Palma, though outnumbered, Taylor had routed the Mexicans under General Arista and inflicted casualties of more than seven to one greater than those of the Americans. Jefferson Davis was gratified at the success of his old chief, and on May 28 he rose in Congress to speak in support of a resolution of thanks to Zachary Taylor for his conduct on the Texas border. Of his onetime father-in-law he declared, "The world held not a soldier better qualified for the service he was engaged in. Seldom, sir, in the annals of military history has there been one in which desperate daring and military skill were more happily combined."

[3] Although Polk's message was derided as "untruthful and frantic" by his most bitter opponents, only two of the forty Senators voted disapproval of it, and fourteen among the 174 Representatives.

Unhappily for his own sake, however, he did not stop with commendation of the General, but took occasion to reply to a gentleman who had "expressed extreme distrust in our army and poured out the vials of his denunciation upon the graduates of the Military Academy." After describing the brilliant results of General Taylor's knowledge of military science, as evidenced in the battles near Matamoros, Davis asked the gentleman to say whether he believed "a blacksmith or a tailor could have secured the same results."

Perhaps the name of Taylor, the subject of the eulogy, may have suggested the choice of tailor as one of the trades mentioned in his impromptu remarks. In any case, it proved most unfortunate and was to bear ill consequences later. For, entirely unknown to Davis, Congressman Andrew Johnson from Tennessee had once been a tailor. Johnson, feeling he had been deliberately insulted, rose in rage and began denouncing "the illegitimate, swaggering, bastard, scrub aristocracy" to which he declared Jefferson Davis belonged. In his fury, Johnson theatrically called upon history, beginning with Adam, who, he declared, was also a tailor, to honor his class of mechanics.

The dismayed Davis at once protested that there was nothing personal intended in his remark. And two days later, sincerely upset by Johnson's misunderstanding, he again apologized on the floor. "Once for all, then, I would say, that if I know myself, I am incapable of wantonly wounding the feelings or of making invidious reflections upon the origin or occupation of any man." He said he pointed out the results of skill and military science, and asked if such achievements could have been expected from men who had not had the advantages of a military education. He had named at random two of the trades of civil life, not because they were less useful or honorable than others. Tactics, like other knowledge, he said, must be acquired. A military education did not qualify for the civil pursuits of life, nor did preparation for any of the civil pursuits, in itself, qualify for the duties of a soldier.

## THE YOUNG CONGRESSMAN

Two public apologies offered sincerely should have mollified the wrath of the touchiest man. But Johnson, being keenly sensitive of his lack of breeding and knowing he had made a fool of himself in accepting an insult which had not been intended, was determined to nurse his grudge. The very gentlemanliness of Davis's eagerness to make amends only accentuated the difference between them. Jefferson Davis had thus made an implacable and ruthless personal enemy. And ever thereafter, Johnson nurtured a smoldering and sometimes explosive hatred of the Southern planter class.

Davis had no further opportunity to salve Andrew Johnson's wounded feelings, for the First Mississippi Regiment was quickly organized at Vicksburg, and he was elected its colonel. Since there was no telegraph service yet and few railways, a special messenger brought the news to Washington in early June. The Davises immediately began packing and making their hasty adieus.

When President Polk, who had been authorized in the emergency to appoint two major generals and four brigadier generals, intimated that he would like to make Jefferson Davis a general officer, the latter declared he preferred an office to which his compatriots had elected him. But he won from the President the promise that he should remain under General Taylor's command for the duration of the war. And he insisted on having his regiment armed with rifles. Though General Winfield Scott "objected particularly to percussion arms as not having been sufficiently tested for the use of troops in the field," Davis got his way. Eventually Davis's men were armed with the new Whitney rifles, recently designed and manufactured at New Haven. Because his regiment was the first to use these firearms, it became known as the "Mississippi Rifles."

The Davises with Mary Jane Bradford left for Mississippi by the same hazardous stage route they had taken in icy December. But now it was late June, and the mountains were wreathed in pink laurel. During the long trip by river boat, Jefferson spent much of his time absorbing a book on military tactics. When Varina reproached him for his lack of attention, he amiably explained to her "the mysteries of enfilading, breaking column, hollow squares, and what-not." The young wife realized that she must ever play second fiddle to her husband's career or whatever he saw his duty to be; she saw that her own happiness would lie in sharing, as far as possible, his life and his vision.

Jefferson and Varina had been married for a year and a half, and it had not always been idyllic for either of them. Because of their opposite temperaments, more than their difference in age, much adjustment was required on both sides. Varina, more complex than he, displayed the mercurial moods of the Kempes. It was hard for her that the Davises never sought sympathy, while the Kempes simply had to have it. The Davises could live companionably with an ideal. The Kempes and the Howells had to have vacations from it. With all of her virtues, Varina was more earthy, more faulty than Jefferson. Whereas the Davises, "people of a mystic and lofty spirituality," were of more heroic mold, the Kempes, though brave, were passionate, choleric people, who loved laughter and the fleshpots.

Naturally fearful of her husband's danger in going to war, Varina was also resentful at leaving Washington just as she was beginning to enjoy it. But she would not stay in the capital during his absence, as he suggested. Magnificent as she proved in meeting tragedies, when Varina could not get her way in smaller things, she often became unwell. Throughout their long married life doubtless Jefferson only partially understood her varied illnesses, though doctors at home and abroad generally diagnosed them as "nervous conditions." But never once did he voice a criticism of her, even to his most devoted relatives.

Now she was indisposed, and Jefferson was concerned about where she would be best contented while he was in Mexico. As the steamboat neared Cincinnati, he wrote on the delicate question to Lucinda, the sister most like himself. He rather hoped Lucinda would invite Varina to stay with her and Mr. Stamps.

Between the lines he pleaded for sympathy in understanding his temperamental young wife, who found the sweet-tempered Eliza a bore. The letter reveals the sensitivity and affection of Jefferson Davis's nature:

July 8, 1846

My dear Sister

    I am on my way to Vicksburg as Colonel of the Regiment raised in Mississippi for the Mexican War. This movement was unexpected though I hope not unnecessary, at least it was felt by me as a real compliment to be thus chosen over a field of comeptitors when absent, and if occasion offers it may be that I will return with a reputation over which you will rejoice as my Mother would have done. Varina and Mary Jane are with me—Mary Jane in fine health. Varina far from well. I wished to leave her in the North this summer but she would not consent. If circumstances warranted it, I would send her to you. To you, and your family alone of all the world could I entrust and rest assured that no waywardness would ever lessen kindness. She regrets very much that she can not see you all, and has never ceased to remember the kindnesses of yourself and the girls and Brother Stamps.

    She will probably stay with her Mother most of the time during which I will be absent. With Eliza she could not be contented, nor would their residing together increase their good feeling for each other. This distresses me as you will readily imagine, but if you ever have an opportunity to understand Varina's character you will see the propriety of the conclusion, and I feel that you will love her too much to take heed of the weaknesses which spring from a sensitive and generous temper.

    My dear Sister, I do not know how it is that I have not written to you often. God knows and I trust you believe there is nothing which I love better.

    I intended and perhaps promised to write to little Netty. Kiss her for me and tell her she must permit her Aunt Varina to become fully acquainted with her, she must judge her uncle's wife by observation and not evade the kindest feeling of a warm heart. Remember me affectionately to Mr. Stamps and Brother Stamps and Jenny and the girls. I will write again. The boat shakes so this is I fear illegible.

Farewell, my beloved Sister—

Your brother<br>Jeffn Davis [4]

[4] To Mrs. Anna Farrar Goldsborough, great-granddaughter of Lucinda Davis and "blood kin" to Varina through her father, I am indebted both for the letter and the differences in family characteristics of the Davises and the Kempes. Mrs. Goldsborough frankly confesses that she herself is more Kempe than Davis, but that she has more admiration for the Davis characteristics.

# CHAPTER XI

# TO THE WAR WITH MEXICO

AT BRIERFIELD, the master made plans for being absent from the plantation for at least a year. He and James Pemberton reasoned long together about the latter's accompanying him to Mexico, as he had to Wisconsin Territory. In the end James himself made the decision: Miss Varina would need him at Brierfield, when she was there or when she was absent, and he felt he could not entrust the plantation management to any other Negro. So Joseph offered his brother a likely black boy named Jim Green for a body servant. When Jeff mounted his Arabian horse Tartar and set off to join his regiment already assembled in New Orleans, the young wife bore up bravely for her husband's sake.

On July 21, Colonel Davis was enthusiastically received by his regiment of nine hundred-odd volunteers. It was an unusual organization, in that it represented the cream of Delta youth, coming from families of wealth and social prominence. Some had brought their personal servants along, as well as hampers of delicacies. His brother-in-law, Joseph Davis Howell, who now towered six feet seven, was among the privates.

The outfit sailed on the *Alabama* on July 26 and landed a week later at blistering Brazos Island in extreme southern Texas. From the commanding general, Colonel Davis received a reassuring and warm letter of welcome.

HeadQts. Ary. of Occupation or Invasion
Matamoras, Mexico, Augt. 3rd, 1846

My dear Col.

I heard with much pleasure of your safe arrival at Brazos Island, with your excellent Regt. of Mississippi Volunteers, & very much regret I cannot at once order your Comd. to Camargo. . . . I can assure you I am more than anxious to take you by the hand, & to have you & your command with or near me. . . .

I expect to leave by the first boat which reaches here from below on her way to Camargo, & should have been highly gratified could I have seen you before I shall have that pleasure—Wishing you continued health & prosperity I remain,

Truly & sincerely
Your Friend
Z. Taylor

Col. Jefferson Davis
  Comdg. Mississippi Vols.
    Brazos Island.

( There could be no shadow of a doubt in Davis's mind now that his onetime father-in-law had only the most kindly feelings toward him.

As soon as tents were set up, the Colonel began putting his soldiers through strenuous drill. It was excessively hot on the sandy neck of land by the sea and the only drinking water was brackish. Some of the young men, unused to hardship, fell ill. But they were all impressed by their commander's own ability to endure rugged circumstances and by his invariable cheer that kept up their morale.

The only time Jefferson Davis is recorded as getting angry with his men was when they raided a cornfield of its roasting-ears, which had just come to succulent maturity. He made them a stern speech and commanded that the rights of private property be absolutely respected. Then he sent money to pay the owner of the crop for the appropriated corn. He was determined that no man or officer in his regiment should return home with a single object of loot, not even a silver spoon.

On August 12, Colonel Davis marched his men nine miles to the Rio Grande to await transports to take them up the river to Camargo. The needless delays occasioned by incompetence higher up were hard for him to bear. He wrote to Secretary of Treasury Walker on August 26: "We have met delay and detention at every point. The quartermasters at New Orleans have behaved either most incompetently or maliciously, and I am now but two days in possession of the rifles ordered forward before I left Washington." Davis was of the opinion, as Taylor was, that politics and jealousy played a part in the various frustrations. Some of the Democrats did not want the Whig Zachary Taylor to succeed too easily or too well because of his presidential potentialities, which had suddenly swelled after the victories of Palo Alto and Resaca de la Palma. And Davis knew that Winfield Scott, the army's ranking general, would do what he could to take the shine off Taylor because he himself aspired to nomination on the Whig ticket.

During the waiting, while the drilling was continued assiduously, Colonel Davis prepared a special manual of arms for his troops and put his officers through a stiff course of instruction. Finally, early in September, the Mississippians were transported to Camargo, where the temperature sometimes registered 112°.

Though General Taylor had moved on to the south, Davis was welcomed at Camargo by several of his soldier friends from Wisconsin days, among them the volunteer colonel, Albert Sidney Johnston, who had become a Texas planter after resigning from the army. Major Bennett Riley, who had received him so casually over a game of solitaire at Prairie du Chien in 1828, was delighted to see him. "Well, my son, here we are again!" the sweating Riley greeted him, and added philosophically, "Good luck to you, boy! As for me—six feet of Mexican soil or a yellow sash."[1]

(General Taylor, who had small regard for volunteers, was so pleased with the bearing and discipline of Davis's troops that he received them almost like regulars. They won the reputation of being "the most orderly, quiet, and best-drilled" of all the volun-

[1] Riley survived the campaign and won the yellow sash of a general officer.

teers. Davis's outfit became a part of the brigade of General John A. Quitman, Northern-born Mississippian, who was both a personal and political friend of Davis.

A few days after Colonel Davis's arrival, General Taylor began the invasion of Mexico with about 6,000 men in his army, half regulars, half volunteers. Without serious interference the Americans pushed forward through hostile territory until they came within sight of the city of Monterey, nestled strategically in the Sierra Madre Mountains. On September 19 the troops encamped about three miles distant in a wood, which they called Walnut Springs. Taylor had gone in advance and measured the defenses of the strongly fortified place, which was garrisoned with 10,000 men commanded by General Ampudia. Though the Americans had not been supplied with heavy artillery, he determined to take the city.

On September 20 the General ordered the attack. First, he concentrated on La Teneria, a massive stone structure protected by a redoubt with artillery; for if he captured this stronghold, he could block communications from Saltillo, the next large town to the south.

In the forenoon, before Colonel Davis and his regiment arrived, one attack by the Americans on Teneria had already been so bloodily repulsed that the Mexicans ran up a new flag in exultation. Three companies of the Fourth Infantry in the advance had been terribly cut up. "Almost in a moment," as the official report admitted, a third of the men fell. The rest, including a young lieutenant named Ulysses S. Grant, then retired. Now the Mississippians and Tennesseans steadily pressed forward under a galling fire of copper grape. When they had approached to within a hundred yards of the fort, they were lost in the smoke. As Colonel Davis himself wrote of the movement: "We were within the effective range of the enemy's fire, but beyond that of our Rifles. I therefore executed a movement which gained ground to the front and left and when the regiment was again formed into line, the troops who had stood upon my right were gone. The attacking force now consisted of the Tennessee and Mississippi regiments; the latter, on the right, was directly in front of the fort."

"With ample courage and enthusiasm the men advanced nearly a mile under the fire of the citadel," wrote Justin H. Smith in *The War with Mexico*, "and before long were under the worse fire of the redoubt in front, but they staggered in the smashing blast of lead and iron, their formation became very irregular and, after a time, though not within effective musket or rifle range, they began to fire at will. Colonel Davis, then some distance in advance, grew impatient at the waste of time, ammunition and life, and as the redoubt stopped firing just then, he cried, 'Now is the time. Great God, if I had fifty men with knives I could take the fort.'"

Davis suddenly decided to charge, although as he states, "I had no instructions, no information as to the plan, no knowledge of any sustaining troops except the Tennesseans on our left." Stirringly he yelled to his troops commanding the charge and dashed forward. The fearless long-legged Lieutenant Colonel McClung, a noted Mississippi duelist, re-echoed Davis's daring with the shout: "Boys, follow me!" With desperate bravery, without bayonets, the men ran after Davis and McClung. Flourishing his sword, McClung sprang over the ditch and mounted the parapet, just a second before Davis. The Mexicans, surprised and panic-stricken at such daring, left their guns and fled to a building three hundred feet in the rear. Davis and McClung, having got in by different entrances, were simultaneously masters of the fortifications as the American flag was run up.

"It seems madness," wrote Dr. McElroy in 1937, "for Davis to have ventured upon such an assault without orders; but he won the fort." Elated with victory, Colonel Davis did not halt long, but urged his men on the charge of the second post, El Diablo, to the rear. Before the place could be taken, for some unaccountable reason, General Quitman sent word ordering Davis to retire. Though Davis remonstrated, as a disciplined officer he obeyed.

The next day General Quitman authorized Colonel Davis to make a sortie with four companies. As he advanced into town, he saw armed bodies of men fleeing through the streets. When he turned the flank of a fort, he found it evacuated and the artillery removed. From some prisoners Davis learned that the enemy had withdrawn to the main plaza, where the cathedral had been turned into an ammunition center.

The flat roofs along the way were lined with Mexican snipers. Davis's men had to force the barred doors of dwellings to reach the roofs and silence the snipers. As the Colonel himself entered one room he found several dark women and children cowering in terror. A mother held up to him her bright blue-eyed baby like an offering, and said pleadingly, "This little one is like you—do not kill it, but take it for your own." Davis had no time to explain or even to pat the baby, but dashed up to the roof to direct the firing against Mexicans shooting from opposite roof tops.

By stages the Mississippians continued to advance until they were within a block of the square. Then they seized a two-story house, and a shooting contest raged for hours. Just as Davis decided to try to take a still higher house "from which it seemed a plunging fire could be thrown into the plaza," again he received orders to retire.

Since Mexican cannon were now trained on the street by which his men had to make their way back, the situation was critical, for every few minutes cannon fire raked the center of the street. Colonel Davis considered the dilemma and the risk; then he ordered his men to follow him and run in groups of two or three between discharges of the cannon and under cover of the smoke. The arrangement made by Davis for crossing the street was that he should go first; if only one gun was fired at him, then another man should follow; and so on, another and another, until a volley should be fired and then all of them should rush rapidly across before the guns could be reloaded. Carrying out this plan, the men got across with remarkably small loss. Though the plaza still remained in the Mexicans' possession, Davis's gallantry and resourcefulness throughout the four days impressed the Mexicans and won special praise from his commanding general. On September 24, after General Worth's division had captured the heights and the bishop's palace, General Ampudia sent a flag of truce asking for parley concerning surrender. Colonel Davis was honored by being put on a committee of three to arrange terms, along with General Worth and Major General Henderson, the governor of Texas.

Davis set down the memorandum of the nine articles of the surrender. The terms of capitulation finally agreed upon by American and Mexican commissioners were decidedly liberal, but by them General Taylor saved many American lives and great expense. The Mexicans agreed to give up the city, the fortifications, the cannon, munitions of war, and all public property. The citadel of Monterey was to be evacuated at ten o'clock the next morning. The Mexican armed forces were to retire beyond a line in the rear of Saltillo forty miles to the south. An armistice of eight weeks was agreed upon as more than ample time to hear from the home governments.

Davis argued cogently that with less than half the forces of the enemy and without siege artillery it would be folly to demand "surrender at discretion," as Governor Henderson had at first urged. General Worth, dubious of Taylor's skill because of his slapdash leadership, agreed with Colonel Davis. Taylor had the hope that the authorities in Mexico would take this capture of Monterey as portentous and offer to make terms of peace.

When the commission had completed its work, the agreed-upon terms of capitulation were written out both in English and Spanish—each to be signed by the commanding generals—Colonel Davis found Ampudia still purposed to delay and haggle. Following an unpleasant interview, Davis at length got the Mexican General's promise that he would give him the document with his signature "as early as he should call for it in the morning." So at dawn next day Davis mounted his horse and started for Monterey about three miles distant from the American camp. General Taylor, an early riser, heard Davis's horse passing his tent, looked out, and called to ask him where he was going. He was amazed to learn that Davis purposed to go alone into the enemy's stronghold. "Not by yourself!" he insisted. Davis smiled and countered, "One man is good as twenty. . . . If they mean foul play, nothing but an army will do." When General Taylor pressed him to dismount to have coffee with him and talk the matter over, Davis smilingly declined: he had already breakfasted.

Just then Colonel Albert Sidney Johnston, acting inspector general, came along and insisted on accompanying his old friend, although he was without proper uniform, since his had been soaked with sea water at Port Isabel. Johnston cut quite a figure in blue jeans and a red flannel shirt, a torn checked coat and a wide-awake hat. He hardly looked like a proper envoy to approach the formal General Ampudia. But in this garb he quickly saddled his horse and rode with Davis to seek the Mexican headquarters on the Grand Plaza in Monterey.

As the friends entered the town the atmosphere became ominous. The flat roofs were lined with armed infantry who glared with hostility at the Americans. Behind the barricade across the street, the gunners were in place with the port fires blazing, and looked as if they would relish blowing the emissaries to smithereens. Davis and Johnston, who were riding at a walk, advanced even more slowly. Johnston suggested they raise their white handkerchiefs, and so they rode up to the battery. Colonel Davis addressed the artillery captain, explaining that he had an appointment with General Ampudia and desired to pass. A soldier was dispatched to the rear. He did not return. At length Davis demanded that a second messenger be sent. He, too, failed to return. A third was sent. The American officers were about at the end of their patience.

While they were halted near a narrow space between the end of the barricade and the wall of a house just sufficient for one horse to pass at a time, an old hag almost caused them to be mobbed by pointing a skinny finger at Johnston and his Texas outfit and hissing derisively, "Tejano!" A menacing throng surged about them just as Ampudia's English-speaking adjutant general opportunely approached on horseback. When Davis remonstrated on the discourtesy he had been shown by being kept waiting so long, the man put his horse in motion as if to go through the passage. Johnston said quickly, "Had we not better keep him with us?" and squared his horse to prevent the Mexican's passing. Then Davis said he would be much obliged if the adjutant would accompany them to the General's quarters. Now, feigning the greatest pleasure in attending the Americans, the Mexican wheeled his horse about and conducted them to Ampudia.

The General received them most ceremoniously, had their horses watered and cared for, and pressed the Americans to breakfast with him. Declining the invitation, Davis reminded him of the document to be delivered. Without further stalling, Ampudia handed it over, already properly signed. The horses were then called for and formal leave taken.

Once again the envoys rode a gauntlet of smoldering hatred and were considerably relieved to reach open country without a bullet in their backs. A mile out of town, when Davis's horse jumped a ditch, the holster attached to his saddle flew open and he discovered his pistol had been stolen while he was with the General. He prized that pistol because it had been given him by his present companion, Albert Sidney Johnston, during the Black Hawk campaign. But with the articles of capitulation in his keeping, he had no notion of risking their loss or any damage to his own skin by riding again through the potential dangers to complain of an orderly's petty pilfering.

On Friday, September 25, as the Mexicans tramped out of the citadel with banners flying, the Americans took possession to the tune of "Yankee Doodle" and the booming of twenty-eight guns from the bishop's palace. Citizens high and low, as well as the soldiers of both armies, noted the contrast between the trim smart uniforms of the Mexicans and the disheveled appearance of the victors, who, as one American remarked, were "about as dirty as they could be without becoming real estate." Zachary Taylor, who laid no stress on personal appearance—Grant says he only saw him twice in full uniform during the Mexican campaign—set the tone of casual sloppiness among his soldiers.

By the twenty-eighth the last of the Mexican troops had departed. In three days' fighting General Taylor had won a city which the Mexicans had regarded as impregnable. It was a minor triumph in American history and the first significant victory since the Battle of New Orleans in the War of 1812. All over the United States victory bonfires flamed in public squares and the name of Zachary Taylor was eulogized by local orators. In the speeches and in the dispatches Jefferson Davis was given a goodly share in the general praise. Dr. Dodd is inclined to believe that "Davis had made a reputation which transcended that of any officer except Taylor himself."

(Regardless of how much laudation Jefferson Davis deserved, a letter from Varina's brother to his mother on October 13 attests to the esteem and devotion of the Colonel's soldiers: "There is not a man in his regiment who would not sacrifice his life to obey him so much has his gallant conduct raised him in their estimation. The degree of power his coolness, courage, and discretion have acquired for him in the army generally would hardly be believed at home. . . . I verily believe that if he should tell his men to jump into a cannon's mouth they would think it right, and would all say, 'Colonel Jeff knows best, so hurrah, boys, let's go ahead.' He is always in front of his men, and ready to be the first to expose himself; and moreover, he has taken them into so many tight places, and got them out safely, that they begin to think if they follow him they will be sure to succeed." )

The public plaudits for Zachary Taylor, the Whig, did not altogether delight the ears of Democratic politicians. President Polk himself was inclined to damn with faint praise, and then to regard sourly the terms of capitulation. Crittenden and others, however, stoutly defended Taylor in the Senate, pointing out all the advantages of the well-supplied enemy over the poorly equipped Americans; while to retreat with sick and wounded, harassed by a mobile infantry, would have been ruinous. Taylor, he said, had chosen the wisest course to escape victoriously, as he did, from the dilemma. Some politicians in Washington, at a safe distance and not caring to consider Taylor's handicaps and lack of equipment, chose to be highly censorious. After considerable wrangling the Government finally set official disapproval on the terms of capitulation and terminated the truce a few days before its expiration.

Davis felt that the United States had now lost "whatever credit had been given to us for the generous terms in the capitulation." Taylor had believed that all "reflecting" men would agree with him in the liberal terms that had saved so many American lives. "Besides," as he wrote his son-in-law, Dr. Robert Wood, "it was thought it would be judicious to act with magnanimity towards a prostrate foe particularly as the President of the United States had offered to settle all differences between the two countries by negotiation."

But President Polk, the politician, found himself in a quandary, because both of the army's top generals were Whigs. He had passed over Scott for Taylor as the less formidable; for while Scott's presidential ambitions were well known, Zachary Taylor had no inclination for political renown. Now with Taylor's sky-rocketing popularity, Polk not only began to cool from his early glowing admiration for "Old Rough and Ready," but he was soon voicing the opinion that, though brave, Taylor did not "seem to have resources or grasp of mind enough to conduct such a campaign." Finally, after failing to maneuver certain unqualified Democrats into the high command, the President surprisingly nominated for the commander in chief in Mexico the Whig for whom he had no liking at all: Winfield Scott.

It was decided in Washington that the attack on Mexico City was to be led by Scott through Vera Cruz and that 80 per cent of all available troops were to accompany him. Taylor was to be left stranded in the north with too few men to do anything in the way of offensive action.

On October 5, 1846, from Monterey Jefferson Davis had written a reassuring note about his physical well-being to Varina, who wanted him to come home. From the portion she quotes in *A Memoir* it was not a particularly affectionate letter: "My health is very good and my ignorance of our future movements as entire as your own. The Mexican general assured us, before the terms of capitulation were agreed upon, that commissioners from the

United States had been received at Mexico. If this was half true a portion of the forces here must soon be disbanded. Your brother is well."

In the meantime she had written him such an alarming letter about the condition of her own health that he felt in duty bound to go to her. In *A Memoir* Varina explains: "After the battle of Monterey my anxiety and depression were so great, and my health so impaired by this and other causes that my husband obtained sixty days' leave of absence which, in those days of slow travel were required in order to spend two weeks in the United States."

On October 19, Colonel Davis left Camp Allen, Monterey, on furlough. He rode away on Tartar, now a well-known figure and a favorite among the troops because instead of returning to camp when the Colonel released him at the fight for Teneria, the horse had followed his master into the battle and stood trembling in an angle of the fort until the fierce shooting was over. Tartar was regarded as a dramatic demonstration of the loyalty horses have for a beloved master. At Brazos, where it was necessary to transfer the high-spirited horse from a lighter to the steamboat, the sailors could not force him on the ship. They struck him sharply to make him leap. Unused to blows, the enraged Tartar snorted and reared. Finally Davis commanded the sailors to let him alone. Then at the ship's edge, holding the bridle, Davis called the horse's name gently with persuasive assurance. Tartar crouched and waited for the moment the lighter and the ship were on a level; then he sprang over the intervening water to his master's side.

Varina does not comment on their reunion at Brierfield where she had come from Natchez to receive her husband, and she makes no further reference to her illness. Apparently she was recovered by the time he had completed the arduous three weeks' journey from Monterey. She may have learned that she had used the wrong tactics to test a Davis's love. His reproaches, however, were generally silent. He did not have to remind her that never would a Davis woman have called her husband back from a war before he had been absent three months, even if she had been dying. Before he met Varina he had had no experience in humoring a woman's whims.

While Jefferson was at Brierfield, he attempted to straighten out some snarls of plantation management his absence had evoked, and he took occasion to make his will. The faithful James Pemberton was to be remembered with land or money—as he chose. In regard to his liberty, James was consulted as to his wishes. His decision was that in case of his master's death he would prefer to belong to and take care of Miss Varina, but if or when death came to her, he wanted to be free. This part of the will was so drawn up.

A different version of the will-making is brought out in the family lawsuit *Davis* vs. *Bowmar*[2] in the 1870's, in which Jefferson Davis endeavored to recover his Brierfield plantation four years after the death of Joseph, who had never given him a deed to the property. It appears here that before Jefferson left for Mexico, he had made his will, which Joseph drew up. Since Varina had been in the family not quite a year and a half, Joseph thought that in case of Jefferson's death their two widowed sisters, Anna Smith and Amanda Bradford, should share his estate, including Brierfield, with Varina. Since Anna had six dependent children and Amanda seven, Jefferson felt that he should help provide for them. The will was drawn accordingly. Presumably Varina learned of the terms after Jefferson was in Mexico. When she did, she was hurt and indignant. Perhaps she made herself ill from resentment. At any rate, in the lawsuit a quarter of a century later she made oath to the effect that she never entirely forgave her brother-in-law. And Joseph in his last will, though he provided for Jefferson's four living children, did not bequeath Brierfield to his brother, presumably to prevent Varina from getting it.

Was it bitterness over the will that brought Jefferson back from Mexico? Evidently the difficulties between Varina and his rela-

[2] The lawsuit, recorded at page 671 in 55 *Mississippi Reports* at the April Term, 1878, of the Mississippi Supreme Court, throws light on a strain in family relations in 1846.

tives he had vaguely feared in his letter to his sister Lucinda written on the steamboat had materialized in a way he had not foreseen. Whether Jefferson, on his return from Mexico, was induced to change his will in Varina's favor is not known. But if he believed it right that his dependent sisters should inherit a potential portion of his estate, it was not in his character to make the change. His wife had much influence on him, but he was ever the master in his house and in his life. The strong-willed Varina could not have loved a man she could dominate.

# CHAPTER XII

# A HERO OF BUENA VISTA

———•◉•———

AFTER a fortnight at Brierfield, Jefferson Davis departed again for war. Fearing that Tartar might be killed, he left the Arabian behind, and this time rode off on Richard, "a handsome bay with black points." In Texas he met up with Colonel Thomas Crittenden, a Kentuckian, who later became a Federal general. Together they traversed the dreary waste land of northern Mexico, taking turns sleeping and watching to avoid assassination at the hands of some lurking guerrilla.

On Monday, January 4, 1847, Colonel Davis rejoined his regiment, which had moved down to Agua Nueva below Saltillo. He arrived just as General Taylor's army was being rapidly depleted by Winfield Scott, who was collecting forces at Brazos preparatory to attacking Mexico through Vera Cruz. Among the officers removed from Taylor's command was Davis's fellow West Pointer, Captain Robert E. Lee of the Engineers. Lee had not been in any of the fighting as yet, for he had left San Antonio to direct road and bridge building on September 28, a few days after the Monterey victory. In fact, this soldier, who was to become a world hero, had on that day for the first time in his career "ridden with troops to march against the enemy." His gallant initiation in battle was to come some months later along the Cortez route in the conquest of Mexico City. On January 17, two days before his fortieth birthday and less than a fortnight after Davis's return to duty, Lee rode away from Taylor's command to join Scott.

Taylor's troops were soon reduced by more than half, and half of those left were raw recruits. He was ordered to concentrate his forces at Monterey. Even though Taylor was as weak in supplies as in men, he had no notion of retracing his steps. He even moved fearlessly, if unwisely, some twenty more miles farther down into Mexico to Agua Nueva. From this place in the lull before the storm, Davis wrote to his wife on February 8.

"We are here on the table-lands of Mexico, at the foot of the Sierra Madre. We came expecting a host and battle, have found solitude and externally peace. The daily alarms of this frontier have ceased; the enemy, I believe, has retired to San Luis de Potosi, and we are waiting reinforcements, while General Scott is taking all who can be seized and incorporates them in his division of the army. We have a beautiful and healthy position, and are waiting only action or such excitement as reconciles man to repose."

The excitement and the activity were not long in coming. Now that most of Taylor's more seasoned troops had been withdrawn to create an army for Scott, the famous Mexican general and current President, Antonio López de Santa Anna, decided the time was ripe for shaking the Americans out of northern Mexico. Santa Anna was a spectacular and tragicomic figure, as full of pomposity as trickery. He had known a series of exiles and recalls, disgraces and elevations. Seven different times he served as Mexico's chief executive. He owed his present high status as dictator and commander in chief of the army to none other than the President of the United States. While in exile in Cuba, the wily Santa Anna had persuaded President Polk to let him through the American blockade of Vera Cruz so that he might "stop the war." He promised as soon as he was restored to power he would make a "good American peace" at the first opportunity, "after the Mexicans had been slightly chastised for their misdeeds." Upon arrival in Mexico, the Mexican government promptly put him in command of the army and expected him to chase the Americans out of the country. At San Luis Potosí he had collected an army of 20,000. All was now in readiness for a smashing victory.

Shortly after Taylor had pushed down to Agua Nueva, Santa Anna started north with his troops and a crate of his prized game cocks. To the sentimental strains of a popular ditty called "*Adios*," the resplendent, sad-eyed General rode out of the city in a lumbering carriage drawn by six mouse-colored mules. With supreme assurance, he began composing an impertinent demand for Taylor's unconditional surrender.

Although "Old Rough and Ready" was a hard man to scare, on February 21, when a lone rider on a fagged horse brought word directly to the General's tent that the mighty Mexican cavalcade was less than a day's march away, Taylor ordered a double-quick withdrawal north to a narrow pass close to a ranch called Buena Vista. Pickets left in charge of protecting stores found they had no time to save them; so they set fire to their wagons, as well as the town's buildings.

Taylor's forces, which numbered only 4,756 officers and men, were in danger of complete ruin. The American press took a dim view of the General's chances of survival. Not only did the enemy's troops outnumber the Americans by almost four to one, but Santa Anna was known to be a shrewd military strategist. Taylor, however, had chosen a situation that strongly favored the defense. And General Wool, in charge of disposing the troops, had drawn them up behind an extraordinary natural network of deep gullies and broad ravines backed by hills.

The morning of Washington's birthday dawned clear. As a rousing breakfast piece the bands played "Hail Columbia," while the watchword "Honor to Washington" was passed from man to man. General Taylor, who had gone to see about the defenses of Saltillo, returned to find Santa Anna charging down the valley from Agua Nueva with an advance force of 2,500 horsemen. Instead of attacking, however, Santa Anna halted to survey the American positions and to wait for the rest of his army to arrive. In the meantime he sent his surgeon general with an arrogant demand for surrender:

You are surrounded by twenty thousand men, and can not in any human probability avoid suffering a rout, and being cut to pieces with your troops; but as you deserve consideration and particular esteem, I wish to save you from a catastrophe, and for that purpose give you this notice, in order that you may surrender at discretion, under the assurance that you will be treated with the consideration belonging to the Mexican character; to which end you will be granted an hour's time to make up your mind, to commence from the moment when my flag of truce arrives in your camp.

With this view I assure you of my particular consideration. God and liberty!

Antonio López de Santa Anna

Taylor's dander rose. He was about to reply in really forcible language when Brevet Major W. W. S. Bliss[1] persuaded him to send back a formal reply, brief and to the point, but preserving the civilities.

Sir: In reply to your note of this date summoning me to surrender my forces at discretion, I beg leave to say that I decline acceding to your request.

With high respect, I am, sir,

Your obedient servant,<br>Z. Taylor,<br>Major-General U.S. Army, Commanding

The Americans braced themselves for an onslaught. They were fortunate in that their ground was such as to hamper Santa Anna's cavalry and artillery and partially to neutralize the Mexican's great superiority in infantry. Santa Anna did not attack until the afternoon. And then there was not much fighting except on the extreme left. By nightfall, however, the Mexicans had gained the summit of a ridge and the Americans had fallen back to the plain at its base. At daybreak of the twenty-third Santa Anna

---

[1] William Wallace Smith Bliss, who later married Zachary Taylor's youngest daughter, Betty, was of inestimable help to General Taylor in Mexico because of his masterly handling of staff work.

resumed the shooting. After some heavy skirmishing the Mexicans moved in three heavy columns on the Americans, whose left broke and was put to flight.

At a critical moment, when the outcome looked peculiarly dismal for the Americans, General Taylor rode old Whitey out on the field in plain view of the troops and exposed himself to the enemy's cannon, utterly cool and calm in the hail of shot. His appearance had a magical effect; the soldiers took fresh heart. Taylor now ordered Colonel Davis forward with the Mississippi Rifles and two extra companies to measure strength against that of General Ampudia, Santa Anna's second in command. As Davis led his men into the battle, he met some of the Indiana volunteers running away pell-mell from the onslaught. He pleaded with them to halt and stick with him. Then, as Major Bradford reported, (Davis "gave the word and like veterans the regiment moved off, under one of the heaviest fires I ever saw, which was returned with equal spirit." Almost immediately Colonel Davis was wounded, a ball entering his heel, shattering bone, and embedding splinters of brass from his spur and shreds of wool stocking deep in the flesh. But ignoring the pain, he attacked with violence. The Mexicans, who thought they had won the victory, were so stunned by the shock of the savage impact that they fell back in confusion and retreated toward the mountain. The batteries of the Fourth Artillery under Captains Braxton Bragg and Thomas Sherman had contributed greatly to saving the morning. As the artillery now retired from the broad ravine to guard the rear, Colonel Davis saw the Mexican cavalry approaching from the left. He realized it was up to him to prevent the enemy from passing to the rear of the American line of battle, where they might capture the batteries. As the enemy advanced, Davis was inspired to devise a formation like an obtuse triangle, which became celebrated in military history as his " V formation." He stationed his soldiers in the form of a V with both flanks resting on the ravine, and allowed the Mexican cavalry to come within easy range on the intersecting ridge, while each American singled out his object.

In his report [2] to General Worth after the battle, written in pencil from his hospital bed in Saltillo, Jefferson Davis told the story:

"The Mississippi regiment was filed to the right, and fronted in line across the plain; the Indiana regiment was formed on the bank of the ravine, in advance of our right flank, by which a re-entering angle was presented to the enemy. . . .

"The enemy, who was now seen to be a body of richly caparisoned lancers, came forward rapidly and in beautiful order—the files and ranks so closed as to look like a mass of men and horses. Perfect silence and the greatest steadiness prevailed in both lines of our troops as they stood at shouldered arms awaiting an attack. Confident of success, and anxious to obtain the full advantage of a cross fire at a short distance, I repeatedly called to the men not to shoot.

"As the enemy approached, his speed regularly diminished, until when within eighty or a hundred yards, he had drawn up to a walk and seemed about to halt. A few files fired without orders, and both lines then instantly poured in a volley so destructive that the mass yielded to the blow and the survivors fled."

The New Orleans *Picayune* reported, "The whole head of the column fell. . . . A more deadly crossfire was never delivered." It was just past noon. Thunder cracked and rain fell in a sudden torrent. Part of the Mexican army retreated to the protection of caves on the mountainside.

Davis continued in his report to General Worth:

"Captain Sherman, having come up with a field-piece from his battery, followed their retreat with a very effective fire until they had fled beyond the range of his gun. Soon after this event, a detachment of our artillery and cavalry moved up on our left, and I was directed to cooperate with it in an attack upon the enemy at the base of the mountain.

---

[2] One of the most interesting items in the vaults of the Confederate Memorial Museum in New Orleans is this report on narrow strips of age-browned paper almost two feet long.

"We advanced parallel to this detachment until it was halted. I then placed my men under such protection as the ground afforded from the constant fire of the enemy's artillery, to which we were exposed, to wait the further movement of the force with which we were to act. At this time, the enemy made his last attack upon the right, and I received the General's orders to march to that portion of the field.

"The broken character of the intervening ground concealed the scene of action from our view; but the heavy firing of musketry formed a sufficient guide for our course. After marching two or three hundred yards, we saw the enemy's infantry advancing in three lines upon Capt. Bragg's battery; which, though entirely unsupported, resolutely held its position, and met the attack with a fire worthy of the former achievement of that battery, and of the reputation of its present meritorious commander. We pressed on, climbed the rocky slope of the plain, reached its brow so as to take the enemy in flank and reverse when he was about one hundred yards from the battery. Our first fire . . . was eminently destructive. His right gave way, and he fled in confusion. . . .

"In this, the last contest of the day, my regiment equalled—it was impossible to exceed—my expectations. Though worn down by many hours of fatigue and thirst, the ranks thinned by our heavy loss in the morning, they yet advanced upon the enemy with the alacrity and eagerness of men fresh to the combat. . . . When hostile demonstrations had ceased, I retired to a tent upon the field for surgical aid, having been wounded by a musket ball when we first went into action. . . .

"Every part of the battle having been fought under the eye of the commanding general, the importance and manner of any service it was our fortune to render will be best estimated by him. . . ."

All through the afternoon the battle had seesawed. Once, through the ruse of a white flag, Santa Anna had extricated his troops from a trapped position while the Americans held their fire. The fearless Taylor had made the mistake of assuming the offensive; he ordered the Illinois and Kentucky volunteers to charge against Pérez's corps of marksmen and lancers, which outnumbered the Americans six to one. The fighting became so violent that the Americans were forced to flee back to their lines. Among the gallant officers who remained to die on the field was Lieutenant Colonel Henry Clay, Jr., son of the great Kentuckian.

Again General Taylor rallied the troops by exposing himself in the thick of the fight. Serene as a man who bore a charmed life, he gave calm commands. Bullets tore through his clothing, slit his shirt and even his undershirt, ripped out the lining of his coat and tore away a buttonhole, but they did no more bodily damage than grazing the skin of one arm. Through the whole bloody afternoon the artillerymen had never flagged, and finally about five o'clock American cannon blasted the Mexicans from the field.

Back in camp, in an almost fainting condition from loss of blood, Colonel Davis was helped from his horse. His boot was filled with blood and the pain was excruciating.

When the report that Jefferson Davis had been killed was brought to General Taylor, he was greatly upset, though he repeated again and again, "I'll never believe it." Sending several messengers to ascertain the truth, he finallly sought out Davis himself. "My poor boy," he said, when he found him in agony, but very much alive, "I wish you had been shot in the body, you would have a better chance of recovering soon. I do not like wounds in the hands or feet, they cripple a soldier awfully." He feared blood poisoning from the bits of brass spur in the wound, which had gone untended for almost eight hours because Davis would not retire from the field. He asked that the Colonel be given most careful attention. So all through the night Davis's friend Captain Eustis sat by his cot and poured a continual stream of cold water gently over the wound, a precaution the surgeon recommended as a prevention against lockjaw.

Though the enemy had withdrawn for the night, no one could say who had won the battle; for the opposing forces occupied almost the same ground as in the morning. Many feared a crushing attack next day. General Wool, among others, advised retreat. But Taylor refused to consider removing that night and began planning his defenses for the next day. Davis was told that the General had checked the casualty list, which reached 673. The Mexican casualties were estimated as almost three times as great.

Despite the dubious victory, it was a night of dread uncertainty for all the camp. When soldiers were roused the next morning for a day's fighting that might prove their demolishment, they were flabbergasted to find that the entire Mexican army had vanished in the darkness, leaving deceptive campfires along the battlefront.

Demoralization had apparently seized the Mexicans; Santa Anna must have been unwilling to face again the destructive fire of American artillery. Without bothering to move his seriously wounded from the field, the great commander had rolled away in his carriage in a cloud of dust far in advance of his tattered soldiers. In every town en route he postured as a national hero, waving two captured American standards to prove his triumph.

When Taylor was apprized of the strange truth of Santa Anna's flight and beheld the abandoned wounded, as well as the wagons and supplies, he duly informed Washington of the victory at Buena Vista.

The American newspapers, having printed chilling stories of Santa Anna's 20,000 soldiers confronting Taylor's depleted force, had prepared the public to expect disaster. Now the amazing news of victory electrified the nation. "Old Rough and Ready" became for the hour as popular an idol as Andrew Jackson had after the Battle of New Orleans. Destiny began to point a finger toward the White House.

Jefferson Davis's heroic fighting and his V formation were accorded a big share in the national praise. Robert Winston, one of his most critical Northern biographers, concedes that "Davis won a fame second only to General Taylor." In faraway Dubuque, Iowa, Davis was acclaimed in superlative terms. Years later the Dubuque *Herald* wrote: "When the news came to Dubuque of the victory over Santa Anna by old Zack, through the tact, skill, and bravery of Colonel Jefferson Davis, who was reported mortally wounded, there was such an enthusiastic celebration and glorification, chiefly on Davis's account, as has never since taken place." Dodd unreservedly affirms that Davis in the noonday battle "saved the day for Taylor." He goes on to say: "The Colonel of the Mississippi Riflemen did other valiant work in this battle —all the time suffering from a painful wound in the foot—but nowhere else was the issue so close and the conduct of his men so heroic."

In his own official report of Buena Vista to the Government, Zachary Taylor wrote:

"The Mississippi Riflemen, under command of Colonel Davis, were highly conspicuous for gallantry and steadiness, and sustained throughout the engagement the reputation of veteran troops. Brought into action against an immensely superior force, they maintained themselves for a long time unsupported, and with heavy loss, and held an important part of the field until reenforced. Colonel Davis, though severely wounded, remained in the saddle until the close of the action. His distinguished coolness and gallantry and the heavy loss of his regiment on this day, entitle him to the particular notice of the government."

While Davis lay incapacitated, the news of Santa Anna's stealthy departure was brought to him. The next day he was removed from the crude makeshift quarters to Saltillo. There that evening he rallied his strength to write a reassuring note to his wife.

"I wrote you a few days since anticipating a battle. We have had it. The Mississippians did well. I fear you may feel some anxiety for me, and write to say that I was wounded in the right foot, and remained on the field so long afterwards that the wound has been painful, but is by no means dangerous. My friend, Mr. Crittenden, will write more on this sheet to brother Joe, and give him more particulars."

Thomas Crittenden wrote to Joseph Davis on several extra sheets, and gave numerous details of the battle that made him proud of his beloved Jeff.

The regiment commanded by your brother won the admiration of all, and suffered, of course, severely, at least one hundred casualties, and among them 40 killed and that when the regiment did not muster 300 men upon the field of battle. . . .

Your brother's wound is not at all dangerous, but in all probability he will not be able to walk for several months, at least without a crutch. Our gallant old General has silenced all fires, front and rear, and proven himself for the hundredth time a hero.

Very respectfully yours,<br>Thos. L. Crittenden.

P.S. . . . I have been with your brother almost daily for several months, and have formed for him a great personal attachment. . . .

The personal attachment spoken of by the Kentuckian was typical of the admiration and affection Jefferson Davis inspired in men and women throughout his life—persons from the lowest rank to those in exalted position. For all of his inbred dignity, Jefferson Davis had a responsive and understanding heart. While outwardly master of his own emotions, he was extremely sensitive to distress in another. And now his physical anguish was somewhat forgotten in his grief over his men who had been killed, and he suffered with those who were painfully wounded like himself. He lamented particularly the death of Henry Clay, Jr., at whose home he had been entertained when a teen-age student at Transylvania. The loss of old friends took away the sense of jubilation he might have felt at the victory.

Three months later, on May 29, the period of enlistment of the First Mississippi Rifles having run out, Colonel Davis sailed with them from Brazos. His wound was far from healed and to move about on crutches gave him considerable pain. It was not a cheerful voyage, for he brought along a heap of pine coffins bearing the remains of his dead regimental comrades and the body of his friend Clay.

When the ship landed at New Orleans eleven days later, Colonel Davis was hailed as "a soldier genius" and "hero second only to Zachary Taylor." As the men disembarked the immense crowd yelled with such shouting as New Orleans had seldom heard. When Colonel Davis appeared on crutches, gaunt from persistent pain, but even more romantically handsome, the crowd went wild. Bands played martial music; cannon were fired; women wept. In Lafayette Square, Seargent Prentiss, the famous orator, eulogized the planter-colonel, his onetime opponent in debate. Never, said the press, had his eloquence more stirred his audience.

Later, as the procession moved to Place d'Armes for an alfresco luncheon, flowers were tossed into Davis's carriage from the balconies along the way. And from the grilled galleries of the Pontalba buildings on the square ladies in summer organdies dropped wreaths and garlands upon the soldiers. In reporting the return of the Mississippi Rifles, the *Picayune* of June 11 confessed that "to attempt to describe the enthusiasm evinced on this occasion was in vain."

Among the letters handed him was a long sweet one from his sister-in-law Eliza welcoming him home to Hurricane and one from the President of the United States, addressed not to Colonel Davis, but to "Brigadier General Jefferson Davis, U.S. Army in Mexico."

The next day Davis and his soldiers boarded a chartered steamboat that stopped at various towns and landings on the river to leave the men at places most convenient to their homes. The Rifles were toasted at every stop. The whole water progress was "one prolonged ovation."

Because of the extensive celebrations at each river landing, the steamboat was a day late in reaching Natchez. Early on the morning of the fifteenth, cannon from the bluff announced the boat was sighted. All the shops and most of the houses were emptied of their people, bent on saluting the heroes. At nine o'clock three hundred schoolgirls "bearing long chains of flowers" formed a double line. Varina, in a state of intense excitement, drove to the landing, accompanied by her parents, her old tutor, Judge Winchester, and Joseph Davis. As Jeff came toward his young wife on crutches, Varina was shocked by his pallor and his gauntness. But respecting his abhorrence of any public display of feeling, she restrained her deep concern.

All through the morning and into the afternoon Jefferson had to endure parades, outdoor feasts, and grandiloquent Southern speeches. On behalf of his regiment and himself, Colonel Davis, according to the Natchez *Weekly Courier,* "delivered a most beautiful and heart-thrilling response." It was all a wearying experience for him, made endurable only because the festivities gave so much pleasure to the Adams County folk. At last, at five o'clock, Jefferson drove out to The Briers in a flower-bedecked carriage to fetch his wife, who had escaped to change into traveling dress. Then through cheering lines of well-wishers, like bride and groom departing on honeymoon, the couple drove down to the river to embark for Vicksburg and home.

In the county seat of Jefferson Davis's own Warren, the celebrations were even more clamorous. The Davises had to spend a full day and night there, while Vicksburg did high honor to the Colonel, who was suffering from the nervous strain of being constantly in the public view, as well as from the wound, which had to be treated by a surgeon.

The next day Joseph drove with them to the blessed remoteness of Hurricane, far out on the peninsula of Davis Bend. They were to remain with him and Eliza until Brierfield could be readied for occupancy. Surrounded by the love of his wife and his brother and Eliza and the devotion of the welcoming Negroes, Jefferson might now relax from the excitements of the demonstrations. But, first, there was the matter of President Polk's letter that had been delivered to him in New Orleans. Jefferson had been ruminating over its contents, which demanded a decision, but he had no time to reply. Both Varina and Joseph read the letter with mingled pride and perturbation.

Washington City,
May 19, 1847

My dear Sir: The Secretary of War will transmit to you, a commission as Brigadier General of the United States Army. The Brigade which you will command, will consist of volunteers called out to serve during the war with Mexico. It gives me sincere pleasure to confer this important command upon you. Your distinguished gallantry and military skill while in the battles of *Monterey* and *Buena Vista,* eminently entitle you to it. I hope that the severe wound which you received at the latter place, may soon be healed, and that your country may have the benefit of your valuable services, at the head of your new command.

I am very faithfully, your friend,
James K. Polk

Varina regarded her husband in his semi-invalid condition, with crutches lying by his side, and was filled with horror at the thought of his ever returning to war. For three days Jefferson debated the matter with the two persons most dear to him. He and Joseph considered "that volunteers or militia had a constitutional right to be under the immediate command of officers appointed by State authority." At length Jefferson wrote to Polk, graciously thanking him, but respectfully declining the appointment on the ground that the Constitution did not give the President power to appoint volunteer officers.

Warren County, Miss. June 20, 1847
To the President:

My dear Sir: Your very kind and complimentary letter of the 19th May last, was received in New Orleans, together with the commission to which you therein referred.

To be esteemed by you as one whose services entitled him to promotion, is to me a source of the highest gratification; which will remain to me undiminished, though my opinions compel me to decline the proffered honor.

I will this day address to the Adjutant-General of the U.S.

Army, an official note informing him that the commission has been received and is declined. . . .

For the gratifying notice you have taken of myself and the regiment I had the honor to command; for the distinction you have been pleased to confer upon me by this unsolicited appointment; and for the kind solicitude you express for my welfare, receive, Sir, my sincerest thanks.

Very truly, your friend,<br>Jefferson Davis

Zachary Taylor, among others, mistrusted the President's rewarding gesture. On June 23, he wrote to his son-in-law, Dr. Wood, in New Orleans, expressing his gratification at Davis's honor: "He richly merits it," but added: "I think it quite likely they gave him the appointment of Brigadier General under the expectation of keeping him out of the Senate."

Varina's only desire now was to have her husband all to herself for at least a little while. Jefferson, whose nature was responsive to every element of plantation life, looked eagerly to assuming again the personal direction of his place. But the interim of respite was apparently to be short, for almost immediately rumors were reaching Hurricane that Jefferson Davis would be appointed to the United States Senate to fill the vacancy occasioned by the death of Senator Jesse Speight.

In the meantime, the fatted calf and concoctions from Eliza's choicest recipes were set before the returned soldier to tempt his appetite and put flesh on his frame. Joseph naturally brought forth his very best Madeira and port. Though Joseph believed in good food, and was something of a gourmet, he had no patience with gourmands. He thought it seemly that the feminine sex should eat sparingly, as befitted their supposed daintiness. Varina paid no attention to him and ate heartily. But to please him his granddaughter Lise, now four and a half, who always sat beside him at table, would take only ladylike helpings. When the meal was over, however, she would steal into the kitchen, where the sympathetic Negroes would stuff her with sweet potatoes, corn bread, cabbage, turnip greens, and pot liquor. Her Uncle Jeff, who knew the secret, smiled because her grandfather was at a loss to understand why Lise grew into such a plump little girl when she ate so daintily.

By July 21 Jefferson and Varina were settled in their own home, for on that day he wrote from Brierfield to Chancellor Stephen Cocke of the Mississippi Superior Court: "I thank you for the interest you take in the appointment of U.S. Senator and am really obliged to Gov. Brown for feelings which by others I had been led to believe he did not entertain for me."

While gratified at the thought of her husband's elevation to the Senate, Varina was sorely concerned with the healing of his wound. The bone had exfoliated, and those splinters that could not be extracted by the surgeon were working themselves out through the flesh, causing disturbances to the whole nervous system, as well as severe pain. Varina could almost wish that not even the world's most resplendent laurels would intrude on the sanctuary of plantation life until her Jeff was completely mended.

In the meantime Varina ran the household with easy and expert efficiency. Jefferson found solace in his home life, and he began to regain his lost flesh. On August 11 the expected letter from Governor Brown reached Brierfield.

> Executive Chamber
> Jackson M. 10th August 1847

Col. Jeff$^n$ Davis
  Warrenton Mi.
Sir

I have the honor to enclose you a commission as U. States Senator to fill a vacancy occasioned by the death of the late General Speight. . . . The people will never cease to remember with pride and gratitude that to you, Sir, and the brave Mississippians under your command, is our State indebted for honors as imperishable as the soil on which you won them; honors, which shall last as long as chivalry is respected or valor has a place in the hearts of men. They expect me to offer you this commission, and it gives me sincere personal pleasure to gratify that expectation. . . .

Very Respectfully<br>Your Ob't serv't<br>A. G. Brown

Joseph was elated at Jefferson's appointment; this was an end to which he had looked in the long evenings of training in the Hurricane library; this was the realization of the promise he had discerned in his youthful brother. Though apprehensive at the thought of a political career, Varina took worldly pride in the fact that Jefferson would enter the Senate before he was forty and that she herself would be a Senator's wife at twenty-one.

Four days after hearing from the governor, Jefferson sent his acceptance:

"It is with a grateful sense of the distinction bestowed, and a a high estimate of the responsibilities which I am about to assume, that I accept the commission you have tendered, with so much of delicate and gratifying encouragement.

"The approbation which you convey of my services in the twenty-ninth Congress is especially pleasing, because therein was manifested my fixed opinion on the taxing and expanding powers of the federal government, my uniformly entertained and often avowed creed of strict construction for the Constitution of our Union."

Now that he and Varina had less than three months more to enjoy the peaceful activities of Brierfield, they accepted with a special thankfulness the days as they unfolded. Jefferson carefully laid out the plans for plantation work during his absence and endeavored to catch up with his correspondence. Ever since leaving Mexico, he had been corresponding with his first father-in-law. He had asked General Taylor's advice about the army and about politics, and the General had counseled him "to pursue that course which you think will be most conducive to your future fame, prosperity, and happiness." In turn, the General received with valued consideration his son-in-law's opinions on the American political situation. On September 27 Taylor wrote to Dr. Wood, "No one can possibly respect the opinions of another more than I do those of Col. Davis and I know he is my most devoted and ardent friend."

A later letter from Taylor to Dr. Wood written from Monterey on October 27 shortly before he left for the United States tells of an illness of Davis and a serious eye infection which was to plague him often.

"I have this moment received a letter from Col. Davis saying he had just, or was fast recovering from a severe attack of sickness, which had very much effected [sic] his eyes, which I deeply regretted to hear; but he said nothing about his wounded foot; he has accepted the appointment of Senator, which is only temporary; the election comes on for four years to complete the late Senator Speight's term in March next. . . . I think there is but little doubt as to his election; he appears however to be indifferent about it. . . ."

Malaria, the perennial curse of the Mississippi Delta, had assailed Jefferson in September, and for more than a fortnight he was laid low. During this time he learned of the fall of Mexico City on September 14, which in effect meant the end of the war with Mexico. Though peace would be established between the alien countries, he saw disturbing signs in measures like the Wilmot Proviso that the crack in the amity of North and South would become greater. He trusted he might be helpful by entering the Senate. He had the hope that the Constitution might save a dangerously critical situation, and no one after John C. Calhoun was a more ardent constitutionalist than himself. Upholding a strict construction of the Constitution was an ideal from which he never wavered or deviated and about the sacredness of which he had not a single qualm throughout his length of days.

Jefferson Davis reached Washington late in November. After a visit with President Polk, he wrote optimistically to Stephen

Cocke: "The President is in good health and in fine spirits, feels confident of being able to discomfort the enemy as signally at home as abroad. . . . I think the Wilmot Proviso will soon be of the things which were."

On December 6, 1847, walking on crutches, Jefferson Davis took the oath in the Senate. Except for his ailing foot, he had recovered his health, and he looked remarkably young for thirty-nine, as well as impressively handsome.

## CHAPTER XIII

## IN THE SENATE

WHEN Jefferson Davis took his seat in the Senate, his valor had been sung abroad and he was received as one of the nation's most lauded heroes. His political rise had been swift, for only four years before he had been thrust into politics on a week's notice as a novice championing a losing side. Now his spoken words were to make him an outstanding figure in what was then an august body.

To be a United States Senator was, of course, a greater distinction than to be a brigadier general, and, at this time, it was far more so, because giants were still in Congress. The aged John Quincy Adams was in the House; Calhoun and Webster sat in the Senate; and Henry Clay was to re-enter it late in 1849. Each of these four notable men was more than old enough to be Davis's father; and within five years they were all dead, as was Davis's father-in-law Zachary Taylor.[1] Of the distinguished statesmen who were to be left alive at the end of 1852, none outshone Jefferson Davis.

When he appeared as Senator, there was perhaps no Southerner or Northerner either who knew the United States as a whole better than did Davis. All through his life—even during the War between the States—he was on terms of warm friendship with Northern men. He was far from being a provincial, and his diction

[1] Adams sank to the floor of Congress with a stroke in February, 1848; Calhoun succumbed in March of 1850, and Taylor, four months later. Webster and Clay, the great Whig rivals, passed away in the same year, 1852.

was more that of a cultivated man of the world than a citizen of the deep South. As Washington and Jefferson—in their separate spheres, the chief figures of the Revolution—were both Southerners with a national vision, so was Jefferson Davis. Not only was he a nationalist, but he was an expansionist, who believed in the swelling destiny of American democracy. Davis did not go as far as the starry-eyed young Brooklyn editor Walt Whitman, who wrote, "it is for the interest of mankind that the power and territory of the United States should be extended—the farther the better," but he envisioned an enlarged nation, one in which the South would maintain its share of prestige.

Because of his special knowledge and training, Davis was put on the Committee on Military Affairs, made a regent of the Smithsonian Institution, and a member of the Library Committee. His first senatorial remarks were made on January 3, 1848, on a bill to increase the army. Despite the necessity of crutches, he yet carried himself with such a "natural air of conscious strength and ease and purpose," and spoke with such persuasive good sense and unconscious magnetism that the Senators and the gallery recognized his quality.

The Davises had taken an apartment in a house next to the United States Hotel, where they had their meals, entering the dining room over a little private bridge. Among others in their "mess" were ex-Governor McWillie of Mississippi, the Burts of South Carolina (Mrs. Burt was a niece of John C. Calhoun), and Senator and Mrs. Toombs of Georgia. Robert Toombs, an ardent Southerner, was a big, burly, good-looking fellow, with glossy black hair. Enjoying the fleshpots with gusto, he also relished the classics, and would roar with delight over each rereading of Molière's satirical comedies. Audacious in his wit and loud-voiced, he yet had the manners of a gentleman, and he was quite vain about his beautiful hands, which he kept perfectly manicured. Varina found Toombs a highly diverting dinner companion. But for the quiet-mannered Jefferson, the Georgian was too expansive an extrovert. Senator Burt, with his dignity and well-bred elegance, was much more to the Davis taste.

While Toombs was an inveterate party-goer, in his first senatorial period Davis rarely accepted invitations except to the houses of friends to whom he was especially attached. It never occurred to him to enhance his popularity by appearing at social functions. "He was so impervious to the influence of anything but principle in shaping his political course," his wife says with a tinge of worldly-wise criticism, "that he underrated the effect of social intercourse in determining the action of public men." The young Varina spent most of her evenings at home, dutifully assisting her husband with his senatorial affairs and taking down letters to constituents. But her husband beguiled her, she assures us, by pausing in the work to regale her with anecdotes and jests, "of which his memory held a boundless store."

As usual, the Davises had brought along relatives. This time it was Varina's sister Margaret and her little brother Becket, who was put in a Quaker school in Alexandria at the brother-in-law's expense. Jefferson never seemed to mind having relatives about. He was generally surrounded by blood kin or in-laws, and continually contributing to some poorer relation's support.

By now Mrs. Davis's father, William Burr Howell, had completely run through his wife's fortune from the Kempes and the Grahames. An indifferent and careless manager, Howell had little aptitude for money-making. But though he was lazy and ineffectual, he was engaging, and his son-in-law was fond of him. To add a monthly stipend to the shrunken and variable family income of the Howells, Davis, on March 18, 1848, recommended his father-in-law for the modest postmastership of Natchez. At this same time General Taylor, who had retired from the army in November, was now actively managing his large plantation, Cypress Grove, and his hundred-odd slaves in the Mississippi county just above Natchez,[2] while the press continued to predict that he would be the next President of the United States. The contrast

[2] In 1842 Zachary Taylor had bought this property of 3,000 acres and 81 slaves, while Baton Rouge was called the family home. He owned other estates with slaves, bank stock in Kentucky, and bonds. On his return from the Mexican War, he was rated as among the fewer than 1,800 Southern planters who owned more than 100 slaves.

between the fathers of the two women Jefferson had married was striking. But there is no record of his criticizing William Howell's lack of business sense or application, though Joseph finally lost patience with his old friend and came to treat him with something like kindly contempt. It would never have occurred to Jefferson not to share with his wife's young relatives—such was an established Southern custom—and besides, he loved children, and delighted in having them about him.

On March 10, eight days before he recommended his father-in-law for the minor position, he was a party to the congressional ratification of the peace treaty with Mexico, which had been signed at Guadalupe Hidalgo on February 2. Though peace had been made between the two nations, sectional strife in the United States itself was becoming ever sharper. The slaveholding states were determined to have their share of influence in the newly acquired, vast territory of California and New Mexico, while the North seemed resolved to keep slavery out of any part of it, in order to hold and increase its advantage in Congress.

That ominous Wilmot Proviso, which Davis had optimistically thought was a dead issue, still haunted congressional halls, though it had twice failed to become a law, in 1846 and 1847. In the late summer of 1846, while Davis was marching toward Monterey with Zachary Taylor, President Polk had asked Congress for $2,000,000 as initial payment on territory that might be acquired by negotiation from Mexico. On a sweltering August evening, after the lamps had been lighted in the House of Representatives, while members sweated profusely, sipped ice water, and fanned themselves with anything handy, a corpulent young Democrat from Pennsylvania named David Wilmot rose and offered an amendment to the "Two Million Bill." It provided that slavery should never exist in any territory (outside Texas) that might be won from the war. Completely unexpected, it was as if a bombshell had exploded in the sultry atmosphere. Wilmot was no Abolitionist, but to strengthen his faltering political position with his protectionist constituents, he devised a measure that seeded a war. The Wilmot Proviso passed the House by a goodly majority, for the North had 50 per cent more representatives than the South. After much wrangling, it was barely defeated in the Senate.

The South reacted to the Proviso with furious indignation. The North had already imposed high tariffs, which the agricultural South was helpless to vote down. With the rapid growth in population from ever-increasing European immigration, the North had seized both political and economic control. If Southern influence was to be completely forestalled in any state formed out of new territory, the South would be placed in abject submission by Northern interests.

Now in 1848 Jefferson Davis found Southern Senators still outraged at the idea of a measure that would deny them the right to take their slaves into territory acquired from Mexico. The volunteers who had fought the Mexicans were largely Southern. The majority of the leading figures were Southern: Taylor, Scott, Wool, Worth, Quitman, Davis, Bragg, and Lee. To forehanded, if hotheaded, men like Robert Barnwell Rhett of South Carolina, the popularity of the Proviso in the North already indicated the necessity of withdrawal from the Union.

In February, 1848, John C. Calhoun, who had opposed the war with Mexico, declared that since the acquired territories were the common domain of all the states, Congress had no constitutional power to forbid the people of any part of the Union from seeking homes in that domain *with their property*. The Southerners, he maintained, had the right already expressed in the Constitution to take their slaves with them into any territory.

In the same month Jefferson Davis forcibly began his fight against the spirit of the Proviso. He insisted that the South should "demand of their political brethren of the North a disavowal of the principles of the Wilmot Proviso, an admission of the equal right of the South with the North to the territory held as the common property of the United States, and a declaration in favour of extending the Missouri Compromise to all states to be hereafter admitted into our confederacy."

"If, on the other hand," he warned, "the spirit of hostility to the South, that thirst for political dominion over us, which, within two years past, has displayed such increased power and systematic purpose, should prevail . . . We shall then have reached a point at which all party measures sink into insignificance under the necessity of self-preservation."

On the Senate floor, Jefferson Davis had no hesitancy in contesting with the most seasoned and venerable statesmen, when he could not agree with them. On March 21, 1848, he answered and bested both his old friend Calhoun and the doughty Daniel Webster on the subject of the Mexican War. When Webster used the term "odious" to characterize the war in which Davis had almost lost his life and had received wounds from which he was still suffering, the Mississippian challenged him with rousing eloquence: "The Senator says this war is 'odious.' Odious! Odious for what?" he demanded, his blue-gray eyes blazing. "On account of the skill and gallantry with which it has been conducted?" He let the irony sink in and then continued.

"Or is it because of the humanity, the morality, the magnanimous clemency which has marked its execution? Odious! Why, in any newspaper which I take up, I find notices of large assemblages of the people gathered together to do honor to the remains of some dead soldier brought back from Mexico. . . . The conductors of the press, without distinction of party, express the highest approbation of the conduct of the army. Where is the odium? What portion of our population is infected with it? From what cause does it arise? It cannot be on account of the origin of the war, the extraordinary unanimity with which it was declared by both Houses of Congress, the eagerness with which our citizens pressed to the service, forbid that conclusion. . . .

"Where, sir, are the evidences of evil brought upon us by this 'odious' war? Where can you point to any inroad upon our prosperity, public or private, industrial, commercial, or financial, which can be, in any degree, attributed to the prosecution of this war?"

A short while later Davis spoke glowingly on resolutions of thanks to General Taylor. "But there stands a soldier whose life has been wholly dedicated to his country—whose services accumulating one by one, have become a pyramid as beautiful for its simplicity as it is sublime for its grandeur."

He was disappointed that Zachary Taylor, with whom he had been in continual correspondence since Buena Vista, had not been able to feel himself a Democrat rather than a Whig. The General, who had never voted in his life, had no history of party allegiance, though he called himself a Whig or "a democrat of the Jeffersonian school." In the previous fall, Davis had become convinced that Taylor could win the presidency in 1848 on the Democratic ticket, and he had reason to fear that the Whigs might nominate Winfield Scott or Henry Clay instead of his father-in-law because of the latter's proslavery sentiments.

On September 27, 1847, Taylor had written Dr. Wood: "I think Col. Davis is mistaken in supposing the Whigs as a body are haling off from me; but if they should do so, it is no reason I should change my opinion in political matters; I shall pursue a straight forward course deviating neither to the right or left so that comes what may I hope my real friends will never have to blush for me, so far as truth, honesty and fair dealings are concerned."

By April, 1848, however, Davis was expecting Taylor's nomination on the Whig ticket and he knew the event would put him in a difficult position. Always admiring his father-in-law's sterling qualities and now personally devoted to him, he could not but hope the General would crown his career with a term in the White House. But being a loyal Democrat, he felt he must support for President whomever his party nominated. On May 22, Lewis Cass of Michigan, also a friend of Davis, was selected.

A fortnight later, Davis received the reports of the Whig convention in Philadelphia with more intense interest. While he felt assured that Taylor would be nominated, he yet had a persistent apprehension of Henry Clay, whom he considered inimical to Southern interests. Clay was not only an accomplished statesman and a shrewd politician, but he had a fatal charm, which Davis himself had felt when he was a schoolboy in Lexington. Now, in his seventy-first year, the brilliant, elegant, Chesterfieldian Clay was still a master at lobbying for Henry Clay. He had announced his candidacy only in April, 1848, and though he had been three times defeated for the nomination, his friends rallied loyally to help him make a last attempt. On the first ballot Clay received 97 votes to Taylor's 111, Scott's 43, and Webster's 22. On the final ballot Taylor won the nomination with 171, while his enemy Scott ended in second place with 60.

Taylor's nomination delighted Davis, though it did put him in a political quandary. It would have been only too natural for him to support his father-in-law, "to walk," as he wrote to his friend Stephen Cocke, "on the broad way and the open gate to self-preferment." Since numerous leading Southern Democrats planned to switch allegiance and vote for Taylor, the General might have expected his son-in-law to do likewise. But to relieve him of any pain the decision might cost him, Taylor wrote Jefferson a long, and very warm letter with his characteristic indifference to syntax. The letter was full of personal matters, revealing his affection for Joseph Davis, and commenting, farmer-to-farmer, on crop conditions.

Baton Rouge Louisiana<br>July 10th, 1848.

My dear Generl,

. . . I am free to say I felt neither pride or exultation at the moment the information was communicated to me, nor have I done so up to this time, & if I know myself when the time arrives, my feelings would not be changed in the slightest degree was I to receive notice of my election to the office in question neither should I be mortified was I instead of my own, to hear of the success of my adversary; for as the time approaches & the prospects increase for my reaching that high office, I find my disinclination to embark in it, & to under take the important duties connected with it greatly to increase. . . . While in the City [New Orleans] met your neighbour & friend across the river, Judge Perkins from whom I was truly gratified to hear your excellent brother his & your excellent ladies had all gone North

& would take Washington in then write when they would turn over the latter to you, remaining themselves some days with you. . . . I believe your brother's required to reestablish his health [3] not only relaxation & rest from his labors but a change to a more northern & less relaxing climate than Mississippi. . . . He ought to go North every season, as the preservation of his health & life, is of more importance to his family, friends & country than all the wealth he could accumulate for the former; particularly as he has already enough to make them all more than independent. . . .

I feel under, my dear General, the greatest obligations for the continued interest you feel and have taken in my reaching the first office in the gift of the American people, in which you and other dear friends, I am confident, take much more concern than I do. . . . I repeat again I have your own advancement more at heart than my own. You are now entering on the stage of action, while I must soon retire from it; you must therefore pursue that course which your good judgment will point out, as far as your honour and the good of the country are concerned, without regard to my advancement. It is sufficient to me to know that I possess your friendship, which is all I ask or wish.

Judge Perkins informed me the corn crops were never better in Louisiana & in Mississippi, & the Cotton promising along the river, but had somewhat been damaged by long and heavy rains, but no doubt there will be more made in the country than can be disposed of; in fact the appearances abroad as regards prices are very gloomy.

Please present my kindest regards to your better half, & to your kind brother & his excellent lady should they be with you . . . . & wishing you all continuing health & prosperity
        I remain
        Truly & sincerely
         Your Friend
          Z. Taylor

[3] Both Joseph Davis and Zachary Taylor were now approaching sixty-four. This is the first record that Joseph's health was impaired.

On July 12, 1848, two days after Taylor sent this intimate and reassuring letter to his son-in-law, Senator Davis was speaking earnestly on the Negro question and constitutional rights, the occasion being the bill to establish territorial government in Oregon. As for the introduction of slavery into Oregon, no Southern Senator had ever asked it, he said. "The fact that the slave is property which its owner may carry into any part of the Union, is that which the South is desirous to see recognized. The words 'slave, or any other property' in the Constitution are conclusive on this point." If the existence of the slave as property be admitted, he asked, what power has Congress to interfere with it? Congress had no power to change the condition of slavery or to strip a man of his right to his property. Entering a territory with his property, the citizen had a right to its protection.

In regard to the status of the Negroes themselves, he spoke the truth as he saw it, mentioning ties of attachment between master and slave which he did not expect the average Northerner to sympathize with or even comprehend.

"Let those who possess the best opportunity to judge the men who have grown up in the presence of slave institutions, as they exist in the United States, say, if their [the slaves'] happiness and usefulness do not prove their present condition to be the accomplishment of an All-wise decree. It may have for its end the preparation of that race for civil liberty and social enjoyment. . . .

"Compare the slaves in the Southern States with recently imported Africans as seen in the West Indies, and who can fail to be struck with the increased improvement of the race; whether physically, morally, or intellectually considered? Compare our slaves with the free blacks of the Northern States, and you will find the one contented, well provided for in all their physical wants, and steadily improving, in their moral condition; the other miserable, impoverished, loathesome for the deformity and disease which follow after penury and vice, covering the records of the criminal courts, and filling the penitentiaries. Mark the hostility to caste, the social degradation which excludes the able from employment of profit and trust, and leaves the helpless to want and neglect. Then turn to the condition of this race in the States of the South, and view them in the relation of slaves. There, no hostility exists against them—the master is the natural protector of his slave; and public opinion, common feeling, mere interest would not allow him to neglect his wants.

"Those who urge that the exclusion of slavery from the Territories does not exclude the slaveholder, because he may dispose of his property before emigration, show such inability to comprehend the attachment which generally subsists between a master and his slaves, that I will only offer to them interest as a motive for the care which is extended to those of the sick, and adequate provision to all. Such is the difference between the condition of the free and slave blacks under conditions most favorable to emancipation. Does it warrant the desire on the part of any friend of that dependent race to hasten upon them responsibilities, for which they have shown themselves so unequal? If any shall believe that the sorrow, the suffering, the crime which they witness among the free blacks of the North have resulted from their degradation by comparison with the white race around them, to such I would answer: Does the condition of St. Domingo, of Jamaica give higher evidence? Or, do the recent atrocities in Martinique encourage better hopes?

"Sir, this problem is one which must bring its own solution. Leave natural causes to their full effect, and when the time shall arrive at which emancipation is proper, those most interested will be most anxious to effect it."

Davis was convinced that if the North would only keep hands off what had become an almost exclusive Southern institution, the solution would evolve of itself, when the Negroes were better prepared to accept the responsibilities of liberty.

Sometime after his July 12 speech, Jefferson Davis received from President-elect Taylor an unequivocable statement on the subject of abolition. "So far as slavery is concerned, we of the

South must throw ourselves on the Constitution and defend our rights under it to the last, and when arguments will no longer suffice, we will appeal to the sword, if necessary." But this Southern-born slaveholder, whom the Whigs had nominated because he was the man of the hour, was known to oppose the extension of slavery. Holman Hamilton, Taylor's best biographer, states clearly that Zachary Taylor was proslavery before his nomination and after he was in the White House "insofar as it appertained to the region where it already existed."

While ever expressing the most sincere hope for unity and conciliation, Taylor did not fail to make clear his determination "to uphold the South's constitutional right to maintain and protect slavery." "The moment Northern radicals go beyond that point when resistence [sic] becomes right and proper," he advised, "let the South act promptly, boldly and decisively, with arms in their hands if necessary, as the Union will in that case be blown to atoms or will be no longer worth preserving."

Though Taylor had been nominated by a party that had only once won a national election—with another war hero, William Henry Harrison, in 1840—he refused to campaign, and would appear publicly only in the two states in which he maintained homes, Mississippi and Louisiana.

As the day of election drew nearer, large parts of the Southern electorate had still not made up their minds, and many wondered what Jefferson Davis was going to do. Since the adjournment of Congress he had remained silent, in retirement at Brierfield. Invited in October to address a general mass meeting at Cold Springs in his childhood county, Wilkinson, he declined because "domestic affliction confines me at home." But he set forth his views in a lengthy letter which was read at the assembly, and published in the Mississippi *Free Trader* of October 26, 1848. He began by emphasizing the imminent crisis in public affairs:

"Seldom, if ever, has there been a period in the history of our confederacy [the United States], more critical and momentous than the present. . . .

"Separating myself as far as possible from the prejudice I may very naturally feel for the creed of my entire political life, it seems to me evident and demonstrable, that the South should fraternize with the Democracy. This is the party of strict construction, of checks and balances, and constitutional restraints. We of the South are the minority and such we must remain; our property, our security in the Union depends upon the power of the constitutional curb with which we check the otherwise unbridled will of the majority."

While avoiding mention of his father-in-law's name, Davis spoke well of Cass and made it clear that he intended to vote, as he had on all past occasions, the Democratic electoral ticket. In the election Taylor won most of the Southern states, but lost narrowly in Mississippi, where Davis's advice was effective. Taylor's friendship for the Senator was in no wise affected, and Davis was really happy that the General would become President of the United States.

The election of slave-owning Taylor did anything but stop radical anti-Southern speeches in Congress, as conservative Northerners with a strong sense of property had hoped. On January 10, 1849, Davis warned the Senate that the Union would certainly be broken up if certain Northern Senators continued their practice of intermeddling with the affairs of the South. "It is an idle waste," he admonished sternly, "and a base abandonment of the duties of members upon this floor thus to squander time which should be devoted to some useful purpose. All this talk about slavery begins and ends and has its middle with the Negro race. I can hear nothing else, sir; of nothing which is progressive in human reform, nothing which does not concentrate itself in this question concerning the African race."

A fortnight later Davis, who was yet optimistic about some harmony in the forthcoming Taylor regime, heard news from Kentucky that disturbed him like an ill omen. On January 30, he wrote to Governor John J. Crittenden of Kentucky: "I regret exceedingly to see Mr. Clay is to return to the Senate. Among many reasons is one in which I know you will sympathize, the evil influence he will have on the friends of General Taylor in the two houses of Congress. Many who would have done well in his absence will give way in his presence. This will introduce a new element in the selection of the General's Cabinet. . . . I hope you will talk fully with General Taylor. He knows little of our public men personally and will have little opportunity to observe them after his arrival. . . . The General will need you and I hope to see you here."

Because he was a leading Democrat and the son-in-law of the President-elect, Jefferson Davis was put on the joint committee of official notification of the election. The official word reached the General at Hurricane where he was staying with Jefferson's brother Joseph and discussing with him likely men for the Cabinet posts.

Varina was in nearby Natchez with her parents, for she had been ailing when the time came for Jefferson to go to Washington in December. The first week in February, 1849, he received a very loving letter dated January 24:

My own darling Husband:

I saw by the papers today that Major Dix had died of the Cholera at Cumberland; and conclude that ere this you are in danger of taking it, Take laudanum and camphor the *first* slight pain you feel. Only come back to me safe in person and I can bear all other evils. Much as I have loved and valued you it seems to me I never knew the vastness of my treasure until now. If you have no fear for yourself, have it for your Winnie, your thoughtless, dependent wife, and guard your health as you would my life. Sweetest, best husband, don't go out at night, don't drink wine, don't eat any fruit. If you feel any temptation to be imprudent just recall the question to your mind if you have any right to blast my life for your gratification of the moment. You were never selfish, then be yourself now, and think of your wife. Jeff, my sweetest, write oftener if you can, though God knows your letters have been very, very frequent. Write to me every day, only three words: "I am well" will suffice, if you have not time for more. My better life, my nobler self, farewell, as ever I am,

    Your devoted Wife

W. Davis

Another letter dated January 25 came the very next day. Varina had heard from Jefferson, who was wondering if she needed him. She replied immediately that the physician had only said that she "must keep very quiet."

You could not assist me in the least unless looking into your sweet eyes would be balm for all wounds—

In the papers you sent me I saw your very forcible little speech in partial answer to Mr. Hale's vituperations against slavery. It was a little too violent, more so than I would have liked to hear you be, however well deserved the censure might be.

Thank you for Dickens' pretty little Christmas tales. If you read it you admired the character of Milly, did you not? I have not been reading much lately, in fact nothing but Mrs. Ellis's Guide to Social Happiness, which as it treats of woman and woman's trials could not interest you, but it will help "Winnie" to be "Wife."

My own bright love, farewell. Kiss wife, and say goodnight. Winnie is Husband's baby and baby is your

        devoted Wife
        Winnie Davis

Jefferson must have been touched by his Winnie's efforts to learn to be a good wife, whatever his reaction to her baby talk. He may have reflected indulgently that she was still only twenty-two. However she expressed it, there seemed no doubt of the ardor of her devotion. And her criticism of his reply to that demagogue Hale was most tactfully offered. She was right to rebuke him, to urge him to be more restrained, whatever the provocation. His young wife was learning to be a statesman, as he had jokingly told President Tyler when the three sipped warm milk together at the fair.

Senator Davis was one of three put in charge of arrangements for the National Inauguration Ball to be given in honor of Taylor and Fillmore. The formal advertisement of February 20, 1849, listed 230 "managers," private and official, of this "splendid compliment to the illustrious President and Vice-President-elect from their fellow citizens without distinction of party." The published notice proclaimed "the decorations will be in a style of elegance, and the supper in a tasteful profusion, hitherto unsurpassed." According to the *National Intelligencer,* among the noncongressional "managers" was Major Robert E. Lee, and among Congressmen was "Hon. A. Lincoln, Ill." For the first time these two famous names were linked together.

On February 27, Davis reported to the Senate that General Taylor wished to be inaugurated on March 5, instead of March 4, because the latter fell on Sunday. And on the Monday of the inauguration, the Senator was among those who escorted Taylor to the stand to lay his hand on the Bible and swear to protect the Constitution of the United States. Varina had arrived in Washington some days before the inauguration. At the ball, where they had places of eminence, she and Jefferson made a striking impression with their distinguished good looks. His Norman type, gold hair and blue-gray eyes, was an excellent foil for her flashing brunette beauty.

During his first weeks in Washington, the President relied a great deal on his Democratic son-in-law's advice. Jefferson was often at the White House, where Betty, the youngest of the Taylor daughters, took charge of the household because of her mother's frail health. Betty, now twenty-five, had ripened into a most lovely young woman. Prettier than Knox, she had the same kind of feminine charm that captivated everyone she met. Although she was a belle from her middle teens, she had remained unmarried until the year before, waiting for the perfect man. She had found him in that estimable Major Bliss, her father's aide in Mexico, who had been admiringly nicknamed "Perfect" at West Point. General Taylor had not opposed this match. He had eaten his oath that no daughter of his should ever marry a soldier; he had seen all three take husbands from the army. Betty was the light of the White House, as well as her father's pet and her mother's mainstay. Jefferson always took special joy in seeing her, because she reminded him of the love of his youth and brought back memories of the clandestine courtship at Prairie du Chien, in which she had loyally co-operated when a girl of eight. He became better acquainted with his little goddaughter Sarah Knox Wood, who was often at the White House, with and without her parents, who now lived in nearby Baltimore. Like Davis, "Old Rough and Ready" was extremely fond of children, and the White House in 1849 "continually rang with children's laughter."

Though the President and the Senator were unusually harmonious in personal relations, there were some ideas on which they could not agree. They continued to be at variance over the *extension* of slavery. Since this was a fundamental point in the ideology of each, Davis's influence began to diminish. Soon that clever Whig leader, William Seward of New York, captured Taylor's ear and was ridiculed in the press for currying favor by presenting Old Whitey, the President's war horse, with a gold currycomb.

Another point of disagreement between the President and his son-in-law was the Cuban question. Taylor was completely "hands-off" in attitude. Davis mistrusted having a Spanish possession lying a few miles from Florida and believed that Cuba, if she could not be purchased, should be free, as she became after the Spanish-American War half a century later.

Through James Buchanan, President Polk had offered to purchase Cuba from Spain in 1848, but the offer was declined. President Taylor would not consider risking embroilment with a foreign power, and he frowned darkly on filibustering. Many patriotic Cubans who chafed under Spanish tyranny felt their only recourse was to seek annexation to the United States by rebellion. The South looked upon the idea with favor, as did the New York *Sun,* which encouraged the disaffection toward Spain in its editorial columns and afforded the Cuban leaders in New York the use of the *Sun* flagpole for their newly designed flag of a free Cuba.

When summer came, the Cuban problem was very much in general conversation. While most of the other congressional guests left the house next to the United States Hotel, the Davises stayed on for some weeks. They had the drawing room almost entirely to themselves, and, according to the custom of the time, on moonlight nights they did not light the lamps because of the intense heat and the insects. One evening Varina walked into the moon-illuminated room to find two men sitting in silence by a window, one youngish and blond, one with silvery hair and beard that brightly reflected the moon's rays. Suspecting they had come to see her husband on business, she moved away to sit at the extreme other end of the room. When Jefferson entered, he and the men conversed in low tones for a long time, and at last he rose, saying, "You must excuse me. I deem it inconsistent with my duty as a senator from my state." As he saw them to the door, he added, "The only man I could recommend to you just now is one in whom I have implicit confidence, Major Robert E. Lee. You might call on him in Baltimore."

When the visitors had gone, Davis confided to his wife that the gentlemen were Cuban patriots and one was the noted General López, head of the Cuban revolutionary junta in New York. They were planning an attack on the island to wrest it from Spanish misrule. López had assured the Senator, as he had the American press, that the Cubans were well armed and looked to annexation to the United States as the only salvation for Cuba's misery. All they needed for victory, he avowed, was a leader. General Worth, Jefferson told Varina, had first been offered the command of the Cuban forces, but he had died before he had made his decision. They now sought Jefferson Davis as their commander to liberate Cuba. If he accepted (according to Mrs. Davis's own statement) the junta would immediately deposit $100,000 in his wife's name, and would give him "another $100,000 or a very fine coffee plantation, when success was achieved." Varina's eyes widened with terror, but Jefferson emphasized that he had declined with finality. In her incalculable relief, Varina came nearer to hysterics than she ever did in her momentous life.

When the agents had pressed Davis to recommend someone else, he had suggested his old West Point mate as the best man for the command. Lee was "conveniently stationed in Baltimore on an army engineering project," and there the Cubans sought him out. "Lee's martial impulses," Douglas Southall Freeman writes, "no doubt were fired by the thought of a campaign in which he would have full opportunity of planning and directing operations." Certainly Lee was tempted; but since he held a commission in the United States Army, he was in doubt as to the question of personal honor. So he came to Washington to discuss the matter with Jefferson Davis.

Varina was alone in the drawing room when Major Lee entered and introduced himself. Her first thought, she says, was that he was the handsomest person she had ever seen, and his manner "was the personification of kindness." When her husband joined them it was the first time these three historic figures, destined to be so closely bound, were together. The soldier and the Senator had a long talk, and they must have recalled the Latin American overtures to Sidney Johnston when they were at West Point together. Both felt assured of the South's sympathy and the approbation of many Northern statesmen who desired a free Cuba. Both realized that a successful conclusion would not only mean financial security for life, but Lee's eternal fame as "the Lafayette of Cuban liberation." Yet neither could consider it consistent with the Major's duty to his Government to accept the command. Lee declined. In the end, the revolution failed; General López was garroted, while several young Southerners of prominent families were executed against a wall.

Would the revolutionary forces have succeeded if Jefferson Davis or Robert E. Lee had led them? Or would the future President of the Confederacy or the South's foremost soldier have had the life squeezed out by the garrote's screw? At any rate, one way or the other, if the commission had been accepted the course of history might have been different.

Jefferson Davis returned to Mississippi a little earlier than he had intended because of a tragedy at Hurricane, which affected his sixty-four-year-old brother more grievously than anything in his life. While out riding one afternoon with his six-year-old grandson Hugh Mitchell, as was his custom, Joseph saw the boy thrown from his pony and instantly killed. He was inconsolable. Hugh had become the bright star of his advancing years. (After Mary's death in Cuba and Dr. Mitchell's removal to Texas, Joseph had legally adopted their three children—Hugh, Joe, and Lise.) Joseph had come to believe in the boy's high destiny as he had in Jefferson's, and the two idolized each other. Jefferson knew from Joseph's letters how greatly he suffered, for Joseph almost never allowed himself the relief of expressing emotion in writing. Now so deep and unremitting was his grief that he could write unrestrainedly, as in a letter [4] of July 21, 1849.

"The rains continue with no change except a greater excess, confining me almost all the time to the house. This may in some degree contribute to a depression of spirit which I never felt before.

"The voices of the children are painful, suddenly recalling my lost boy. Indeed, everything reminds me of him. At the barns, in the woods or fields, objects are associated with him that is gone, and forever.

"I have suffered other afflictions, other hopes have been blighted, but whether from the time of life when fewer objects engage my attention and care, or whether from my more intimate association with him I know not, but nothing has weighed down my spirit like this."

When Jefferson and Varina arrived in Mississippi in the late summer, they did all they could to comfort Joseph and to divert

[4] This particular letter from which parts are quoted was written to Dr. Mitchell. It is in the possession of Mrs. Mary Lucy O'Kelley, the doctor's granddaughter.

him by talk of Washington. But Jefferson confessed that he was not happy about the first five months of Taylor's administration. To his constituents the Senator had to express misgivings about the state of the Union. Calhoun had recently given his famous address in favor of secession if the Wilmot Proviso was ever adopted. On October 12, Davis wrote a public letter to the South, concluding: "The generation which avoids its responsibility on this subject sows the wind and leaves the whirlwind as a harvest to its children. Let us get together and build manufacturies, enter upon industrial pursuits, and prepare for our own self-sustenance."

Thus eleven years before the dread possibility of a war between the states became a reality, Jefferson Davis was urging the South to set up factories and organize industries. The South did not heed his advice; indeed, no significant industrial movement stirred the region until some three-quarters of a century later.

## CHAPTER XIV

## FATHER-IN-LAW IN THE WHITE HOUSE

ON MONDAY, December 3, 1849, the Thirty-first Congress held its first session. Jefferson Davis was made chairman of the important Committee of Military Affairs by a vote of 32 to 5 for all other nominees, a tribute to his recognized abilities. Shortly he revealed his vision of a greater America. Not only did he champion the cause of a railway to the Pacific, but he looked into the future of the nation's political planning and suggested a Panamanian railway, which would carry international commerce across the isthmus and be of inestimable value for the defense of Pacific seaboard states. It was during this session that William Prescott, the famous historian, in estimating the caliber of that Senate pronounced Davis "the most accomplished of its leaders."

But Davis had little opportunity to use his constructive talents, for the fires of antislavery agitation began to dim all other Federal issues. The congressional year of 1850 was as tense as Washington had ever known. The vast territorial acquisitions from Mexico proved a mighty bone of contention. The North still wanted to make political use of all the territory. To Jefferson Davis and the South it was a matter of survival to check the sectional aggression of the North, with its augmenting power to increase the protective tariff rates for Northern industry and its threat to disrupt the South's agricultural economy by wiping out the institution of slavery.

Now the status of each newly organized territory in regard to slavery had to be settled. On these decisions depended the chance of the South to keep the North from controlling the Senate, as well as the House. And as the Federal Government extended its power, invariably favoring Northern interests, Davis foresaw the dribbling away of political liberty, as well as prestige, in the South.

After taking office President Taylor had asked California to organize its own government and apply for admission to the Union. Because of the discovery of gold near Sacramento in 1848, the breakneck rush of adventurers to California in 1849 raised the population sufficiently for statehood before the area could be organized as a territory. Most of the fortune seekers came from New England and other Northern states and were strongly opposed to competing with possible slave labor. In November, 1849, a California convention met and adopted a free state constitution, and Taylor was prepared to abide by the decision not to admit slaves. The South felt it was to be cheated of the finest fig in the basket. Robert Toombs arose in Congress and declared with passion: "If you seek to drive us from California, I am for disunion."

Heightening the tension at the beginning of the Thirty-first Congress was the expressed attitude of Vermont. Her legislature had declared slavery a crime and announced that it should not be permitted any longer to exist in any territory or under any jurisdiction of the United States. Her Senators and Representatives were instructed to endeavor diligently to execute Vermont's wishes.

Several decades earlier, because she found slavery unprofitable, Vermont, like most of the Northern states, had sold her slaves to traders for resale in the South. As Henry Clay himself pointed out, the North was now contending for a mere abstraction, while in the South the principle involved "their property, their prosperity, and even their peace." For the 3,900,000 slaves suddenly freed would involve a mighty policing problem, as well as ruin to the planters by depleting their capital.

On January 10, 1850, Jefferson Davis rose to answer Senator

Hale of New Hampshire, who, while supporting Vermont's stand, at the same time spoke piously of the praiseworthy nobility and general superiority of his own constituents. Davis was disgusted with this calculated insincerity, for Hale had announced on the floor only a few days before that all those petitions and memorials were mere devices intended for electioneering purposes and professed that this harmless agitation really meant nothing more than an effort to secure votes. Davis loathed such tricks to cajole the people "back home." He rebuked Hale for his folly and rashness, the demagoguery of which his constituents had perhaps been victims. Then he deplored the terrible waste of vital energy in Congress which these sectional recriminations caused—and he emphasized the danger of continued insult and threat. He made reference to the incendiary publications of the New York Anti-Slavery Society, which, he said, he believed sent out more printed matter than the Senate. Their pamphlets poured into the South to stir up the Negroes as they had poured into California to influence legislation against slavery.

"It is a melancholy fact that morning after morning, when we come here to enter into the business of the Senate our feelings are harrowed up by the introduction of this exciting and profitless subject, and we are compelled to listen to insults heaped upon our institutions. Sir, there is no man who comes here to represent his constituency for high and useful purposes, and who feels upon himself the obligation of his oath to defend the Constitution of the United States, who would act thus from day to day for the purpose of disturbing the useful legislation of the country, for no other purpose than to insert another brand into the flame, which every reflecting, sober man now sees threatens to consume the fabric of our government. . . .

"For one, sir, my purposes are to keep down this species of excitement both here and at home. I know the temper of those whom I represent, and they require no promptings to resist aggression or insult. . . . We, sir, are parties to the Union only under the Constitution, and there is no power known in the world that could dictate to my little State a Union in which her rights were continually trampled upon by an unrestrained majority. . . .

"I regret that Vermont has not now such constitutional scruples as actuated her in the War of 1812,[1] and that she does not keep her resolutions within her own limits . . . as she attempted to keep her troops during that War."

The Senators and the gallery who heard Davis knew the beating of his heart was steady, and even men who disliked him respected his integrity. For he had "that centralizing force of mind that gives strength and unity to character." Jefferson Davis was not "in politics" as men are "in business." Politics as politics had little to do with him. His very nature rebelled against anything that savored of the demagogue. In State Rights he had something like a religion to fight for. As General Morris Schaff, one of his Massachusetts biographers says, "If ever a public man's life was built up around sincerity, that of Jefferson Davis can lay claim to the tribute."

No one has made such a claim for Henry Clay, who had been returned to the Senate in December. On January 29, the very tall and very thin old gentleman with the lofty bald brow proposed his carefully planned scheme for compromise between the North and the South. His omnibus measure provided for: (1) the admission of California as a free state; (2) the organization of New Mexico and Utah on popular sovereignty principles; (3) prohibition of slave sales in the District of Columbia; and (4) a more effective fugitive slave law.

The proposal created something like a furore. Virtually no one would accept it in its entirety, and it was destined to be debated all through the winter, the spring, and the summer. Davis promptly assailed the Compromise as a proposal to the South to surrender at discretion. With all his eloquent might he fought the bill in the Senate. He exposed the hollowness of a measure which he said gave the South nothing. Davis saw the program as "an invitation to still more intolerable exactions by an implacable

---

[1] By the rest of the country Vermont and Massachusetts were considered extremely unpatriotic and almost treacherous in the War of 1812.

and ever increasing sectional majority." If the North really desired a reasonable settlement, he begged that the Missouri Compromise, with the line 36° 30', be extended to the Pacific.

"I here assert that never will I take less than the Missouri Compromise line to the Pacific Ocean," he said, "with specific right to hold slaves in the territory below that line; and that before such Territories are admitted into the Union as States, slaves may be taken there from any of the United States at the option of the owners. I can never consent to give additional power to a majority in this Union; and I will never consent to any proposition which will have such a tendency, without a full guarantee or counteracting measure being connected with it."

On March 4, 1850, the desperately ill John C. Calhoun was scheduled to give a prepared speech. But he was too weak to rise from his bed to go to the Senate to hear his speech read by a friend. To save the Union, the statesman called upon the North to yield equal rights in the newly acquired territory. He appealed for a pledge to stop turbulent agitation of the slave question. He suggested a Constitutional amendment calculated to restore to the South its former position of self-defense. In conclusion, he pleaded: "If you of the North will not do this, then let our Southern states separate and depart in peace."

The next day, by a superhuman effort of will, he came to the Senate to answer some unfair attacks on the speech and to make one last appeal for brotherly love and magnanimity. Knowing of her devotion to Calhoun, Vice-President Dallas had sent for Mrs. Davis. He put her on a stool between two of the Senators' chairs, quite near Calhoun's seat. She had just sat down when the old man entered like some ancient ghost swathed in flannels and supported by a Senator on either side. Cadaverous, his eyes aflame with fever, he gave Varina a burning hand as he passed, and whispered, "My child, I am too weak to stop." When he reached his place, before he sank into his seat, his "eagle glance swept the Senate in the old lordly way."

Henry Foote, the elder Senator from Mississippi, rose to attack the Calhoun speech. Foote was an excitable little man, and though

wellborn, given to coarse and offensive language. Able and
shrewd, Foote hated Jefferson Davis venomously and opposed
virtually anything the younger Senator advocated. Until recently
he had been intensely proslavery, but, in 1850, sensing the change
in the wind, he had come out for a compromise and Union at
any cost. Many Southern Senators despised him as a turncoat.
With brutal lack of consideration for Calhoun's enfeebled condition, Foote began baiting him and kept it up for more than an
hour. As Calhoun was forced to rise again and again to protest
some twisted interpretation, several Senators murmured aloud
their indignation. "Shame! Shame!" cried Thomas Hart Benton.
"No brave man could do this infamy." Jefferson Davis and several
others attempted to interpose and save Calhoun the exertion of
replying, but to no avail. Each time Calhoun rose, he bent further
over his desk, as his strength ebbed. Though his remarks were
pointedly clear, the voice grew weaker and weaker. When no one
could force Foote to relent and it seemed that Calhoun might
die on his feet, friends nearest to him bore him half-conscious
from the chamber.

On March 7, 1850, Webster made his famous speech in favor of
Clay's Compromise. It is still considered a masterpiece of oratory,
"the only speech in the nation's history known by the date of its
delivery." The Senate had never been more crowded. The floor
was jammed like the galleries. The walls were lined with humanity. There were not six inches of available space left anywhere. Privileged ladies in their best attire were squeezed in
between Senators' chairs on the floor. Some scrounged together
on the steps of the Vice-President's high seat.

"I speak today for the preservation of the Union. 'Hear me for
my cause,'" Webster began in his cello-toned voice. Almost immediately he took up a point in the speech of Calhoun's read on
March 4. Just then, to everyone's astonishment, Calhoun himself
was brought in and half-carried to his seat. Webster had to go
on. He claimed Calhoun had once written: "Texas must be obtained for the security of the slave interest of the South."

"Another view is distinctly given," Calhoun answered.

"But the honorable member did not disguise his conduct or his motives."

"Never, sir, never," Calhoun cried, and as he attempted to explain he tottered and dropped into his seat.

In a tender human gesture, Webster stretched out his arms magnanimously to Calhoun and said with emotion: "What he means, he is very apt to say."

"Always, always," the sick man gasped his last words in public. The Senate stood while he was carried out.

There were tear-filled eyes on every side as Webster resumed his speech. The Massachusetts Senator was never more magnificent than in his plea for harmony. But he infuriated his radical constituents at home, who reviled him until his death two years later.

Calhoun could hardly bear to die when his mind was clouded by dark forebodings. He told Beverly Tucker that he should die happy if he could believe the Union would be preserved. But he had no real hope. Rallying his ebbing strength, he astounded the Senate by taking his seat on March 11, the day Seward proclaimed with a rasping cry, "There is a higher law than the Constitution," and then proceeded to denounce the opinion of the Supreme Court which had just sustained the Fugitive Slave Law in the Prigg case. Davis, like many another Senator, glanced toward the almost-dead Calhoun, who leaned back with scorn on his face, his lips clamped in silence. When he was taken home, he remarked of Seward, "With his ideas, he is not fit to associate with gentlemen." He felt the Union was "doomed to dissolution" —and set the time "within twelve years."

Before the month had slipped into April, the great and troubled spirit of John C. Calhoun was stilled forever. The Senate was subdued with mourning, for the grand old statesman was esteemed by all parties. The whole South regarded Calhoun's passing as a major misfortune. The people of his own state idolized him to such an extent that it was commonly said, "When Calhoun took snuff, all South Carolina sneezed."

It was not until April 22 that the body was taken by water

to Charleston for burial. Jefferson Davis was chosen a member of the escort of honor to accompany the casket. Crowds jammed the Washington docks where the steamer *Baltimore* was heavily draped in black. To the muted strains of martial music and the tolling of church bells, a distinguished procession followed the hearse drawn by twelve black horses.

Frederika Bremer, the world-famous Swedish novelist, who happened to be visiting in Charleston when the *Baltimore* arrived, attended Calhoun's funeral. "He was laid away," she wrote, "like some divinity." She tells that 3,000 persons marched behind the casket, which was placed "so high on a catafalque that it seemed impossible for it to pass under triumphal arches." Calhoun was laid to rest in the west churchyard of beautiful St. Philip's, facing the graceful white spire.[2]

Jefferson Davis was deeply affected by his old friend's death, and he knew that now a greater burden of defending State Rights lay upon his shoulders. He was to follow Calhoun, as Coit says, "in trying to save the South, to save the Union, to save the federal principles of the Union. . . ." On his return to Washington he was outstanding among those who eulogized Calhoun in the Senate. Webster congratulated him warmly on his oration, commending him especially for the comparison "like a summer-dried fountain when our need was the sorest." Smilingly Davis confessed, "That was the only line that was not mine; that was Sir Walter Scott's."

With the death of Calhoun, Senator Davis definitely assumed leadership of the Southern Democrats in the interminable debates on the Compromise. He continued to demand as the first condition of agreement that the line of 36° 30′ should be extended to the Pacific. In regard to the proposal of the stronger law for the return of fugitive slaves, Davis proclaimed it "a dead letter

[2] The author visited St. Philip's churchyard in March, 1954. Above the great block of marble inscribed "Calhoun," a flowering crab apple was in full bloom and birds were singing in its branches. He could agree with Jonathan Daniels, who said so well: "Nowhere on earth is there a sweeter or nobler place for sleep."

in any state when the popular opinion is opposed to such rendition."

For some months it looked as if the Compromise could not pass. President Taylor was not friendly to it, and Northern extremists led by Seward were as opposed as the Southerners. Every time the powerful Seward assailed the Compromise, he gained still more strength with New York voters. But it was in Jefferson Davis that Clay found his chief opponent.

President Taylor's faith in Davis's ability to curb Clay's influence is attested by Charles Anderson, friend of the Taylor family from babyhood, who was a guest at the White House. (Anderson himself confesses "an idolatrous devotion" to Mr. Clay.) "I was repeatedly amazed," he writes, "at Gen Taylor's almost infatuation of admiration and esteem for Col Davis. . . . Upon one occasion I remember he was complaining to me of the treatment of himself by Mr. Clay in the recent canvass. . . . The President, after speaking in simple and earnest admiration—even indeed to my own satisfaction, added, 'But . . . there have been changes lately—Mr. Clay can't rule, in Congress, the Nation, as he used to do. *Now there is Mr. Davis of Mississippi, the Senator.*' [3] I looked at him in some amazement, with this mental question to myself— Is it possible that he would compare Jeff Davis to Henry Clay in the Senate?—Well, I am perfectly sure that he did so estimate him, and in downright earnest simplicity too. Such was his admiration and esteem for Mr. Davis."

Davis believed, as Clay's early biographer later asserted, that "Clay was at heart in favor of the Wilmot Proviso." Once staring at Clay with steady accusation, Davis said bitterly but quietly: "Does he lend his hand to arrest the progress of the flood? No, he comes here representing the Southern interests which are at stake, surrenders the whole claim of the South, and thus gives support to abolitionism which no Northern man could have afforded." But despite the political antagonism between them,

---

[3] The italics are Anderson's. His manuscript is in the possession of Professor John A. Kelly of Haverford College, who inherited it from Zachary Taylor's great-grandson, Trist Wood.

Clay repeatedly testified to the talents and the fearlessness of the Mississippian. "My young friend," he habitually addressed him, and always with respect.

Again when Davis had been unusually critical of some subtle twist in Clay's reasoning, the old Kentuckian began: "My young friend from Mississippi—" He broke off, and then went on in a voice tremulous with emotion, "I trust he will permit me to call him my friend, for between us there is a tie, the nature of which we both well understand." He paused again, and for a moment his eyes filled with tears. Davis knew he referred to his cherished friend, Henry Clay, Jr., who had fallen at Buena Vista not far from his side. When Clay had first met Davis after his return from Mexico, the father had told him, "My poor boy usually occupied about one-half of his letters home in praising you." Though Clay seems to have felt a sincere attachment to his son's friend, he could never win him, for Davis mistrusted his political wiles.

While Davis could not approve of Clay the politician, he could reciprocate his friendly feelings as a man. Some hours later when Davis secured the floor, he apologized for the sharpness of his criticism. "I did not," he said, "intend to arraign in an offensive sense the consistency of my friend from Kentucky, as I am permitted to call him. I not only accepted the appellation when he applied it to me, I accepted it gratefully and I felt the remarks which came from him in a suppressed voice more deeply than I can express. Between us there is a tie of old memories, an association running back to boyhood days, near and dear, and consecrated so that death alone can sever it. It is one which he well knows and I can never forget."

But Davis saw clearly that Clay's proposal for a stronger law concerning the return of fugitive slaves to their legal owners meant virtually nothing; for already the Northern press was crammed with appeals to refuse to obey the existing Federal laws in such cases. They had been put in to appease the border states which were mainly the ones from which slaves were assisted to escape; they had small relation to Mississippi and the lower South.

Davis demanded only the continued protection for slave property, which the Constitution clearly had given. "Less than that equal protection the South can never take, unless its people are willing to become an inferior class, a degraded caste." And he never relented in insisting that the North give the South "equal rights in the new lands acquired from Mexico."

Once in private talk, after Webster had been denounced in New England as a traitor for favoring the Compromise, Clay, with all his beguiling charm, said to Davis: "Come, my young friend; why don't you join us in these measures of pacification? Let us together rally Congress and the people to their support and they will assure us at least thirty years of peace." Davis regarded him coldly. "I cannot consent," he said, "to transfer to posterity a question which is ours, when it is evident that sectional inequality, which will be greater then than now, will render hopeless any justice."

When Frederika Bremer, who had now come to survey the Washington scene, saw Jefferson Davis in the Senate at this time, she described him to her sister in Sweden as "the inflammable Mississippi, that is to say, a young man of handsome person and inflammable temperament who talks violently for 'Southern Rights.'"

Varina was quite eager to meet this foreign authoress whose simple novels of Swedish home life had captivated the world. Though her husband had gone out in society even less than was his custom in the busy months following Calhoun's death, Varina persuaded him to accept an invitation to Mrs. Seaton's high tea on July 2 in honor of Miss Bremer. Varina was excited at the thought of greeting one of her favorite authors in the flesh. Jefferson confessed that he had read little of Miss Bremer and could recall nothing except some ugly girl's embarrassment over her long nose. Since the heroine was homely, he laughingly said, he had small interest in her.

Varina had little idea of what to expect in the celebrity whom Hawthorne had described as "the funniest little fairy person whom one could imagine," adding that she was "worthy of being the maiden aunt of the whole human race." When she was presented on Mrs. Seaton's spacious back veranda, Varina was amazed at the reality. Miss Bremer was tiny, with a long red nose just like her heroine Petraca. "Her complexion was rosy red; her small eyes, the palest blue." The extraordinary outfit she wore was as ornate as she herself was plain. Her gown was a lace cape reaching from neck to feet and lined with purple silk. On her little head sat a huge cap of frilly white lace, dotted with innumerable butterfly bows of purple ribbon. But her manner was disarmingly natural and debonaire; and the expansive kindliness of her heart transcended her odd appearance.

The gentlemen were somewhat put off by the spinster's eccentric quaintness and almost unintelligible English; so immediately after tea Davis with the others strolled down into the back garden for cigars, while Varina sat on the moonlit gallery with the ladies in an admiring circle about the lioness. Daniel Webster arrived late from a stag dinner party to join his wife. When he was presented to little Miss Bremer, the mighty Senator stood before her in the full magnitude of his white linen evening attire and said invitingly in a voice loud enough to be heard down the corridors of the Senate, "Madame, you have toiling millions; we have boundless area." Miss Bremer looked up at him with profound deference and replied sweetly, "Yes, very mooch." For once the great man was nonplused and could go no further. Fortuitously Davis came up and took him off to join the gentlemen for a smoke. When Varina, who had had no opportunity to chat alone with Miss Bremer, got home that night she confessed to Jeff that never again would she long "to look with the naked eye" upon her favorite writers.

Like other congressional and diplomatic couples, the Davises would sometimes appear at the White House Saturday afternoon parties. During Taylor's regime a part of the executive mansion was then open to the public; and on the lawn, where a military band furnished music, the President would stroll about informally among the guests. On rare occasions, when she was feeling strong enough, Margaret, his wife, would accompany him. But Betty Bliss was always in charming evidence at these Saturday receptions. At the last one the President gave, Frederika Bremer attended, and found the young Mrs. Bliss "at twenty-six, unspeakably agreeable and lovely, with a quiet, refined manner."

A few days later, a bulletin of July 5 announced that the President was indisposed. It was rumored that something he had eaten had disagreed with him after he had stood bareheaded for two hours in the broiling sun listening to windy Fourth of July orations delivered by Senator Henry Foote of Mississippi and others. A combination of fresh cherries and iced milk was reported to have caused the disturbance, called cholera morbus by some, and by others, acute gastroenteritis. Jefferson Davis suspected that psychological complications had aggravated the condition. The President was gravely disturbed about the state of the Union; its problems depressed his heart, for he could see no solution. Since May, he had been unwontedly tired, and Davis knew that for all his seeming robustness he was susceptible to intestinal disorders.

At this critical time Davis had more than personal reasons to be deeply concerned about his father-in-law's illness, for though the President possessed no great talent for statesmanship, he was esteemed by both sides for the purity of his character and the reasonableness of his thinking. Davis believed that if anyone could keep the country from splitting asunder, it was Zachary Taylor.

On July 7, Davis was relieved to find that the President had rallied and was considerably better. But on the ninth, in the midst of a dull proslavery speech by Senator Butler of South Carolina, several persons with grim countenances entered the Senate. One spoke in an ominous whisper to Daniel Webster, who rose and, with an apologetic gesture, begged to interrupt Butler because of grave news. A deathlike stillness gripped the chamber as Webster remained speechless for some moments. Then in a voice full of emotion he announced: "I have a sorrowful message to deliver.

A great misfortune threatens the nation. The President of the United States, General Taylor, is dying, and may not survive the day." The dismayed Senate straightway adjourned.

Jefferson Davis went direct to the White House, where he found Ann Wood, the eldest daughter, and her physician husband, together with the Joseph Taylors. Betty was quite overcome with grief; Mrs. Taylor could "not stand or sit without support." Through the afternoon and into the evening the President lay dying, vomiting now and again, but completely conscious. At ten o'clock that night, as he began sinking fast, his wife and daughters, with the three sons-in-law, Wood, Davis, and Bliss, were gathered close about the bedside. Just before he lost consciousness, Zachary Taylor begged his wife, whom he had loved with passionate devotion, not to grieve or weep. "I have endeavored," he said, "to discharge all my official duties faithfully—and I trust in God's mercy. I regret nothing, but I am sorry to leave my dear ones and friends." A little after half-past ten, Davis saw the old soldier, whose life had been so strangely interbound with his own, take his last breath.

The capital was plunged in grief. So was the nation. As Horace Greeley's *Tribune* said, "Taylor endeared himself to the people to a degree few public men attain." Thomas Hart Benton, the leonine old Senator from Missouri, later wrote much as Davis now felt: "His death was a public calamity. No man could have been more devoted to the Union, or more opposed to the slavery agitation; and his position as a Southern man . . . would have given him a power in the settlement of those questions which no President without these qualifications could have possessed."

At the funeral service in the East Room on July 13, Jefferson Davis was seated to the left of the bier with Dr. Wood, Colonel Bliss, the grandsons, and Joseph Taylor. Webster and Clay, who were pallbearers, sat not far away. In the procession that followed the casket to the Congressional Burying Ground, two things must have stirred Davis with bitter and poignant memories. One was the climax to the army's role in the obsequies: vainglorious, obese Winfield Scott, mounted and wearing a "towering plume of yellow feathers." The other was Old Whitey, America's most famous living horse, stepping proudly to the booming of the cannon, while inverted spurs swung on the empty saddle.

Except for Scott, perhaps the only man who could regard the passing of Zachary Taylor with some gratification was Henry Clay. Francis Preston Blair wrote that he seemed "very happy." Without a tinge of sorrow, Clay recorded in his journal: "I think the event will favor the passage of the Compromise Bill."

At Taylor's sudden death the odds for Clay's measure were changed. Millard Fillmore, now President, was strongly under Clay's influence. He put pro-Compromise men in his cabinet and gave his personal support to the measure. With the death of "Old Rough and Ready," who was a kind of national balance wheel, the opposing forces went to work with new energy.

For almost three years after Taylor's demise Davis was to have no intimate contact with the White House. The very evening following the funeral, Mrs. Taylor, who could not bear the sorrowful associations, moved to the home of William Meredith, Secretary of the Treasury, and left shortly for Baltimore to stay with the Woods. Taylor's widow was not content to let his body remain in Washington. She thought he belonged to Kentucky, where he had spent his boyhood and found his bride. So in October, Colonel Bliss accompanied the casket by train over the mountains and by boat down the Ohio to Louisville. There, in the family cemetery in the Jefferson County earth he loved, Zachary Taylor found his final resting place,[4] not far from the spot where his daughter Sarah Knox had pledged her troth to Jefferson Davis.

[4] Two years later Mrs. Taylor passed away in Pascagoula, Mississippi, and was buried beside her husband in Kentucky.

# CHAPTER XV

# BITTER DEFEAT AND HAPPY INTERLUDE

AT A CONVENTION of Southern political leaders at Nashville in midsummer 1850, the Resistance Movement proved far less strong than had been anticipated. The foremost "fire-eaters," Robert Barnwell Rhett of South Carolina and William Yancey of Alabama, who claimed to interpret the sinister writing on the wall, contended that the South's best move would be to secede immediately if Clay's bill passed. But they could not rally the convention to their side. Chief Justice Sharkey of Mississippi, chairman of the convention, sprinkled cool water on every suggestion of radical action. Nothing positive resulted. Rhett and Yancey lost face. And Rhett, who had been given Calhoun's chair in the Senate, soon found the situation in Washington so unpalatable that he resigned and sought solace in his South Carolina plantation.

Secession was never desired by Jefferson Davis. "If I have a superstition which governs my mind and holds it captive," he had said in Congress on June 27, 1850, "it is a superstitious reverence for the Union." Davis ever drew a sharp distinction between nullification and secession. As long as a state remained in the Union he could not countenance any violation of federal law constitutionally adopted. On the other hand he repeatedly maintained with forceful conviction that Mississippi or Massachusetts or any other sovereign state had the *right* to withdraw from the Federal Union.

# BITTER DEFEAT AND HAPPY INTERLUDE

Until congressional adjournment in the fall, Davis was an active and frequent speaker in the Senate. All his suspicions about the inefficacy of a strengthened fugitive slave law were being confirmed. Public opinion in the North was vociferously against it. The Northern states virtually nullified the old laws; for their citizens would storm jails, rescue captured slaves, and rush them to Canada. Davis was convinced that certain Northern Congressmen had voted for the law not because they wanted fugitive property restored to legal owners, but merely to augment the antislavery agitation for personal political profit.

In the end the Compromise forces proved the stronger; many Southern Congressmen went over to their side. Though the bill as a whole was defeated, by the end of September, 1850, broken into pieces, it became the law of the land. Several of the most prominent Southern Democrats, among them Jefferson Davis, put themselves on record in the *Congressional Globe* as protesting the passage of Clay's measures.

At the adjournment of Congress, Davis returned to Mississippi not only disappointed but deeply disturbed about the South's future. The critical year of 1850, with its almost continuous dispute and excitement, had been a hard one for him. In the end the South had really got nothing from the war with Mexico, while the North's dominant position had been strengthened. Two of his best and most powerful friends, Calhoun and Taylor, had died of the strain. Davis was glad to lose himself for a while in the problems and pleasures of the plantation.

But first he had to clarify his position on four questions of great moment in 1850, as he had been asked to do by the Woodville *Republican*. His answers published in the Mississippi *Free Trader* made his stand clear.

"I. If any have, falsely and against the evidence before them, attempted to fix on me the charge of wishing to dissolve the Union, under existing circumstances, I am sure your information and intelligence has enabled you to detect the shallow fraud. II. If any have represented me as seeking to establish a Southern

Confederacy . . . my whole life, and every sentiment I have ever uttered . . . give them the lie. III. If any have supposed, gratuitously (they could not otherwise), that my efforts in the Senate were directed to the secession of Mississippi from the Union, their hearts must have been insensible to the obligations of honour and good faith which I feel are imposed upon me by the position of an accredited agent from Mississippi to the Federal Government.

"Your fourth question, therefore, is the only one which I feel you could have addressed to me, as your Representative, for any other kind of purpose, than to give me an opportunity thus summarily to dispose of baseless slanders."

To that fourth question, as to whether he was in favor of resistance to the recent acts of Congress, Davis replied that the South should stand firmly upon her ancient constitutional rights and should be prepared "to go out of the Union, with the Constitution, rather than abandon the Constitution, to remain in an Union."

Mississippi approved his opinions, and, on the next to the last day of 1850, elected him to the Senate for a full term of six years.

In the midst of absorbing state duties, he never ceased to be mindful of personal obligations or to do thoughtful things for members of his large family. To Varina's parents he would send barrels of potatoes and jars of sausage, along with gifts from his wife like pillow slips, a comfortable, socks for her father, a dress for her mother. On a trip to Washington in early April, 1851, Jefferson stopped in New Orleans to see his mother-in-law, who was living in the suburbs in very poor circumstances. Her amiable husband was descending from failure to failure. "Hope, hope—" Mrs. Howell said in quiet resignation—"I live upon hope." While it hurt him to see her humiliation and her heroic courage, the sight of Jeff cheered her. "My dear son, as dear to me as any child I have," she could say sincerely. They talked intimately of Varina, and on April 7 she wrote her daughter: "Jeff says your health is better than he ever saw it. He thinks you *now* the finest woman he knows. You cannot know how gratified he felt—the manner he said it was feeling and full of pride and affection."

On April 3, Jefferson had sent a gift along with a tender letter to his eldest sister, Anna Smith, who had been like a mother to him when he was a baby and at whose home Sarah Knox had died. The gift was a cameo brooch which he had had made especially for her.

My dear sister:

I send you a cameo likeness [1] and hope then to make my peace with you for the failure to present you on a former occasion with a daguerreotype. It is set in a breast-pin that it may be brought very near to you, and that in this manner I may have renewed the happy days of childhood where my sweet sister held me in her arms. During this summer I expect to visit you. In the meantime accept my love and present me affectionately to all of our family. Your brother,

Jeff

He did visit Mrs. Smith later in the year, under circumstances not conceived of in the spring, for a drastic upset ensued in his political career. In Mississippi, General John A. Quitman was the Democrats' anti-Compromise or Resistance candidate for governor. He proclaimed himself for nullification, a doctrine to which Jefferson Davis never subscribed. Dreading the consequences of radical action, many Mississippi Democrats, under the influence of turncoat Senator Foote, joined with the Whigs to create what was called the Union party. A political strategist and a keen judge of public opinion, the fiery Foote was a master at party manipulation. Resigning his senatorship, he became the rival candidate for governor, with the endorsement of the Whig leaders Clay and Webster. The preservation of the Union was made the issue. Foote began a bold, abusive campaign against Quitman, who suffered from an arrest by the United States Government for some

---

[1] The cameo was inherited by Mrs. Smith's daughter, Mrs. Lucy J. Boyle, and left to Varina Ann Davis. The letter is in the New York Public Library.

support he had given López in the abortive Cuban revolution. Quitman was no match in debate or harangue for Foote, who held him up to ridicule. A canvass on the question of holding a state convention to pass on the Compromise of 1850 was defeated by a majority of 7,500 in favor of the Compromise. Obviously this vote meant the defeat of Quitman, who was forced to withdraw from the race.

In the face of such a majority, there was only one Democrat who might defeat the Unionist candidate. In the crisis Senator Davis was appealed to. Davis had contempt for Henry Foote and regarded him as thoroughly unprincipled in his methods as in his opportune political switches. He could not bear to see the little opportunist triumphing over the Democratic party he had deserted. Although he had served only six months of his six-year term in the Senate, Davis sacrificed his prized seat and allowed himself to be named the Democratic candidate on a strict constructionist view of the Constitution.

Despite the numerical tally against the Democrats, Davis had reason to believe that he would win. For on November 30, 1850, the legislature of Mississippi had published resolutions, signed by the governor, the president of the senate, and the speaker of the house, censuring Foote's conduct as United States Senator, while commending that of all the other national representatives. The last paragraph of the resolutions read as follows:

"*Be it further resolved*, That the course of the Hon. Jefferson Davis, as Senator, and Hons A. G. Brown, Wm. McWillie, W. S. Featherston, and Jacob Thompson, as Representatives in Congress from this State in their firm and consistent support, and able advocacy of the rights and honor of Mississippi and the South, in all the questions before Congress at its late session involved in the slave controversy, is approved; that the course of the Hon. Henry S. Foote on all these questions is not approved; and this Legislature does not consider the interests of the State of Mississippi committed to this charge safe in his keeping."

But smart Foote had shrewdly judged the temper of the masses, and fate played into his hand, for when the time came for Davis to present his case to the people, he was incapacitated.

Back at Brierfield in the heat of September, 1851, Jefferson Davis came down with malaria. The fever brought on an acute inflammation of his left eye. Ulceration of the cornea seemed imminent.[2] For weeks, unable to bear rays of light in either eye, he slept in a darkened room by day and arose only after sundown. In semidarkness, to take his mind off the agony, Varina would read aloud from books of large print.

In the meantime Foote was stumping the state and sneering at "General Davis." "Where *is* General Davis?" he would shout, and pause for effect. "I challenged him to meet me face to face before the people of Mississippi. Where is he now? I do not know where he is *now*, but I do know where he was in Washington during the late Compromise debates: in the same truckle-bed with Seward and Chase and Hale, the abolitionists! . . . While Clay and Webster, with my humble assistance, were standing shoulder to shoulder for the Union, General Davis and the Northern radicals were hobnobbing to break it up."

Less than three weeks before the November election, emaciated and extremely weak, wearing goggle spectacles and with the bad eye bandaged, Jefferson left Brierfield to assist in his own canvass. It was too late to cover much territory by carriage or horseback. Foote's intensive and extensive campaign had been as unscrupulous as it was noisy, according to Mrs. Davis. In the eastern counties, which her husband could not reach, Foote's cohorts circulated a rumor of Davis's death, with the result that many of his admirers in outlying precincts did not bother to ride to the polling centers.

The election resulted in Davis's defeat by 999 votes. Because he had so greatly reduced the majority of 7,500, friends chose to regard the narrow margin as a personal triumph. But Davis himself suffered keen humiliation, for he had stated that he would

---

[2] Eventually he did lose the sight of the left eye.

consider the election as a vote of confidence from the people of Mississippi. His bitterest enemy in the state and the nation had been the victor. The shrill-tongued Foote crowed blatantly.

In responding to the urgent call of his party, Jefferson Davis had done himself out of more than five years' unexpired term as Senator. On the surface it seemed that he had made a costly error and seriously damaged his political career, though it was generally conceded that if he had been physically able to campaign for six weeks instead of three he would have won. However, there were enriching compensations in the plantation life, and Davis determined to turn his bitter defeat into a kind of blessing.

Settled comfortably in the quiet of Brierfield, Davis recovered his health, eschewed political affairs, and waited for the proper time to show Foote in his true colors. Foote had returned to Washington on December 1 and temporarily resumed his seat in the Senate, "where he strutted as the vanquisher of Jefferson Davis." He even attacked the absent Davis on charges of conspiracy to disrupt the Union and was severely reprimanded by several Senators who reminded him that Davis was not there to defend himself. At the same time Foote loudly supported the cause of Kossuth, the Hungarian patriot, who was urging intervention on behalf of his oppressed country. "Those who are not for freedom are for slavery!" Foote yelled. Southern Senators, who regarded Kossuth's visit as a trick of the Abolitionists to indulge in a new form of antislavery propaganda, now began to accuse Foote of being an Abolitionist. By the time Foote became governor of Mississippi on January 8, 1852, the Democratic bolters were thinking they had made a bad bargain. On that same day, the Democratic state convention met at Jackson, and "Get rid of Foote" became the campaign slogan.

As a delegate from Warren County, Jefferson Davis attended, quiet, assured, with all his dignity and health. He heard Foote scream, "I defy and denounce the Secession Democratic party. . . . Die they must and die they will! Their putrid political carcasses shall yet lie about the state in heaps, like piles of chickens in the street that have died of the gapes."

Davis appealed to the Democrats for unity; begged them to reconcile their personal feelings for the good of the country. Then he attacked Foote, "the changeling by nature, the changeling by choice," and linked his name alliteratively with "fraud and falsehood." In reference to disunion and secession he reiterated they were the last resort. "The assertion of a right," he said, "was no evidence of an intention to use it." Calling Foote a demagogue, Davis claimed he was "as full of intrigue and selfishness as he was destitute of truth and principle."

Davis had never really excoriated anyone before in public. Virtually the whole Democratic party of Mississippi backed him again. From Representative A. G. Brown in Washington, he got the capital's impression of his attack on Foote. In a letter of March 1, Brown wrote: "The Universal opinion is that the little dog deserved all he got, but it is equally as universal that no more credit could be obtained in thrashing him than in kicking a polecat. People here regard the prospect of Foote's return to the Senate with such horror as children feel when told that ghosts of the dead are coming back. If there is a single senator who would be glad to see the little creature back I do not know who it is." [3]

Early in 1852, the new house for Varina, which had been years in the planning, was at last completed. It was not huge like Hurricane or elaborate like the mansions of Natchez. But it was dignified and appealing. White and spreading, it had a pleasing symmetry with balancing wings, each bearing its separate veranda. Twelve Doric columns supported the roof of the façade. Designed particularly for Southern comfort, the windows and outer doors extended from the floor almost to the high ceilings. Numerous chimneys punctuated the roof, for there were open

---

[3] Foote found the governor's chair full of tacks. In December, 1853, when the legislature defeated him for the Senate, he resigned in a fury, shook the Mississippi dust from his boots, and moved to California.

fireplaces in every room, and white marble mantels in the parlors and dining room. Wherever Varina made her home, she had the reputation of providing for the comfort of her family and guests.

During the last stages of construction, while Jefferson was absent on business, Varina stayed in the older cottage and personally supervised the work. At the last minute she made changes in the construction of the kitchen, for which she was reprimanded by Joseph, who wanted to spare his brother the extra expense. But she let Joseph know emphatically that she intended to have the kitchen, her special province, according to her heart's desire.[4]

Jefferson tried never to take sides in the contentions between his young wife and his aging brother. But the submerged jealousy between them troubled him; for in personal relationships he was more strictly peace-loving than either Joseph or Varina. However, each knew better than to criticize the other to Jeff. The practical Varina had something special to resent, for Joseph had not actually deeded the property to his brother, who had been cultivating the land for more than fifteen years. The idealistic Jeff had complete confidence in his brother's good faith and good intentions, and, as it turned out after the war, it was fortunate that the property had not been recorded in the name of the man who became President of the Confederacy.

When they were settled in new Brierfield House, Varina ran the household with smooth efficiency. Unlike her spendthrift father, she was an economical manager, and with her keen sense of values, she could always make an excellent appearance on small outlay. The respite from political activities Jefferson acknowledged as a soothing balm. The defeat may have had a salubrious effect on his ego, for heretofore almost everything had been handed him on the proverbial silver tray, however much he deserved the honors. At any rate he had time now to take stock of himself and to let the springs fill.

[4] According to one story, Joseph wanted two kitchens in the house, one for the Bradfords, who he insisted should occupy half of the house. This is the 1874 testimony of David Lanmaster, connected with a firm of contractors who had built a ginhouse on Brierfield.

In a figurative and literal sense Jefferson began again to cultivate his garden. He knew the ineffable quality of relaxation that comes from digging in the earth. With Varina at his side he planted roses and flowering shrubs, and set out live-oak seedlings. The unpredictable slow pageant of river traffic which flowed along the very border of their front garden was diverting by day and by night. Beyond the cultivated fields and orchards were the romantic dark bayous, which they never ceased to find fascinating with the changing patterns of white cranes and blue herons. The shooting of wild fowl and game in season was excellent. The couple rode horseback daily, and sometimes on forest roads they would race each other on mounts almost exactly matched in speed. When they rode slowly they could distinguish the different odors, perennial and seasonal: the moss, wild crab apple, plum blossom, sassafras, cedar, sage.

The Negroes, with their infectious sense of fun, their original use of language, and their uninhibited expressions of affection, were a constant source of pleasure to the master of Brierfield. Everywhere he rode about the plantation his people were eager to greet him. Riding through the quarters, he would lean down from his horse to shake the hand of some venerable, retired cotton picker. Pickaninnies vied with each other to take Marse Jeff's horse when he returned home. There was not so much difficulty in getting the Negroes to work when the master was on the premises, for they took delight in hearing his praise.

Jefferson attempted to make adjustments in the losses inherent in absenteeism. His invaluable and beloved James Pemberton was dead, and no white overseer ever proved as able as he. The qualities which an overseer should possess, according to Varina, were "divine patience and ceaseless vigilance and industry, utter self-abnegation and an inflexible will." James Pemberton had seemingly been endowed with these attributes, together with a Negro's native shrewdness in judgment of character and classification of men. White overseers complained that they could not make the Davis Negroes work without punishment, because they were spoiled. Not under any circumstances would Jefferson Davis allow his slaves to be whipped; and if told anything derogatory against one of them, he would invariably say, "I will ask him about it," and let the Negro speak in his own defense. He insisted his people be kept healthy and happy, even if smaller crops were produced.

Varina was not altogether without sympathy for the overseers' complaint, for she learned that Negroes were adept at malingering; and, not being as indulgent as her husband, if a slave was reported ill, she would sally forth to the quarters with a large jar of quinine powder in one hand and a quart bottle of castor oil in the other.[5] It amused Jefferson to note that the mere sight of his young wife's unpalatable but efficacious remedies would often revive the ailing one, and he would light out for the fields, sometimes with a sidelong grin.

With the new year Jefferson's contentment was the more complete because after almost seven years of marriage Varina was expecting her first baby in July. On May 5, 1852, Payne and Harrison, in New Orleans, sent him a bill for eleven and a half yards of bird's-eye diaper, $9.08.

In this year of 1852, when Jefferson was savoring the seductions of plantation life, Harriet Beecher Stowe published a novel called *Uncle Tom's Cabin* which created an immediate sensation. Within the first year of publication 300,000 copies were sold. The novel was more or less a fictionalized Abolitionist tract, full of harrowing details of brutality and sadism, calculated to make the blood boil with indignation. The hero was a kindly black man, the very soul of gentle Christian virtues, whose counterpart could certainly be found on numerous plantations. The villain was a Northern-born white overseer named Simon Legree. Throughout the book the Negro in general was idealized and his wretchedness in the South greatly exaggerated. Although Mrs. Stowe herself had visited on a highly respectable Southern plantation and knew

---

[5] Varina's grandson, Jefferson Hayes-Davis, gave the author this picture of his grandmother, as she gave it to him in her New York apartment when he was a Princeton undergraduate just after the turn of the century.

true facts, for source material she relied chiefly on an Abolitionist book, *Slavery As It Is, the Testimony of a Thousand Witnesses,* published in New York back in 1839 and widely circulated by the American Anti-Slavery Society. It was rumored that she kept this tract, as some pious ladies did the Holy Bible, in her sewing basket by day and under her pillow when she slept.

Though in her own way Mrs. Stowe pointed out some of the useful and kindly aspects of slavery, the South was shocked at what it considered a libel of the grossest misrepresentations. Southerners generally regarded the novel as the epitome of the insults the North continually hurled. Jefferson Davis deplored its publication, for its melodramatic stirring of already troubled waters. And he must have contrasted the horrors depicted by the New Englander with the well-being and harmony of his people at Brierfield.

Enjoying his quiet comforts, far from the scene of action, he took only a moderate interest in the Democratic national convention which met at Baltimore on June 1, 1852. But his excitement bounded when he learned that his friend Franklin Pierce was the surprise nominee for President. When on the fourth day it had seemed that no leading candidate—Cass, Buchanan, Douglas—could ever satisfy all factions, Virginia had suggested the New Hampshire lawyer. Pierce's name met with such instantaneous enthusiasm that on the 49th ballot he was chosen almost unanimously.

Jefferson soon learned some special details of the nomination through a letter which George H. Gordon, who attended the convention, wrote to their mutual friend Carnot Posey.

"Tried every way in our power to get Jeff Davis then for vice President—but could not succeed in doing so. But I assure you he holds a very high stand in the Union both as a man of talents and of high toned integrity and worth. If he lives he will I have no doubt be President some day. He possesses that kind of reputation which will continue to grow and increase. Wm. R.

King of Alabama [6] was nominated on the second ballot by nearly a unanimous vote. After the nominations the Convention proceeded to adopt the democratic platform which I think covers fully every thing the South could desire—and with all it is strictly correct in my humble opinion. It passed with but one single individual voice against it in the vast assembly. . . . The nominations are received with universal joy everywhere then. All admit that Pierce is as sound on all Southern questions as any Southern man. Some of the abolition papers have commenced on him already saying he is fully committed to the South. . . ."

What effect, if any, the prophecy that he would be President some day had on Jefferson Davis we cannot know. But since Pierce was cordial to the South and held the same constitutional principles as he himself, Davis could not have been more pleased with the nomination. Throughout his career Pierce had advocated the constitutional right of African slavery. The Compromise of 1850 was no longer an issue; it was accepted as a finality by all parties, and was to play no role whatever in the presidential campaign.

In the midst of Jefferson's pleasure over Pierce's nomination, Varina gave birth on July 30 to a boy child. At last Brierfield possessed an heir. He was named Samuel Emory after Jefferson's father. There was unbounded jubilation on Davis Bend. The Negroes had a holiday, and every one came to the house bringing some gift, a chicken or a new-laid egg, a bouquet, some fruit or yellow yams. Each one made a simple speech of thanks for the birth of the little master who would "take care of we and be good to we." In turn the Negro women kissed the newborn infant, a demonstration that would be considered outrageously unsanitary in these sterilized days, but in 1852 was lovingly looked upon as a harmless, natural expression of affection.

Davis felt impelled to do some campaigning on behalf of his old friend Pierce. His ardor was further stimulated because

[6] William Rufus King had been pro-Compromise, and certainly no anti-Compromise man could have been nominated in 1852.

Winfield Scott was the Whig candidate. The thought of "Old Fuss and Feathers" in the White House was utterly repellent to Davis. In October he made several campaign speeches in Mississippi and Louisiana. He "scrutinized" Scott's military conduct "for the purpose of ascertaining what talent he possessed for the cares and offices of state." He charged Scott with being "quarrelsome," a man "unable to get along with his subordinates" and one who "showed a disposition to appropriate the lion's share of the laurels which the army had won."

In praising Pierce he had access to all the facts of Pierce's career in a biography of the Democratic nominee just published in September. The author was Nathaniel Hawthorne, already famous for his recent *Twice Told Tales* and *The Scarlet Letter*. Hawthorne had become one of Pierce's most intimate friends at Bowdoin College, which the writer had entered in 1821 as a strange, shy young man with a beautiful face and a faraway air. The perceptive Hawthorne knew Pierce thoroughly. Because his admiration for his character was unbounded, Hawthorne produced a campaign biography, though it was entirely out of his line and hurried writing always caused him distress.

Pierce's early career had been remarkably promising. Five years after his graduation from Bowdoin College in 1824, where Longfellow as well as Hawthorne had been a college mate, he became a member of the New Hampshire legislature. At twenty-nine he entered the United States House of Representatives. At thirty-three he became the youngest member of the Senate. On volunteering for the war with Mexico, he was appointed a brigadier general and fought under Scott. After the war he had quietly engaged in private law practice.

Davis knew, as Hawthorne avowed and gave evidence, that Pierce had done "everything in his power, actively and passively, to avoid the perilous and burdensome honor of the candidacy." But he had accepted the nomination, "which had made him perceptibly sad for days, as the will of Divine Providence." In his letter of acceptance, Pierce spoke hopefully of the fact that his name was first presented by Virginia, regarding it as an omen "pointing to the overthrow of sectional jealousies, and looking to the permanent life and vigor of the Union."

It was in the spirit of that optimistic phrase that Jefferson Davis campaigned for his friend. When Pierce defeated Scott by an enormous electoral majority, 254 to 42, and carried all but four states, Davis was perhaps never more elated in his life. Not in thirty-two years had there been such a victory. With the Democrats in power again, he believed the South might get justice and the Union be saved.

# CHAPTER XVI

## SECRETARY OF WAR

NEAR mid-December, 1852, a letter arrived from the President-elect that threatened to break the peace of Brierfield, though it was gratifying to Jefferson Davis's heart.

>Concord N. H.
>Dec. 7, 1852

My dear General:

As the news of your illness filled with anxiety your friends in this northern region, so the intelligence of your convalescence has brought relief and joy. We earnestly hope that before now you have regained your elasticity and vigor. You will not be surprised, that, under all the circumstances of our early acquaintance and present positions respectively, I much desire to see you, and to avail myself in connection with the duties and responsibilities before me of your advice. Can you gratify such desire without too great inconvenience? I wish to converse with you of the South and particularly of the formation of my Cabinet. I am not permitted to know, that you would accept a place in it if desired and I do not ask an interview on the ground, that I have arrived at any fixed conclusion upon the subject, but, because I wish to talk with you, as a friend, in relation to matters of high concernment not only to myself, but to you and every man, who had at heart the best interest of our party and the country, and because I feel an assurance that whether our views coincide or not, from you I shall receive a friend's free and useful suggestions. . . .

Your friend,<br>Frank: Pierce

When Varina saw Pierce's letter, she feared what her husband's reaction would be to this implied offer of a Cabinet post. The Davises had never been so happy in their eight years of marriage as now; Varina was beginning to feel that her Jeff belonged to her rather than to the nation. With the new baby and the pleasant new house she could not bear the thought of Washington excitements and tribulations. She entreated her husband to consider deeply before he relinquished the peace of Brierfield. In his resumption of farming Jefferson had become so contented that he was loath to disrupt the harmonies of his daily living to re-enter the discords of public affairs. As he wrote in his old age: "Happy in the peaceful pursuits of a planter, busily engaged in cares for servants, in the improvement of my land, in building, the time passed pleasantly away until my retirement was interrupted by an invitation to take a place in the cabinet of Mr. Pierce. . . . Although warmly attached to Mr. Pierce personally, and entertaining the highest estimate of his character and political principles, private and personal reasons led me to decline the offer."

Varina became ill; her condition was aggravated, if not caused, by worry. On December 27 Davis wrote to his friend, giving a negative answer. A few days later the Pierces were involved in a tragedy that grieved Davis deeply.

January 6, the President-elect, with his wife and eleven-year-old son, Bennie, boarded the morning train at Andover, Massachusetts, to return to their home in Concord, New Hampshire, to make final preparations for Washington. They had proceeded no more than a mile when there was "a snap and a jar" and then a violent shock as their coach tumbled down a steep embankment and rolled over in the field below. In the wreckage the injured father found his little boy with his cap still on, unconscious, as he thought. When he removed the cap he saw that the skull was horribly crushed. Bennie was already dead, the only person killed outright in the accident.

The sight of the mangled boy, whom they both had worshiped since the death of Frank, their other son, at the age of four, shattered them both. Jane Pierce went virtually out of her mind with grief. Pierce had reconciled himself to the arduous responsibility of his great office, which he had not wanted, by the belief that the position would help Bennie in his career. Now he looked upon the presidency with something like horror. His wife turned the screw of his anguish by deciding God had taken the lad so that he would not interfere with his father's duties in the White House. The son's life, she insisted, had been the price exacted for the exalted honor.

While numbed by grief and distracted by his wife's suffering —"the misfortune had paralyzed her energy entirely"—Pierce was compelled to select a Cabinet, and he hardly knew where to turn. Five days after Bennie's funeral he wrote again to Jefferson Davis at Brierfield for help.

Andover, Mass.<br>Jany. 12, 1853

My dear General,

I presume you may already have heard of the terrible catastrophe upon the rail road, which took from us our only child, a fine boy 11 years old. I am recovering rapidly from my bodily injuries, and Mrs. Pierce is more composed today, tho' very feeble and crushed to the earth by the fearful bereavement. Your letter of the 27' ulto: came last night, and the ever present consciousness of my own desolate condition made me tremble for you, my friend, when I read what you say of the health of your family. You say nothing of your own health, but I infer that it is fully restored and thank God for it. I have no right to put you to trouble and could not think of asking you to leave your home unless you can do so without anxiety. I may go to Washington by the middle of Feby: but my movements are involved in uncertainty. How I shall be able to summon my manhood and gather up my energies for the duties before me it is hard for me to see. Politicians seem to have troubled themselves very much on account of the friendly relations supposed to exist between us. It is pleasant to believe that they are unselfish and uncalculating relations not likely to be disturbed. I have no heart to write now, and intend to do no more than to acknowledge with thanks your noble spirited letter, and to assure you how truly

I am yr friend
Frank: Pierce

The moving letter made Davis long to go to Pierce at once. But family problems and personal business matters, as well as illness, demanded his presence at Brierfield. Intuitively Varina had little confidence in Jefferson's ability to decline whatever his friend asked of him if they met face to face.

Soon Pierce wrote again, begging Davis, if he would not accept a Cabinet position, at least to come to his inauguration and give him some advice. Though torn by indecision and his wife's entreaties, Jefferson felt he could not refuse his friend's plea. And by the end of January the health of the family must have been restored, for a letter [1] of that date from Varina's father, W. B. Howell, mailed at New Orleans begins: "Dear Jefferson, Varina's letter gave me assurance of your general good health with that of the family at large." It is a long, wearisome letter full of complaints of things gone wrong, requests for Jefferson to secure evidence from court records on this and that, recitals of various business schemes, vague hopes of employment, and hints for cash advances. After lengthy explanations about trust deeds and worthless notes and speculations in property ("I live in hopes yet to be

[1] This letter in the New York Historical Society is highly revealing of the ineffectual character of Davis's father-in-law and also of the sort of family problems with which the forbearing, long-suffering Davis was confronted throughout most of his life.

satisfied with the purchase and to make all right with you"), he concludes:

> I was hailed on Saturday by General Harrison direct from Washington—spoke of his belief you would be offered a Cabinet position—thought it would be War Department. . . .
> Give my best love to V— Kiss our little Sam and my love to Becket [2] charging him to study hard & make a man of himself while the opportunity last—
> as ever your friend et cetera<br>W. B. Howell.

The portfolio of war was something Jefferson Davis would like to have; he was peculiarly equipped for such a position. But he was still reluctant to leave the plantation.

Finally the President-elect telegraphed Davis urgently requesting his presence in Washington, saying he himself would arrive about February 20. When Pierce arrived in the capital, he found that all the men he wanted for Cabinet ministers—Marcy, Cushing, Guthrie, Dobbin, Campbell, and McClelland—had arrived except Jefferson Davis, who was then summoned a second time by telegraph. Davis wired that he would come to the inauguration. By the night of February 22, all Cabinet plans were settled as far as Pierce was concerned, except for Davis's acceptance of the secretaryship of war. The matter had to be inconclusive. But the press got the list of names and printed them correctly, though not with complete accuracy as to the positions the men would occupy. At noon of March 4, when Pierce entered the official carriage to drive to the Capitol, Davis, whose train had been delayed, had not arrived.

Except for the shadow of Pierce's personal tragedy, which still hung about him at the inauguration, the regime of the fourteenth president began auspiciously on March 4, 1853. At forty-nine Franklin Pierce was the youngest chief executive to have reached

---

[2] The Davises still had Becket Howell with them and were happy to relieve the father of the lad's support.

that high estate. He yet had a "slender, boyish figure," and he was considered the best-looking President the United States had ever had. His handsome face was very pale, according to Mrs. Roger Pryor, who witnessed the proceedings, and "his countenance wore an expression of weary sadness." He had not been able to shake off his grief. In the ceremonies Pierce broke two precedents: he did not "swear" allegiance, but "affirmed" it; then, with the snow falling on his bare head, he removed his overcoat and "declaimed" his inaugural address, without manuscript or even a scrap of note. Mrs. Pryor speaks of "the indescribable charm for which he was conspicuous." The source of that charm and of his captivating voice and manner, she affirms, lay "in genuine kindness of heart." It was that good heart above all else that drew Jefferson Davis to him. And Mrs. Davis, who later came to love Pierce devotedly, declared "all sympathies seemed united in him."

In his address, Pierce hinted strongly at the desirability of acquiring Cuba; he pledged himself to defend the Monroe Doctrine; and he pleaded for the preservation of the nation. On these subjects Jefferson Davis was in firm agreement, though he was not on hand to hear the words.

When the President awoke in the White House the next morning (Saturday), he was relieved that the Senate was adjourned until Monday, for Davis had still not arrived and he feared that "persuading him to accept a ministerial post would be difficult." The big event of the crowded day was Davis's arrival. "It took all Pierce's persuasive powers," says his biographer Nichols, "to prevail upon him to enter the cabinet." Davis was as sincerely reluctant as Pierce had been to disrupt the quiet tenor of private life. To exchange peaceful plantation rhythms for official duties in Washington was not easy. But Pierce convinced him he really had need of him in the Cabinet, as well as needing his counsel and sympathetic friendship. Caleb Cushing and others persuaded Davis that there was absolutely no one else of his caliber to head the War Department. Recommendations for the Cabinet positions had to go to Congress on Monday. If Davis had come a few days before the inauguration, he might have declined. Now he accepted his fate.

On Monday, March 7, Pierce sent his Cabinet nominations to the Senate. Ex-Governor Marcy of New York was named Secretary of State and Caleb Cushing of Massachusetts Attorney General. From the first, these two, together with Jefferson Davis as Secretary of War, were recognized as the strong men of a Cabinet more distinguished for harmony than for brilliance. That the Cabinet remained intact without a single change during the entire term was a rare thing in American annals and due in large measure to Pierce's own amiable and conciliatory nature.

Davis's closest friend in the group was Cushing, a man of more than considerable learning. A youthful prodigy, he had been graduated from Harvard at seventeen and could still recite the *Iliad* from memory. Attractive both in manner and address, Cushing could converse with many foreign diplomats in their own tongue. The gentleman from Massachusetts and the Mississippian took pleasure in each other's company, in discussing literature as well as practical affairs of state. They were almost matched in energy. Cushing, however, possessed such mental agility that he was sometimes considered intellectually unreliable. In his friendship with Davis, "the consistent man," Cushing found what he needed—"the influence of a more single and stable judgment to keep him from divergency."

Marcy, the New Yorker, whom Davis did not altogether like because of his earlier attitude toward Zachary Taylor during the Mexican War, was the only dyed-in-the-wool politician among the four Northern and three Southern Cabinet members. But Marcy was very able, and he was noted for his philosophic calm. Big and burly, with beetling brows, he could on occasion be quite formidable. He had one established rule for living that Davis would have done well to follow. Every morning before Marcy reached his office, his secretary would cull the papers and the correspondence. All the complimentary things said about him were placed uppermost in the center of his desk. Adverse newspaper mention or criticism in unsolicited letters went into the wastebasket or at the bottom of the pile. So Marcy would laughingly say he could not but think well of himself and stay serene, since he read virtually nothing but compliments. Not so Jefferson Davis, who was so sensitive to criticism that he would spend untold time in trying to explain himself or his actions to some critic. This compulsion to set detractors right was undoubtedly a flaw in his nature, for in later life it consumed much vital energy.

At forty-five Jefferson Davis was now at his prime and enjoying excellent health. Uncommonly well-equipped for his Cabinet position by his West Point schooling, his frontier service, and his noteworthy feats in the Mexican conflict, he became one of the outstanding war secretaries in United States history. Dodd considers only Calhoun his equal in that position. "And," he says unequivocally, "the new Secretary was the foremost Southern Democrat," adding that "morally there was hardly a more commanding character in the country." Carl Schurz, the German-born publicist, recorded an impression of Davis at this period that has been much quoted:

"I had in my imagination formed a high idea of what a grand personage the War Minister of this great republic must be. I was not disappointed. His slender, tall and erect figure, his spare face, keen eyes and fine forehead, not broad but high and well shaped, presented the well-known strong American type. There was in his bearing a dignity which seemed entirely natural and unaffected, that kind of dignity which does not invite familiar approach but will not render one uneasy by lofty assumptions. . . .

"A few years later I heard him deliver a speech in the Senate, and again I was struck by the dignity of his bearing, the grace of his diction, and the rare charm of his voice—things which greatly distinguished him from many of his colleagues."

In mid-July Davis accompanied the President, with two other Cabinet ministers, Cushing and Guthrie, on a kind of whirlwind royal progress through some Northern states. In four consecutive days Davis made five speeches: at Wilmington, Delaware; at Trenton and Princeton, New Jersey; and at Philadelphia and New

York. In all of them he reflected a glowing optimism, and everywhere he was greeted with resounding applause.

In the first speech, at Wilmington on July 15, Davis paid tribute to the new President. "He is a glorious patriot. He knows no North, no South, no East, no West; and will abide by all the obligations and enforce all the rights and privileges of the Constitution. With such a President as this, I feel that a view lies before us of prosperity and peace in the future, of expanding commerce, of increasing fraternity at home, until that miserable faction [the rabid abolitionists] which has disturbed the peace of the Union shall be crushed beneath the heel of patriotism, which long since should have ground it unto dust."

At Trenton he spoke of Pierce's declaration of political faith as "a harbinger of peace, because it assures us that those great principles upon which our government rests are to be the guiding star of the administration—that there is to be a strict construction of all the powers of the federal government, which leaves to the people in each locality the power to administer their own affairs." And he warned the crowd against "the danger of consolidation, centralization, and the re-establishment of despotism upon the liberties of the people."

In industrial Pennsylvania, Davis's Philadelphia speech attracted enthusiastic attention because of allusions to the Pacific railway project, in which he had been the leading spirit when Senator. Pennsylvania, he said, was "tied by lightning to every portion of the United States and with her coal and iron she was about to establish commercial relations with the shores of the Pacific." Though a Democratic administration was constitutionally opposed to internal improvements at national cost, Davis justified the project of joining East and West by a transcontinental railway on the grounds of national defense and national unity. The outbursts of cheering which greeted his remarks lasted many minutes. When his hearers were still again, he reminded them that he himself belonged to the strict construction school "which never turned to the right nor to the left to serve any purpose of expediency." At the conclusion of his speech, James Buchanan, the Pennsylvania statesman, responded with approbation for the Secretary of War's sentiments on a Pacific railway and emphasized President Pierce's concurrence in Davis's views on this great national project.

On July 19, at a banquet tendered the presidential party at the Crystal Palace in New York, where a world scientific convention was being held, Davis took an international theme, and advocated free trade. "I most cordially rejoice," he said, "in the manifestations around me, which seem to indicate an increase in the fraternity of nations. . . . The earth was given to man for his domination. It has been perverted from the great object of the Creator by vice and ignorance among men, who, warring one with another have forced nations to employ their industry upon things not adapted to their condition, climate, and soil, at the sacrifice . . . the loss of time and productiveness." Here he was interrupted by such a burst of applause that he had to make a long pause before he reached the vital and basic point in his message. "Throw open the ports of all the world," he urged. "Let the civilized nations represented here declare we are one brotherhood and that whatever can be produced more cheaply in another country shall be brought thence. Thus we will have a bond of peace that will not be in the power of unwise rulers ever to break."

"Free trade," he stressed, "was a cornerstone in the foundation of our political temple. It was placed there by the hands of sages, philosophers, and patriot soldiers. . . . I believe that the sun of truth has risen upon the globe, and will, in time, lead us to see . . . that it is for the comfort, peace and salvation of the civilized earth, that there shall be untrammelled, unbroken free trade."

The foreign delegates in New York were greatly impressed by the Secretary of War's remarks. When Davis returned to Washington his political stature had taken on new inches.

In 1853 Jefferson Davis was thus a voice crying out for a more even distribution of the good things of life as a way to keep the world at peace. But that call was to go unheeded, since oncoming

Republican administrations, dominated by Northern industrialists and financiers, erected higher and tougher tariff walls.

While Davis was traveling with the President and receiving plaudits in eastern cities, Mrs. Davis was making a series of visits to family members in Mississippi, showing off the infant Samuel. The Secretary of War had been making his temporary home with his niece Mary Bradford, who had accompanied them to Washington on that perilous winter journey in 1845, when he first went to Congress. After the early death of her first husband, Robert Sayre, Mary had married a Philadelphian, Richard Brodhead, who was now a member of Congress (and later Senator). The Brodheads had taken a furnished house. On May 7 Mary had written to "Aunt Varina"—as she called her in fun, since they were the same age—urging her to come on to Washington. In the letter she had given her many feminine hints. "Uncle Jeff looks very well of his neuralgia. He has been working too hard going without lunch— Aunt Varina, why don't you pack up & come? I am crazy for you to be here. About the house there is no trouble. Gory is a pearl beyond price— Bring blankets. Moths would get into them at Brierfield— If you live here all the time for four years you will need to bring a great many things. All that we use here—table linen, silver, glass—belong to the house— But think what a help you will have in Yankee me!" As a postscript she added: "Jewelry is worn much more than it has been in many years— Green is the fashion color in New York—"

But Varina, who planned to bring some of her relatives along, preferred to wait until Jefferson had found a furnished house large enough for his family. Late in the summer of 1853 she left for Washington by way of New Orleans and Mobile. With her went her sister Margaret, her ten-year-old brother Becket, and the baby and nurse. She stayed but one night in either city, for a virulent yellow fever raged along the Gulf Coast. In New Orleans Betty Bliss's admirable husband lay critically ill with the disease, and by the time Mrs. Davis reached the capital the Colonel was dead.

In Washington Varina found Jefferson completely happy and at the top of his form as Secretary of War. He seemed to be the President's most intimate friend in the capital. And she quickly discerned that her Jeff was already becoming, as Eckenrode says, "the dominant personality of the administration." She felt that they had four happy years ahead of them, far happier than she had dared anticipate.

Jefferson Davis, who was not a very demonstrative man, was quite carried away by his little boy Samuel, a precocious child with "a lovely personality." He was such a friendly tot, possessing a confiding, caressing hand, which stole so naturally and securely into the hand of a grown-up. The boy took at once to his father, who did not try to disguise the inordinate pride a man who has reached his prime feels in a first-born son. When the Secretary came home from the War Office, his first thought was always the boy. The little fellow would wait patiently by the front door for his father's expected return to get the first kiss.

Jefferson was greatly pleased too, with his young wife's maturing. Now, at twenty-seven, Varina had distinction, with poise and grace, as well as a striking brunette beauty. Some of her intellectual inferiors, however, were not drawn to her, for it was not easy for her to be completely polite to bores and pretentious persons. Varina abominated the striving, the meanness, the pettiness encountered in social intercourse. In her huge dark eyes would sometimes appear a steady level expression that disconcerted both stuffed shirts and affected ladies. But she earnestly tried to school herself in self-control by watching her husband, who was really more charitable with human weaknesses than she, and inherently more democratic.

While the Secretary of War was becoming better acquainted with his son and heir, Mrs. Davis was meeting Cabinet ministers and getting to know the Pierces. The First Lady was still so overwhelmed with her tragedy that she had not yet been able to appear at a public function. Her depression was intensified by some obscure ailment, which was probably of neurotic origin, though some believe she was tubercular. Jane Pierce was a tiny woman, bearing a striking resemblance to Elizabeth Barrett Browning, then at the height of her fame. A daughter of President Appleton of Bowdoin, she was intelligent and well-read. Though gentle and retiring, she had a keen sense of the ridiculous, which Mrs. Davis thought saved her from utter melancholia. Mrs. Pierce felt surprisingly at ease with the warm young Southern woman and welcomed her friendship, for Varina was extremely sensitive to the needs of the ailing or the sorrowing, as she was ever a tower of strength to her own family in hours of affliction.

Sometimes Varina would find the President's lady alone in an upstairs sitting room, writing pathetic little notes in pencil to the dead Bennie, apologizing for never having revealed to him the full depth of her devotion. Or she would discover her bent over the blinding fine print of Thornton's *Family Prayers*, which always was in evidence on a center table in the oval library. With her perceptive understanding and sprightly talk, Varina did much to brighten the cold and cheerless atmosphere of the White House. And one day she was inspired to bring little Samuel with her. Jane Pierce took an immediate fancy to the responsive child. She began taking him on her afternoon drives, her sole diversion. Often Varina rode with them, but when she was engaged, Mrs. Pierce would send for the boy to be brought to her. After an hour's drive with the prattling, but well-behaved child, the President's lady would return home in a happier frame of mind.

Although Mrs. Pierce's companion, Mrs. Abby Means, a widow of her uncle, acted as hostess at the public receptions, there was little entertainment at the White House. So the social prestige of the administration, as Dr. Nichols says, rested chiefly on Mrs. Davis, Mrs. Marcy, and the daughters of Secretary Guthrie, who, like Cushing and Dobbin, was a widower.

But despite the lack of festivity in the White House, Washington social life was quite gay during the Pierce regime. Southerners controlled society as they had done since the inaugural of George Washington. A correspondent for the New York *Herald* wrote: "With their natural graces and their inherited taste and ability in social affairs, it was natural that the reins should fall to them. They represented a clique of aristocracy."

The Davises, who had no fortune, entertained well, in the best of taste, but without extravagance. They were interested in persons of merit and achievement; their dinner lists were largely composed of persons of distinction and old friends. Any friend or acquaintance who turned up in Washington was sure to receive a warm welcome from the Secretary of War. Except for formal dinners, Varina rarely knew an hour ahead how many would sit down at table. Often she would receive by messenger a penciled note like the following from the hospitable Jefferson:

Dear Wife

Geo E. Payne formerly of New Orleans will dine with us today— I told him to come round at 4½ o'clock say. Dinner at 5— *Family dinner*

Your Husband

Monday

Varina was little more attracted by the glitter of fashion than was her husband. She frankly preferred the conversation of men. While she made herself very charming, she was never in any sense a coquette and she could be scornful of the seductive airs and vivacious graces of some of her Southern sisters. Jefferson was the ideal host, easy, gracious. He was a good listener as well as an excellent raconteur, with a gift for both humor and wit. Though more of a man's man, with his handsome face and charm of manner he made a captivating dinner partner.

The Davises did everything possible to make life happier for the President. With them Franklin Pierce was entirely informal and dropped in just after breakfast, or any time. At the Davises he could relax, shake off the gloom of the White House, talk and laugh, as he had when Jefferson first knew him in the 1830's. To one of Pierce's temperament, the natural warmth of Southern hospitality was an immense relief and pleasure. Because the whisperers were saying that the South was running the administration, Pierce would sometimes call after dark on foot, unattended, to see the Davises or the Clement Clays of Alabama. He really liked the exercise of walking, as much as he did riding his black horse, named "Union."

One day the President and his Cabinet went in a body to Fortress Monroe, Virginia, to review the troops. The wives of the Cabinet ministers and of several Congressmen were invited, among them Mrs. Clay, who described the occasion. The Secretary of War was in charge of the maneuvers; his "spirited figure, superb horsemanship, and war-like bearing" attracted great admiration. "At night," wrote Virginia Clay, "the Fort and the waters beyond were lit up by a pyrotechnic display of great gorgeousness, and enthusiasm rose to its highest when, amid the booming of cannon and the plaudits of happy people, an especially ingenious devise blazed across the night sky the names of Franklin Pierce and Jefferson Davis!"

# CHAPTER XVII

## ACCOMPLISHMENTS IN THE WAR OFFICE

EXCEPT for Winfield Scott, the army personnel had from the first looked upon Davis as "their own man"; they had urged his appointment "with hearty, unanimous approval," as the American consul in Panama wrote him. In the fall of 1852, Davis's friend Robert E. Lee had been appointed superintendent of the Military Academy at West Point. The two exchanged ideas for bettering the physical plant as well as the quality of instruction. In the operations of his department, Davis infused an energy hitherto unknown. He advocated a system to improve the discipline and efficiency of officers, and raised their salaries to something more nearly commensurate with amounts men of their caliber would be receiving in civil positions. He recommended improvements in the recruiting service and other reforms calculated to curtail desertions, which had risen to 16 per cent since the war with Mexico. He got the pay of privates increased and their living conditions bettered. Fascinated by the theory of warfare, though ever deploring its practice, Davis renovated and rejuvenated the whole army. He strengthened the medical corps. He introduced the light infantry system of tactics, rifled muskets, and the Minié-ball. He advised Congress that the manufacture of arms for the United States Army should be under the control of the War Department for economy, uniformity, and efficiency rather than in the hands of corporations represented by lobbyists. He therefore urged the establishment of a new national armory on the West Coast. Advocating a thorough exploration of western frontiers, he set in motion meteorological and geological surveys. He was vigorous in directing pending projects of harbor and river improvements. Davis's capacity for work amazed his wife and all but undid his aides. Sometimes he would forget to eat luncheon entirely, and in times of special pressure might arrive home for dinner as late as 2 A.M.

During the first year of Davis's administration the enlargement of the Capitol was actively prosecuted under his direction. His engineering department had charge of bringing an adequate supply of fresh water to Washington from the Potomac Falls through a nine-foot conduit. The great stone aqueduct with a span of 220 feet, known as John Cabin, was constructed largely under Davis's direction.[1]

Perhaps greater than his army reforms or improvements in the capital were the series of "reconnaissances of routes" for projected railways to the Pacific Coast which Jefferson Davis launched. One of the young officers whom he first appointed to the exploratory task was a talented and personable young captain named George B. McClellan. On the Secretary of War's recommendation, plans were eventually drawn for four strategic roads. As McElroy says, the skill shown in the surveys "is evidenced by the fact that they correspond approximately, to the lines actually built, with governmental assistance: the Northern Pacific, Union Pacific, Kansas Pacific, and Southern Pacific." In his *History of the War Department,* Ingersoll calls this work of Davis "the most valuable contribution to commerce and to science that had ever been prepared from actual surveys and reconnaissances in the field."

Within ten weeks of Pierce's inauguration, a new trouble with Mexico had arisen—a disagreement as to some 45,000 square miles

[1] When the aqueduct was finished in 1861, in the beginning of Lincoln's regime, Jefferson Davis's name as Secretary of War was inscribed under that of Franklin Pierce as President. The next year, on the order of Secretary of Interior Caleb Smith, the name of Davis was chiseled away. In 1909, after great pressure had been brought on him by club women, President Theodore Roosevelt ordered the name reinscribed on the tablet.

just south of Gila River, flowing through New Mexico and Arizona, and about which the Treaty of Guadalupe Hidalgo was not clear. Mexico threatened to renew the war rather than surrender her claim. President Pierce called in Jefferson Davis for counsel. The Secretary of War promptly recommended James Gadsden of Charleston as just the man to send as minister to Mexico to treat and to purchase the disputed territory. Gadsden had seen distinguished service in the War of 1812 as aide-de-camp to Andrew Jackson and he was now president of the South Carolina Railroad.

Davis, always progressively railroad-minded, saw the opportunity of constructing a transcontinental railway that could avoid the expense and the difficult engineering problems of crossing the Rockies. The land lying south of the Gila possessed plains ideal for rail laying. Such a railroad (along the present route of the Southern Pacific) Davis knew could provide transportation between the newly discovered gold fields of California and the supply centers of the East, and at the same time permit the South "to partake of advantages of the China trade" and thus better Southern economy in its losing competition with the North. His agents in Mexico informed him that Santa Anna was in sore need of cash to keep his soldiers loyal, and Davis believed the disputed territory could be bought at a bargain price. Pierce appointed Gadsden minister, and worked with Davis and Marcy on instructions.

For six months Gadsden negotiated, first with Santa Anna and then with a commission appointed by the Mexican president. Finally on December 30, 1853, the Gadsden Purchase treaty was signed. For the meager sum of $15,000,000 (later reduced to $10,000,000) the administration not only squashed the threat of a new war, but secured for the United States full title to 45,535 square miles of territory. Though the extent of the real estate was somewhat disappointing to the War Secretary, it was the best Gadsden could wangle.

President Pierce sent the treaty to the Senate on February 10,

1854. He had some difficulty in getting it ratified, partly because of a fight over what became known as the Kansas-Nebraska Bill, which vied for the center of congressional attention. But after five months of debate, at the end of June, 1854, the treaty was ratified and possession of the land changed hands. There was still Northern resentment to the deal. The New York *Herald* scoffed that the treaty was negotiated for the benefit of Jefferson Davis, who, it claimed, held property near the new boundaries that would greatly increase in value when the new railroad was built.

Although some Northern historians have taken the attitude that the Gadsden Purchase "did not mean very much to us anyway,"[2] its subsequent advantages and benefits inordinately surpassed Jefferson Davis's expectations. That tract of land, near the center of which lies Tucson, Arizona, has proved of considerable economic profit to the United States. It has already returned over $4,000,000,000 in revenue from its mining properties alone. The payroll of the Southern Pacific Railroad in Tucson today annually exceeds the price paid to Mexico. The Gadsden Purchase territory, which cost the United States about thirty-four cents an acre, has a mighty wealth potential, not only in minerals, but in tourist trade, livestock, and agriculture. Again Jefferson Davis had evinced a foresight which proved of value to succeeding generations.

On the morning of Sunday, January 22, 1854, Jefferson Davis made a simple decision for which he has been severely criticized. A few days after the completed treaty with Mexico arrived in Washington, while the Secretary was at home taking his ease and enjoying fatherly play with his little boy Samuel, Stephen A. Douglas was announced. The dynamic Senator from Illinois had come on an urgent mission. He wanted the Secretary of War to intercede with the President to grant him an immediate interview even though the day was Sunday; Pierce had always fol-

---

[2] The Gadsden Purchase is not even mentioned in Bassett's *A Short History of the United States* (885 small-type pages). In fact, Bassett devotes only half a sentence to Jefferson Davis's services as Pierce's Secretary of War (page 486).

lowed a firm rule never to discuss business of any kind on the Sabbath.

Davis had not been at all intimate with Douglas, though he had known him since that December day of 1847 when they had both entered the Senate for the first time. Called "the shrewd Yankee" in Illinois, Senator Douglas had, in fact, been born in Vermont. Almost five years younger than Davis, his political advancement had been incredibly swift. The very year he began to practice law in Illinois he was made state attorney general at the remarkable age of twenty-one. At thirty-four he had reached the United States Senate, following four years in the House. His marriages were highly advantageous. First he had married a Southern heiress to plantations with more than a hundred slaves. For his second wife he captured one of the capital's famous beauties, Adèle Cutts, a great-niece of Dolly Madison.

Like Davis, Douglas had advocated the annexation of Texas, supported the war with Mexico, favored the acquisition of Cuba, and in general followed the Democratic party's policies. Still Davis regarded him as a political opportunist, daring and facile. The man was unusually plausible, as well as brilliant, but Davis, like almost everybody else in Washington, believed he was ruled by a consuming desire to be President. So he was on his guard this Sunday when his favor was begged by the short, powerfully built man, with the massive jaw and the great beautiful eyes that veiled his ruthlessness. But the "Little Giant," as the press designated him, had shrewdly brought along as backers perhaps the three most powerful Southern Senators: Davis Rice Atchinson of Missouri, and James Maury Mason and R. M. T. Hunter, both of Virginia. This delegation was shortly followed by two of the top Southern Representatives: John C. Breckinridge of Kentucky and Philip Phillips, a brilliant Jewish lawyer from Mobile, Alabama. It was imperative, Douglas explained, to gain the administration's support for his revised Kansas-Nebraska Bill, which was to be presented the very next day in the Senate.

In December of 1853, a bill for the organization as a territory of the vast tract west of Iowa and Missouri known as Nebraska had been submitted to the Senate Committee on Territories, of which Stephen A. Douglas was chairman. An attempt to make Nebraska into a territory had recently been defeated by Southern Congressmen, because the land lay north of 36° 30', which according to the Missouri Compromise made it free soil. While Missourians desired the land west of them as a state, they would not stomach Abolitionist control of it. Senator Atchinson of Missouri, who had declared he would see all the Nebraska land sunk in hell before he would let it become a free soil territory, promised Douglas he would vote to make the land a territory, but only on condition settlers be allowed to decide the slavery question for themselves.

To keep an illusion of balance of power and to concede a principle to the South, Douglas had advocated the creation of two territories—Nebraska and Kansas—the implication being that the southern half, Kansas, would be settled by slaveholders.

On January 4, 1854, Douglas had reported on his territorial measure calculated to win Southern proslavery support. The settlers themselves in the new territory, he proclaimed, should decide whether or not they should have slavery. This was merely a reframing of Cass's "squatter sovereignty," dignified now with the term "popular sovereignty." At the last hour Senator Dixon of Kentucky pressed for an amendment that would definitely repeal the slavery section of the Missouri Compromise. Douglas was forced to accept it, for he believed that this was the only sure way to get Southern sanction. And he also saw a golden opportunity to gain Southern sympathy for his presidential ambitions. He was impelled to get the bill passed, for he was beseiged by constituents to create the territory so that Chicago might conceivably become the starting point of the first projected railroad line to the Pacific. And he himself was intrigued by the opportunities for land speculation. But up to now Douglas had not consulted the President, for his dramatic move was partially designed to win for himself the next Democratic presidential nomination. He knew, however, his bill had no chance in the Senate without administration support. So he had come to the man who had the most influence with Franklin Pierce.

Davis hesitated to ask the President to break his Sabbath rule and he hesitated to disturb sleeping political dogs. Everything was going peacefully with the administration—Pierce's election had been won by a big majority upon the distinct acceptance of the Compromise of 1850 as a finality and the implied commitment not to reopen the slavery question. To Davis, Douglas now represented his revised measure as contemplating merely the assertion of the rights of property, including slavery, within territories. The ultimate admission of Kansas as a slave state, the accompanying Southern Senators declared, was the South's only chance to stem the tide of Northern domination.

Davis reflected that if the North had been willing in 1850 to extend the line of 36° 30' to the Pacific, as he had urged, all this new agitation, as well as all that of Clay's Compromise, would have been avoided. At last, however, he yielded reluctantly to the importunity of Douglas and the Southern legislators and called at the White House. Pierce at length received Douglas, though with noticeable coolness. The Senator made the bill sound very plausible. Finally the President promised his approbation, thereby, as it turned out, ruining his own chance of succeeding himself in office. But he insisted the delegation consult with Secretary of State Marcy and get his sanction before the bill was presented in Congress. Douglas did call at Marcy's house, but happily finding the Secretary was dining out, he made no further effort to reach him.

In the detachment of age, Davis wrote of the incident from Beauvoir in 1886: "The President knew nothing of the measure until it was explained to him in that interview. Then he gave his assent because it was in conformity with his opinion of the constitutional power of Congress, and because the Missouri Compromise was regarded as virtually repealed by the refusal in 1850 to recognize its binding force in the division of recently acquired territory. To this extent, and this *only*, was it an administration measure, and the committees left the President with the ability to say that he concurred in the propriety of the measure."

Though the administration considered the principle of the Kansas-Nebraska Bill correct, both Pierce and Davis had forebodings that mischief might result, which indeed it did. On March 3, 1854, Douglas got his measure accepted by the Senate. On May 30, Pierce made it law by signing it. At the time, he expressed the vain hope that the slavery agitation would now subside forever.

With perspicacious hindsight, some historians believe that this decision of Davis made on the third Sunday of January, 1854, was a climactic event in his life and a most disastrous one. They argue that Douglas, prompted by his personal ambition and under the pretense of conceding a principle to the South, introduced a measure which did perhaps more than anything else to precipitate disunion. Jefferson Davis was gulled, they think, and, worse, instrumental in the gulling of his best friend, the President. Douglas, they affirm, was to show his true colors when in the next administration he led the attack against the conciliatory Buchanan, who struggled to get Kansas into the Union as a slave state.

It is obvious that Douglas did not expect his bill to be of much practical value to the South. He foresaw the western plains occupied by eastern homesteaders who would raise wheat and cattle, and not by cotton-planting slaveowners. To the aroused antislavery contingency, Douglas replied frankly that there was no great cause for alarm, for slavery would not function well in these new acres. He always insisted his bill provided the only practical way to get the territory organized and he himself took full responsibility for it.

Davis may have been deceived and he may have acted unwisely in persuading the President to discuss affairs of state with Douglas. But if he was tricked, so were the ablest Southern Senators, and so were the Representatives who voted for the bill. And if the "Little Giant's" intent was diabolically selfish, he was ultimately hoisted with his own petard. For the passing of the bill aroused slumbering dogs: Abolitionists howled that slavery was to be forced on all states. Douglas was so repudiated and reviled that he declared sardonically he could travel all the way from Boston to Chicago by the light of his own burning effigies. The Kansas-Nebraska Act also turned many Northern Democrats against Pierce and helped bring about the birth of the Republican party. In the end, the South gained nothing more than a concession to principle and a mounting animosity in the North.

In the spring of 1854, despite the first anti-Democratic repercussions from the Douglas bill, everything in Jefferson Davis's personal and professional life was proceeding with remarkable harmony. He had never been happier. Then, little Samuel, the radiant joy of the house, sickened with some undiagnosed disease. For three weeks the father and mother watched the child's decline with anguish. On the last day of June, before he had reached his second birthday, the boy died. The father was crushed and silently inconsolable in his grief; he had come to adore this firstborn son for whose future he had such hopes. This was the first deep sorrow Jefferson Davis had known since the death of his young bride Sarah Knox nineteen years earlier. But this time he could not mourn in secret, for hundreds offered sympathy. Outwardly he accepted the loss like a stoic, for he believed above everything else in firm self-control. But Mrs. Davis wrote that for weeks afterward "he walked half the night, and worked fiercely all day," and a child's crying in the street would cause him acute distress.

The Pierces, who loved the little boy almost as one of their own, could best commune with the parents' sorrow. The last of August, 1854, the President persuaded the Davises to go with him and Jane on a vacation to Capon Springs, Virginia. The summer had been unduly hot, even for Washington; the thermometer often stood at 95° and the nights afforded no relief. In the cool mountain air of Capon Springs, secluded from the hurly-burly, the four enjoyed a revivifying time together.

But the pleasurable respite was short. For on their return to official duties on September 9, Davis found that New England was resenting the President's enforcement of the Fugitive Slave Act as much as the passage of the Kansas-Nebraska Act. Threatening letters arrived at the White House, like this one beginning: "To the chief slave catcher of the United States— You damned infernal scoundrel." The powerful states of New York, Ohio, Indiana, and Pennsylvania also showed signs of grave dissatisfaction with the administration.

Davis was disturbed at the urgency of fanatics who were demanding immediate emancipation. On Independence Day, just two months earlier, while Davis was struggling with his grief over his son's death, William Lloyd Garrison had publicly burned a copy of the Constitution of the United States, denouncing it as "a covenant with death and an agreement with hell."

To the annoyance of some of the intellectual upper-class Abolitionists, this former shoemaker's apprentice, newspaper compositor, and editor of the first American temperance journal, had assumed leadership of the radical antislavery men. Garrison was now definitely in the ascendancy, though in 1829 his denunciation of New England slave traders, who still plied their outlawed profession, had landed him in jail. And in 1835, when mauled by a Boston mob for his railings, he had to be rescued by the police and kept in jail for his own safety. But in 1854 he could burn the Constitution with impunity and consort with his social betters like Wendell Phillips and Thomas H. Higginson and join them in urging dissolution of the Union, as the three of them were to do openly at an antislavery convention held in Worcester, Massachusetts, in January, 1857.

In the fall elections of 1854 the Democrats lost heavily. Although every Northern state but two had voted for Pierce in 1852, the Democrats now carried only two non-Southern states— New Hampshire and California.

Mounting virulence of Northern reaction against Douglas, the foremost Democratic leader in that region, made the South doubt if she could ever get what she regarded as justice. Many Southerners expressed the determination to secede if the Kansas question was finally decided against them. Even a conservative paper like the Richmond *Dispatch* wrote: "If forced to go out of the Union, the South can go with colors flying, with arms in her hands, and with all the honors of war."

The year closed with an acute disappointment for Jefferson Davis and the President in the failure to acquire Cuba, particularly so since an "incident" for the initiation of proceedings had created itself. At the end of February, the *Black Warrior,* a merchant ship that flew the American ensign and traded between Mobile, Havana, and New York, had been seized off the Cuban coast. On the charge that the port rules had been violated, she was unlawfully forced to render up her cargo of $100,000 worth of cotton, and the captain was heavily fined. Public opinion was thoroughly aroused at this latest "insult to the American flag," and especially when the Secretary of State submitted to the President sixteen detailed instances of Spanish contempt for United States' rights in Cuban waters.

Like Davis, Marcy was convinced that a Spanish possession so close to United States shores would be a continual menace to her commerce in the Caribbean. On April 3, he had instructed Pierre Soulé, American minister to Spain, to negotiate the purchase of Cuba. Already Soulé had demanded a heavy indemnity settlement of the *Black Warrior* claims within forty-eight hours. Though Spain's royal family was eager to sell, the angry government did not deign to reply to the minister's peremptory note. In the early fall Soulé was ordered to Paris to meet with the American ministers to France and Britain, John Y. Mason and James Buchanan. On October 18, from a seaside resort town in Belgium, the three diplomats issued the famous Ostend Manifesto. With a remarkable lack of diplomacy and no concealment of motives, the document declared, in effect, that the United States Government would pay a fair price for Cuba if Spain was inclined to sell promptly; if not, the island might be seized without compensation.

The Secretary of State was naturally shocked at such bald frankness and shortly recalled Soulé, chief author of the document. Outside of diplomatic channels, Spain had already settled the claims of the *Black Warrior's* owners. Because the North opposed the purchase of Cuba on the ground that it would become a state with Southern interests, Congress now shortsightedly refused to grant the President funds for the purpose. The best opportunity for acquiring the "Pearl of the Antilles" had been muffed. For another fifty years Cuba remained a Spanish possession. Through no fault of the President or his Cabinet, the administration had failed in one of its important objectives. Davis's long-cherished hope of acquiring Cuba was lost. Almost half a century later it took a costly war under a Republican administration merely to free the island from Spanish rule.

After their return to Washington from the Virginia resort, the Davises moved into Edward Everett's large house of twenty rooms at the corner of F and Fourteenth Streets. Although doors had to be repaired and wallpaper replaced, Varina found it much more convenient for entertaining. Because she was *enceinte* and not feeling well in October, her mother came up from Natchez to stay with her. Mrs. Howell was charmed with Washington and its social life. On October 31, 1854, she wrote her husband her impressions and an account of the family's health.

"No one has been more kind to me than Mr. and Mrs. Pierce. The society here is really delightful. Everybody is well read and well informed. You are well entertained if you only sit still and listen. Talent makes the aristocracy *here*—money has its admirers too—but talent outranks it. Jeff leaves tomorrow for a short trip to West Point by way of relaxation from duty. He will be absent five days. His health is about as usual—he has escaped his usual attacks of fever this fall for the first time since he has been in public life—he looks well though thin— We play backgammon every night late and sometimes too late. Varina's health and spirits are much improved—though she suffers sometimes from toothache—a natural consequence I think of her *situation* [3]—and a cough which her physician says is altogether nervous. When she has the one, the other is entirely relieved."

The Secretary of War went to West Point in early November to visit Robert E. Lee, the superintendent, and to look into the Academy's most pressing needs. Davis was surprised to find that Lee, who was only a year and a half older than he, had "so many gray hairs on his head." He had aged considerably since taking the position in the fall of 1852. "He confessed that the cadets did exceedingly worry him," Davis wrote many years later in the *North American Review*, "and then it was perceptible that his sympathy with young people was rather an impediment than a qualification for the superintendency." Though Lee believed in strict discipline, it was hard on him to dismiss cadets for demerits or for failure to keep up in their studies.

Davis was glad that the son of his friend Henry Clay, Jr., who had died on the battlefield of Buena Vista, had been allowed to resign instead of being dismissed. Lee had had no end of trouble with an unconventional cadet named James McNeil Whistler, nicknamed "Curly," a witty youth, who stood number one in drawing, but who attracted demerits like a magnet and was no more organized to be a soldier than Edgar Allan Poe had been. Whistler's Scotch mother had once made a strong personal plea to the Superintendent not to expel her boy, laying his vagaries of temperament to rheumatism. So Lee had given "Curly" another chance. But later, in a chemistry recitation, when the cadet had defined silicon as a gas, his professor had written him down as hopelessly deficient in chemistry and Whistler's career as a soldier ended soon afterward. His mother, whom he was to immortalize in his most popular painting, had to reconcile herself to her son's becoming an artist.

[3] This letter, which the author discovered in Colorado Springs, definitely establishes the year of the first daughter Margaret's birth as 1855. It is recorded variously in Mrs. Davis's *Memoir*, in church memorial windows, on Mrs. Hayes's tomb. Disliking birth dates, Mrs. Hayes effectively obliterated the year of her own birth in the family Bible and all books where it appeared.

ACCOMPLISHMENTS IN THE WAR OFFICE 273

Lee's own personable nephew Fitzhugh had been one of his problems because of a tendency to night prowling; he had barely escaped expulsion by court-martial. But his son Custis had been a source of joy and parental pride; like his father, he graduated number one in his class.

After his conferences with Superintendent Lee, the Secretary of War got Congress to appropriate $22,000 for the riding hall, and adequate sums for cavalry stables and for the enlargement of the cadets' hospital and officers' quarters. An appropriation for $15,000 was made for a gashouse and the installation of gaslights in the cadet barracks.

The year of 1855 was a happier one for Jefferson Davis than 1854 had been. He concentrated on his job as Secretary of War; there are few references to political questions in his letters of the period. On February 25, Varina gave birth to a daughter, who was christened Margaret Howell and who was to become the new apple of her father's eye. Gloom in the White House began to lift with Jane Pierce's first real public appearance on New Year's Day, 1855, when she received with her husband at what was called a presidential levee. In the glitter of gaslight her black velvet gown and diamonds accentuated her extreme pallor and though she made a gallant effort to be gracious, everyone who saw her was touched with sympathy. While Mrs. Davis had not been able to attend that reception, a new baby did not long interfere with hospitality in the Davis home, and Varina continued to relieve Mrs. Pierce of much semiofficial entertaining.

Despite sectional strife in the press, fresh flare-ups of the slavery question, severe criticism of the administration, and the preponderant Northern majority in the House, Jefferson Davis had little difficulty in getting from Congress what he wanted for his department. The authorized full strength of the army, he pointed out, was only 14,216 and these few troops—the total in service seldom reached 12,000—were expected to protect not only the seacoasts and international borders, but to guard an extensive frontier in the West against 40,000 unfriendly Indian warriors. He asked for four more full regiments, two of cavalry and two of infantry. An act of Congress authorized them on March 3, 1855. That same day the Secretary of War announced the names of the colonel and lieutenant colonel of the new Second Cavalry: Albert Sidney Johnston, his college days' idol, and Robert E. Lee, a soldier in whose abilities his faith was never shaken. It was really a promotion for Lee, who had held only a brevet rank at the Academy. Davis thought service in the field would be a welcome change from the confining halls of West Point, and, besides, he wanted the best men he knew to head the newly created regiments in the West.

On April 2, two days after Lee made his adieus at West Point, the Secretary of War wrote a joint letter addressed to "Major R. Delafield, Major A. Mordecai and Captain George B. McClellan, U.S. Army," informing them they had been selected a commission of three to visit Europe and observe the war between Britain and Russia, which was then at its height in the Crimea. They were to obtain useful information on "the practical working of the changes which have been introduced, of late years, into the military systems of the principal nations of Europe."

Among the manifold subjects to which Davis particularly desired them to direct their attention were:

"The organization of armies and of the departments, for furnishing supplies of all kinds to the troops, especially in field service.

"The fitting up of vessels for transporting men and horses, and the arrangements for embarking and disembarking them. The medical and hospital arrangements, both in permanent hospitals and in the field. . . .

"The composition of trains for siege operations—the kind and quantity of ordnance. . . .

"The composition of bridge trains; kinds of boats, wagons, etc.

"The construction of casemated forts and the effects produced on them, in attacks by land and water.

"The use of camels for transportation, and their adaptation to cold and mountainous countries. . . ."

In returning from Russia, Davis said, the commissioners would have an opportunity to observe the military establishments of Prussia, Austria, France, and England. The lengthy list of subjects and objects they were to study reveals his detailed knowledge of military problems.

Davis also wrote personal letters to the members of the new commission, inviting them to dine with him and to meet the ministers of the various countries they were to visit.

Despite a two-year exchange of numerous acrimonious letters, the aged Winfield Scott, commanding general of the army, came down from New York to the dinner. Scott had caused Davis complicated trouble by remaining in New York and refusing to have army headquarters in the seat of government. From Davis's second month as Secretary of War, the General had been a pricking thorn in his flesh, continually bombarding him with complaining letters. The quarrel had begun in May, 1853, when Davis backed up the accounting officer of the Treasury Department in his rejection of a voucher for the transportation of Scott and a servant at sixteen cents a mile on an unauthorized journey.

At the dinner the obese old General dominated the conversation, as he invariably did. Davis heard him instruct Count de Sartige, the French minister, in the art of cooking terrapin, and then expound to the entire table the proper mode of chasing buffalo on the western plains. *Sotto voce,* the Count expressed sympathy to Mrs. Davis for Scott's labors in having, "according to the necessity of his nature, to teach the whole company at once." Misunderstanding something the young Captain McClellan was saying to the person beside him, Scott shouted across the table to set him right. McClellan blushed furiously, as he was wont to do, and his blushing, Mrs. Davis noted, made him look even younger than he was.

Many persons questioned the choice of so young a soldier as McClellan for so important a mission as that to the Crimea. But Davis's faith in the Captain's powers of observation was justified; in three months McClellan learned enough of the Russian language to read works on military science, and, ironically, he also gained invaluable military knowledge that he was to use against the Confederate forces a few years later. Davis's appreciation of the young Captain, Mrs. Davis says, was an instance of her husband's happy faculty of discerning the merits of young people and by his charm of manner "drawing" them into sympathetic communication with him. "There was," she writes, "a refined assumption of equality and co-intelligence between himself and them, which conciliated them at once."

The Secretary of War had been concerned about military transportation between Texas and the defenseless Pacific coast. In an effort to provide quicker and better transportation than the 120 days the journey took overland, in March, 1851, as senatorial chairman of military affairs, he had recommended an appropriation of $30,000 for the purchase of camels and the hire of Arab drivers. Some of the Senators regarded the proposition as ludicrous, and the appropriation was denied. But Davis did not give up the idea, for, together with Major H. C. Wayne of the Quartermaster's Department, he had made extensive study of various breeds of camels and he was convinced of their adaptability to the arid regions of West Texas, New Mexico, and Arizona. He knew that the camel could carry enormous loads and travel much faster than horses over rough ground. The beast could exist for days without water and required only the poorest forage. President Pierce backed him in his camel experiment, and on March 3, 1855, Congress passed a bill for the purchase of camels for military transport.

Davis gave detailed instructions to his emissaries about their selection and ordered them to prepare a thorough report on the camel's needs, the nature of its likely diseases, and so forth. On February 15, 1856, the ship *Supply*, which the Secretary had sent to bring the stock to America, sailed from Smyrna. The cargo comprised thirty-three camels: nine dromedaries from Egypt, twenty Arabian camels, and four others of different species. All the females that were not already with young were covered by males before departure so that the herd might increase quickly.

On May 10 at the mouth of the Mississippi River the camels were turned over to Major Wayne and transferred to the steamer *Fashion*. On May 14 Wayne unloaded the animals at Powder Point, Texas. Then after a period of rest and acclimatization he began his tests. In September he sent horses and camels to San Antonio for supplies: six camels brought as much as twelve horses could haul in wagons in almost half the time. In November he proved that camels could travel without fatigue muddy roads on which horses could not pull wagons at all, and that they could climb with ease mountain trails where no wagon could go.

Despite all the fun poked at Secretary Davis for his introduction of camels, at the end of 1856 in his annual report, he could declare that the experiment was succeeding.[4]

Beyond Davis's dedication to making his department outstandingly efficient and progressive in major manifestations, he spent much energy on minor problems and quite unimportant persons. Perhaps it might be considered a weakness that his good heart put him at the service of any private who desired an interview. Sometimes desperate persons would call at his home to tell a tale of woe or to make some plea. One morning, before the household was stirring, a frantic, disheveled young woman arrived with two offspring to appeal a court-martial sentence given her soldier husband. Davis dressed, came downstairs, and talked patiently with the poor creature for half an hour and then brought her into the breakfast room, a squalling baby in her arm and a sniffling little boy led by the hand. Before the astonished Mrs. Davis could speak, her husband announced pleasantly that they had company for breakfast. He ordered a chair placed for the mother, and then led the boy up to Varina and said sooth-

---

[4] Secretary of War Floyd, under Buchanan, convinced of the camels' value on the southwest deserts, asked for the purchase of 1,000 additional beasts in his report of December, 1858, but Congress refused his request. Up to 1861 camels were used by army quartermasters. Some were made use of by the Confederate Post Office Department. At the close of the War between the States the Federals advertised them for sale and many were bought by traveling circuses. The extension of the railroad to the Pacific eventually made the camels obsolete.

ingly: "My little man, here is a lady who knows how to comfort crying boys."

After quiet was restored and breakfast eaten, the little ones were entrusted to Varina's care while her husband took the soldier's wife to the President to make her appeal. After a few hours, the woman returned with a note from the Secretary of War, asking that the family be served an early dinner, the children be given a dollar each, and the butler sent with them to the station to pay for their passage home and to put them on the right train.

Sometimes Varina would grow impatient at her husband's indulgence. Once when she expressed her annoyance at his patience with an intrusive half-demented fellow who often called at the house, he replied gently, "It is a dreadful fate to be distraught and friendless." When this particular individual was later committed to an insane asylum, Davis sent him stationery to indulge his compulsion to write lengthy letters to persons in high positions, and he himself charitably answered the man's missives.

Varina felt that Jefferson's tender kindness was sometimes betrayed into misplaced sympathy, as in the case of a beggar woman who sat before the War Department building, season in, season out, knitting stockings. Each day the Secretary had his skeptical messenger take her a coin, and in the winter he asked Varina for a cushion to keep the old woman from catching cold. The sums of money he gave to individual charity cases worried his chief clerk, Colonel Campbell, but not as much as the fact that the Secretary of War grieved over their distresses after they were gone.

Davis believed quite literally that it was more blessed to give than to receive. One morning, just as the family was finishing breakfast, the President himself arrived in gleeful mood to tell them that the first expedition under Commodore Perry to Japan had returned and that the Japanese government had sent bales and boxes of presents: lacquerwork, jars, vases, parasols, jade figurines, rugs, wall hangings. He invited Mrs. Davis to come to the White House and "abstract" some of the exquisite things, since they belonged to no one. Mr. Davis quickly interposed. "In that case, my wife knows they do not belong to her."

"Well, then, General," said Pierce, "I have a present for you—a dog." When Davis asked what he could do with a dog in town, Pierce replied, beaming, "Oh, if it crowds your big house, you can put it in a tea-saucer."

That evening a White House messenger arrived with a diminutive creature in his pocket. It resembled an hour-old puppy, but its head was shaped like a bird's with a blunt beak and popped eyes. It was jet black, except for one band of white around the body. A label about the neck said his name was "Bonin." The Secretary of War accepted the strange, forlorn little dog as his pet, and became its champion and defender against servants, who stumbled over it, and against his wife, who found it a nuisance. When Varina would complain of Bonin, the Secretary would bow with mock politeness and offer to "build a house for myself and my dog."

All the Davis guests had to see the curious new pet who really did find a tea saucer an ample bed. One of the most interested was Professor Henry of the Smithsonian Institution, who was a frequent and favorite guest. Davis enjoyed absorbing learning from this genial scientist, as he did from Louis Agassiz and Professor John le Comte, who sometimes accompanied him. When Surgeon General Totten, whom the Davises admired both as a physician and a friend, was present, everyone was scrupulously careful to respect his strange idiosyncrasy: whenever the name of a person he disliked was mentioned, he unfolded a large handkerchief and sneezed into it spasmodically until something diverted his attention. When Charles O'Conor, the New York lawyer, brought his bride to Washington, the Davises entertained them. It was at this time that Mr. O'Conor conceived the esteem for Mr. Davis that later prompted him to volunteer his services as lawyer in the court trial of 1867.

When the President presented his second annual message, Jefferson Davis was gratified to note a portion of about two hundred words that could be considered the political credo of Franklin Pierce. Whether or not Davis had a direct hand in framing the sentences, he was wholly in accord with the sentiments expressed. And he may have surmised how blessed the United States would be if future chief executives would follow the spirit and letter of Pierce's inspirational political faith:

"Our forefathers of the thirteen united colonies in acquiring their independence and in founding this Republic of the United States of America, have devolved upon us, their descendants, the greatest and the most noble trust ever committed to the hands of man, imposing upon all . . . the most sacred obligations. We have to maintain inviolate the great doctrine of the inherent right of popular self-government . . . to render cheerful obedience to the laws of the land, to unite in enforcing their execution, and to frown indignantly on all combinations to resist them; to harmonize a sincere and ardent devotion to the institutions of religious faith with the most universal religious toleration . . . to carry forward every social improvement to the uttermost limit of human perfectibility, by the free action of mind upon mind, not by the obtrusive intervention of misapplied force . . . to preserve sacred from all touch of usurpation, as the very palladium of our political salvation, the reserved rights and powers of the several States and of the people; to cherish with loyal fealty and devoted affection this Union, as the only sure foundation on which the hopes of civil liberty rest."

Davis devoutly believed in carrying forward social improvements to the limit of human perfectibility by the free action of mind on mind. He never swerved in holding the reserved rights and powers of the several states and of the people as the safeguard and security of America's political salvation. And he cherished the Union with a devoted affection, even after events, which he struggled to prevent, had fractured its unity.

# CHAPTER XVIII

# A "STRENGTH AND SOLACE" TO PRESIDENT PIERCE

—◦◉◦—

DAVIS had watched the Democratic prospects continue to brighten ever since five of the largest Northern states had returned to the party in local elections in October, 1855. He paid scant attention to press speculations that he himself or William Marcy might be the nominee in 1856 if the President declined to stand for a second term, and he was happy when Mr. Pierce finally announced in November his willingness to be a candidate. In all probability Pierce would have been nominated and elected if matters in Kansas Territory had proceeded with reasonable order. But the newly opened land was in turmoil.

Immediately after the passage of the Douglas bill the race to win Kansas commenced. Missourians began moving across the border and a few of the more prosperous ones brought their Negro slaves with them. It was generally presumed that the Territory would ultimately be admitted as a slave state. In the East, however, branches of the Emigrant Aid Society, sponsored by the Abolitionists, kept offices open night and day to facilitate the movement of antislavery pioneers to the Kansas prairie. By March of 1855 the Territory's population numbered 8,500, including 242 slaves. In that same month, Governor Reeder called for the election of a territorial legislature. A proslavery assembly gathered at Shawnee Mission and framed a constitution to suit its special purposes. The Pierce administration recognized the legality of this legislature, but the free-soilers would not. They held their own constitutional convention at Topeka and drew up a document prohibiting slaves in the Territory.

At the beginning of 1856, Kansas possessed two rival governments, both created by fraudulent voting. Several governors sent in sequence from Washington had brief and turbulent regimes. With no settled authority, the region was soon plagued with marauding adventurers, who made things unpleasant for honest homesteaders. The town of Lawrence was raided by some pro-Southerners, who burned a hotel and wrecked two Abolitionist newspaper offices. Though Jefferson Davis had feared trouble might result from the passage of the Kansas-Nebraska Act, neither he nor perhaps anyone else had envisioned rioting and bloodshed.

In the spring of 1856, Davis first heard of an obscure man who was to play a strangely sinister role in United States history. Among the Kansas settlers was a fanatical, Connecticut-born Abolitionist named John Brown, whose grim life had been a series of failures, due mainly to his own fractious and violent disposition. He had moved from state to state and successively had failed at sheep ranching, tanning, land speculating, and a variety of other ventures. His terrible personal discontent and his avowed hatred of slavery were grist to the antislavery mill. With his five sons, Brown had come as a bankrupt into Kansas, ostensibly to establish a homestead but really to agitate against supporters of slavery. Living at Osawatomie, near the town of Lawrence, he had got himself appointed an officer in the emergency forces recruited to defend Lawrence, and then began muttering that "the time for action has come."

Though, according to Oswald Garrison Villard, there had been no previous killings in the neighborhood, and only five definite proslavery offenses, John Brown with four of his boys and two other rowdies made a raid on the cabins of two Southern families, the Doyles and the Wilkinsons, living on Pottawatomie Creek. On the night of May 24, 1856, Brown and his gang massacred five men without warning or mercy. With diabolical fury they slashed them to pieces with knives. They then hauled the mutilated bodies to the public road and left them there as a ghastly warning to all who professed proslavery sentiments.

The slaughtered men did not themselves own any slaves, and at no time were there more than three hundred Negroes in the whole Territory. Even Brown's biographer, Villard, condemns his crime without equivocation: "It must ever remain a complete indictment of his judgment and wisdom; a proof that . . . he had neither true respect for laws or human life."

The killers were never brought to trial, and Northern papers played down the atrocity. In retaliation proslavery men in Kansas attacked the Brown partisans and destroyed the Osawatomie settlement. Men on both sides were killed, including one of the Brown boys. Having launched his feud, John Brown himself slipped out of Kansas. In the East he was sheltered and feted by Abolitionist zealots, who were eventually to supply him with arms to launch a black insurrection in Virginia.

Sectional violence in 1856 was not confined to the plains of Kansas; it occurred on the floor of the United States Senate. On May 19, a few days before the Brown massacre, Charles Sumner of Massachusetts delivered a vituperative speech, which came to be entitled "The Crime against Kansas." He sprayed particular venom on South Carolina and made a scurrilous personal attack on that state's courtly old Senator Butler, who was absent. When Sumner finished his mordant denunciation, a painful and ominous silence pervaded the chamber. Then Michigan's General Cass rose to express his shocked disapproval. He deplored the speech as the "most un-American and unpatriotic that ever grated on the ears of the members of this high body." It was a noble rebuke. But it made no impression on the supercilious Sumner, who proudly rated his speech "the most thorough phillipic ever uttered in a legislative body."

Sumner's self-satisfaction was rudely shattered when he received a public thrashing. Representative Preston Brooks, a nephew of Butler, felt impelled to avenge the insult to his state and to his uncle. After adjournment two days later, Brooks entered the hall with a stout cane. Walking down to Sumner's seat, he faced him, reproached him, and then specifically explained his special mission: he had come to chastise him for slandering his relative. Then he proceeded to beat Sumner over the head and shoulders with the cane. Brooks said later he had not meant to injure him, only to whip him and disgrace him. Before other Senators could intervene, he belabored Sumner severely, broke the cane in two and finished with the butt. Sumner was injured sufficiently, or pretended to be, as some investigators insist, to remain out of his Senate chair for three years.

The Northern papers went quite wild over Sumner's whipping, particularly those that had tried to suppress the true facts of the John Brown massacre and to make light of his offense.

While many Southerners publicly expressed deep regret at Brooks's attack, others were frankly gleeful at the dramatic defense of the South's honor. Some of Sumner's own Northern colleagues took a modicum of pleasure in his discomfiture, for they regarded him as a vain, pedantic, self-loving poseur. Davis realized that Brooks had done the proslavery forces considerable harm, and his rashness may have gained followers for the new Republican party. As it turned out, by inadvertently stretching the stature of Charles Sumner to martyrdom, Brooks really strengthened the man's later position in the Senate, where he did not fail to take abundant revenge both during the war and the reconstruction.

In June, 1856, the Republican party held its first national nominating convention at Philadelphia. Though the party was scarcely two years old, it had become so strong that a majority of the Northern state governments were already under its control. The name "Republican" had been adopted at a Jackson, Michigan, mass meeting on July 6, 1854. The new party was established on "the sole issue of the non-extension of slavery." It was this tenet that now combined many Free-Soilers and Know-Nothings, radical Whigs and some Democrats together with avowed Abolitionists. "Bleeding Kansas" became the favorite theme for impassioned oratory. At Philadelphia radicals of the combined party, zealous in their antislavery crusade, won the nomination for John Frémont, who had earned renown for his "conquest" of California and his valuable explorations in the Rockies. Frémont was Savannah-born and Southern-educated, but after he left the South he had become intensely anti-Southern. Georgia's Robert Toombs was the first to alert the region: "The election of Frémont would be the end of the Union. . . . The object of Frémont's friends is the conquest of the South."

Because of agitated press accounts of the feuding in Kansas, neither the friends of Pierce nor those of Douglas could secure the Democratic nomination for their leader. The Kansas-Nebraska Act had, in fact, spoiled the presidential chances of anyone connected with it. So the delegates settled on sixty-five-year-old James Buchanan, who had spent the recent disturbed years out of the country as ambassador at the Court of St. James's. His running mate was chosen, not from a cotton state, but from Kentucky: John C. Breckinridge, a moderate follower of Henry Clay.

Since Pierce could not get the nomination, Davis was satisfied with Buchanan. The two were on excellent terms. Davis liked Buchanan's reasonableness and conservatism, and he admired his gentlemanly qualities. The Pennsylvanian had always been cordial to the South; his record and sentiments regarding slave property were as "spotless as those of John C. Calhoun himself."

In the November elections of 1856, Buchanan won by 174 electoral votes to Frémont's 114 and the 8 of Fillmore, candidate of the American party and the now almost defunct Whig party. It was no sweeping victory for the Democrats, because the popular vote of the two rival candidates outnumbered theirs. The danger to the republic which Davis feared had only barely been averted. "We had reached the crisis," Buchanan said just after his victory. ". . . Republicanism was sweeping over the North like a tornado. . . . Had Pennsylvania yielded, had she become an abolition State . . . we should have been precipitated into the yawning gulf of dissolution."

In 1856 the Republicans, who were to proclaim such ardent

sentiments about "Union" in 1861, were widely denounced as "disunionists," because they were entirely sectional. Jefferson Davis had, in fact, looked upon the formation of a purely regional party as a kind of secession in itself. "They [the Republicans]," he said four years later, "seceded in the last Presidential election, went off as a section, organized for themselves, and attempted to force a sectional candidate, supported entirely by a sectional vote. That was secession, practical secession."

Though the Democratic victory did not by any means free Davis from anxiety for the future, it gave hope that with vigilance and unrelaxed effort the Union might be saved. Davis believed he could help by returning to the Senate when his Cabinet term was over. He therefore wrote his friend Stephen Cocke that he would be gratified "for special reasons" if Mississippi would bestow the election upon him. But he insisted he was too engrossed with the War Department to make any effort in his own behalf. Though warned he must speak for himself on Mississippi soil, he firmly declined. When the state legislature finally voted on the matter, Jefferson Davis was again elected Senator, the new term to begin the day he ceased to be Secretary of War.

In midsummer of 1856, to save Varina, who was with child again, from the city heat, Davis took a house in the country about three miles from the capital. It was a pleasant change for the children—the baby Margaret and "Jeffy D" Howell, Davis's little brother-in-law and namesake, who was now living with him. The Pierces would often come down with the Secretary on week ends for relaxation and intimate talks. The President unbent in the country and threw off his worries. He took special delight in Margaret, now a precocious eighteen months, sometimes called Maggie, but more often Pollie. To the end of his life Franklin Pierce recalled an amusing incident of girl-biting-dog. One day when Maggie was alone with the President, the dog hurt her feelings by snapping at her. Holding back her tears, she bided her time, and lay quietly down beside the animal until he was sound asleep. Then she bit him sharply on the nose "in retaliation."[1] Ten years later when visiting Jefferson Davis in prison, Pierce retold the story, with fresh amusement.

On the whole, for Jefferson Davis personally, that exciting year of 1856 was a harmonious one. The President and he were, if possible, more devoted friends than ever. Members of his immediate household remained in good health. The War Department functioned smoothly and Congress attested its confidence in the Secretary's recommendations.

The one plaguing fly was Winfield Scott, who kept up his prolonged bickering. Perhaps no one in his life, not even Henry Foote, got under Jefferson Davis's skin like "Old Fuss and Feathers," who was notoriously difficult to get along with. Scott's army record had been punctuated by controversy and exhibition of irascibility since the days of his first lieutenancy when he was court-martialed for criticizing a superior officer, about the time Jefferson Davis was born. In army circles his curmudgeonly reputation was a byword. To Davis he proved an inveterate troublemaker, taking up an incalculable amount of the Secretary's valuable time. He naturally disliked vain, pompous, paradeful men, and Scott's attempt to belittle and undermine Zachary Taylor in Mexico had given him a contempt for the General.

The irritations had begun shortly after Davis took office. Scott persistently disobeyed orders from the War Department and ceaselessly pressed claims for money which regulations did not warrant. The quarrels reached a blistering height in the first half of 1856 when Davis, irritated beyond endurance, let go discharges of anger and scorn that he approximated only twice in his later career: once with Britain's Lord Russell, and again, in old age, with a brash young man named Theodore Roosevelt.

The preceding July, when Davis had questioned the Commanding General about an action he considered highly unwarranted, Scott had replied in an accusatory epistle of thirty-six paragraphs,

[1] In August, 1953, Margaret's son Jefferson Hayes-Davis told the author that his mother actually bit off a tiny bit of the dog's nose, but that his grandmother Varina had refrained from saying so in her *Memoir*.

ending with the insult: "Notwithstanding the representations of your beneficiaries and sycophants, military and civil, that you stand so intrenched in the favor of the President that any appeal against your caprice and injustice would be sure to lead to an aggravation of the injury . . . I ask that this letter may be laid before the President." Davis promptly referred the letter without comment to the President. And the next day he received from Scott a three paragraph postscript loaded with fresh gall.

Davis might have briefly disposed of the General's lengthy complaints and insults, but because Scott was determined to make the correspondence official and public, the Secretary felt impelled to justify himself in a detailed reply. "While I am not at all reluctant to spread on the records of the Department a full history," he wrote, "I regret the length of the discussion which the necessity of replying to your charges imposes upon me." Amassing a battalion of facts and figures, he answered the enumerated "provocations and aggressions" in twenty-seven documented foolscap pages, which he trusted would satisfy and silence the Commanding General.

His hope was vain. Scott launched a new campaign calculated to tarnish not only Davis's character but his shining record in the War Department. Thoroughly exasperated, Jefferson Davis wrote the Commander "in extremely strong ink," as Saint Catherine of Sienna once wrote to an erring Pope:

"Considering it a public duty to repel the undeserved censure you have cast upon the administration of the Department over which it is my fortune to preside, I . . . have not sought to conceal the indignation which your gratuitous and monstrous calumnies could not fail to excite. . . .

"Another instance of your capacity in the same breath to beg for sympathy and utter slander, is your accusation that I have endeavored 'to provoke a duel with an old soldier known to be so lame in both arms as to write with difficulty and pain.' Those ignorant of the fact that the great disability of which you complain was the result of a fall upon the pavement in New York, would naturally infer from the introduction of the phrase 'old soldier' that you were by wounds received in battle disqualified for self-defence, and every generous heart that believed your assertion would visit with indignant censure the unmanly attempt to involve a wounded veteran in personal combat. . . .

"Your petulence, characteristic egotism, and recklessness of accusation have imposed on me the task of unveiling some of your deformities. To do this I have been compelled to draw from some portions of your history not written by yourself, and if I have succeeded in making you see yourself as others see you, it may prove a useful service to my successors in relieving them from the annoyances to which I and my predecessors have been exposed in their official connection with you. . . .

"It is sincerely to be hoped that those who follow you in the honorable profession in which you have been eminent, notwithstanding your fame has been clouded by grovelling vices, will select for their imitation some other model than one whose military career has been marked by querulousness, insubordination, greed of lucre and want of truth."

Scott was only temporarily silenced. On May 21, he called Davis "an enraged embecile" in the beginning of his letter, and in the final paragraph he rose to an almost eighteenth-century proficiency in satirical vilification.

"A late celebrated wit, to illustrate the overweening self-confidence of a British secretary, (still living) said, 'he was ever ready to couch an eye, operate on the bladder, or take command of the Channel fleet in the midst of an enemy.' It is believed that an American Secretary can be named, who, without having served an apprenticeship to either of those functions, is rash enough to unite them all to his present office, and take upon himself the part of chief criminal judge into the bargain. . . ."

This time Davis's reply was both terse and final. The letter contained only two sentences and ended thus:

Having early in this correspondence, stamped you with falsehood, and whenever you presented a tangible point, convicted you by conclusive proof, I have ceased to regard your abuse, and as you present nothing in this letter which requires remark, I am gratified to be relieved from the necessity of further exposing your malignity and depravity.

Very respectfully Yr obt Serv<br>
Jeffn Davis<br>
Secretary of War

Davis had fallen into the wasting error of trying to explain and justify himself, to make his attacker see and admit the truth. But it was his integrity, his insistence on verity that compelled him to persist in detailed proof. And he could, if driven to the limit by insistent misrepresentation, indulge in stinging rebuke.

Scott passionately resented Davis's outstanding success in the War Office; his mocking comparison of Davis to the self-confident British secretary was due to the fact that more and more responsibility was thrust on the War Minister because of his demonstrated abilities. The Washington correspondent of the *Daily Delta*, in a routine report of January 3, 1857, attested to Davis's achievements.

"Both Houses of Congress were in session yesterday, and several interesting communications were received by the Executive departments. The Secretary of War gave a detailed report of the disbursements through his office, which in the aggregate amount to the enormous sum of $19,991,261.70 in one year. Some idea of the fine capacity and sterling integrity of General Davis, as an Executive officer, may be formed by the fact that this vast sum of money has been disbursed by him without one word of complaint having been heard from any quarter. From the confidence reposed in him by Congress, nearly every appropriation for any kind of internal or public improvement has been placed under his supervision and direction; and so successful has been his administration of public affairs that the War Department, formerly insignificant, has now a patronage greater than any other department of the Government, controlling, as it does, at least one-third of the entire appropriations by Congress."

In December, 1856, the Secretary of War had submitted his last annual report to the President. It was comprehensive and minutely detailed like all the others. He reported that the commission of three he had sent abroad had returned in April after a year's absence. Besides surveying battlefields in the Crimea, they had inspected arsenals, camps, and military schools at St. Petersburg and Moscow. They had visited Prussian and Austrian military establishments and seen the government foundry for cannon in Belgium. They had been particularly impressed by the modern skill of Russian engineers in constructing fortifications.

The report touched on a wide variety of subjects from seacoast defenses and settlement of Indian difficulties on the western plains to a carefully estimated cost per mile of a railway from San Diego to Fort Yuma and the construction of a road from the Great Falls of the Missouri to intersect the road leading from Walla Walla to Puget Sound. Dredge boats on the Great Lakes and tunnels through California mountains were subjects of consideration. The Secretary discussed the machinery that had been erected for removal of the masonry of the old Capitol dome and the vast quantity of marble bought for the new portico. In his report Davis did not fail to reflect credit on the mechanics for their good workmanship on both the Post Office and Capitol extensions.

While the Secretary of War was preparing his last recommendations to the administration, another man with the same surname as the Commanding General was playing a significant if silent role on the public stage. This was Dred Scott, the Negro involved in the famous Supreme Court decision that bears his name.

Dred Scott was a slave owned by Dr. John Emerson, a U. S. army surgeon, who had taken him from Missouri on a military assignment to Rock Island, Illinois, and later into Wisconsin Territory. In 1838 the servant had returned to Missouri with his master. After the death of the physician, he sued Mrs. Emerson for his liberty in 1846. His lawyers argued that he was free because he had resided in a free state and also in a free territory. Scott won his case in the lower court of Missouri, but the decision was reversed by the state supreme court. In the meantime the widow had married a Massachusetts Abolitionist named Chaffee, who had political ambitions. To keep an Abolitionist from appearing in federal courts as a slaveowner, Scott was sold to Mrs. Chaffee's brother, a New Yorker, John F. A. Sanford.[2]

Jefferson Davis followed the developments in the case with peculiar interest, for to him the Constitution was at stake. In the Federal District Court in Missouri, Sanford contended that because Scott was a Negro, he was not a citizen of Missouri and therefore could not sue. When the judge ruled against Scott, the case was appealed to the Supreme Court of the United States. In February, 1856, it was lengthily argued, and then argued again in December, to be deliberated upon until February 15, 1857. In the interim two of the Northern justices, Curtis of Massachusetts and McLean of Ohio, both of whom had presidential aspirations, let it be known that they proposed to present separate dissenting opinions in which the constitutionality of the Missouri Compromise would be championed. Their intention changed the shape of things and the case had to be postponed until each of the nine judges could prepare a separate opinion.

While Jefferson Davis, like the entire nation, was eagerly awaiting the Supreme Court's action on Dred Scott, his wife gave birth to a son on January 16, 1857, and almost died. That January was unprecedentedly cold. Snowstorm followed snowstorm. On Sunday, two days after the baby's birth, while Mrs. Davis lay desperately ill, a climaxing blizzard paralyzed the capital; it was worse than anything in the oldest citizen's experience. No trains

[2] Allan Nevins explains further that Mrs. Chaffee had tried to make some mercenary use of Scott by hiring him out to various families, but because the old man was ailing and inefficient he could not hold his jobs. Since Mrs. Chaffee and her brother were loath to look after their slave, he was largely dependent on the charity of descendants of his first owner. Dr. Nevins thinks the freedom suit, initiated first in 1846, may have been prompted by some lawyer who hoped to share in the collection of wages in arrears. If Scott had won his case, Sanford might have been forced to pay retroactive wages.

could get into or out of the city. In some places snow lay six feet deep. Men had to beat down the snow so that a neighbor could get across F Street to Mrs. Davis's bedside. President Pierce himself braved the drifts on foot to inquire about her. Several times he sank to his waist. At one spot it took him almost an hour to fight his way through a block and a half of snow. When he arrived at the Davis house and fell into a chair exhausted, he said he had had to come himself because he did not believe any of the White House servants would have pushed through.

Jefferson Davis was greatly touched by the President's solicitude. But because the Chief Executive was a loyal and devoted friend, he was not as surprised at his hazardous journey as he was at a special gracious gesture on the part of William Seward, the South's mighty foe. Though Seward had never met Mrs. Davis, when he heard she was near death and that Mrs. Hetzel, a neighbor of his who was nursing her, could not procure any kind of vehicle to get back to her through the blizzard, he ordered his own valuable pair of horses put to a sleigh. After some almost disastrous mishaps, the equipage finally got the nurse to Mrs. Davis. To the end of their lives, though political bitterness made it difficult, the Davises never ceased to be grateful for Mr. Seward's kindness.

At nine o'clock on March 4, before the rest of the Cabinet arrived to say good-by to the President, Jefferson Davis came in for a last intimate talk. Both men were moved. "I can scarcely bear the parting from you," Pierce told his Southern friend. "You have been strength and solace to me for four anxious years and never failed me."

After his return from riding in the carriage with Buchanan to the inauguration ceremony, Pierce went to the home of a friend. Later in the day, he received a heart-warming letter from his loyal Cabinet. In turn, Jefferson Davis and each of the retiring Secretaries received a copy of a farewell letter in which Pierce thanked his advisers for their unfailing and cheerful co-operation, which had lightened his official labors. In the last paragraph he took occasion to include a brief evaluation of his administration, which should be pondered fairly by those who decry the Pierce regime.

"You may, I think, recur with just pride to the condition of the Country during the four years now about to close. It has concededly been a period of general prosperity; defalcations on the part of federal officers have been almost entirely unknown:—the public treasury with more than twenty millions of dollars constantly on hand has been free from the touch of fraud or speculation:—long pending foreign questions, have been amicably and advantageously adjusted:—valuable addition has been made to our already vast domain and peace has been maintained with all the nations of the earth without compromise of right or a stain upon the national honor.

"Whatever of credit pertains to the Federal executive in the accomplishment of these results is attributable in great measure to the fidelity, laborious habits and ability of the heads of the different departments.

"In my final retirement from active participation in public affairs I shall observe the career which awaits you individually with the interest of constant and unabated friendship."

No more than Franklin Pierce did Jefferson Davis conceive of the extraordinary responsibilities and the tragedy that were to mark his own future career.

As he read the President's summation in full, he must have taken a certain special satisfaction; for he was generally recognized not only as an unsurpassed Secretary of War, but also as a chief motivating force of the good that was accomplished in this honest administration. But he may also have recalled that if he had not been overpersuaded by Douglas and the Southern Senators that Sunday morning in January to secure an interview with the President, the ferment of the Kansas situation might have been avoided. In the light of later events, it was perhaps the only thing in four constructive years for which Jefferson Davis might take blame.

Despite the verdict of many historians with an anti-Southern bias, the Pierce regime was as commendable as any since Andrew Jackson's. For honesty, it ranks below none; under it, prosperity abounded, and, most importantly, it held the Union together by giving the South hope of fair play.

By the time of Buchanan's inauguration, Mrs. Davis was recovered; the baby, who had been given his father's name, was flourishing; and Jefferson Davis was a reasonably happy man.

# CHAPTER XIX

# "HOW FAR ARE YOU TO PUSH US?"

WITHIN twenty-four hours after he had ceased to be Secretary of War, on March 4, 1857, Jefferson Davis took his seat in the Senate. And, on March 7, the Supreme Court rendered its decision on the Dred Scott case. By a six to three majority, it was declared: (1) a Negro cannot become a member of the political community created by the Constitution and be entitled to the rights of federal citizenship; (2) the Missouri Compromise law prohibiting slavery in a part of the national territory was unconstitutional.

In delivering his own opinion, Chief Justice Roger B. Taney, a Marylander and always a Union supporter, stated that no Negroes were citizens of the states when the Constitution was adopted and that the language of the Declaration of Independence did not include them in the term "the people of the United States." Taney and five associate justices, all Democrats and one of them a Northerner, maintained that while citizenship could be conferred on a Negro by a state within its own limits, "it cannot confer the rights of citizenship as a member of a Union."

This latter opinion was what Davis, like Calhoun, had contended since 1847. And neither Davis nor Pierce had ever believed in the constitutionality of the Missouri Compromise. So Davis was highly gratified that the Supreme Court upheld a strict construction of the Constitution. Douglas and his Northern Democratic followers felt vindicated. The South was jubilant. Enraged

Republicans bitterly attacked Taney, one of the ablest and longest-serving of all chief justices. Yet even in antislavery Boston the old established families agreed with the Dred Scott decision. As Catherine Drinker Bowen says, "New England had a firm belief in property. Though slavery might be morally wrong, slaves were assuredly property, and property had to be protected." Like the Kansas-Nebraska Act, the momentous decision put all fair-minded New Englanders in a hard case; they were torn between "sacred property" and "sacred freedom."

While the Republican press of New England invented new epithets of abuse, the Southern papers answered the recriminations by asking, "What about your own wage slaves? What about those five thousand white women in their early twenties who work unconscionably long hours in the Lawrence cotton mills?" Our Negroes, except in crop times, they pointed out, have a lot of leisure. You work your white workers to early old age or to their graves, but we take better care of our African slaves, for it is profitable as well as humane to keep them in good health. And we never turn out our old, ill, and useless Negroes; we have a law which forbids the freeing of a slave who has become a financial liability.

At the close of the congressional session, in which Jefferson Davis carefully avoided any reference to slavery, he and the family returned to their Mississippi plantation, where he had spent so little time since 1852. Now in May of 1857 he was received with great enthusiasm. Big barbecues in his honor were given in Vicksburg and in Jackson; everywhere he appeared he was accorded an ovation. He went about among his constituents endeavoring "to harmonize their views" and continuing to speak for the Union. Then he mended the neglected business of his plantation and sent his wife and children to Mississippi City on the Gulf to avoid risking the late summer fevers that came to the Delta.

While there, Varina found an ideal place for a summer home and was eager to purchase three acres along the shore. On August 31, 1857, she wrote her husband at Brierfield about her discovery.

My dear Banny: [1]

. . . I shall probably fence in three acres of the lot . . . and of course put a board fence around it. I shall sow Bermuda Grass or rather sod Bermuda all over the part cleared. And if we purchase the new lot, leave it to amuse you when you come down. It is covered with a thick growth of young live oaks—two of the grandest pines on the coast and some rich magnolias, and live oaks full size for this place. This is the handsomest lot I have ever seen—maple—hickory, magnolia, live oak, jupon, pine and sweet bay in a dense shade—

Then she gave him a recountal of the children's doings:

Jeffy!!! . . . He's the sweetest thing you ever saw and good as gold—not at all precocious however—and I am thankful for it. Maggie is very little less fleshy than she used to be in Washington—and the smartest thing I ever saw. She calls out to go bathing and when she gets in plays about like a fish. . . .

Take care of yourself, my own old Ban, and write when you can. God bless and keep you is the prayer of your devoted wife

W. D.—

Leaving the plantation in reasonably good condition in the fall and relying on the good judgment of the intelligent Montgomery Negroes to assist the white overseer with problems as they developed, Davis went to join his family at Mississippi City. Here he fell in love with the Gulf Coast region, where he was to spend his old age.

On October 12 at Mississippi City he made his final speech to his constituents before returning to the Senate. He deplored the bungling of the *Black Warrior* affair and the resultant failure to purchase Cuba. He expressed the hope that if William Walker, the daring young adventurer from Tennessee, succeeded in his filibustering expedition in Nicaragua that the Government would take advantage of his success and "act with firm hand." He ad-

[1] Why she called him "Banny" she never explained and none of the descendants have any idea. But strangely her grandchildren always called *her* "Banny," while Mr. Davis was called *Papa*, in the French manner.

mitted that popular sovereignty, as it had turned out in Kansas, had been disappointing. He now favored taking a position which should have been consistently maintained: that the Government must protect slaves in the Territory as it did every other species of property. The Supreme Court's ruling on Dred Scott, he said, had made this position clear and legal.

Davis never gave up his belief in the desirability of acquiring Cuba. He thought it would be well if the United States owned all the land from the Canadian border to the Isthmus of Panama, and he was convinced that United States citizenship would prove a progressive benefit to the peoples of Mexico and Central America. On the Senate floor Davis had supported President Buchanan heartily when he recommended the purchase of Cuba at the most favorable opportunity and asked Congress to vote money for the purpose.

In December, 1857, the slavery clause of a proslavery constitution drawn up at Lecompton, Kansas, by a minority of the settlers was voted on and approved. The proceeding was irregular, because free-state men had largely abstained from voting. Buchanan, however, used his influence to induce Congress to admit Kansas as a state with this constitution recognizing the legality of slavery. He defended the Lecompton convention on the grounds that the free-state men, whom he regarded as professional rebels against the authority of the Federal Government, would have voted against it merely to keep trouble stirring.

"Kansas," Buchanan declared, in view of the Dred Scott decision, "is at this moment as much a slave state as Georgia or South Carolina. It has been solemnly adjudged by the highest judicial tribunal known to our laws, that slavery exists in Kansas by virtue of the Constitution of the United States." He argued that speedy admission of Kansas as a state would "restore peace and quiet to the whole country," while rejection would be keenly felt by the fourteen states where slavery existed. He felt that the South deserved conciliation.

Six days after Buchanan's message of February 2, 1858, urging the admittance of Kansas as a state with the proslavery constitution framed at Lecompton, Jefferson Davis rose to praise the President as a patriot and a statesman. And he took occasion to chide a Republican Senator who had attacked the President in "miserable slang." "It may serve the purpose of a man who never looks into his own heart, to find there any impulses of honor," he said feelingly, "to arraign everybody, the President and the Supreme Court, and to have them impeached and vilified on his mere suspicion. It ill becomes such a man to point to Southern institutions as to him a moral leprosy, which he is to pursue to the end of extermination, and perverting everything, ancient and modern, to bring it tributary to his own malignant purposes."

Then measuring his words carefully, he spoke in a cool, quiet tone: "Sir, we are arraigned day after day as the aggressive power. What Southern Senator, during the whole session, has attacked any portion, or any interest, of the North? In what have we now, or ever, back to the earliest period of our history, sought to deprive the North of any advantage it possessed?" After a long pause to let the words sink into the minds of his Northern opponents, he said challengingly: "Had you made no political war on us, had you observed the principles of our confederacy . . . that the people . . . left perfectly free to form and regulate their institutions in their own way, then, I say, within the limits of each state the population would have gone on to attend to their own affairs, and have little regard to whether this species of property [slaves] or any other was held in any other portion of the Union. You have made it a political war. We are on the defensive. How far are you to push us? . . ."

In all probability the bill would have passed and with it the crisis, if Stephen A. Douglas, the begetter of the original Kansas-Nebraska measure, had not now roundly denounced Buchanan for favoring Southern interest. Jefferson Davis and Douglas's Southern adherents were shocked at what they regarded a turncoat hypocrisy. They realized finally that Douglas was for the West and the West only. By attacking Buchanan on the Kansas question, Douglas had, however, regained the favor of the Northern Democrats—though he lost completely the trust of the South. In no uncertain terms Davis called him "a double dissembler," and he could never again believe in his integrity.

Douglas's vigorous efforts against the bill helped to kill it in the House. But it did pass the Senate, where Davis defended it stoutly, by a vote of 33 to 25. When Douglas himself voted with Seward and the antislavery Senators, speculations arose that the Republicans might take up Douglas and make him their leader. The ambitious "Little Giant" had created a rift in the Democratic party which no solder could ever mend and which was to be the South's undoing and his own.

Under the strain of sectional antagonisms and the heavy weight of responsibility resting upon him to preserve some sort of unity, Davis's health began to break down. Though suffering again from severe facial neuralgia, he refused to give up. Even in poor health, Davis was the best speaker and debater the South had in Buchanan's regime. While often intense he was no firebrand, but reasonable, sagacious, extremely knowledgeable, and magnetically persuasive. An antislavery editor like Horace Greeley of the New York *Tribune*, wrote frankly: "Mr. Davis is unquestionably the foremost man of the South today. Every Northern Senator will admit that from the Southern side of the floor the most formidable to meet in debate is the thin, polished, intellectual-looking Mississippian with the unimpassioned demeanour, the habitual courtesy and the occasional unintentional arrogance, which reveals his consciousness of the great commanding power. . . . He belongs to a higher grade of public men in whom formerly the slave-holding democracy was prolific."

The great burden of being chief supporter of the Southern cause had been sustained at a deplorable drain on his health. Finally, at the end of that controversial and exciting February of 1858, Davis became gravely ill. In a thoroughly run-down condition he caught a cold which developed into severe laryngitis; neuralgia of a most painful sort paralyzed one entire side of his face, and his left eye became dangerously inflamed. For weeks he was forced to lie in a darkened room, virtually without power of speech or sight, and provided with a large slate for communication. He suffered agony from a swollen pupil, which seemed as if it would burst. Because of his anguish he could scarcely bear to take nourishment. The alarmed family physician brought the eminent Philadelphia specialist Dr. Hayes to see him. To have the eye examined, the patient had to sit in streaming sunlight, when even candlelight gave him great pain. As Varina held her husband's hand while the examination was in progress, Dr. Hayes murmured in astonishment, "I do not see why this eye has not burst." Davis groped for the slate and scrawled, "My wife saved it." Varina says all the triumphs of her life are concentrated in the "blessed memory" of that moment. When she told the questioning physician that her patient was never irritable, ever deplored causing trouble, and endured torture such as no one but herself dreamed, he said, "Such patience is God-like."

Davis was more concerned about his little brother-in-law and namesake, Jeffy D, who lay in the room above ill with scarlet fever. The boy had been born while the Colonel was fighting in Mexico and christened after he was reported mortally wounded. He had lived with the Davises a good part of their married life and was loved like their own. When Davis insisted on being taken up to see the boy, his wife remonstrated, because he himself had never had the disease. But ever fearless about his own personal welfare, the sick man had himself led upstairs one day when she had left the house. When Varina returned, she was horrified to find her bandaged husband sitting on Jeffy D's bed, an arm under the boy's head, telling bear stories in a whisper.

The Senator did not lack visitors to help him beguile the tedious weeks of pain in a dark room. Lord Napier, the British minister, was a favorite caller at the Davis bedside. Napier had none of the stiffness of the traditional English diplomat,[2] but radiated a sympathetic friendliness, as well as robust good spirits. Though forty-seven, he seemed youngish, and Mrs. Davis says

[2] Mrs. Roger Pryor felt otherwise, and writes amusingly of her first meeting with Lord Napier.

he came "like a healthy, tender boy" to brighten the sickroom. Senator Clay of Alabama would sit with him for long night hours to give Mrs. Davis a rest. Colonel Hardie would read to him and take down letters, while Mrs. Davis got an hour's fresh air in her carriage.

Men of all shades of political opinion came to chat with him including such antislavery men as Colonel Edwin Sumner. William Seward came almost daily. He was an incomprehensible man to the Davises, because he was so different in intimate private life from his public political self. He had proved a friend in need when he sent his sleigh through the snowbound streets, and when Mrs. Davis had met him later she had liked him very much. Seward seemed strangely drawn to his foremost Southern opponent. His solicitude was genuine. Once when it appeared that Davis would have to have the diseased eye removed, he turned to the wife with tears in his own eyes and said feelingly: "I could not bear to see him maimed—he is such a splendid embodiment of manhood."

Seward would tell the patient significant things that happened in senatorial debates and speak of "your man" and "our man." One day when Davis remarked how much he himself was inspired by the attention and sympathy of his audience, Seward surprised him by confessing that he found it somewhat of a relief to speak to empty benches. "For," he affirmed, "I speak to the papers. They can repeat a thousand times if need be what I want to impress upon the multitude."

One day when the touchy subject of slavery was brought up, Varina challenged Seward. "How can you, Mr. Seward, with a grave face, make those piteous appeals for the Negro that you do in the Senate? After being a schoolmaster in Georgia, you surely don't believe the things you say." For a moment he eyed her quizzically, and then with a smile admitted: "I do not. But these appeals, as you call them, have potent effect on the rank and file of the North." Jefferson Davis could not refrain from expressing surprise. "But, Mr. Seward," he said earnestly, "do you never speak from conviction?" "Nev-er," came the frank reply. Davis was so shocked that he raised his blindfolded head from the pillow and half sat up. "As God is my judge," he said impulsively, "I never speak from any other motive." To Seward's ears his words were not self-righteous or priggish; they were merely a simple expression of truth. He put his arm about Davis's shoulder and gently laid his head back on the pillow. "I know you do not," he said with tenderness. "I am always sure of it."

In no sense did this complex, kindhearted man, so full of contradictions, seem to resent "the daily beauty" in Davis's life, nor was he in the least apologetic that expediency ruled his own career. In private he made no pretense to ideals or illusions about politics.

Seward continued to call until the patient's good eye had cleared sufficiently to bear light. He said the walk was good for him and that Davis's conversation relieved his boredom. He backed up Mrs. Davis's objections to her husband's insistence on addressing the Senate on an appropriation for Dallas Bache's coast survey. Though still extremely weak, Davis was determined. "I must go if it kills me," he said. "It is good for the country and good for the friend of my youth." So he drove in a closed carriage with Varina beside him, holding a little basket containing beef tea and wine to revive him after his speech. Though very pale and emaciated, he spoke with his accustomed clarity and effectiveness, and left the Senate immediately in an almost fainting condition.

Davis insisted after that on going to the Senate at least for an hour every day. But his convalescence was so slow and his appetite so negligible that his physician prescribed a sea voyage or a change to a more northerly latitude. Davis thought of Europe where his friend Franklin Pierce was now with Jane and Nathaniel Hawthorne. On April 4, 1858, he dictated a letter to Pierce:

"I had the pleasure some days since to receive your very welcome letter. It found me suffering under a painful illness, which has closely confined me for more than seven weeks and leaves me at this time quite unable to read or to write, and my wife has kindly undertaken to act as my amanuensis. I am much surprised that you should have received nothing from me, and find in your unshaken confidence under such seeming neglect another assurance of that friendship I so deeply cherish and of which I have received so many proofs. . . . Mrs. Davis, and myself have rejoiced much at the reported improvement in Mrs. Pierce's health and strength, and if the session of Congress were now at an end I think we should sail for the south of Europe, and probably see you there. I am advised to take a sea voyage somewhere, but I do not feel at liberty to go away during the session of Congress and have not decided definitely upon what we shall do after Congress adjourns, except that I will not return home to encounter malarial exposure during the summer, or fall."

In May, in the brief hours he was able to stay in the Senate each day, Davis spoke on a variety of subjects: on the bill concerning fishing bounties, on the legislative appropriation bill, on the Texas boundary bill, on a river and harbor bill, on a civil appropriation bill. Still unable to write or read and with his head bandaged, out of his prodigious memory he presented facts and figures in logical sequence and brought sagacious counsel to the assembly.

On Tuesday, the eighth of June, when the Senate was considering the army appropriation bill, Senator Judah P. Benjamin, a brilliant New Orleans lawyer, criticized a minor point Davis was making on breech-loading arms. Davis, still suffering from neuralgia, said with asperity that Benjamin was attempting to misrepresent a very plain remark. "The Senator's manner is not at all agreeable," Benjamin said. The tempers of both men flared and almost got the better of them. Benjamin felt that Davis had given him a sneering reply and had implied that the Louisianian was a "paid attorney." When he got home Benjamin, in the heat of his anger, sent a note by James A. Bayard challenging the Mississippi Senator to a duel. Davis, completely calmed down, was amazed when he read the note. He tore it up, declaring, "I will make this right at once. I have been wholly wrong."

The next day Davis went to the Senate to make suitable amends in public. After his manly apology, in which he took complete blame, Benjamin "replied handsomely" and the affair ended. The incident increased their mutual respect. They became the best of friends and Benjamin was to prove Davis's most trusted minister in the Confederate cabinet.[3]

Now his physician insisted that Jefferson Davis must have an absolute rest immediately. Because a trip to Europe seemed impractical, the Davises decided on Maine, for in Portland they had friends of both political persuasions, and Dallas Bache was in the New England mountains making experiments. Since Davis ever had an affinity with the sea and always improved on salt water, they chose the sea route. With Maggie and Jeff Jr., they sailed from Baltimore at the end of June.

As soon as the ship reached the ocean and the dissensions of the land were left behind, Jefferson Davis began to mend. By the time they reached Boston, he could lay aside his eyeshade in the late afternoon. After Boston, where the family changed to a packet boat, he began to mingle cheerfully with his fellow passengers, and on the Fourth of July he yielded to their importunity and made a little speech urging peace and adherence to Union and Constitution.

When they arrived at Portland, Davis was struck by the beauty of the town's superb situation on a peninsula promontory with the deep harbor locked by scores of verdant islands. He found the climate salubrious and the hospitality extremely cordial. Only four days after his arrival, citizens honored him with a serenade. It was hardly the sort of courtesy a Southerner with widely known proslavery sentiments would have expected in a Puritan

---

[3] The above version of the flash quarrel between Davis and Benjamin is substantially as that told by Robert Douthat Meade in his authoritative biography *Judah P. Benjamin, Confederate Statesman*. Mr. Meade noted the words "paid attorney" were only "reported" as something Mr. Davis said, and not official.

The exchange of words and the apology are recorded in *Congressional Globe*, 1st Session, Thirty-fifth Congress, pp. 2775-82.

Carl Sandburg mistakenly writes on page 240 of his one-volume biography of Lincoln that Davis "for nothing much . . . challenged Senator Benjamin to a duel," the opposite of the fact.

state where, only six years before in the little college town of Brunswick, Mrs. Stowe had written *Uncle Tom's Cabin.* When the music ceased, the Senator appeared on the steps of Madame Blanchard's guesthouse and was greeted with rousing applause. He began in his mellifluous voice: "Vanity does not lead me so far to misconceive your purpose as to appropriate the demonstration to myself; but it is not less gratifying to me to be made the medium through which Maine tenders an expression of regard to her sister Mississippi."

The burden of his impromptu talk was that the national sentiment and fraternity, which made us one people, could keep us one people. But he spoke of less imponderable things like a railroad to the Pacific—a theme that lay close to his heart—and of the time when the country should have need perhaps of three or more. "The building of the road," he said, "will require the efforts of a united people. The bickerings of little politicians, the jealousies of sections, must give way to dignity of purpose and zeal for the common good." He condemned sectionalism: "The acts of representatives and senators affect the whole country and their obligations are to the whole people. . . . One who would confine his investigations to any section," he declared, "would be morally unfit for the station. . . . Has patriotism ceased to be a virtue," he asked, "and is narrow sectionalism no longer to be counted a crime?" He ended by thanking the Portlanders from the heart for "the gentle kindness, the cordial welcome, the hearty grasp, which made me feel truly, and at once, though wandering far, that I was still at home."

The citizens were charmed by the Mississippi planter and his handsome wife, and showered them with attentions during the following weeks. Jefferson Davis enjoyed the clambakes given in his honor. He liked "basket-parties," for which each lady brought her culinary specialty and the picnic feast was spread in some wooded island. He took pride in little Maggie's immediate popularity with the townfolk. She was a responsive, beautiful child, who would run away to call on neighbors and to visit old seamen, who told her fabulous stories.

As the days of rest and simple entertainment followed each other, Davis's health improved rapidly. Later in the summer he went with his family to visit Professor Bache and his scientists, who were working on Mount Humpback. They traveled by railroad car to Bangor, then took the stagecoach as far as it went, and finally boarded an ox-pulled sled Bache had sent to fetch them up to the mountain plateau, where the white tents were pitched.

The quiet life on the cool remote mountain was peculiarly revivifying for Jefferson Davis. He rambled about the unfamiliar terrain with his little girl on his shoulder; he helped her pick "ghost flowers," Indian pipes, among deep green mosses. Sometimes he watched the scientist make experiments in triangulation, and listened to Bache's clear explanations. In the evenings his host would read aloud from the latest books sent to him regularly, or the company would listen to selections from Verdi's recent operas on a large imported music box. The profound silence of the mountaintop was strange to Davis, accustomed at Brierfield to the ceaseless clamor of insects on summer nights. Here, where a leaf's fall could be plainly heard, the soporific quiet proved a potent balm to his frayed nerves. The pervading quietude among loving friends made him forget the political clamors of Washington and the swelling animosities on opposite sides of the Mason-Dixon Line. This blessed visit to Benjamin Franklin's great-grandson was the last respite of perfect peace Jefferson Davis was to know until his twilight years at Beauvoir on the Gulf shore.

When Davis returned to Portland, his recuperation seemed complete. On a visit to the State Fair at Augusta, when pressed to make a speech, he began by saying he had come as an invalid seeking the benefits of the Maine climate, preceded by a reputation which was expected to prejudice them unfavorably. "I have everywhere met courtesy and considerate attention from the hour I landed on your coast to the present time." He attributed their manifest kindnesses to that "sentiment which would cause you to recognize in every American citizen a brother." Then he touched

## "HOW FAR ARE YOU TO PUSH US?" 309

deftly on almost every facet of Maine's way of life, exhibiting a remarkable knowledge of its timber, its agriculture, and its various breeds of cattle. He praised the horsewomen who had just performed at the fair, complimented the state's industries, and commended its schoolhouses.

"In looking upon the evidences you have brought of mechanical and agricultural improvements," he said, "I have viewed it with the interest of one who felt he had a part in it, as an exhibition of the prosperity of his country. The whole Confederacy is my country, and to the innermost fibres of my heart I love it all, and every part. . . . My first allegiance is to the State of which I am a citizen, and to which by affection and association I am personally bound; but this does not obstruct the perception of your greatness, or admiration for that which I have found admirable among you." His sentences and paragraphs flowed easily and fell into place with graceful sequence. His diction was not provincial; he did not speak with a Southern drawl, but like a man of wide cultivation. When he finished, the Maine Yankees felt that he was one with them.

Everywhere he went, Davis proved a winning ambassador of good will from the South. Twice again he spoke at Portland. At the Belfast Encampment, the hero of Buena Vista reviewed the troops. He made a speech on the field and then spoke at the banquet that closed the encampment. Bowdoin College, situated in Harriet Beecher Stowe's beloved Brunswick, conferred upon him an honorary doctor of laws degree.

Leaving a host of new-made friends in Maine, the Davises returned by way of Boston. They had intended to spend only a day, but the baby Jeff was seized with a violent attack of croup that almost proved fatal. They were forced to remain at the Tremont Hotel. Strangers as well as old acquaintances called to offer sympathy and service and the Davises got a taste of Boston kindness and solicitude. One inclement night when the baby was critically ill, a lady in coat and house dress knocked on their hotel-room door, introduced herself as Mrs. Harrison Grey Otis, and announced with the smiling assurance of a true Boston aristocrat that she had come to spend the night and do the nursing while Mrs. Davis got some greatly needed rest.

After Jeff's illness had passed the crisis, the Davises were shown Boston and entertained in the best homes. When a committee of Democrats asked Jefferson Davis to speak in famed Faneuil Hall, he was surprised, but he gladly accepted the opportunity to explain the Southern view in Massachusetts. One of the committee who urged him to speak was Benjamin F. Butler, then a State Rights Democrat, but within five years perhaps the most hated of the Federal generals.

On October 11, the "Cradle of Liberty" was packed to the doors, with the aisles full, to hear the Southern statesman. On the stage sat prominent men with distinguished family names, like Robert C. Winthrop and Edward Everett. In a half-hour introduction Boston's Caleb Cushing presented Senator Davis glowingly as "a citizen of the Southern States, eloquent among the eloquent in debate, wise among the wise in council, and brave among the bravest in the battlefield." He spoke from personal observation of "the surpassing wisdom of Jefferson Davis in the administration of the government. Such a man," he said, "you are . . . to hear as a beautiful illustration of the working of our republican institutions in the United States, which as in the old republics of Athens and of Rome, exhibit the same combinations of the highest military and civic qualities in the same person. . . . Such a man may not only aspire to the highest places in the executive government of the Union, such a man may acquire . . . the combination of eminent powers, of intellectual cultivation, and of eloquence, with the practical qualities of a statesman and general." Tremendous cheering greeted this introduction.

"As Mr. Davis took the stand," reported the Boston *Morning Post* of October 12, 1858, "a scene of enthusiasm was presented which defies description. Those who held seats in the galleries rose *en masse,* and joined with those standing on the lower floor in extending a cordial, very cordial, greeting to the honored guest from Mississippi."

"Countrymen, brethren, and Democrats," Davis saluted his

hearers and charmed them with his first utterance. Then in that stronghold of Abolitionism he dared to speak boldly in defense of the institution of slavery, as it then existed.

"Why then, in the absence of all control over the subject of African slavery, are you so agitated in relation to it? With pharisaical pretension it is sometimes said it is a moral obligation to agitate. . . . Who gave them the right to decide that it is a sin? By what standard do they measure it? Not the Constitution; the Constitution recognizes the property in many forms, and imposes obligations in connection with that recognition. Not the Bible; that justifies it. . . . Is it in the cause of Christianity? It cannot be, for servitude is the only agency through which Christianity has reached the Negro race.

"If I were selecting a place where the advocate of strict construction of the Constitution, the asserter of democratic state rights doctrine, should go for his test," he said with compelling emphasis, "I would send him into the collections of your Historical Association. . . . Such was the proud spirit of independence, manifested in your colonial history, such, the great stone your fathers hewed . . . and left, the fit foundation for a monument to state rights!"[4] He ended with a moving, solemn plea that the ties which had bound the colonies together in their early days of trial be not broken now.

From most accounts, Davis completely captivated his audience at Faneuil Hall. His friends say he was at his absolute best as an orator that night. "A better, a fairer, a more thoughtful or earnest speech he never made," wrote the Union General Morris Schaff, and added, "He was the last great slaveholder that ever stood on that historic platform and talked out of his heart to the people of Boston."

In New York, Jefferson Davis stopped to speak in Palace Garden, and succinctly interpreted the political crisis as "a con-

[4] He refrained from reminding them that Massachusetts had threatened to secede when Louisiana was purchased and again when Texas was admitted to the Union. He did not say that from 1803-04 to 1815 New England was constantly in the habit of speaking of the dissolution of the Union, her leading men deducing this right from the nature of the compact between the states.

test upon the one side to enlarge the majority it now possesses and a contest upon the other side to recover the power it has lost. . . . If," he said, "one section should gain such predominance as would enable it, by modifying the Constitution and usurping new power, to legislate for the other, the exercise of that power would throw us back into the condition of the colonies. And if in the veins of the sons flows the blood of their sires, they would not fail to redeem themselves from tyranny, even should they be driven to resort to revolution." In William Seward's New York, the Mississippi Senator warned the electorate against the danger of pushing the South too far, and was resoundingly cheered.

Davis had naturally expected to be assailed by the Abolitionists for his defense of slavery. But he had no more anticipated the Republicans calling him "a propagandist for disunion" than he had foreseen that certain Southern editors would rake him over the coals for "praising the Yankees." He had been far too chummy with Northerners to suit some of his own constituents, too well received, too gracious in thanks for their kindness, too complimentary of New England ways and accomplishments. Some suspected him of currying favor with the Yankees to make a bid for the presidency.

On November 16 Davis was back on home soil clarifying his position before the state legislature and, in a measure, on the defensive. "Was it expected," he asked, "that to public and private manifestations of kindness by the people of Maine, I should repel their generous approaches with epithets of abuse?"

In answering a specific criticism from a different kind of opposition, he affirmed: "Neither in that year [1852] nor in any other have I advocated a dissolution of the Union, except as a last alternative, and have not considered the remedies which lie within that extreme as exhausted, or ever been entirely hopeless of their success." Senator Davis took pains to explain that he did what he could in New England to counteract impressions injurious to the South such as that created in the last presidential canvass when one of the Maine Senators actually convinced many voters that if Buchanan were elected, slavery would be forced upon that state. He pointed out the insidious propaganda of Seward, which he feared might stir up an armed conflict.

At the Republican state convention at Springfield, Illinois, on June 16, 1858, Abraham Lincoln, candidate for the United States Senate, had made a statement that was noted throughout the land. To a line taken from Jesus—"A house divided against itself cannot stand"—he had added, "I believe this government cannot endure permanently half *slave* and half *free*." Four months later, on October 25, a fortnight after Davis's Faneuil Hall address, William Seward had strikingly echoed the Lincoln hint of eventual war when he said, "Shall I tell you what this collision means? . . . It is an irrepressible conflict between opposing and enduring forces, and it means that the United States must and will, sooner or later, become either entirely a slaveholding nation or entirely a free-labor nation." He sought to alarm his auditors—and, through the printed report of his speech, the entire North—by proclaiming that the purpose of the South and the Democratic party was to force slavery on all the states of the Union. "Absurd as all this may seem to you," Davis told the legislators, "I have reason to believe that it has been inculcated to no small extent in the Northern mind."

Davis warned Mississippi against the "dangerously powerful" Seward, "mastermind of the so-called Republican party," who grossly misrepresented the slave system and whose "irrepressible conflict" phrase caught the public attention like some abracadabra of black magic. But he expressed the belief—it was a vain one indeed—that if a "Northern army should be assembled to march for the subjugation of the South, they would have a battle to fight at home before they passed the limits of their own state." He assured the South of its many powerful friends in the North, despite the rank growth of the hostile Republican party. "I hold the separation from the Union by the state of Mississippi to be the last remedy, the final alternative," he reiterated. "In the language of the venerated Calhoun, I consider the disruption of the Union as a great, though not the greatest, calamity."

But he made it clear that his optimism was not merely fatuous, and counseled his constituents to make prudent preparations for whatever contingency might arise.

"The maintenance of our rights against a hostile power is a physical problem and cannot be solved by mere resolutions. . . . Such preparation will not precipitate us upon the trial of secession . . . but will give to our conduct the character of earnestness of which mere paper declarations have somewhat deprived us; it will strengthen the hands of our friends at the North, and, in the event that separation shall be forced upon us, we shall be prepared to meet the contingency with whatever remote consequences may follow it.

"It seems now probable that the Abolitionists and their allies will have control of the next House of Representatives, and it may be inferred from their past course that they will attempt legislation both injurious and offensive to the South. . . .

"If [in the next election] an Abolitionist is chosen President of the United States, you will have presented to you the question of whether you will permit the government to pass into the hands of your avowed and implacable enemies. . . . In that event, in such manner as should be most expedient, I should deem it your duty to provide for your safety outside of the Union of those who have already shown the will, and would have acquired the power, to deprive you of your birthright and reduce you to worse than the Colonial dependence of your fathers."

Thus Jefferson Davis, one of the best-trained military men in the nation, gave the same advice to Mississippi that he had invariably given to the United States: the best safeguard for peace is preparation.

While Davis earnestly counseled coolness and sought pacification in New England, in Mississippi, and in Washington, extremists on both sides carelessly flourished firebrands. Yancey of Alabama and Spratt of South Carolina now did the Southern cause inordinate harm by defiantly advocating a reopening of the slave trade. Abolitionists, already fevered with moral indignation and hatred, cried out for vengeance. Inflammatory broadsides and

## "HOW FAR ARE YOU TO PUSH US?" 315

pamphlets calling for violent action were posted and circulated in New England and Midwestern states. One ill-phrased pamphlet, among scores that might well have excited Southern apprehension, read thus:

"One plan is to land military forces in the Southern States, who shall raise the standard of freedom and call the slaves to it and such free persons as may be willing to join it. One plan is to make war openly and secretly, as circumstances may dictate, upon the property of the slaveholders and their abettors, not for its destruction, if that can be easily avoided, but convert it to the use of the slaves. If it cannot be converted, we advise its destruction. Teach the slaves to burn their masters buildings, to kill the cattle and hogs, to conceal and destroy utensils, to abandon labor in seedtime and harvest, and let the crops perish. To make slaveholders objects of derision and contempt by flogging them whenever they shall be guilty of flogging their slaves."

If these violent Abolitionists had their way, the planters were to be turned out of their homes and Negroes installed; or if this arrangement could not be effected, dwellings were to be burned, crops and cattle destroyed, and everybody, including the slaves too, left to perish of starvation. Though the majority of Southerners perhaps considered such incendiary resolutions the mere raving of fanatics, a minority gave them manifest credence.

While Abolitionists cried aloud for bloody vengeance, and the Yanceys declaimed alarums and defiance, while Seward spread his subtle political oil and Douglas schemed for the presidency with a seemingly "rule or ruin" callousness, Washington danced, as if trying to drown fears in a Lethe of lavish diversion. Never had official society been more given to elegant entertaining.

## CHAPTER XX

## SOCIAL LUSTER AND DOMESTIC CARES

WITH the installation of the aging Buchanan as President and the coming of young Lord Napier as British minister, society in Washington had taken on a brilliant luster. The lovely, cultivated Lady Napier was perhaps the most popular foreign hostess the capital had known, while the President's niece, Harriet Lane, was as competent as any White House mistress since Dolly Madison. Miss Lane's years in European capitals had given her poise and sophistication. Possessing natural tact, she had developed a sure diplomatic sense which was invaluable as sectional antagonisms sharpened.

Under the inspiration of the wealthy, aristocratic Napiers, Southern women were uncommonly busy at entertaining. It was almost as if they were having a last fling before the deluge. What Nicolay and Hay speak of as "the blandishments of Southern hospitality" lifted the capital—in Virginia Clay's estimation—"to the very apex of its social glory."

Commenting on contemporary American society, the Marquess of Lothian wrote:

"It is only in that part of the Union [the South] that you can find anything approaching to the country gentleman of England. It is only there that you can find families which, holding the same lands generation after generation for a long period of years, have acquired the self-respect, the habits of command, and the elevation of character which arise in a society which has been for some time in the possession of power, and the refinement which generally follows upon the possession of hereditary wealth. . . . The blood of the old cavaliers of England, coursing in the veins of the Virginians and Carolinians, was as much reproduced in them as that of their opponents, the Puritans, was reproduced in New England.

"There may be a difference of opinion as to which of the characters, Cavalier or Roundhead, is the best; but there can be no doubt which is the most attractive. . . . Still more powerful was the influence of the Southern ladies. . . . They bore the bell in grace and refinement, and besides, had about them that air of superiority which may possibly make its possessors detested, but which, when it has anything to rest upon, seldom fails to make itself acknowledged. . . . Over fashion the South bore almost unquestioned empire."

This was a period when women made the most of glamour. Three of the top Southern society leaders, besides Mrs. Jefferson Davis, later wrote their memoirs, rich in colorful comment: Mrs. Clement Clay of Alabama, *A Belle of the Sixties;* Mrs. Roger Pryor of Virginia, *Reminiscences of War and Peace;* and South Carolina's Mrs. James (Mary Boykin) Chestnut, *A Diary from Dixie.* Two of the most beautiful belles of the day were from Washington itself—the "quality folk" of Washington in those days always considered themselves Southern—brunette Thérèse Chalfont and fair Adèle Cutts. The former, regarded as the beauty par excellence of the time and of all preceding administrations, had married George Pugh, young Democratic Senator from Ohio, while Addie Cutts, daughter of a poor department clerk, but a great-niece of Dolly Madison, was the second wife of Senator Stephen A. Douglas.

In these years of elegance and conspicuous expenditure, the well-to-do, like the European-educated Mary Chestnut, ordered their clothes and adornments from Paris. The serving of dinners became a fine art. Treasured family recipes for terrapin, oysters, canvasback duck, quail—particularly those of hostesses from Maryland, Virginia, Louisiana—delighted gourmets among the foreign diplomats. Though Mrs. Pryor insists that nobody esteemed riches and that only position, talent, beauty, and charm were the requisites for the best society, lavish sums were expended on hospitality. The daughter of Georgia's Senator Toombs confessed to Mrs. Clay that her father spent $21,000 annually, a very large sum for those days. California's wealthy Senator Gwin, who came originally from Mississippi, was reputed to spend as much as $75,000 a year.

Shortly after the Napiers' arrival, the Gwins gave an elaborate costume ball that became legendary. The Senator's lady appeared gorgeously as the queen of Louis XIV. Since no one was masked, the incomparable Thérèse Chalfont Pugh created a sensation in black gauze and spangles as "Night," while her companion, the radiant Addie Douglas, made a lovely foil as "Dawn." Mrs. Jefferson Davis went as Madame de Staël and indulged in "the caustic repartee to which the role entitled her." To those who understood the language, she spoke in French; to those who did not, in broken English. Her husband was amused to note that whoever dared to match wits with Varina in either language got the worst of it, but he was sometimes apprehensive that her ready tongue might make an enemy.

The Napiers, with whom the Davises were on unusually friendly terms, constantly entertained: musicals, afternoon receptions, simple teas, resplendent evening parties, and dinners where the men were served on silver plates and the ladies on gold. In honor of Queen Victoria's birthday in 1858, the Napiers gave a ball with a sumptuous supper, which glittered in the memory of all who attended. Foreign ministers wore the court dress of their nations with all the decorations of gold stars, crosses, and ribbons they could muster. The hostess was "superb" in white brocaded satin and tiara of diamonds and emeralds. While Nina Napier was the perfect wife of Britain's emissary, it was not her generous hospitality that made her so beloved. Varina Davis and a few others found a key to her gracious aura in her private boudoir. There, on a table among silver and gold objects encrusted with coronets, stood a rosewood bookrack holding a Bible and five books with metaphysical titles. Religious contemplation had different effects on Lady Napier and Jane Pierce; while it made the President's Puritan wife brooding and somber, it gave the English noblewoman a sweetness and light that pervaded the atmosphere wherever she appeared.

Washington society in the late '50's was so alluring that the septuagenarian Washington Irving, still America's most widely read author, spent far more time in the capital than on his Hudson River estate. Another favorite social figure was also a New Yorker—the sculptor Thomas Crawford, who was commissioned by Virginia to make a heroic statue of George Washington for Richmond's Capitol Square.[1]

Perhaps the most popular of all the men in society was Virginia-born A. Dudley Mann, perennial diplomat and "a sophisticate with every Christian virtue." Jefferson Davis and he were drawn to each other when they first met. Later Davis admiringly called him "a perfect man," and Mrs. Davis says "they loved like David and Jonathan until extreme old age."

Because the Davises had less money than many of their friends, Varina entertained more simply, but with marked distinction. Mrs. Roger Pryor, whose own rich house was "filled with good Virginia servants," pays tribute to the "social influence" of Varina Davis, whom she calls "one of the most brilliant women of her time, greatly sought by cultivated men and women."

In *Recollections of Jefferson Davis*, Mrs. Hezekiah Sturges, daughter of a Representative from New York, described an evening with the Davises, when she was a teen-age girl on her first visit to Washington. They were having a small dinner for which her father had accepted an invitation before her arrival the day of the party. He called on Senator Davis to ask if he might bring his daughter. Mr. Davis, loving young people, was delighted—he was continually adding to guest lists at the last hour, often to his wife's consternation. The girl was enchanted by the Mississippian's courtesy. She was surprised that he talked with a "distinguished

[1] This statue was completed in 1861, and Jefferson Davis stood before it when he gave his second inaugural address on Washington's birthday, 1862.

German military man," who had been on a military mission to Mexico, in German and then broke easily into Mexican patois. After dinner the Davises took their guests to a concert at Carusi Hall to hear Ole Bull, the great Norwegian violinist. Before leaving Mr. Davis showed them the advertisement, which read: "Ole Bull will perform some of his finest music, and little Signorina Patti and Maurice Strakoch will diversify the evening's entertainment."

The young girl from New York sat in one of the boxes with Mr. Davis and watched him almost as much as she did the performers, noting that "his attention was that of enraptured admiration" and commenting in later years that "Mr. Davis was a lover of art in all its forms and phases." "Ole Bull," she declared, "was superb." And when Patti, "the wonder child" in a filmy white dress with blue silk sash, "beautiful as a dream fairy," sang an aria from *La Somnambula*, hats, as well as flowers and lace handkerchiefs, were tossed upon the stage.

At large "mixed" parties, guests were careful not to talk of the "irrepressible conflict" Seward had prognosticated. In 1859, they conversed about the latest books from abroad: Tennyson's *Idylls of the King*, Thackeray's *The Virginians*, and *Adam Bede* by a young man called George Eliot, for no one then knew that the author was a woman named Mary Ann Evans. They talked of concerts, of Adelina Patti, the little Italian-Spanish soprano, who was a musical sensation at sixteen and who seemed destined to take the place of the "Swedish nightingale," Jenny Lind, now in her late thirties. They discussed the latest roles of Charlotte Cushman, America's foremost actress, who at forty-three was at the height of popularity.

A host had to be cautious in Buchanan's time not to send a Southern lady in to dinner with an Abolitionist. Mrs. Clement Clay, scintillating wife of the Alabama Senator, avowed she would decline to accept even a pronounced Republican as her escort to table. She had steadfastly refused to permit William Seward to be presented to her. Asked about attending some function he was giving, she impetuously declared, "Not to save the

Nation could I be induced to eat his bread, to drink his wine, to enter his domicile, to *speak* to him." At the Gwin costume ball, Mrs. Clay says Seward took the occasion of her impersonation of the comic character "Aunt Ruthie Parkington" to present himself; they exchanged half a dozen sentences. While Mrs. Clay was an extremist and something of a show-off in her Democratic loyalties, her friend Mrs. Douglas could be coolly cutting to one who dared to disapprove of her Illinois husband.

In his farewell years in Washington, Davis may have again recalled his father's advice expressed so feelingly in that last letter of his written when Jefferson was fifteen: "Use every possible means to acquire useful knowledge as knowledge is power the want of which has brought mischief and misery on your father in his old age—that you may be happy & shine in society when your father is beyond the reach of harm is the most ardent wish of his heart." Without effort Davis shone in society whenever and wherever he appeared. But in the midst of its diversions he could not be called content. Beguiling will-o'-the-wisps did not make him unmindful of treacherous quagmires that seemed to lie ahead. In mid-January, 1859, he wrote something of his anxiety to Franklin Pierce, one of the few persons in the world to whom he could bare his heart. And he made it clear that his chief solace was not in the allurements of society, but in the company of his adoring little girl, who was then almost five.

Washington, D. C.<br>Jany. 17, 1859

My dear friend,

Your letter relieved me of an anxiety created by the absence of any recent intelligence concerning you.

We are dragging on here in a manner significant of no good to the country. Each day renders me more hopeless of effecting any thing for the present or prospective benefit of the country by legislation of Congress. Even more than heretofore members and Senators represent extreme opinions and may increase but cannot allay the ferment which gave to them political life. I am gratified by the view you take of my New England tour. The abolitionists and the Disunionists combined to assail me for the speeches made there. I hope the Southern assailants have been scotched and the others may rail on to their content. That tour convinced me that the field of useful labor is now among the people and that temperate, true men could effect much by giving to the opposite section the views held by the other. The difference is less than I had supposed.

Your old friends in Missi. have not forgotten you and are ready to show their appreciation of you on the first occasion. Many said to me that your nomination for the Presidency was their first wish and best hope.

. . . Our children have grown rapidly and the little girl is now quite a companion to me when at evening I go home to forget the past and postpone the future. . . .

You may scold me roundly as I deserve for not writing to you more regularly, but do not I pray you fail to give me credit for good resolves and do let me hear from you as often as your convenience will allow.

As ever your friend<br>Jeffn: Davis

Louis Trezevant Wigfall, Senator from Texas, was amazed one day, when he went to see Mr. Davis on some grave matter of state, to find the dignified statesman "in his library, lying flat on his back with two of his little children crawling over him." With him, it was not an uncommon way of relaxing.

During the early part of 1859, the only incident of a political nature that might have given Jefferson Davis a little gratification was the receipt of a letter from Keene, California, about his old foe Henry Foote, who had sought a new western pasture after being discredited in Mississippi. It had been written on January 4, by a man named Lewis Campbell.

"You will remember that the Hon. Henry S. Foote, having finished his political career in Mississippi removed, some years since to California and, on his arrival there, announced to the people that he should take no further part in political matters, but should wholly devote his time & talents to the duties of his profession.

"But soon afterwards he joined the Know Knothing party . . . and became a prominent candidate for the United States Senate.

"In the Legislature elected in California there was a large majority of Know Knothings in the house and a majority in the Senate of only *one*. The house voted to proceed to the election of United States Senator, but the Senate by *one* majority refused to go into joint ballot, the election was postponed and Foote failed to be elected.

"He was greatly enraged; threatened that he would stump the State, appeal to the people, and put down the Traitors who had defeated his election.

"You may be interested to know who it was that had the independence to defeat Foote: it was none other than a New Hampshire Democrat, by the name of *Flint*, whose *heart* was so *hard* and *will so stubborn* that he would not vote for Foote, because he believed him to be, what he has since turned out to be, an unprincipled Demagogue unworthy to be trusted by any Party. . . .

"Seeing it stated in the papers that Foote had written a Letter censuring yr political course and commenting severely upon yr late speech at Jackson Miss I have taken the liberty to write you and let you know who is entitled to the credit of keeping the garrulous, windy and wordy Foote out of the United States Senate. . . .

"This is not intended for the public eye. Pardon me for writing you so much, at length, about a matter in which you may take but little interest. . . ."

Davis must have taken considerable interest in learning details of Henry Foote's defeat and that he was behaving true to form on the other side of the continent. But the narrow margin of defeat reminded him that "the snake was scotched, not killed."

In the first two months of the Senate session, Davis carefully kept off the question of slavery. Though he spoke on many subjects, he put his most forceful energy into urging the passage of a Pacific railroad bill. He proved that a Southern route which avoided the Rocky Mountains would be by far the cheapest to construct. He wanted the railroad to California to begin at

Memphis, so that the commerce of the West would be loaded into the holds of Mississippi River boats from New Orleans. He envisioned, too, a railroad from Memphis to Charleston, via Montgomery and Atlanta, to connect with Atlantic Ocean traffic and thus save weeks of water transport. But Douglas was pressing for Chicago as the eastern terminus of the Pacific railroad, while Senator Green of Missouri was maneuvering for St. Louis.

In March, the bill had not got beyond the discussion state before alarming news of the Mississippi River floods presented Davis with a most disturbing dilemma. Dire destruction was threatening Brierfield. Brother Joseph was incapacitated by illness. Jefferson's presence at the plantation was imperative and urgent. It was a relatively small matter to postpone pressing for his precious railroad bill, but how could he possibly absent himself from Varina, who was expecting another baby in April? Painful reflections crowded upon him by day and by night. It was like a relived nightmare to recall how close his wife had come to death when little Jefferson was born. Varina herself made the decision; she insisted that he must go to protect their plantation home and the Negroes and succor his aging brother.

With misgivings about what lay before him and behind him, and in the forced hope that he might be able to return before the confinement, Jefferson Davis set out for Mississippi. He first went to Memphis to ascertain the state of the river there and above and to get a better idea of the dread exigencies. When he reached Brierfield on March 22, he found everything at an awesome standstill, awaiting his arrival. He plunged straightway into the work of building levees. The first letter he received from Varina after his arrival was filled with bits of desultory family and capital news.

Washington<br>April 3, 1859

My dear Husband—

. . . I see by the papers that you reached our home the 22nd for which I am thankful.

Eliza Bache came on to see me about some business the day before yesterday and is staying with me. She has cheered me more than I can express. All my friends are very kind in coming in frequently, as my feet don't permit me to walk now.

The weather here is lovely, warm enough to dispense with fires.

Maggie is more changed than any child I ever saw. She continued to run away to Mrs. Phillips every few hours and Mrs. P. amused her guests making her curse, until I had to whip her three times—since which she is perfectly biddable, good tempered.

The Napiers left here for Annapolis a few days since, but the late arrival of Lord Lyons has induced the fear that the ship has been lost in the severe gales. They are coming back tomorrow to the Corcoran wedding, which is to be a small Rothschild's affair.

I enclose you some cotton seed, and a letter that will explain them.

Don't feel uneasy about me. I am pretty well and quite hopeful. *Pray keep out of the sun and night air,* and try to take my heart trouble lightly, so long as our little home circle is complete. That God may help you and keep you safe is the nightly prayer of your devoted Wife, W. D.

It was a consoling letter; Varina was keeping up her courage. Jefferson must have smiled at her warning him to keep out of the sun, when he was directing men from sunrise to sunset.

Another longer letter written a week later assured him that she was attending to everything as best she could. But she had given up hope of his returning in time for the birth. She understood how much would have to be arranged for on the plantation after the flood subsided.

Washington
April 10, 1859

My dear Banny:

I received your letters of the 24th and 25th yesterday, it being the first news of you since you left Memphis.

All this time I have been hoping that the high water accounts were exaggerated by the papers. . . . I am glad I persisted in urging you to go home. I have not the least doubt that your presence has averted a crevasse. I hope that you may be able still to do so. But the state of watchfulness and uncertainty must keep you in a nervous condition. I was just going to break out in a series of useless regrets that at the only home we have we cannot be together, but it is useless, and idle, and does not tend to make either of us feel happier. Your return . . . must necessarily depend upon so many contingencies and I must reconcile myself to look upon it as the church does Easter i.e. a moveable feast.

Little Jeff is constant to a degree, I have never seen in a little dear baby before. He shouts fifty times a day—"I love my Daddy, I love Mr. Davis, I do!" He and Maggie ran away day before yesterday and were discovered across the street taking a stroll hand in hand "like the babes in the woods," as Maggie says. Dr. Lawson's garden is a perfect blessing to us, they trot around there all day long, and Eliza [the nurse] seems to enjoy having them penned up securely in so large a stamping ground. I am doubly glad because the scarlet fever is very prevalent. . . .

Maggie and Jeff are both as well as possible, only Jeff is burnt quite red, his cheeks look so red they would do honor to a winter apple. He is singing from the minute he gets out of bed until his mouth is stopped with his own delicate mixture of fish roe and molasses.

Being rather more helpless than usual, my friends are very kind. . . . They come very often to see me, which relieves me of many weary hours, for now I am unable to go out but for a little while in the carriage and find it impossible to see strangers as I can't bring them upstairs. Strange to say the most affectionate remembrance I have had was from dear Lady Napier, who has knitted me some little socks and not only written to me from Annapolis, but written to friends for news of me. Lord Lyons [the new British minister] is very taciturn and very stupid, so the people say who have seen him. . . .

I have sent off over two thousand speeches etc. The Boston, Jackson etc. speeches are now in the process of being franked. My time of trouble is so near that I cannot look a day ahead, so I am getting the envelopes ready—

I have deposited a $1000 check from Payne and Harrison in Riggs' bank and paid Mr. Ledyard $285 for the cameos. Mrs. Hetzel [2] will take charge of my money matters and household affairs and children, etc, when I can do so no longer—so don't feel uneasy about us all.

I was in hopes your and my anticipations of Brother Joe's condition would not be justified and regret to hear that they were surpassed by the reality. . . . I shall hope to see you by the first of June, should we all be spared and trust you may induce him to come with you. You must try to spend your birthday with us.

The things most urgent in the garden I think cannot be done until the fall—trimming the roses, planting new ones, dressing and replenishing the new asparagus bed near the backyard, and dressing and dividing the strawberry bed. The quinces want cultivation—

God bless you, my dear Husband, much more love than can be expressed, is in the heart of your

Waafe
W. D.

By the time Jefferson received this long, full letter signed Waafe—love talk for wife—the river was spreading disaster for miles about. On April 17 nearly every acre of Davis Bend was under water. Jefferson sent the cattle to the hills at Grand Bluff. He had holes bored in the floors of Brierfield so that the water would not carry the house away from its foundations. Ropes were attached to the best pieces of Varina's furniture to be lifted by pulleys toward the ceilings if necessary. The next day, in the midst of all his tribulations, with Brother Joseph seriously ill, Jefferson put a sick slave girl on the river boat, sending her to New Orleans for treatment. To his father-in-law, who was temporarily living in that city, he wrote a hurried note of explanation.

Brierfield
April 18, 1859

. . . Julia Ann, the daughter of Hagar, who will be recollected by Mrs. Howell, has been since last winter suffering from a

[2] Mrs. Hetzel had nursed Mrs. Davis through the critical illness when Jeff Jr. was born.

nervous rheumatism and I have concluded to send her down to Dr. Cartwright. Fearing that Dr. C. might be away I have consigned the girl to you, but pray that you will take no further trouble than to see that she is properly disposed of under the Doctor's care. . . . The girl was usually good in every sense of the word as applied to a field hand and had from infancy been very healthful.

On the Third, Varina reported the children and she were in better health than for sometime previous

Very affectionately

Jeffr: Davis

The day after he dispatched Julia Ann to the New Orleans doctor, Varina, more than a thousand miles away, was delivered of another son. She had written him a letter on April 17, which he received a week later and before he learned of the child's birth. It was a moving, poignant letter, revealing Varina's courage and resourcefulness, along with her fear, and her profound love for her husband and the boy Jeff, whom she idolized.

Washington April 17, 1859

My dear Banny,

. . . One morning Jeff ate two large mutton chops for breakfast.

Jeff is the "friend of my bosom, the balm of my life," as I felt he would be from the minute he was born. If I should not live to tell him so you must when he can understand it, but every day I pray to rear him.

The only person I have seen in high spirits for some days is Mr. Buchanan, who paid me a very long and very pleasant visit yesterday, congratulating himself that there was no news—thank goodness.

If I am not taken sick before Wednesday I shall have franked 2780 envelopes, and about five hundred ready. It gives me pleasure to be doing something which seems to bring us nearer to each other. I do so long to see you, my dear Husband. It saddens me to realize that there is so very much in one's being the first love

of early youth. Often since you have been away this time I have experienced that queer annihilation of responsibility, and of time, and gone back fourteen long years to the anxious loving girl, so little of use, yet so devoted to you—and nothing but my grey head,[3] swollen feet, and household cares awake me from the dream. But indeed I am becoming sentimental, and if this reaches you in broad sunlight, busy with the levees, answering the negroes questions, or with weak eyes when you don't want to read bad writing you will wish my romance had been indefinitely postponed, so I can only promise to run off no more, but assure that hourly my prayer is that "the Lord bless thee and keep thee"
Your affectionate Wife
V. Davis.

Jefferson may have been somewhat surprised that in those times when *enceinte* ladies were quite shy about their condition, Varina had received the President two days before her confinement. Perhaps in reading the letter, when he came to the line about "being the first love of early youth," Jefferson may have wondered if Varina was referring to Sarah Knox rather than to herself. He was aware that she had never entirely rid herself of jealousy of the girl who had first won his heart when he was young. He may have had a guilty pang, for he knew that some of his family believed—as descendants do today—that Sarah Knox was the love of his life. Yet Varina had done everything in her power to make him a good wife; and as the years passed and troubles came in battalions, his love for her increased with his admiration.

On April 24, 1859, Davis wrote from Brierfield to his father-in-law that his "anxiety for Varina was uncontrollable." "I have sent off last evening the residue of my stock," he said, "and am hastening to leave for Washington, as soon as provision is made for the negroes, who I am unwilling to send away. The water runs with strong current across the main ridge which was dry in the flood of 1828 and was considered above any possible rise of the river—"

[3] Varina was only thirty-three at this time.

On his return to Washington he found Varina had had no serious complications with the delivery, but she was far from well. So he decided that the family should spend the hot months in Allegany County, Maryland, the nearest and most convenient mountain region. The baby was named Joseph Evan for Jefferson's brother and his grandfather. Joseph, with Eliza and the grandchildren Lise and Joe Mitchell, came to see his namesake in June.

After a slight operation on his eye, the Senator settled his family and his relatives at Oakland, Maryland, and returned to Washington business. A letter from a Vicksburg friend written on June 7 had brought welcome news: "The river is falling rapidly—an inch in 24 hours, with every reason to look for an increase in the rate." But Jefferson would have to return to see that the plantations were restored to some running order, though the crop prospects for the year were ruined. After calling at the Executive Mansion to pay his parting respects to President Buchanan, he spent the week end happily with his family at Oakland and then started for Mississippi on June 26.

Except for a rattlesnake in the vicinity which had eluded him, Jefferson was free now from worry over his loved ones' welfare. But Varina was fearful of his Delta sojourn in chills-and-fever season. Shortly after he arrived at Brierfield he received a solicitous letter written on July 2 in answer to one of his from Cincinnati. Eliza Davis was much improved by the mountain air, Varina wrote. She herself had been confined to the house by a boil, but it had burst and she was walking again. The landlord kindly sent cream to their rooms every day.

How I do look forward & long for the time when we may walk about here together, if God only gives you back to me safe. My little Joe seems blessed to me, and all the sweetness of our happiest hours seems to have returned with his birth and I hate to give you up even for a day. May God keep you safe, my only love, and give you to me again in health— But please don't stay long— I feel so unwilling for you to run so great a risk. Do remember that you are a part of a powerful party and therefore can be spared but you are all to your wife and babes. But I get so worked up and so frightened when I think of your danger I am hardly coherent. . . .

The rattle snake is defunct—20 drops of chloroform on a rag killed it instantly, I am sure you will feel easier. . . .

And now my precious good Husband, farewell, and may God have you in the hollow of his hand and you to my arms is the hourly prayer of your devoted Waafe

W. D.

While dealing with plantation problems, Davis had to prepare, without benefit of amanuensis, an address to be delivered at the Mississippi Democratic convention at Jackson on July 6. Because of the diverse attitudes of his own people it was a most difficult speech to prepare. While the word "secession" had been generally avoided at conventions, in street conversations and about the family hearths it was a heated subject. Davis had to be cautious how he went about cooling seething tempers. At the same time he had to prepare his constituents for grave dangers ahead, and to impress the fatuous with the imperative necessity of defeating Mr. Seward's anti-Southern party.

Outstanding among the paragraphs in one of the longest speeches of his career, which the New York *Daily Tribune* later printed in full, are the following:

"We are necessarily cognizant of the fact that the unity of the people of the States is disturbed by a sectional, fanatical hostility, as irrational as it is vicious. However well it may serve to fan the flame of local excitement, and to promote the personal ambition of an aspirant, the idea of incompatibility for the purposes of our Union because of different systems of labor in the States, is palpably absurd, and would be suicidal if the purpose avowed were attainable. Though the defense of African slavery (thus it is commonly called) is left to the South, the North are jointly benefited by it. Deduct from their trade and manufactures all which is dependent upon the products of slave labor, their prosperity would fade. . . .

"Ours is an agricultural people, blessed with a fruitful soil and genial climate; the elements unite with man to render his labor profitable. We have, under these circumstances, no inducement to engage in a general competition with those who, for want of land and by rigor of climate, find in the workshops their only industrial employment. . . .

"A party too powerful to be unheeded, and marked, as nations are distinguished, by territorial limits, is now organized for the destruction of the labor system of the South, and seeks to obtain possession of the General Government, that its machinery may be used in aid of their war upon our existence as a sovereign State. . . . It is not the political division of a people because of different opinions upon matters of joint interest; but is in the nature of foreign war waged for conquest and dominion. . . .

"Our countrymen have two paths before them, either of which the majority of the States and of the people are free to choose. The one leads by the way of usurpation and tortuous construction, through discord and civil strife, to the destruction of this best hope of republican government. The other through peace and prosperity, by the perpetuity of the institutions we inherited, mounts to an eminence which looks down on a continent of equal sovereign, confederated States. We are near, I believe, to the point at which that selection is to be made. . . . To us it has been reserved to witness the organization of a party seeking the possession of the Government not for the common good, not for their own particular benefit, but as the means of executing a hostile purpose toward a portion of the States.

"The success of such a party would indeed produce an 'irrepressible conflict.' To you would be presented the question, will you allow the constitutional Union to be changed into the despotism of a majority, will you become the subjects of a hostile Government or will you, outside of the Union, assert the equality, the liberty, and sovereignty to which you were born? For myself, I say, as I said on a former occasion, in the contingency of the election of a President on the platform of Mr. Seward's Rochester speech, let the Union be dissolved. Let the 'great, but not the greatest of evils' come. For as did the great and good Calhoun, from whom is drawn that expression of value, I love and venerate the Union of these States—but I love liberty and Mississippi more. . . .

"Is there one of you who would support a Southern candidate for the Presidency, who avowed his purpose if elected to use the power of his office to crush or to assail a domestic institution of the Northern States? I pause not for an answer; the patriotism you have exhibited on every trying occasion renders a reply unnecessary. . . .

"I trust that a sanguine temperament does not mislead me to the belief that the mists of sectional prejudice are steadily though slowly floating away. . . . But . . . the fate of the sluggard will be ours if the promise of success does not wake us to additional preparation, energy and effort."

While warning against contingencies—and indirectly pleading with the North for a more generous attitude—in the last minutes of his address the Senator endeavored to impress his hearers with a hope that "the mists of sectional prejudice" were dissolving. It is a little hard to believe that his own faith was as sanguine as he implied.

In the midst of the impending national crisis, Jefferson made arrangements at Hurricane for a long absence of Joseph, who had decided to go abroad for pleasure and health. Among his own countless problems at Brierfield was the case of Julia Ann. In answer to his inquiries about her improvement he received a loving, but touching, letter from his mother-in-law.

New Orleans<br>July 14, 1859

My Dear Jeff

I am glad to see you are safe at Brierfield and do *not* intend remaining long—although I am very anxious to see you, and have a thousand questions to ask about my dear children and yourself Yet I do not wish to have you here, even for a few days, at this season— The City, however, is perfectly healthy for the acclimated— Not a case of yellow fever so far—at what moment it may break out we dont know— As soon as I received your letter I sent for Cartwright to know if Juli Anne could be sent up—he came this morning and pronounces her well—he says she is wonderfully changed in her appearance and understanding, *for the better*. . . . he says he wishes the issue kept open and running until the peas and plaster he sends are used up—he also wishes her to be put to work as customary—her leg to be dressed once a day— There is a small bill at the Apothecaries of 13 or 14 dollars which I will send to Mr. Payne for settlement— Tell Hagar she is a good girl & has behaved herself well—

I had a letter from Varina dated 4th and giving a good account of her continued improvement in health. . . . She says the children are in fine health and that my little Joe is a beauty—Maggie growing more and more beautiful every day—Master Jefferson not so good as he was, but a great boy never-the-less—I feel my separation from you all more & more every day of my life, but nothing is done without God's will—I try to submit myself as cheerfully as possible to my privations let them be ever so grievous— Sometimes find myself saying it is very hard, and wondering Why it is so ordered, but at such times I am so very miserable and suffer so intensely I am glad to submit myself to *his Will*, and to pray for grace to keep me soul and body under his care continually. . . . [Her spirits had been lifted by reading some books on the Apocalypse and the end of time by a man named Cumming.] I never was happy in my life before—I never had such a clear view of my duties and responsibilities as I now have—I never lived *above* the world before— Let me prevail upon you, my dear son, as dear to me as any child I have, to read those books. . . .

Becket is well but thin—he is six feet and an inch—a steady, good obedient son— Jennie has grown very much and is slender and delicate in her form— She plays almost as well as Varina did on the piano and has a fine voice— She is a good child and a great comfort to me— She was confirmed a short time ago by Bishop Polk—who by the by is a great friend of mine and when I see him he often talks of you with much affection—and desires to be always affectionately remembered to you. . . . I have just remembered, my dear Jeff, that your eyes are not strong, and will have mercy upon you. All here send much love to you and hope

to see you in the fall— That God may bless you my dear Jeff and all that belongs to you, is the daily prayer of
Your affectionate<br>Mother

The strain Jefferson had been under since March was so intense that on his return to Maryland at the end of July, he became seriously ill. But he was relieved to hear from Ben Montgomery that Julia Ann, who had been under treatment in New Orleans for three months, had arrived home "apparently much improved."

Joseph departed for Europe accompanied by an entourage: his wife Eliza, the seventeen-year-old Lise and her brother Joe, Mary van Bentheysen, a niece of Eliza's who had been brought up at Hurricane, Joseph's "body servant" and secretary, Eliza's colored maid, and another maid for the girls. As soon as they reached Europe a courier was added to the party. The Mississippians made quite a stir when they entered the grand hotels of Paris, Brussels, Rome. When Joseph took "a water cure" in Switzerland, he was greatly impressed by its efficacy. With the case of Julia Ann's rheumatism and nervous affection in his mind, he decided it was just the thing for his Negroes at Hurricane. So he hired the Swiss doctor who attended him to return to Mississippi with him and install various types of water cures. The physician's wife was engaged to teach French to Lise and Joe and whatever great-nieces and great-nephews happened to be staying at Hurricane.

On Joseph's return to the plantation, he built a two-story hospital[4] for his people, in which the doctor arranged all sorts of therapeutical baths. Jefferson was surprised on his next visit to Hurricane to see groups of darkies treading barefoot through the dew at dawn. It was a part of the cure. The neighboring planters were astounded to learn that the Davis Negroes were being given mud baths. But Joseph never ceased in his endeavors to improve the lot and health of his slaves, until the destructions of war rendered him powerless to help them.

[4] The hospital was not destroyed by the Federal troops. After the war, when Lise Hamer inherited Hurricane, she gave the building to the Colored Methodist Church. The upper rooms were used by different societies of the church. Lise's imposing washerwoman, who weighed 250 pounds, was the Mother of the "Sisters and Brothers of Love and Beauty."

## CHAPTER XXI

# THE DEMOCRATIC PARTY
# SPLITS ASUNDER

A PEACEFUL lull and more kindly feelings seemed to pervade the land in the Indian summer of 1859. It appeared as if the mists of violent sectional prejudice might really dissolve and that the brighter dawn Jefferson Davis had anticipated in his Jackson speech would break. But then on October 20 a dreadful deed stirred up enmity in the farthest corners of the republic.

In Canada, with twelve white men and thirty-four Negroes, John Brown conspired to force emancipation of Southern slaves by violence. Brown grandiosely purposed to use bloodshed to liberate the blacks, secure them in the mountains, and defeat any Southern state militia or Federal forces sent against him. He would seize Southern planters as hostages to compel emancipation. From here and there, Brown collected money to buy guns and pikes, with which the slaves could bash the skulls of their masters. Then he formulated a crude constitution by which the conquered South would be ruled.

Responsible men in high positions contributed cash to his lawless ends, generally in cloudy ignorance of the prime intention. Such well-known men as Gerrit Smith, Theodore Parker, and Dr. S. G. Howe, all of Boston, gave Brown financial assistance. Even Salmon P. Chase, then Governor of Ohio and later Secretary of Treasury and Chief Justice of the Supreme Court, had subscribed twenty-five dollars to Brown's use in December, 1856. In his biography of Chase, Albert Bushnell Hart quotes a letter of September

10, 1857, from Brown to Chase—after the massacre at Osawatomie—asking him for bigger money: "From Five Hundred to One Thousand Dollars for *secret service and no questions asked*. I want the friends of Freedom *to prove me now herewith*." Whether Chase provided further cash or not is not known, but after the Harpers Ferry raid, the New York *Herald* directly charged Chase with being a party to the conspiracy.

In the fall of 1859, like the rashest megalomaniac, Brown was ready to begin an invasion of the South with twenty-one men besides himself, including three of his sons and five Negroes. He expected his forces to snowball, as the slaves rushed to his liberating standard. The first point of attack was to be Harpers Ferry, Virginia, where the southernmost Federal arsenal was situated. According to a later report of President Buchanan, Brown had purchased in the North "200 Sharpe carbines, 200 revolver pistols, and about 4,000 pikes." Secreting his little army and his store of weapons at the Kennedy farm in Maryland just across the Potomac from Harpers Ferry, John Brown bided his time and carefully laid his plans.

On Sunday night, October 16, 1859, he made his attack, surprised the watchmen, bound them, and took possession of the arsenal, the armory, and the rifle factory. Next he seized some sleeping citizens as hostages and sent a raiding party to the plantation of Colonel Lewis Washington, great-great-nephew of the General. His men captured the planter, put arms into the hands of his amazed slaves, and told them they were free. They brought Colonel Washington, along with a sword Frederick the Great had given his famous relative, to the engine house, where the other hostages were incarcerated. An embarrassed, bewildered detachment of Washington's Negroes were set to guard their master and the other white prisoners.

The first citizen Brown's gang killed was a highly respected free Negro named Shepherd Heyward. He was coming to his work as baggagemaster of the little station at half-past one in the morning, and when he did not halt at command, they shot him in the belly. He lay in agony unattended until he died.

With muskets to pass out along with pikes, Brown called on the slaves to arise in rebellion. When the mystified blacks did not respond, Brown was greatly perturbed at such apathy. In the meantime the early morning train had carried the alarm to the next towns, and newspapers were describing the event in excited exaggeration. "Five hundred," "a thousand" Abolitionists and Negroes had seized Harpers Ferry. The countryside armed itself. Brown fortified the engine house to withstand a siege. By the time the first volunteers and militia arrived, a few more citizens, including the kindly old mayor, had been killed. All through Monday Harpers Ferry was in a state of terror. Colonel Robert E. Lee, with Lieutenant J. E. B. Stuart and a detachment of marines, was dispatched by special train from Washington.

When Brown refused to surrender on Lee's terms, the Colonel gave an order for the marines to batter down the door. In a quarter of an hour it was over. Brown was captured, bleeding, but not killed. One of his sons was dead; another, mortally wounded; the third had escaped.

John Brown and six insurrectionists were brought to trial at Charles Town, Virginia. The nation was excited to fever pitch; the South quite frenzied at the lengths to which antislavery men would go. In New England, Gerrit Smith "conveniently" went insane, and old Dr. Howe piously "denied all godly connection with the raid." But some Abolitionist orators and editors, in their utterances, became as fanatically ridiculous as Brown himself in his daring action. Wendell Phillips, the highborn declaimer, derided Virginia as an inferior civilization and compared her to "a pirate ship." "And John Brown sails the sea a Lord High Admiral of the Almighty with his commission to sink every pirate he meets on God's ocean of the nineteenth century."

On October 31, a jury found John Brown guilty of treason against the State of Virginia, of inciting slave rebellion, and of murder. His execution was set for the first week of December. Though no one could complain that the trial was not fair, stirring rumors of rescue began to circulate. Armed bands were reported to be forming in Ohio. Governor Wise of Virginia warned Salmon

Chase, the Abolitionist governor of Ohio, "If another invasion should assail the State of Virginia, I shall pursue the invaders into any territory, and punish them wherever they can be reached by arms."

Colonel Lee was sent to Charles Town to see that the hanging went off without demonstrations. But the desperadoes, supposed to be collecting, did not appear. Perhaps, in any case, John Brown would himself have scorned rescue, because as he shrewdly insisted, he would be worth more to "the cause" dead than alive. Execution would give him a sure place in the chronicles. Certainly, he received the noose coolly, with unflinching stoicism; and to some it seemed he grimly relished his star role in the dramatic event of December 2.

When Brown's neck was broken, churches in some Northern towns were draped with black, bells tolled, cannon fired, and a murmuration of prayers went up for his soul's passing. The South was aghast when Ralph Waldo Emerson, the sage of Concord, became blasphemously foolish by comparing Brown's "glorious" scaffold to the cross of Calvary. An apotheosis was initiated to transform a fanatical criminal into a saint as well as martyr. In the words of Stephen Benét:

> *The North that had already now begun*
> *To mold his body into crucified Christ's*
> *Hung fables about those hours.*

When Jefferson Davis heard of Brown's attempt to incite a slave rebellion, he was deeply disturbed, not so much because of this isolated case, but because of the effect it would have on Southern people. For, as President Buchanan wrote: "In the excited condition of public feeling throughout the South this raid of John Brown made a deeper impression on the Southern mind against the Union than all former evils. . . . It was the enthusiastic and permanent approbation of the object of his expedition by the Abolitionists of the North which spread alarm and apprehension throughout the South."

The political atmosphere was dangerously charged when the

Thirty-sixth Congress assembled in December, 1859, a few days after Brown's execution. Kansas was still in crisis, with desultory shootings occurring. Order was kept only by the presence of Federal troops Buchanan had sent to preserve outward peace; without the soldiers a little civil war might already have been waxing. The ominous shadow of a greater sectional war hung like a pall over the capital.

Many Northern papers accused certain United States Senators of being party to Brown's conspiracy. Seward was proved to have contributed money to John Brown's cause, but he avowed he had no idea what the money was to be used for. In the Senate, almost immediately after the execution, resolutions on the Harper's Ferry Invasion were introduced to sift the matter and to pass condemnation on the subversive act of aggression. Stephen A. Douglas promptly declared it was his "deliberate conviction that the Harper's Ferry crime was the logical, inevitable result of the doctrines of the Republican Party." Some of the Northern Senators, however, like Trumbull of Illinois and Wilson of Massachusetts, tried "to embarrass" and postpone the proceedings by introducing all kinds of extraneous matter. They launched into lengthy discussions of the Kansas situation, rehashed the whole theory of slavery, and even proposed to ship all the Negroes in America back to Africa at taxpayers' expense.

On December 6, Jefferson Davis, who had been put on the investigating committee, took the obstructing Senators sharply to task. He made repeated use of the word "invasion," which appeared in the title of the resolutions. "The great consideration," he emphasized, "is the invasion of a State to disturb its domestic peace, the preservation of which is a purpose which stands prominent among the great objects for which our Union was formed. . . . That word 'invasion' once had a signification which carried the mind simply to foreigners alone. God forbid we should ever come to learn that it means likewise a portion of our own brethren." The last words touched many perturbed hearers as both a supplication and a foreboding.

The second day following, after a Northern Senator's prolonged effort to sidetrack the import of the resolutions, Davis spoke again, with quiet indignation and a certain measure of pained contempt.

"Mr. President, when recently a murderous raid was made into the State of Virginia; when insurrection and rebellion against the Government, the laws, and the Constitution, raised its odious crest, it was to be expected that when the Senate assembled it would seek to find what was the cause in order that it might apply the appropriate remedy. . . . The Senator from Illinois [Trumbull], however, introduced a proposition to embarrass the inquiry by presenting a collateral matter unconnected with any purpose which could be involved in this investigation. . . . Having first embarrassed the inquiry, he follows it up to-day with a long speech which goes into the question of slavery, taking the side of anti-slavery; and this when the country is already disturbed by the invasion of a State by a murderous gang of Abolitionists?

". . . What has a question, ethnological, social, and political, to do with the consideration of a foray like this? We had a right to expect that every Senator would be prompt to explore the cause and to apply the remedy to such an evil. . . .

". . . The men who have given money, the men who had had meetings and encouraged such acts are accomplices before the fact; and those who approve it now, those who attempt to cover it now, are criminal after the fact. . . ."

Looking in the direction of a group of radical Republicans, Davis spoke of a reputed conspiracy extending clear into England, to foment servile insurrection, and he attempted to bring forcibly to their minds the horror of such a dire event. He told of the British hireling adventurer, known as Colonel Forbes, who had been engaged by Abolitionists to create and lead a civil war in Kansas and who had turned "willing witness" against his employers when his promised salary from American antislavery funds was not promptly paid.

". . . It was foretold in England long before occurred this treasonable act, that insurrection among the slaves of the South would happen, and the disappointment must be, that the only rebellion of the slaves was against the incendiaries who got possession of them, and from whom they escaped to return to the protection of their masters.

"Mr. President, in the case before us, the object undeniably was to incite to insurrection the ignorant slaves who were peacefully living in the relation of domestics to their Southern masters. . . . The Negroes, as domestics, have access at all hours through the unlocked doors of their masters' houses; and if their weak minds should be instigated to arson, murder, and rapine, the confidence of their protectors would render the first act of crime one of easy perpetration. How much deeper, then, is the crime of him who would incite a slave insurrection than was that of the immoral, infamous minister of Great Britain, who armed the savage Indians against our ancestors. But how much better would he be than the criminal involved, who, in the hall of Federal legislation, would seek to obstruct inquiry or to dull the sword of justice in favor of him whose crime connects with all that is most abhorrent to humanity, the violation of every obligation to the social compact, the laws, the Constitution, the requirements of public virtue and personal honor."

Such a strong speech coming from a man of Jefferson Davis's rectitude and acknowledged integrity must have made those excusing legislators squirm unless they were conscienceless. Their persistent roundabout, implied defense of Brown made the abortive raid loom up as a foreshadowing of the kind of subjugation and vengeance an increasing faction anticipated. Davis was as unprepared for this unexpected reaction of certain Northern Senators as he was amazed at glorification of the deed by supposedly sober-minded intellectuals of high repute. If an unemotional man like Emerson, a onetime professing minister of God, could rapturously compare Brown's gibbet to the cross of Christ, what justice could the South expect from less temperate Northern brethren? It would be extremely difficult for Senator Davis to still the fears of his constituents and make them believe in amity with the North.

The Brown raid, together with the excusing justification, had virtually killed the hope of compromise. Harrowed by both rage and grief, realizing the depth and virulence of the sectional hatred, the South was impelled toward secession by its passionate extremists with their "we-told-you-so" and "this-is-only-the-beginning" kind of talk.

While the nation was seething, a seditious work called *The Impending Crisis in the South: How to Meet It*, which had been first published in 1857, was reissued in large quantities. "No book," said Buchanan, "could be better calculated for the purpose of intensifying the mutual hatred between the North and the South." The author was a North Carolina-born man named Hinton Rowan Helper. As a drastic way of abolishing slavery, he called not for a black insurrection, but for a revolt of the "poor whites" against the slaveholders. It was his purpose to stir up jealousy and resentment in the Southern "have-nots." Helper pointed out that of the 6,184,477 persons in the slave states in 1850, only 347,525 were slave owners, and he declared poor whites were regarded with less esteem than Negroes. He urged nonslaveholding Southerners to band together politically to defeat all proslavery candidates. He advocated no fraternizing whatever with proslavery men in society, "no fellowship with them in religion." To create economic embarrassment, he advised nonslaveowners to boycott proslavery shops and all hotels and restaurants served by slaves; to refuse to pay fees to proslavery doctors and lawyers; and to discontinue subscriptions to proslavery newspapers.

Then with insolence and mocking prophecy he addressed the slaveholding citizenry:

"But, sirs, slave-holders, chevaliers, and lords of the lash, we are unwilling to allow you to cheat the negroes out of all the rights and claims to which, as human beings, they are most sacredly entitled. . . .

"What are you going to do about it? Something dreadful, of course. Perhaps you will dissolve the Union again. Do it, if you dare. Our motto, and we would have you understand it, is 'The abolition of slavery and the perpetuation of the American Union.' If, by any means, you do succeed in your treasonable attempts to take the South out of the Union today, we will bring her back tomorrow; if she goes away with you, she will return without you."

To intelligent readers of any persuasion the ominous significance of the last clause stood out as if italicized. When many Northern Congressmen gave the book the stamp of approval by buying copies of a condensed version called the *Compendium* to use as political propaganda, Jefferson Davis was much disquieted.

Sick at heart over the mounting hatred on both sides and the deplorable waste of time caused by fruitless discussions of African slavery, Davis worked hard at the nation's business during the early months of the congressional session. He spoke often and tellingly on such variegated measures as the bill to abolish the franking privilege, on the sale of arms to the states, the consular and diplomatic bill, the pay of the navy, contracts made by the Secretary of War, the Military Academy appropriations. His amazing fund of information, his detailed knowledge of an incredible variety of subjects never failed to impress his colleagues, the galleries, and the stenographers.

E. V. Murphy, an official stenographer of the Senate, who was just beginning to practice his shorthand during Mr. Davis's last senatorial years, made an interesting comment on the Mississippian at the time of his death. "He was a nervous, energetic speaker, and very impressive," Murphy recalled to a Washington reporter. "He spoke rapidly and forcibly, as if he were thoroughly in earnest. This earnest force made him highly effective. He gave everyone who saw him the impression he was a born leader. . . ." In reply to a question about Senator Davis's personal characteristics, Murphy said:

"He was courteous and kind to all. He gave strangers the impression that he was reserved and unapproachable, but this was not so. His quick nervous temperament made him easily nettled

## THE DEMOCRATIC PARTY SPLITS ASUNDER 345

and when he was disturbed he would sometimes make a sharp retort, but he would apologize for it the next moment. . . . I recollect particularly how kind Mr. Davis was to all the employees of the Senate. He knew them personally and would ask after them and their families, if they had any. He was a favorite with all the employees for another reason, and that was because he would always endeavor to secure extra compensation for them."

Bearing out Murphy's opinion, by way of apology to one of the Republican Senators at whom he had pointed some rather stinging remarks, Davis said on the floor: "If yesterday there was anything in my language which personally reflected on that Senator, it was not so designed. I am aware that I am very apt to be earnest, perhaps some would say excited, when I am speaking, and it is due to myself that I should say now, once for all, that I do not intend ever to offer discourtesy to any gentleman. By no indirection, by no equivocal expression, do I ever seek to injure the feelings of anyone."

In this strained year of 1860, the coming presidential nominations intensified the national tension by creating antagonisms within the political parties themselves.

Though Jefferson Davis has been falsely accused by antipathetical historians of seeking the 1860 Democratic nomination for himself, not in any written evidence or reported conversation is there a suggestion that this is true. Clement C. Clay, who had good reason to profess that Davis was "as intimate and confidential with him as with any person outside his own family," wrote: "He never evinced any such aspiration by word or sign." Davis himself states unequivocally in his *Rise and Fall of the Confederate Government* that he had no more desire to be President of the United States than he did of the Confederacy. He was more than content to hold the office of Senator from Mississippi—"one which I preferred to all others."

"So far from wishing to change this position [of senator] for any other, I had specially requested my friends not to permit my name to be used before the Convention for any nomination whatever.

"I had been so near the office for four years, while in the cabinet of Pierce, that I saw it from behind the scenes, and it was to me an office in nowise desirable. The responsibilities were great; the labor, the vexations, the disappointments, were greater. Those who have intimately known the official and personal life of our Presidents cannot fail to remember how few have left the office as happy men as when they entered it."

There is plenty of testimony, however, that under other circumstances Davis might well have had the nomination forced on him as Pierce did. Even the Republican politician James G. Blaine, who later libeled Davis viciously, wrote in *Twenty Years in Congress* that Davis "had been growing in favour with a powerful element in the Democracy of the free states, and but for the exasperating quarrel of 1860 might have been selected as the presidential candidate of his party."

Davis had staunch admirers throughout the North, from Massachusetts to Iowa. A Western friend well expressed the sentiment of thousands: "Among all the prominent men before the country, you have the highest reputation for decision of character and unfaltering will. I sincerely hope that by the time the Charleston convention assembles, public opinion will fix upon Jefferson Davis as the man of the time."

Franklin Pierce, whom Davis himself preferred for the nomination, wrote him on January 6, 1860:

"I have just had a pleasant interview with Mr. Shepley, whose courage and fidelity are equal to his learning and talent. He says he would rather fight the battle with you as a standard-bearer . . . than under the auspices of any other leader. This feeling and judgment . . . is, I am confident, rapidly gaining ground in New England. Our people are looking for 'the coming man'—one who is raised by all the elements in his character above the atmosphere ordinarily breathed by politicians—a man really fitted for this emergency by his ability, courage, broad statesmanship and patriotism. Col. Seymour arrived this morning and expressed his views in this relation in almost the identical language used by Mr. Shepley."

In these letters, one from a private citizen and one from an ex-President, were struck two lines that etched the true public character of Jefferson Davis: "The highest reputation for decisions of character and unfaltering will," and "one who is raised by all the elements in his character above the atmosphere ordinarily breathed by politicians."

Two days after his January 6 letter, Pierce wrote again, late in the night, to say good-by just before he sailed to Nassau. At this time Jefferson Davis might well have wished himself leaving the disturbed land with its seemingly unsolvable problems, which kept him relentlessly busy by day and sleepless by night.

In the midst of the senatorial proceedings of January 30, while Nicolson of Tennessee was reading a tiresome speech "on the everlasting negro question," Davis stopped listening and took the opportunity to answer Franklin Pierce's letters. In the casual writing, he touched on family matters, and his concern over national affairs.

Senate Chamber<br>Jany. 30, 1860

My dear friend,

We are yet, as when you sailed, talking in the Senate and wrangling for organization in the House. . . .

Govr. Dana of Me. is still here and much concerned lest our party should be divided at Charleston. I have not been able to show him how the question could be adjusted by "resolution," but have told him of the only way I have seen, and which is that of nominating the man who will be accepted by both sections without a platform.

Yesterday we had our youngest boy christened Joseph Evan and wished we could have had you and Mrs. Pierce to wish a "God speed" on the journey of life. . . .

The prospect for our country is not less gloomy than when you left. The condition in which Genl. Cushing said men should provide for storm seems to be rapidly approaching—I will stand by the flag and uphold the constitution whilst there is possibility of effecting any thing to preserve and perpetuate the Govt. we inherited—beyond that my duty and my faith binds me to Mississippi & her fortunes as she may shape them. I hope on for the kind Providence that has preserved us heretofore and still labor at my [post] as a member of the general Govt.

Please present my kindest remembrances and most friendly wishes to Mrs. Pierce. . . .

Hoping to hear from you often, I am as ever truly yrs.

Jeffer: Davis

Davis did not consider the dynamic Democratic Senator from Illinois as one who could be accepted by both sections, for Douglas advocated a platform unpalatable to the South. Though Davis believed Douglas probably had more adherents than any other potential candidate, he knew there were numerous Democrats in the North, as well as in the South, who were decidedly antipathetic to the "Little Giant." Throughout the early spring of 1860 Davis was receiving letters from all over the country urging him not to support Douglas.

A prominent Maine jurist, J. D. Dickerson, wrote on March 17: "I beg to say first and ever, that the assertion that Mr. Douglas is the only man that can carry the requisite number of electoral votes at the North is false. . . . I trust, therefore, that the South will stand firmly, and not be cajoled or driven into the nomination of Mr. Douglas at Charleston, for, if nominated, it must be by southern votes. The national men at the North could not but regard the nomination of Mr. Douglas as a repudiation of themselves by the South for their fidelity to southern rights."

From an unimportant man in Des Moines named Jacob Jones, Davis got much the same warning and also a shrewd observation on Douglas's seeming ambivalence. "But what is strange to me is, the Douglas Democracy boast they are more opposed to slavery than the Black Republicans are, they claim to have secured, the

Freedom of Kansas, they all claim they would oppose the extension of slavery in the Territories, as citizens of the same, for they all denounce the institution of slavery as bitterly as the Black Republicans. . . . But Mr. Douglas's position in regard to his squatter sovereignty is deceptive, and more fatal, for his principle invites the Slave holder to come into the Territories, to be unceremoniously kicked out again. . . . Can the South rely upon the Douglas Democracy?"

And from M. D. Haynes, Treasurer of Mississippi, came a note expressing in execrable syntax that state's strong aversion to the Douglas candidacy. "Douglas could not get a Respectable Electoral Ticket in Miss if Nominated at Charleston— There isn't 7 leading men in the State that would Serve— They would feel themselves personally degraded to do So— Such is the General feeling in Miss— There are a few men, mere camp followers, who, perhaps, would want Miss to vote for Douglas if nominated— But I apprehend the Charleston Convention will act Sensibly & tell him to go— I do not believe he Could even carry Illinois in a Presidential Canvass— It would be worse than Suicidal to nominate him— It Certainly Cannot be done—"

Though he preserved friendly relations with Douglas, Davis felt about him very much as did the Treasurer of Mississippi. He could not trust him. No more did scores of leading Democrats on both sides of the Mason-Dixon Line. Southern extremists like Rhett and Yancey were violently anti-Douglas. Prominent New England conservatives like Caleb Cushing and Edward Everett were stoutly against him. President Buchanan opposed his candidacy for personal as well as national reasons.

In an effort to defeat Douglas for the nomination, the national committee had deliberately chosen for the convention the Southern city in which the "Little Giant" was least liked. Because Davis feared Douglas might disrupt party unity and risk disunion to gain his ends, he departed from his well-known practice of not attempting to influence a convention while a member of Congress. Though he refrained from attending in person, he made it clear he felt Douglas should be defeated, unless he relinquished his "squatter sovereignty" tenet. His real quarrel with Douglas boiled down to the question of Federal protection of slave property in territories, which the Illinois Senator disputed. When the delegates convened in historic Charleston on April 23, 1860 (by chance, it was Douglas's forty-seventh birthday) a struggle ensued over that one controversial plank in the platform. The Southern delegates abided by Davis's insistence on Federal protection of all property in the territories. The Northern delegates remained relentlessly committed to Douglas's hands-off—"squatter sovereignty." On this single contention the Democratic party split asunder. If Douglas had given in, he would surely, despite powerful opposition, have been the Democratic nominee and, with a unified party behind him, he might have realized his consuming ambition to be Chief Executive. But Davis—and the Lower South—could not give up a principle they felt was upheld by both the Constitution and the Supreme Court in the late Dred Scott case.

The fiery Yancey was the leading speaker to proclaim that the Federal Government must protect slavery in the territories. Douglas would not subscribe to the doctrine and said without clarification that the party would abide by future Supreme Court decisions. Doubtless he felt that by opposing Federal protection of slavery he would win a host of Northern votes that would otherwise go to the Republicans.

When on April 30 by a narrow majority of 37 out of 303 total votes the convention finally adopted Douglas's vague platform, William Yancey delivered a diatribe against "Northern invasion of Southern rights." Then he presented an ultimatum: the platform of the Lower South must be accepted or Alabama delegates would withdraw. When the Douglas delegates remained firm, Yancey and the Alabama delegation dramatically walked out. They were followed by delegates from most of the cotton states except Georgia. With the departure of Georgia the next day, Alexander H. Stephens dismally prophesied war within a year.

With most of the Lower South delegates departed, Douglas's cohorts could not muster the two-thirds majority for nomination required by Democratic party rules. The Massachusetts delegation, forty-nine strong, steadfastly cast its vote for Jefferson Davis in fifty-seven sequent ballots. One of the Massachusetts men, Benjamin F. Butler (later called the "Beast of New Orleans"), who had heard Davis speak in Faneuil Hall, believed that he was the man who could unite the Northern and Southern Democrats. "I am proud of having voted as I did," Butler declared afterward in Congress, ". . . I believed that Mr. Davis would be the strongest, most available candidate the Democratic party could run; and if nominated he would defeat the Republican candidate."

Particularly in light of the Bay State's unswerving support, this question presents itself: If the Lower South delegates had not bolted, would Jefferson Davis have eventually secured the nomination? Was he, as Butler always believed, the man who could have reconciled the opposing factions? Perhaps few would dare defend the affirmative of this putative speculation. But if nineteen of the Douglas-committed delegates had switched and voted for the Davis platform, it is possible that Davis would have been nominated—Pennsylvania with its swelling numbers was reputed to be ready to join Massachusetts. Dodd says that "it may be fairly argued that he [Davis] might have been the choice of the convention had the majority report of the committee on the platform prevailed." Mrs. Davis always entertained the fond belief that if Jefferson Davis had appeared before other Northern audiences "with his heart and hand open to them as he had in Boston, he might have saved the Union and prevented the war."

At last, after prolonged balloting, when neither Douglas nor anyone else could be nominated, the convention adjourned. A new meeting was scheduled for June 18 in Baltimore and an appeal was sent to the cotton states to select new delegates. The withdrawn Southern delegates, however, had met in private, adopted the platform Davis favored, and planned their own nominating convention at Richmond.

In the interim, on May 8, Jefferson Davis, still hoping to bring Douglas around, took the argument into the Senate. He spoke frankly of the unhappy division that had entered the ranks of his party. He had noted the triumphant grins on Republican faces when the telegraphed news reached the Senate. "We saw the enemies of Democracy," he said, "waiting to be invited to its funeral." He pressed the Senate to vote on his modified Resolutions on the Relations of the States, which had been submitted originally on February 2 and revised on March 1.

On urging a vote, Davis stated in clear terms what he wanted and expected. He asked that when personal and property rights in the territories are not properly protected, Congress should intervene and provide the means to secure an adequate remedy in each case. "I ask that the Territorial Legislature be made to understand beforehand that the Congress of the United States does not concede to them the power to interfere with the rights of person or property guaranteed by the Constitution."

Because Douglas had declared on the floor of the Senate that he would not accept the Democratic nomination if the platform demanded congressional protection of slave property in the territories, Davis smiled a trifle scornfully at the man's self-esteem. "Does the Senator consider it modest," he chided, "to announce to the Democratic convention on what terms he will accept the nomination, but presumptuous in a state to declare the principle on which she will give him her vote?" He paused, and added wryly to the delight of the chamber, "It is an advance on Louis Quatorze."

Day after day ensued long, wearisome arguments, with numerous Senators interpolating and offering amendments to each section of the resolutions. But the debate was really between Davis and Douglas. Bitterness sometimes cropped out. Douglas looked upon Davis as the man who was barring his way to the White House, while Davis felt he was battling for the very life of the Democratic party.

"What may be the fate of the Democratic party," Davis said, "if it suffers that division to which the Senator [Douglas] refers, I cannot say. It has achieved many a glorious victory in the cause of its country. It can claim credit for the acquisition of every acre of territory which has been added to our original domain. It leaves behind it the legacy . . . of a glorious past. If it is to be wrecked by petty controversies in relation to African labor; if a few Africans, brought into the United States, where they have advanced in comfort and civilization and knowledge, are to constitute the element which will divide the Democratic party and peril the vast hopes . . . I trust it will be remembered that a few of us have stood by the old landmarks of those who framed the Constitution."

In the end a goodly majority voted with Davis, passed the resolutions seriatim, affirmed the doctrine that neither a territorial legislature nor the United States Congress could prohibit slavery in the territories, because they were a common possession of all the states. The acceptance of the Davis Resolutions by the Senate amounted to the Democratic party's repudiation of Douglas just as he was expecting to be nominated for the presidency at Baltimore.

In mid-May when the Republicans met at Chicago their hopes were red-hued because of the Democratic ruptures at Charleston. The nation as a whole confidently expected William Seward, the recognized party head, to be nominated. However, various delegates were committed to Salmon P. Chase, to Simon Cameron, or to Edward Bates of Missouri, because of the latter's conservatism on the slave question and his enthusiastic support by Horace Greeley. A fifth candidate, whose managers could claim the support of only one state a week before the convention's opening, was a dark horse named Abraham Lincoln. He had not long since gained national reputation in a famous series of debates with Stephen A. Douglas, in which he had proved a sharp opponent, with a homespun wit that convulsed his hearers. Lincoln was as fortunate in the choice of convention town, Chicago, as Douglas had been unlucky in Charleston. He was on home ground, where whooping Western exuberance made the raw atmosphere quite different from what it would have been in any of the three great northeastern cities.

A huge wooden building called the Wigwam had been erected

for the great occasion. Judge David Davis, Lincoln's three-hundred-pound chief manipulator, had taken the third floor of the best hotel, Tremont House, for headquarters, and in the words of Carl Sandburg, "rooms for his staff of Lincoln hustlers, evangelists, pleaders, exhorters, schemers." In the parlor liquors of all kinds were set out, along with thousands of cigars for the delegates and people of influence. Chicago's 100,000-plus population was swelled by more than 30,000 Westerners who had come to root for one of their own sons.

Thurlow Weed, in charge of Seward's campaign, dispensed hospitality at Richmond House to the thousand cheerers he had brought from New York, as well as all other pro-Seward politicians. The Lincoln followers let the Seward men have prominence until the adoption of a platform, but they never ceased cajoling and trading behind the scenes.

While Lincoln's managers were exhausting themselves with ballyhoo, dodges, and trades, he was sending them restraining notes and tempered telegrams from Springfield, refusing to commit himself or be bound. Finally, in private conference, when they became exasperated with their candidate's caution, David Davis quashed the matter by telling the other manipulators, "Lincoln ain't here, and don't know what we have to meet, so we will go ahead as if we hadn't heard from him, and he must ratify it." They won over state delegation after state delegation by "paying their price" and "promising them anything," including Cabinet posts.

On May 17, Lincoln's friend Lamon made a little deal with the printer of seat tickets. Long after midnight men worked "signing names of convention officers to counterfeit seat tickets," so that next morning Lincoln supporters could fill up the hall. On May 18, at sunrise the thousands of Lincoln shouters were rushed through the Wigwam doors until they filled the seats and jammed much of the standing room. Only a small proportion of Seward's cohorts could squirm their way in. The infuriated majority of Seward men could only mill about outside with the mob of 30,000 strangers who had come on cheap excursion tickets to yell for their favorite son, "Good Old Abe, The Rail Splitter."

At punctuated handkerchief signals from the platform, when Lincoln's name was mentioned, bedlam broke loose. As a local character boasted, "The idea of us Hoosiers and Suckers being outscreamed would have been bad. Five thousand people leaped to their seats . . . and the wild yell made vesper breathings of all that had preceded. A thousand steam whistles, ten acres of hotel gongs, a tribe of Comanches, might have mingled in the scene unnoticed."[1]

On the first ballot, in which Seward received 173½ votes, Lincoln got 102, while the three other candidates were in the neighborhood of 50 each. The surprising initial strength of the Illinoisan had a potent effect. Though Seward needed only 60 additional votes for a majority, he never got them. Lincoln's campaign managers bargained smartly for votes, pledging Cabinet posts without his sanction or knowledge. On the third ballot Lincoln received a majority. And then came the proverbial landslide, with tumultuous shouting and the booming of cannon to announce (as it turned out) one of the fateful events in America's history and doom to the South.

The East seemed as unprepared for Lincoln's nomination as the South. Boston, says Catherine Drinker Bowen, had looked upon him as a "mere local politician, adroit in stirring up the hatred of one section of his country against the South." The *Boston Post*, she says, admitted only to his "talent for demagogical appeal." Wendell Phillips asked contemptuously, "Who is this huckster in politics?" But Douglas, who had measured his enemy, knew him as "a strong man of his party—full of wit, facts, dates—and the best stump-speaker, with his droll ways, in the West."

The horrified South considered Abraham Lincoln as the embodiment of Republican ill will. Though he professed a hands-off

[1] The description of the Chicago Republican convention is based on and largely taken from Carl Sandburg's *Abraham Lincoln* and W. E. Barringer's "Campaign Technique in Illinois—1860," *Transactions,* Illinois State Historical Society, 1932, pp. 203-281.

policy as to the institution of slavery within the states that already had it, the South had no confidence in his protestations. Besides, he was considered crude and vulgar, just as cultivated New Englanders and a large portion of the Northern press proclaimed. Southerners were filled with a chilling fear that Lincoln would attempt to remold their culture "in the Yankee pattern."

Another presidential convention, of those who still clung to the old Whig party, together with some remnants of other minor conservative organizations who could not stomach radical Republicanism, held a meeting in Baltimore on May 19 and nominated John Bell of Tennessee and Edward Everett of Massachusetts. The new Constitutional Union party, as it was called, drew its major strength from the border states.

A few days before the Democratic convention met at Baltimore, Davis wrote Pierce a letter in which he revealed his low spirits.

"We all deplore the want of unanimity as to the candidate among our Southern friends and I do not see any satisfactory solution of the difficulty. The darkest hour precedes the dawn and it may be that light will break upon us when most needed and less expected. . . .

"If Northern men insist upon nominating Douglas we must be beaten and with such alienation as leaves nothing to hope for in the future of nationality in our organization. . . .

"I have never seen the country in so great danger and those who protect it seem to be unconscious of the necessity. If our little grog-drinking, electioneering Demagogue [Douglas] can destroy our hopes, it must be that we have been doomed to destruction."

The contending Democratic factions at Baltimore were by no means reconciled. The Douglas supporters would not permit the Lower South's original delegates to sit. Bitterness tinctured the confusion. On the fifth day the chairman, Caleb Cushing, gave up and retired; most of the delegates from Virginia, North Carolina, and Tennessee walked out. Yet Douglas persisted. With the hall cleared of his opponents, he got what he wanted. Alabama's

Benjamin Fitzpatrick was nominated to be his running mate; but when he promptly declined, Herschel V. Johnson of Georgia was chosen in his place.

The Charleston fracture was bad enough, but the one at Baltimore was disastrous. The cotton state delegates, first meeting at Richmond on June 11, convened at Baltimore on June 28, for the nominations. They named Buchanan's handsome Vice-President John C. Breckinridge of Kentucky and Oregon's Joseph Lane as their standard bearers. Breckinridge gave the keynote of the South's unhappy state when he said ruefully to Mrs. Davis immediately after his nomination: "I trust I have the courage to lead a forlorn hope."

At the most critical time in the party's history, the Democrats were now split three ways, for many stood with the Whigs. On the other hand the Republicans were cemented by two sectional appeals: antislavery and protection. The two great subjects of contention, slavery and high tariffs that would protect Northern industry, had brought East and West together. Above the Mason-Dixon Line the men who wanted protection were willing to attack slavery and the men who hated slavery would swallow protection. "The efforts of the Republicans' wirepullers and caucusmongers," wrote the observing Marquess of Lothian, "contrived to unite all the scattered elements out of which a party could be formed in the North—Puritans and Roman Catholics, Abolitionists and nigger-haters, foreigners and natives—into one compact body, united on the principle of opposition to the South. . . . Now, for the first time since the Union began, there was seen the new phenomenon of a distinctly-avowed Northern party. The South could not avoid seeing what would happen if this party were to get the upper hand."

The Scottish nobleman saw that the "irrepressible conflict" between North and South had been delayed only by the fact that the Democratic party was strong enough to hold in the infuriated extremes of both sections without allowing them to come in collision. "It was originally the party of State Rights as against the

Union," he said; "it became the party of State Rights for the sake of the Union." But now it was hopelessly divided in itself.

With the triple split of Lincoln's opponents, Davis was convinced that the Republicans were bound to win despite Douglas's inordinate belief in his own magnetic power. In a desperate effort to forestall the election that many Southerners swore would be the cue for secession, Davis asked Senator Bell, the Constitutional Union candidate, and Vice-President Breckinridge if they would be willing to withdraw if a Democrat more generally acceptable to all parts of the country could be decided upon. Both gentlemen authorized Davis to say that they would. Then laying by all pride for the sake of union, in humility Davis called on Douglas to ask if he would consider withdrawing. In the *Rise and Fall of the Confederate Government* Davis wrote:

"When I made this announcement to Douglas—with whom my relations had always been such as to authorize the assurance that he could not consider it as made in an unfriendly spirit—he replied that the scheme proposed was impracticable, because his friends, mainly Northern Democrats, if he were withdrawn, would join in the support of Lincoln, rather than of any one that should supplant him [Douglas]; that he was in the hands of his friends, and was sure they would not accept the proposition.

"It needed but little knowledge of the status of parties in the several states to foresee a probable defeat if the conservatives were to continue divided into three parts, and the aggressives were to be held in solid column. But angry passions, which are always bad counselors, had been aroused, and hopes were still cherished, which proved to be illusory."

Heartsick at the debacle of the Democratic party, Davis worked hard through June, addressing Congress on various appropriation bills: legislative, army, naval, and civil. He also spoke eloquently for justice for the deserving Choctaw tribe of Indians, whom the Government had treated shabbily.

As he journeyed to Mississippi at the adjournment of Congress, he was aware that he would have to face constituents who regarded the situation as hopeless. Considering the gloomy prospects of the coming election, he wondered how secession could possibly be prevented if Lincoln won.

"Why did not the South secede?" asked Lord Lothian across the Atlantic, voicing the opinion of numerous thinking Britons. "She had suffered enough from the Union to have learned, that whatever its advantages might be for the North, it was of no advantage to her; and every session proved that the chance of equal legislation was growing less and less, for the majority had neither mercy nor good faith. . . . The South clung from sentimental motives to the Union; and she persisted in hoping against hope that things would grow better."

# CHAPTER XXII

# SOUTH CAROLINA SECEDES

ON ELECTION DAY, November 6, Jefferson Davis duly cast his vote in Warren County and awaited the national tally with some of the perfervid anticipation that gripped the country from Maine to Texas. When the official count was published, Abraham Lincoln had received 1,866,352 popular votes as against some 2,800,000 for his opponents. Douglas had 1,376,957 votes, Breckinridge 849,781, and Bell 588,879.[1] Since the rivals together had almost a million more votes than the Republican candidate, the will of the majority clearly opposed Lincoln's presidency. Yet in that curious political arrangement known as the electoral college, Lincoln won by an impressive margin. Douglas, who was less than half a million behind Lincoln's popular vote, received only 12 electoral votes in all: Missouri's 9 and 3 of New Jersey's 7. Though he had doggedly insisted that he alone could win over the Republicans in the North, he received only three-sevenths of the electoral vote of a single Northern state, New Jersey. He stood at the tail end of the candidates; Bell had 39 electoral votes, Breckinridge 72, and Lincoln 180.

Professor Randall, Lincoln's able biographer, points up the significant fact that Lincoln was elected "not because of a lack of union among his rivals, but because of advantageous distribution of his votes among populous states." In New York, for instance,

[1] These figures are reported by Edward Stanwood and accepted by Lincoln's biographer, J. G. Randall. Slightly variant totals are given by other sources.

though in the popular vote Douglas received 312,510 to Lincoln's 362,646, the state's entire 35 electoral votes were all counted against him.

Lincoln, who did not receive a single vote in ten of the Southern states, was obviously a sectional as well as a minority president. Wendell Phillips, one of the most vocal of the long-time Abolitionists, now announced with defiant satisfaction: "No man has a right to be surprised at this state of things. It is the first sectional party ever organized in this country . . . it is not national—it is sectional. The Republican party is a party of the North pledged against the South." To the Douglas Democrats and even to some Republicans, Mr. Lincoln was, in the phrase of his admirer Thomas Beer, "an amiable freak who had been rushed into office by the mob." But President he was to be and the South was mightily stirred up. Jefferson Davis took the news of the Republican victory with grave misgivings.

Mrs. James Chestnut, wife of the Senator from South Carolina, who was traveling on a train on November 7, recorded in her diary some feelings of the hour. When a man in her coach received a telegram announcing the returns, "the excitement was very great. . . . Everybody was talking at the same time— One, a little more moved than the others, stood up—saying despondently— 'The die is cast— No more vain regrets— Sad forebodings are useless. The stake is life or death' . . . and some one cried out: 'Now that the black Republicans have the power I suppose they will Brown us all.'"

The manifestations in the Southern states which followed the Republican victory, Davis later wrote, "did not proceed from chagrin at their defeat, or from any personal hostility to the President-elect, but from the fact that they recognized in him the representative of a party professing principles destructive to their peace, their prosperity and their domestic tranquility." One of the inevitable fears was that more John Browns would spring forth to stir up insurrection among the blacks. And now that Lincoln had control of patronage, would he not put Republicans in Southern post offices and would not the mails be flooded with incendiary propaganda?

The South had endured the North's taunts and insults—"not indeed without a murmur"—but she still had endured them. And she had borne the domination of the Northern majority in a way which adversely affected her economics and gave every indication of growing worse. As Lothian, the free-trade Britisher, saw it, the South "had submitted to bear far more than her share of the taxes of the Federation. She had seen the money that was forced from her against her will expended in bounties to Northern manufacturers, and in plunder for Northern office-seekers. She had seen trade carried away from her borders, her coasts neglected. . . . She had seen her rivals fattening on her spoil, and glorying in the triumph as well as the advantage of doing so. But never before had she seen a party whose war-cry was to be, the North versus the South. . . ."

Three days after the election, Davis received at Brierfield a letter from Robert Barnwell Rhett, Jr., hotheaded editor of the Charleston *Mercury*, asking his opinion about the attitude of Mississippi in case of immediate and separate secession by South Carolina. Perplexed as how to answer, Davis replied on November 10 that his home was so isolated that he had no intercourse with those who might aid him in forming an opinion as to the effect produced on the mind of the people by the election. But he doubted whether South Carolina should withdraw from the Union without assurance that the cotton states would follow.

"The planting states," he wrote, "have a common interest of such magnitude that their union, sooner or later, for the protection of that interest, is certain. United they will have ample power for their own protection, and their exports will make for them allies of all commercial and manufacturing powers. . . . My opinion is, therefore, as it has been . . . to bring those states into cooperation before asking for a popular decision upon a new policy. . . . I have written with the freedom and carelessness of private correspondence, and regret that I could not give more precise information."

Davis's letter was certainly not calculated to stimulate Rhett or anyone else to hasty action. The only comfort Davis could give Rhett was in the line: "If the secession of South Carolina should be followed by an attempt to coerce her back into the Union, that act of usurpation, folly, and wickedness would enlist every true Southern man for her defense."

On the very day Davis wrote from Brierfield, South Carolina's legislature called for a "Sovereignty Convention" to meet seven days later. That same day Senator James Chestnut resigned his seat in the Senate; the other South Carolina senator followed on November 13.

Davis shortly received a summons from Mississippi's Governor Pettus to confer with him and the other congressional representatives to consider whether the state should pass an ordinance of secession or endeavor to hold South Carolina in check for some later concerted action. Davis opposed immediate and separate state action. He declared himself against secession as long as any hope of a peaceable remedy remained. "While holding," he wrote later, "that the right of a State to secede was unquestionable, the knowledge I had gained, as Chairman of the Military Committee and as Secretary of War, had made me familiar with the entire lack of preparation for war in the South; and, unlike most of my associates, I did not believe that secession would be peaceably accomplished, but that war would surely ensue between the sections." However, he affirmed that he would stand by the decision of the majority.

His confreres regarded him as "too slow" and correctly asserted that "he was behind the general opinion of the people of the State as to the propriety of prompt secession." According to his intimate associate, Senator Clay of Alabama, Jefferson Davis took no active part in planning or hastening secession. "He reluctantly and regretfully consented to it as a political necessity for the preservation of popular and State rights."

Before the conference in Mississippi ended, Davis received a telegram signed by two Cabinet members urging his immediate return to Washington: Buchanan was preparing a message to be presented at the forthcoming session of Congress and sought his advice. Davis's colleagues, perhaps glad to have him gone, advised him to comply.

Just as he was leaving for Washington, Davis received a letter from his wife dated November 15, 1860, giving him a glimpse of the state of confusion and unrest in the capital.

My dear Husband—

I trust from the newspaper accounts you are quite well, and Mr. Wigfall tells me you were in good spirits when he saw you, and looking well.

. . . I dined at Mrs. Woods today and they asked a great many questions about you. There is interest felt here to know what you are doing or will do. I always say I don't know, and can't guess, that there is one thing we do know, and that is that we quit here the 4th of March. . . . People talked so impudently of disunionism before me that I hunted up my old white satin flag: "If any man calls me a disunionist I will answer him in monosyllables. Jeff. Davis," and declared I'd hang it up and quarrel with the first person who said a word. Mr. Buchanan has taken it, however, and vows I shan't have it again. There is a settled gloom over everyone here. . . . *Everybody is scared*, especially Mr. Buchanan. Humphries is eminently conservative and quite metropolitan. Wigfall is talking—and so on to the bitter end. Hunter opposed secession. Jake Thompson is prepared to go with the majority for everything. Toombs's blathering about a resignation (in future). No one rings like the true metal so much as Constitution Browne, who is enthusiastic and thoroughgoing, repudiates Mr. Buchanan openly, assuming secession responsibility.

Good bye, dear Husband. I hardly think you care to hear from me since you don't write, though you have been so busy. I won't stick to that. May God direct you right, prays

Your wife,<br>W. D.

Arriving in Washington, Senator Davis promptly called on the President, who read to him a draft of his forthcoming message.

Davis made certain suggestions for its modification, which Buchanan accepted, though he subsequently changed some. In the consultation Davis stood firmly on the ground of State Rights. He was disappointed to find that Buchanan, good Democrat and supporter of Breckinridge, had now come around to Webster's view expressed long before that a state had no right to secede. Davis reasoned with him, but to no avail. Buchanan had fallen under the influence of the Northern members of his Cabinet.

In his message to Congress December 3, the President blamed the Abolitionists for the national crisis. He affirmed that the existing peril arose from incessant Northern agitation, which had shattered family security in the South. "Many a matron," he said, "retires at night in dread of what may befall herself and her children before the morning." All that the South asked for, he emphasized, was to be let alone to manage its own domestic institutions. He did not believe the last presidential election, of itself, afforded just cause for dissolving the Union. He insisted that justice required that some overt act be awaited before resorting to such a remedy. While denying the validity of the right of secession, he concluded that it was "not a valid Federal power to make war upon a seceded state." He was convinced that even if the power of coercion existed, it would be unwise to exercise it in fraternal conflict. "Our Union rests upon public opinion," he said, "and can never be cemented by the blood of its citizens shed in civil war."

Buchanan was clearly torn between his Southern sympathies and his Unionism. His policy was to conciliate insofar as he could. But Davis could not persuade him to come out unequivocally for the constitutional right of secession, and his Northern advisers could not get him to threaten force. However odd and anomalous his viewpoint seemed, Buchanan held fast to it as a means of preserving peace, at least through his own regime. He lost friends in both camps and brought upon himself contemporary ridicule and an undeserved bad epitaph in history.[2]

[2] Auchampaugh's *Buchanan* and Harper's *Parallel Source Problems in American History*, edited by McLaughlin, Dodd, Jernegan, and Scott, substantially improve this epitaph.

On December 10, in answer to a resolution for investing the Federal Government with greatly increased physical powers, Jefferson Davis pleaded in the Senate for better understanding.

"I call upon all men who have in their hearts a love of the Union . . . to look the question calmly but fully in the face that they may see the true cause of our danger, which . . . I believe to be is that a sectional hostility has been substituted for a general fraternity, and thus the Government rendered powerless for the ends for which it was instituted. The hearts of a portion of the people have been perverted by that hostility, so that the powers delegated by the compact of union are regarded, not as means to secure the welfare of all, but as instruments for the destruction of a part, the minority section. How then, have we to provide a remedy? By strengthening this government? By instituting physical force to overawe the States, to coerce the people . . . to pass under the yoke of the Federal Government? No, sir. I would have the Union severed into thirty-three fragments sooner than have that great evil befall constitutional liberty and representative government. Our government is an agency of delegated and strictly limited powers. Its founders did not look to its preservation by force. . . . The chain they wove to bind these States together was one of love and mutual good offices. They had broken the fetters of despotic powers . . . and their sons will be degenerate indeed if . . . they forge and rivet upon their posterity the fetters which their ancestors broke. . . ."

Then facing the Republican section of the Senate, he put a stirring earnestness in his appeal: "Give us that declaration, give us that evidence of the will of your constituency to restore us to our original position, where mutual kindness was the animating motive, and then we may hopefully look for remedies which may suffice." He closed by begging them to live up to the obligations of good neighbors and friendly states united for the common welfare.

When he finished, however, he felt little assurance that his words had touched the hearts of his opponents. And in casual letters from numerous outsiders he found the very opposite of

## SOUTH CAROLINA SECEDES

reassurance. From Otter Creek, Illinois, came a letter written on December 12 by one Sidney Noble, who had been born in Mississippi.

"Twenty Seven years of residence in this State has convinced me that the south will never get her constitutional rights in the Union. I have seen enough to convince me that every constitutional man in the north will be ere long driven out of office, and a constitutional man will never again be elected to the office of President unless the south takes a determined course to have her rights or go out the union, such a course on the part of the south is the only thing that will cause the north to reflect, yet I have but little faith that such reflection will ever do any good, with such Leaders as Lincoln who became soured toward the South, who hates slavery as bad as any abolitionist, these fanatics have their mission to perform and that is to destroy the best government ever formed by man. . . .

"O sir nearly all my relation are in the south and the Idea is horrible to think of that the south must be taxed and fight the battles of the country and yet be denied equal right in the territories, it seems the north wants the south to raise cotton and shugar rice tobaco for the northern states, also to pay taxes and fight her battles and get territory for the purpose of the north to send her greasy Dutch and free niggers into the territory to get rid of them. At any rate that was what Elected old Abe President. Some professed conservative Republicans Think and say that Lincoln will be conservative also but sir my opinion is that Lincoln will deceive them he will undoubtedly please the abolitionists for at his election they nearly all went into fits with Joy. . . .

"There are a good many good Democrats in the north but our Leaders have yielded to northern fanaticism little by little untill the field has been taken and we are powerless for good."

In the meantime, while rumors of likely secession of Southern states circulated, many of Lincoln's friends urged him to make some statement that would calm the fears of the South. But he refused, saying he stood on public utterances he had already made, and the people concerned could look in newspaper files for his expressed sentiments.

Except for the absolutely relentless among the Abolitionists, the whole country was longing for some simple statement from the President-elect. But Lincoln said not a word in his own voice, though he gave secret advice to some Republican cohorts that would have added to the South's agitation if she had known it. On December 11, he said privately to Congressman William Kellogg of Illinois: "Entertain no proposition for a compromise in regard to the extension of slavery. The instant you do they have us under again; all our labor is lost. And sooner or later it must be done over. Douglas is sure to be again trying to bring in his popular sovereignty. Have none of it. The tug has to come, and better now than later. You know I think the fugitive-slave clause of the constitution ought to be enforced—to put it in its mildest form, ought not to be resisted." [3]

On December 14 Jefferson Davis was invited to the apartment of Reuben Davis of Mississippi to meet with a group of Senators and Representatives from nine Southern states to discuss the subject on everybody's mind. A joint address entitled "To Our Constituents" had been prepared by two of the legislators. "The argument is exhausted. . . . In our judgement, the Republicans are resolute in the purpose to grant nothing that will or ought to satisfy the South. We are satisfied the honor, safety, and independence of the Southern people require the organization of a Southern Confederacy—a result to be obtained only by separate state secession."

Jefferson Davis pondered the matter, and then after making some verbal alterations, signed the document. Several pointed out that a show of strength and resolution among leaders from nine states might impress those opposed to any compromise with the South. However, it was not easy for Davis to go along with a decision favoring secession, for he felt coercion and war would be

[3] More of the same attitude is expressed in Lincoln's *Works,* Vol. I, pp. 657-660.

the result. The strain brought on an attack of his old bête noire, neuralgia.

Three days later Davis read an editorial by Horace Greeley in the New York *Tribune,* which gave him a lift of hope. "If the cotton states shall become satisfied that they can do better out of the Union than in it," he said, "we insist on letting them go in peace. . . . We must ever resist the right of any state to remain in the Union, and nullify or defy the laws thereof. To withdraw from the Union is quite another matter; and whenever any considerable section of our Union shall deliberately resolve to go out, we shall resist all coercive measures to keep it in. We hope never to live in a Republic whereof one section is pinned to another by bayonets." Then he pointed up the logic Davis himself later often reiterated: If the Declaration of Independence justified the secession of three million colonists in 1776, why did it not justify the secession of five million Southerners from the Federal Union in 1861?

Back in Springfield, Illinois, the President-elect was not thinking in accord with the foremost Northern editor of the day. Yet the nation was dismayed at the prospect of secession and looked to Congress to do something to hold the Union peaceably together. The Senate now created a committee of thirteen to supersede the exploratory work already being done by a House committee of thirty-three. As a foremost leader of his section and a conservative, Jefferson Davis was asked to serve along with Toombs and Hunter, as one of the three members from the cotton states. Douglas and John J. Crittenden, Kentucky Whig, headed the five non-Republican committeemen from the border states and the North, and Seward was prominent among the five Republicans. At first, Mr. Davis declined to serve because he had signed the document "To Our Constituents," but he was finally prevailed upon.

"If," he said in yielding, "in the opinion of others, it is possible for me to do anything for the public good, the last moment while I stand here is at the command of the Senate. . . . If there be any sacrifice which I could offer on the altar of my country to heal all the evils, present or prospective, no man has the right to doubt my readiness to make it." And no one who knew the facts did doubt. As Dr. Eckenrode affirms: "No man labored with more intensity to preserve the Union than Jefferson Davis."

The venerable Crittenden, who had assumed the mantle of the Great Compromiser, was made chairman. At the first meeting on December 20 Davis proposed that no recommendation be made to the Senate in which a majority of the Republicans did not agree. Crittenden presented a carefully prepared paper covering all the disputed subjects. He proposed contemplated amendments to the Constitution, including the following: the prohibition of slavery in all territories north of 36° 30' and the protection of slavery south of that line; a denial of the power of Congress to abolish slavery in the District of Columbia, which lay between the slave states of Maryland and Virginia; remuneration for escaped slaves by communities in which the Federal fugitive slave laws might be violently obstructed. To meet the North's demands, the South was willing to abandon the Dred Scott decision of the Supreme Court and the provision of the Constitution that guaranteed the right of introduction and protection of slavery in all the territories. But the first proposition to extend the line of 36° 30' to California as the final boundary between slave and free states became the controversial issue. The Republicans would not commit themselves until they heard further from President-elect Lincoln.

Christmas decorations for the Yuletide celebration of "peace on earth, good will to men" were all in evidence in the capital by that December 20 of 1860. One of the big social events of the season, scheduled for the afternoon, was the marriage of Representative Bouligny of Louisiana to the daughter of a wealthy Washington grocer named Parker. It took place at the large Parker mansion, which had been converted into "a conservatory filled with blossoming roses and lilies," and adorned with illuminated fountains. Jefferson Davis did not feel like attending, but almost everybody else who was anybody did. A special chair had been arranged for President Buchanan, who was greatly worn by the pressure put upon him and the harsh criticisms of the press of both sides. On this gala afternoon, though he had obviously aged in the last few months, the President was in fine form and insisted he "had never enjoyed better health nor a more tranquil spirit." Before coming to the celebration he had written that morning: "I have not lost an hour's sleep nor a single meal. I weigh well and prayerfully what course I ought to adopt."

Mrs. Roger Pryor, the beautiful wife of the young Representative from Virginia, paid the old gentleman special court by standing behind his chair as guests came up to pay their respects. When the crush in the drawing room had diminished as the crowd moved to another part of the house to view the presents, all of a sudden there was an extraordinary commotion in the entrance hall. Turning to Mrs. Pryor, Buchanan said with concern, "Madame, do you suppose the house is on fire?" As if she had received a command, Mrs. Pryor slipped away through the nearest door to the hall to investigate. To her amazement she found Representative Lawrence Keitt of South Carolina leaping up and down in high elation, waving a telegram over his head and crying out, "Thank God! Thank God!" Mrs. Pryor seized hold of him, saying, "Have you lost your mind, sir? The President hears you and wants to know what is the matter."

"Oh," he exclaimed joyfully, "South Carolina has seceded. I feel like a boy let out of school."

Mrs. Pryor returned to the President's side and said in a low voice, "It appears, Mr. President, that South Carolina has seceded." Buchanan turned deathly pale, sank back into his chair and grasped its arms. Then he whispered, "Might I beg you to have my carriage called?"

Mrs. Pryor first sent his aide to him and then ordered the presidential carriage. She had her own equipage called, found her husband, and drove away heedless of bridal pair, wedding cake, champagne, adieus. She summed up the fateful hour thus: "This was the tremendous event which was to change all our lives—to give us poverty for riches, mutilation and wounds for strength and health, obscurity and degradation for honor and distinction, exile and loneliness for inherited homes and friends, pain and death for happiness and life."

Aware of dissenting voices in his own state, Jefferson Davis had hardly expected such unanimity as the 169 convention delegates displayed at Charleston. There was not one negative vote. On that momentous December 20, a young Charlestonian named W. A. Burk, assistant to the secretary of the convention, was sitting at the secretary's desk a few feet from the speaker, Maxey Gregg, when "in a death-like silence" the ordinance was passed. Burk immediately rose, raised a window, and announced the event to the crowd blocking Broad Street below. Their enthusiastic shouts were echoed almost immediately by the chimes of St. Michael's, followed by booming of cannon on the water front. The city went wild with joy. Family feuds were ended and people who had been at enmity for years met like brothers. A duel scheduled for three o'clock was called off and the principals reconciled. Women were as jubilant as men. When night came the city was illuminated, bonfires blazed, fireworks dazzled the sight, impromptu orations were delivered at top voice. Then a queer thing occurred, the memory of which was to impress Burk to his dying day. At a quarter of an hour before midnight, while the citizens were still frenzied in their demonstrations, the sky was "clear as crystal, not a cloud to be seen, the stars shown bright as jewels." Suddenly came a deafening crash of thunder, and blinding lightning dimmed the man-made illumination. As crash followed crash in quick succession, the sky became "pitchy dark." A cloudburst deluged the streets with a relentless fury. The celebrants dashed for shelter, "their hilarity turned to awe."

On arriving at home, Burk found his mother in tears. She placed a trembling hand on his head, as if in blessing to save him from disaster. "May God preserve you," she said, "through the coming struggle. You know not what you do. We of the South are few, the North are many. Our subjugation is only a matter of time; even nature seems against us." For a moment the ardent young man was repelled, as if his mother were a traitor. The next day when he opened his Charleston *Mercury* he was astonished to see dispatches from Montgomery and Baltimore, as well as from New York, headed "Foreign News." He realized that he was no longer a citizen of the United States, but of the "Republic of South Carolina." [4]

With complex emotions Jefferson Davis read reports of the reception of the news in various other Southern cities. In the first high excitement the public shouted approval, without giving a thought to potential consequences. When, in New Orleans, an actor on the stage of the Varieties Theatre announced South Carolina's secession, the audience went into such a paroxysm of glee that the show had to be called off. The people rushed out, joined a street assemblage, sang the "Marseillaise" in French and in English. The bust of John C. Calhoun, decorated with the cockade, was brought forth like some holy image on a feast day and paraded through the streets. Davis wondered if any compromise could now halt a chain reaction of seceding states. Though he had signed the document advising his constituents to prepare for secession, he desired delaying action, for he refused to give up hope that some acceptable measure might be effected.

Unwell as he was, he met with the Committee of Thirteen every day from December 21 through Christmas Eve. He did not know then that the man back in Springfield was exerting an extraordinary influence on the Republican members of the committee.

"Lincoln," says his most recent biographer, Benjamin P. Thomas, "took upon himself the grave responsibility of blocking compromise." When important Republican Congressmen, in an endeavor to save the Union, sought Lincoln's advice, he admonished them to "stand firm." "Hold firm, as with a chain of steel," he wrote Representative Washburne. If any sort of territorial compromise was adopted, he said he felt convinced that a year

---

[4] The vivid details of the reaction in Charleston are told by Col. W. A. Burk in an article in *The Confederate Veteran* for January, 1890. This was the first of his series of articles on *The Secession of South Carolina*. Burk had also been assistant secretary of the Democratic national convention held earlier in 1860.

would not pass before the Southern states would be demanding acquisition of Cuba as a condition upon which they would remain in the Union. Concerning fugitive slaves or slavery in the District of Columbia he cared little one way or the other, but he was utterly immovable on the extension of slavery anywhere, even in those territories lying south of 36° 30'.

Shortly after Congress convened Lincoln had asked Seward to be his Secretary of State. That master politician hesitated to accept, wondering how far he would be able to control the less experienced Illinoisian. He sent his astute political backer Thurlow Weed to Springfield to take Lincoln's measure at close range. While Weed was sounding out the President-elect, South Carolina seceded. Instead of the event appalling Lincoln, as it did many Republican leaders, he took occasion to send word by Weed to Seward not to agree to the Crittenden Compromise, which might have preserved the Union without resort to war.

As letters to his wife reveal, Seward had been wavering, and now he was strongly disposed to avoid the "irrepressible conflict." The message from Lincoln, however, induced Seward to change his view of the situation and to vote against a settlement. "The popularity of the great war President," Dodd writes, "has made students of the subject overlook his responsibility for this momentous decision." "The Republican President-elect," he adds in criticism, "was almost alone in his firm stand on this point. . . . Lincoln deliberately chose the horn of the dilemma which meant war." Though Lincoln may not then have expected war to result from his inflexible attitude, no one has ever claimed that he would have acted differently, even if he had foreseen that war would be the outcome.

The Republicans were grimly influenced by Lincoln's cool suggestion: "Stand firm. The tug has to come, & better, now than any time hereafter." Was "tug" his homely synonym for a dread word? Whatever "tug" meant, stiffened by commands from the new master, the Republicans were obviously determined, as Salmon P. Chase avowed, to "use the power while they had it and prevent a settlement." Crittenden denounced the Republican purpose to prevent any pacifying adjustment; but his venerability, eloquence, and undoubted Unionism had no effect on the Republican Senators.

December 25, 1860, was as gloomy a Christmas as Jefferson Davis had known. The merrymaking of his children could not banish a heavy sense of foreboding. Yet perhaps the arrival of the three commissioners from South Carolina due the next day might mark some amicable change in the strained relations. They were coming to treat concerning the surrender of forts still held by the United States, to balance business accounts with the Federal Government, and get formal recognition of their state as a separate commonwealth. All were men of high reputation and well known to Buchanan: blue-blooded Robert W. Barnwell, Harvard graduate, college president, and former United States Senator; James H. Adams, Yale alumnus of Massachusetts stock; and James L. Orr, graduate of the University of Virginia, onetime speaker of the House of Representatives and an outstanding conservative.

Before the commissioners had time to present themselves to the President on December 26, Trescott of the War Department called Davis out of the Senate and gave him disturbing news. Together with Senator Hunter, they hurried to the White House and saw Buchanan at once. "Mr. President," Davis said, "I have a great calamity to announce to you." He told him that Major Robert Anderson in command of Fort Moultrie in Charleston harbor had spiked the guns there, burned the carriages, and under cover of night removed to redoubtable Fort Sumter, which was out of range of the shore batteries. "My God!" the President exclaimed. "Are calamities never to come singly?" He avowed, with God as his witness, that the deed had been done without his orders or knowledge.

Because South Carolina regarded Anderson's move as an act of war, the authorities had immediately possessed the remaining Federal forts. Davis urged Buchanan to order Anderson back to Moultrie and publicly to disavow his act. Buchanan could not bring himself to do so, and made the affair a Cabinet matter. The majority of the Cabinet decided that Anderson had not disobeyed orders. When Buchanan had originally refused to give up the forts as South Carolina demanded, his Secretary of War, John B. Floyd, a Virginian, had instructed Major Anderson to "avoid every act that might tend to provoke aggression," but to "hold possession of the forts" and to defend himself if attacked. Since the combined garrison of the three harbor forts, Moultrie, Sumter, and Castle Pinckney, was only large enough to defend one of them, Anderson had "used his discretion." Knowing that Fort Moultrie could be taken with ease, while Sumter, a block of rock in the middle of the channel, was virtually impregnable, he had secretly removed his force there from Moultrie, while Charleston was sleeping off Christmas revelry. His action, as he insisted later, was motivated by a desire to prevent a clash that might launch a war. As it turned out, the decision brought calamity in its wake. "That green-goose Anderson," Mrs. Chestnut called him for being so ill-advised. But Anderson is not to be blamed for what proved a catastrophic decision. The idea of civil war held horror for him. A Kentuckian by birth, with a Georgian wife devoted to the South's cause, Major Anderson was yet a soldier of the United States and strongly opposed to disunion. Perhaps no one was to go through a more harrowing conflict between allegiance and sympathy than Jefferson Davis's old friend of West Point and frontier service days.

When South Carolina's commissioners were received by the President on December 28, they reminded him of his implied promise to their Congressmen not to change the status of Federal fortifications in Charleston harbor. He did not deny the nature of his promise, but he would not accede to their demands. He asked time to consider and "to say his prayers."

Jefferson Davis insisted that Buchanan had the power to prevent other Southern states from following South Carolina if he only had the courage to act. He reasoned with the President, urged him to withdraw the troops from Sumter. But this time his advice was rejected. Many years later Davis wrote: "Mr.

Buchanan was an able man, but a very timid one. If he had had the nerve to deal with the situation, as its gravity demanded, I doubt exceedingly whether any other State would have followed South Carolina into secession. Had he withdrawn the troops from Sumter, it would have been such a conspicuous act of conciliation that other states would not, I believe, have called conventions to consider the question of secession."

Davis attributed some of the President's irresolution to his fear that Abolitionists in his home town would burn his beloved house, "Wheatland," as they had threatened to do if he made any further concessions to the Southerners. The Northern press was reviling him daily and demanding strong action against the South. The New York *Tribune* questioned his sanity; some editors suggested impeachment. While Davis could appreciate that now at threescore and ten Buchanan naturally looked forward to his home as an abiding place for his last years, he felt he was too much influenced by his "increasing dread of Northern excitement."

On December 29 Secretary of War Floyd resigned, ostensibly because Buchanan refused to withdraw the Sumter garrison. Whatever his reason,[5] it was an unfortunate move for the South, because the President shifted to that important position Joseph Holt, his Postmaster General, who later became virulent in his anti-Southern attitude. Holt, though Southern-born, was not trusted in the South. On hearing of his appointment Senator Wigfall presumed to telegraph a friend in Charleston, "Holt succeeds Floyd. It means war. Cut off supplies from Anderson and take Sumter as soon as possible." Happily the bad advice was not taken.

On the last day of the year Buchanan gave his final decision to the South Carolina commissioners. He refused to order any change in the military status of Fort Sumter, and he showed no inclination to give formal recognition to the new commonwealth. In their disappointment over failure, the commissioners sent the

---

[5] Secretary of War Floyd had been criticized for reputed mishandling of departmental funds.

President a stiff note in which they justified South Carolina's action and upbraided him in such harsh terms that he refused to accept their document.

In the post-Christmas meetings of the Committee of Thirteen the Republicans had declined all overtures to pacification. When Douglas demanded of them, "Tell us what you do want, what you will do," they remained stonily silent, offering no terms of conciliation whatever. Finally, on the last recorded ballot, when the Republicans persisted in voting against the admittance of any new state south of 36° 30′ with slavery, Jefferson Davis, too, voted against the Crittenden measure, as he had said he would if a majority of the Republicans voted nay. On New Year's Eve the Senate gravely received the report that the Committee of Thirteen had failed to agree upon any general plan of adjustment. In marked fairness, Lincoln's biographer, J. G. Randall, points out as "a fact of vital importance" that "in 'this fateful hour' . . . Lincoln and Seward refused to accept any compromise which did not recognize the impossible Wilmot proviso."

No sun emerged on New Year's Day of 1861 to bring a ray of brightness to the capital. Rain poured drearily on Democrats and Republicans alike when they came to the President's reception that afternoon. The music, the flowers, the forced smiles, the best attire of the ladies could not dispel gloom in the individual and collective hearts.

Two days later while the disappointed Crittenden prepared to present his Compromise directly to the Senate, and then, if necessary, to submit it as a referendum to the nation's electorate, Stephen Douglas declared in the Senate with ringing denunciation that "the sole responsibility of our disagreement, and the only difficulty in the way of an amicable adjustment, is with the Republican party." [6]

[6] On March 2, two days before Lincoln's inauguration, Douglas reaffirmed his position and said that if the Crittenden proposition had been passed early in the session, it would have saved all the states except South Carolina. While he confessed it was not in accordance with his own cherished views, he said no man had labored harder than he to get it passed. And he affirmed that Senator Davis "was ready at all times to compromise on the Crittenden proposition."

The first significant event of 1861 concerned an ill-advised enterprise that speeded secession in individual states. On orders from General Winfield Scott a ship was loaded secretly with arms, provisions, and two hundred men to go to the relief of Fort Sumter. To deceive the Charleston authorities, an unarmed merchant vessel, the *Star of the West*, which made a regular run from New York to New Orleans, had been substituted for the Federal warship *Brooklyn*, which followed at a discreet distance to render aid with its cannon if necessary. After the ships had sailed on January 5, the President, fearing consequences, suddenly countermanded the order. It was too late. Jacob Thompson, the last remaining Southern member of the Cabinet, alerted Charleston so that its batteries were on guard.

On the morning of January 9, as Jefferson Davis was stepping into his carriage to go to the Senate, a telegram was handed him announcing the attempt of the *Star of the West* to reinforce and provision Sumter. When the ship approached the harbor a warning cannon ball was sent across its bow. When it did not heave to, two shots were fired into the hull itself. The *Star* then turned about and limped back to New York. Stirred by the danger-packed news, Davis told the coachman to drive him to the Executive Mansion. For the last time he appealed to Buchanan to take "such prompt measures as were now evidently necessary to avert the impending calamity." The result of his appeal Davis found utterly unsatisfactory, though Buchanan determined that no more Federal moves against South Carolina should be made during his few remaining weeks in office.

Had Major Anderson fired from Sumter, a war might have been launched then and there. Fortunately, though orders had been sent to him to return any fire from Charleston batteries, he had not received them. Each side naturally claimed the other was the aggressor. South Carolina regarded the expedition as an invasion of an independent state by a foreign power. Washington resented the firing upon a ship bearing the Stars and Stripes. Though the *Star of the West*'s failure was ridiculed by the newspapers, the explosive potentiality of the Sumter situation was only too obvious.

But Buchanan did not dare to recall Anderson's garrison, and, besides, he was chafing from the galling criticism of the South Carolina commissioners in their January 2 letter. Davis came away in a low state of mind. He felt the end was near. His old friend Buchanan, he believed, had forfeited any claim which he might have on the South's "forbearance and support." "During the remainder of Mr. Buchanan's administration," Davis wrote later in his *Short History of the Confederate States of America*, "things went rapidly from bad to worse, and the veteran statesman retired to private life, having effected nothing to allay the storm that had been steadily gathering during his administration." He added bitterly, comparing Buchanan's and Lincoln's administrations: "Then timid vacillation was succeeded by unscrupulous cunning, and, for futile efforts without hostile collision . . . were substituted measures which could be sustained only by force and bloodshed."

That afternoon in the Senate, Davis insisted on bringing before the Senators a certified copy of the commissioners' letter so that the nation might hear South Carolina's cause. And he took it upon himself to rebuke the President publicly.

On that same crowded January 9 Jefferson Davis's own state seceded. But since he received no official notification of the Mississippi ordinance, he did not mention the fact the next day when he made what he supposed might be his last speech in the Senate. Because of the swift rush of events he gave up speaking, as he had originally intended, on the abstract question of Constitutional rights and dealt with events. It was a long speech running to something like 15,000 words when printed in the *Congressional Record*. While some of the paragraphs may seem too formal in their construction, they covered an intense emotion. Davis's admirers hung breathlessly on his words. Even the majority of the radical antislavery Senators gave him grave and respectful attention. In his last few minutes on the floor, when he pleaded with the North not to make war on its brothers, Republicans were moved as well as Democrats.

"I have heard, with some surprise, for it seemed to me idle, the repetition of the assertion heretofore made that the cause of the separation was the election of Mr. Lincoln . . . but no individual had the power to produce the existing state of things. It was the purpose, the end; it was the declaration by himself and his friends, which constitute the necessity of providing new safeguards for ourselves. The man was nothing, save as he was the representative of opinions, of a policy, of purposes, of power, to inflict upon us those wrongs to which freemen never tamely submit. . . .

"I have striven to avert the catastrophe which now impends over the country, unsuccessfully; and I regret it. For the few days which I may remain, I am willing to labor in order that that catastrophe shall be as little as possible destructive to public peace and prosperity. If you desire at this last moment to avert civil war, so be it. . . . If you will but allow us to separate from you peaceably, since we cannot live peaceably together . . . then there are many relations which may still subsist between us . . . which may be beneficial to you as well as to us.

"If you will not have it thus; if in the pride of power, if in contempt of reason and reliance upon force, you say we shall not go, but shall remain as subjects to you, then, gentlemen of the North, a war is to be inaugurated the like of which men have not seen. . . .

"Is there wisdom, is there patriotism in the land? If so, easy must be the solution of this question. If not, then Mississippi's gallant sons will stand like a wall of fire around their State; and I go hence, not in hostility to you, but in love and allegiance to her, to take my place among her sons. . . .

"Towards you individually, as well as to those whom you represent, I would that I had the power now to say there shall be peace between us forever. I would that I had the power now to say the intercourse and the commerce between the States, if they cannot live in one Union, shall still be uninterrupted; that all the social relations shall remain undisturbed; that the son in Mississippi shall visit freely his father in Maine, and the reverse; and that each shall be welcomed when he goes to the other, not by himself alone, but also by his neighbors; and that all that kindly intercourse which has subsisted between the different sections of the Union shall continue to exist. It is not only for the interest of all, but it is my profoundest wish, my sincerest desire, that such remnant of that which is passing away may grace the memory of a glorious, though too brief, existence. . . .

"To-day it is in the power of two bad men, at the opposite ends of the telegraphic line between Washington and Charleston, to precipitate the State of South Carolina and the United States into a conflict of arms. . . .

"And still will you hesitate; still will you do nothing? Will you sit with sublime indifference and allow events to shape themselves? No longer can you say the responsibility is upon the Executive. He has thrown it upon you. He has notified you that he can do nothing. He has told you the responsibility now rests with Congress; and I close as I began, by invoking you to meet that responsibility, bravely to act the patriot's part. If you will, the angel of peace may spread her wings, though it be over divided States; and the sons of the sires of the Revolution may still go on in friendly intercourse with each other . . . and the happiness of all be still interwoven together. Thus may it be; and thus it is in your power to make it."

When Jefferson Davis had finished, the applause in the galleries was so tumultuous that the presiding officer shouted that the sergeant at arms would remove all disorderly persons. After quiet had been restored, a deep hush pervaded the Senate. The silence was finally broken by Lincoln's friend Trumbull, the Republican Senator from Illinois. He rose to attack Davis's speech, for he feared the effect its moving eloquence might have on his cohorts. He was contemptuous of any appeal to let the seceding states go in peace, and scornful of the idea of withdrawing the small Federal garrison from Sumter to prevent an overt clash. "Then," said Davis in the last reply he was ever to make to an opponent in the United States Senate, "I have to say to the Senator, his ideas of honor and my own are very different; that I should hold the man to be a scoundrel who did not desire to have a garrison withdrawn, if he believed that garrison might produce bloodshed and could not do good."

# CHAPTER XXIII

## FAREWELL TO THE CAPITAL

THE DAY after Mississippi's withdrawal, Florida passed an ordinance of secession. Alabama followed on the eleventh. On January 12, when four states had withdrawn from the Union, Senator Seward, who was as responsible as any man for the disrupted state of affairs, made a strong speech urging moderation. The ominous situation he had helped create for the aggrandizement of his own political power and that of his party loomed up now as a new Frankenstein monster over which he had no control. He argued that this Union could not be maintained by force and that a Union of force was despotism. But his conciliatory gesture was too late to halt secessions. On the nineteenth Georgia withdrew. Eight days later Louisiana severed ties with the Union. Because of the powerful opposition of old Governor Sam Houston, Texas did not secede until the first day of February.

After Jefferson Davis's prolonged speech in the Senate on January 10, his effort to restrain display of emotion helped to bring on an incapacitating malady, which almost blinded him with pain. Three days later, confined to bed, he roused himself to answer an urgent letter from Governor Pickens of South Carolina.

"A serious and sudden attack of neuralgia has prevented me from fulfilling my promise to communicate more fully by mail than could safely be done by telegraph. I need hardly say to you

## FAREWELL TO THE CAPITAL

that a request for a conference on questions of defense had to me the force of a command; it, however, found me under a proposition from the Governor of Mississippi, to send me in the organization of the State militia. . . . I cannot place any confidence in the adherence of the administration to a fixed line of policy. The general tendency is to hostile measures, and against these it is needful for you to prepare. I take it for granted that the time allowed to the garrison of Fort Sumter has been diligently employed by yourselves, so that before you could be driven out of your earthworks you will be able to capture the fort which commands them. . . .

"To shut them [the garrison] up with a view to starve them into submission would create a sympathetic action much greater than any which could be obtained on the present issue. I doubt very much the loyalty of the garrison, and it has occurred to me that if they could receive no reinforcements—and I suppose you sufficiently command the entrance to the harbor to prevent it—that there could be no danger of the greatest intercourse between the garrison and the city. . . .

"We are probably soon to be involved in that fiercest of human strife, a civil war. The temper of the Black Republicans is not to give us our rights in the Union, or allow us to go peaceably out of it. If we had no other cause, this would be enough to justify secession, at whatever hazard."

Five days later, still suffering, he wrote Governor Pickens regretting that he was unable to come to Charleston for a consultation because the Governor of Mississippi had claimed his immediate presence. And on the twentieth he wrote him again, urging against any ultimatum to the Sumter garrison.

". . . The opinion of your friends . . . is adverse to the presentation of a demand for the evacuation of Fort Sumter. The little garrison in its present position pressed on nothing but a point of pride, and to you I need not say that war is made up of real elements. . . . I hope we shall soon have a Confederacy, that shall be ready to do all which interest or even pride demands, and in the fullness of a redemption of every obligation. . . . We have much of preparation to make, both in military and civil organization, and the time which serves for our preparation, *by its moral effect tends also towards a peaceful solution.* . . .

"The occurrence of the *Star of the West* seems to me to put you in the best condition for delay, so long as the Government permits that matter to rest where it is. Your friends here think you can well afford to stand still so far as the presence of the garrison is concerned, and if things continue to speak with a voice which all must hear and heed . . . permit me to assure you that my heart will be with you, and my thoughts of you."

From his sickroom Senator Davis had been ruminating over what he would say the next day, January 21, when he made official announcement to the Senate that Mississippi had withdrawn from the Union. He had agreed with Senators Mallory and Yulee of Florida and Fitzpatrick and Clay of Alabama that the five should each make their separate adieus on the same day. But before he finished jotting down notes for a public farewell, he wrote private letters to two of his Northern friends: Franklin Pierce in New Hampshire and Iowa's General George W. Jones, currently the United States minister to Colombia. To these men he felt that he could speak from the heart, and in writing to them it was as if he were bidding good-by to all his personal friends in the East and in the West.

To the Iowan, now far away in Bogotá, he wrote:

"Mississippi has seceded from the Union & I am on the eve of taking my final leave from the general government. . . . This I am sure will excite regret but cannot cause you surprise. I am sorry to be separated from many true friends at the North, whose inability to secure an observance of the Constitution does not diminish our gratitude to them for the efforts they have made. The progress has been steady towards a transfer of the government into the hands of the abolitionists. Many states like Iowa have denied our rights, disregarded their obligations, & have sacrificed their true representatives. To us it became a necessity to transfer our domestic institutions from hostile to friendly hands, & we have acted accordingly. There seems to be but little prospect that we will be permitted to do so peacefully, but if the arbitrament must be referred to the sword we have resolved to meet it & confident in the justice of our Cause, we trust in the God of our fathers & the gallantry of their sons. I know you will sympathize with us although you cannot act with us, that we shall never find you or yours in the ranks of our enemies—"

To the New Englander Franklin Pierce, whom he loved above all other men except his brother Joseph and Sidney Johnston, he wrote:

"I have often and sadly turned my thoughts to you during the troublous times through which we have been passing and now I come to the hard task of announcing to you that the hour is at hand which closes my connection with the United States, for the independence and Union for which my Father bled and in the service of which I have sought to emulate the example he set for my guidance. Mississippi, not as a matter of choice but of necessity, has resolved to enter on the trial of secession. Those who have driven her to this alternative threaten to deprive her of the right to require that her government shall rest on the consent of the governed, to substitute foreign force for domestic support, to reduce a state to the condition from which the colony rose. . . .

"When Lincoln comes in he will have but to continue in the path of his predecessor to inaugurate a civil war, and, leave a *soi disant* democratic administration responsible for the rest.

"Genl. Cushing was here last week and when we parted it seemed like taking leave of a Brother.

"I leave immediately for Missi. and know not what may devolve upon me after my return. Civil war has only horror for me, but whatever circumstances demand shall be met as a duty and I trust be so discharged that you will not be ashamed of our former connection or cease to be my friend. . . .

"Do me the favor to write to me often, address Hurricane P.O. Warren County, Missi.

"May God bless you is ever the prayer of your friend."

Jefferson Davis was not only convinced that these two tried friends could never be counted in the ranks of the South's enemies, but he felt sure that scores of thousands of other Northern men and women who had some true understanding of the South would always remain friendly. Carl Sandburg in *A Lincoln Preface* bears him out: "In all essential propositions, the Confederacy had the moral support of powerful, respectable elements throughout the North." And he points out that in a Northern electorate of four million, "probably more than a million voters believed in the justice of the cause of the South as compared with the North."

Because of his own belief in the understanding heart of a goodly proportion of Northerners, Jefferson Davis continued to hope that the weight of their opinion might even still prevail over political ruthlessness and avert catastrophe.

Though his physician insisted he was in no condition to leave his room and feared that the strain of speaking in public would have grave results, Mr. Davis determined to appear in the Senate the next day. Knowing the will of her husband, Mrs. Davis felt sure he would go in spite of the doctor's orders and his own debility. He spent a wakeful night in remembrance and foreboding. To tear himself away from ties of Union to which he was bound emotionally caused Jefferson Davis extreme mental anguish. His father had fought in the Revolutionary War; three of his brothers had risked their lives in the War of 1812. From the age of sixteen until he was thirty-five his years were spent in the armed service of his country. The world had attested his valiancy in the war with Mexico, in which he had barely escaped death. The better part of fifteen years had been lived in Washington as United States Representative, Senator, and Secretary of War. Now he was resigning an office most congenial to his temperament, and one which no man on that contemporary stage had filled with more conspicuous ability.

Some time after six, when she found her husband fixed in purpose, Varina sent a servant with a friend to hold two seats in the visitors' gallery for herself and a companion. The word that Jefferson Davis was to make his last appearance as a United States Senator on January 21 had resounded around the capital; the city vibrated with anticipation. Streets leading to the Capitol were soon jammed with carriages of ladies and gentlemen who had sent servants to hold places for them. By nine o'clock even sofas in the corridors were occupied. And with no thought given to fire hazards, aisles of the gallery were packed. Some ladies sat on the floor against the walls, their hoops decorously collapsed about them. The diplomatic corps with their wives occupied seats in the press gallery. The excitement of the crowd was as intense as in the old days when Calhoun or Webster was scheduled to make some notable speech. When Mr. Davis arrived the throng was so dense before the Capitol and on steps and porches that he had difficulty in getting through. He gave no heed to the word "traitor" that was muttered by some as he passed. Dressed faultlessly in black broadcloth with a black satin waistcoat, he wore a black silk handkerchief knotted like a stock about the high white collar. The toll of insomnia and pain showed on his sensitively modeled features. Gaunt hollows appeared beneath the sculptured cheekbones, but a steady light illuminated the deep-set gray-blue eyes.

The other four Senators preceded him in their official announcements: Yulee, Mallory, Clay, and Fitzpatrick, in that order. The place of honor and emphasis had been reserved for Jefferson Davis. It was a little after twelve when he rose to speak. He stood very erect, as was his custom, but there was no stiffness, no haughtiness in the posture. He was a man holding his head above adversity and grief, but his attitude was one of natural grace. Though pale and touched by sorrow, there was no more handsome or distinguished face in the Senate chamber. Strangers may have wondered, was this a face for a man of revolution? Was it not "too refined, too spiritual, or too purely intellectual?" Saunders, the British miniaturist, who had painted Lord Byron, insisted that though Jefferson Davis might have military shoulders his head was that of a poet. His head might have belonged also to a philosopher. In any case, his face was one of obvious integrity and self-mastery, the face of a gentleman, a noble face.

Inconspicuous in the gallery, dressed in black, Mrs. Davis, who had slept not at all because of the dark visions of war with its attendant bloodshed and ruin, regarded the complex mood of the tense, well-dressed spectators. Some of the people had come as if to a theatrical performance. Some had come to witness a historical event. But most of them looked upon the occasion with funereal solemnity. She wondered how many could possibly discern, beyond the cool exterior of her husband, his absorbing depression and his heart's desire for reconciliation.

For some moments Jefferson Davis remained silent, as a profound and complete stillness in the audience paid him tribute. When he uttered his first words they were so low and weak that his hearers instinctively strained forward. But the first words were not really important since the formal information they imparted had been known generally for twelve days.

"I rise, Mr. President," he said, "for the purpose of announcing to the Senate that I have satisfactory evidence that the State of Mississippi, by a solemn ordinance of her people, in convention assembled, has declared her separation from the United States. . . . The occasion does not invite me to go into argument, and my physical condition would not permit me to do so, if it were otherwise; and yet it seems to become me to say something on the part of the State I here represent on an occasion as solemn as this."

For a moment he paused, as a wave of emotion gripped him. "Had he been bending over his father, slain by his countrymen," Mrs. Davis says, "he could not have been more inconsolable."

As he proceeded his voice became stronger, and soon the mellifluous quality and the old force, for which his public utterance was known, returned in full measure. Each syllable carried to the farthest corners of the hall. He made it clear that because he had always advocated, as an essential attribute of state sovereignty, the right of a state to secede from the Union, that even if he had not thought Mississippi had justifiable cause, he would have been bound by her action. "But," he said with emphasis, "I do think she has justifiable cause and I approve her act."

"Secession is to be justified upon the basis that the States are sovereign. There was a time when none denied it. . . .

"If it be the purpose of gentlemen, they may make war against a State which has withdrawn from the Union. But there are no laws of the United States to be executed within the limits of a seceded State.

"I well remember an occasion when Massachusetts was arraigned before the bar of the Senate, and when the doctrine of coercion was rife, and to be applied against her, because of the rescue of a fugitive slave in Boston. My opinion then was the same that it is now. . . . I then said that if Massachusetts . . . chose to take the last step which separates her from the Union, it is her right to go, and I will neither vote one dollar nor one man to coerce her back; but I will say to her, God speed in memory of the kind associations which once existed between her and the other States."

He reminded those who had invoked the Declaration of Independence to maintain the position of the equality of the races, that by the words "all men are created equal," Thomas Jefferson had clearly meant the men of the political community of the time. The phrase, which had been composed by a Southern planter and slaveowner, did not include Negroes, who were not then regarded as citizens.

"Then, Senators," he said, referring to abstract principle, "we recur to the principles upon which our Government was founded; and when you deny them, and when you deny to us the right to withdraw from a Government which, thus perverted, threatens to be destructive to our rights, we but tread in the path of our fathers when we proclaim our independence and take the hazard. This is done, not in hostility to others, not to injure any section of the country, not even for our own pecuniary benefit, but from the high and solemn motive of defending and protecting the rights we inherited."

His voice took on a note of deepest sincerity, when he said: "I am sure I feel no hostility toward you, Senators from the North. I am sure there is not one of you, whatever sharp discussion there may have been between us, to whom I cannot now say, in the presence of my God, I wish you well; and such, I am sure, is the feeling of the people whom I represent toward those whom you represent. I, therefore, feel that I but express their desire when I say I hope and they hope for peaceable relations with you, though we must part. They may be mutually beneficial to us in the future, as they have been in the past, if you so will it. The reverse may bring disaster on every portion of the country, and if you will have it thus, we will invoke the God of our fathers . . . we will vindicate the right as best we may."

There was no defiance, no bravado in the words—only the quiet determination to play the manly part if forced to combat. After a long pause, he swept the Senate with a glance marked by loving kindness. "In the course of my service here, associated at different times with a great variety of Senators, I see now around me some with whom I have served long; there have been points of collision, but, whatever of offence there has been to me, I leave here. I carry with me no hostile remembrance. Whatever offence I have given which has not been redressed, or for which satisfaction has not been demanded, I have, Senators, in this hour of our parting, to offer you my apology for any pain which, in the heat of the discussion, I have inflicted. I go hence unencumbered by the remembrance of any injury received, and having discharged the duty of making the only reparation in my power for any injury offered.

"Mr. President and Senators, having made the announcement which the occasion seemed to me to require, it only remains for me to bid you a final adieu."

The genuineness of his sorrow and his appeal for peace held his hearers spellbound. There were wet eyes on the Senate floor, as well as audible weeping in the galleries. Many Republican Senators sat staring grimly, as if now for the first time they fully accepted the fact that catastrophe stalked the land.

As Jefferson Davis made his last exit from the Senate of the United States, everyone realized that the nation had cracked apart. But that night while he struggled to go to sleep, his wife heard him murmuring: "May God have us in His holy keeping, and grant that before it is too late peaceful councils may prevail."

The Davises took their time in departing from the capital, lingering a week while Mr. Davis's strength returned and friends came to bid them good-by. Rumors had been circulating that extremists among the Republicans were agitating to arrest Jefferson Davis and the other "traitor Senators" before they left the capital. Davis would have welcomed arrest for the general effect it might have on the country at large, which, according to Dr. Dodd, believed "that any State had a right to secede when its special interest seemed to be in imminent peril." If arrests had been made and the cases tried, the courts would most likely have decreed the absolute right of a state to secede; for the Supreme Court was known to adhere to the doctrine of State Rights. "Indeed it was thought," as Davis himself wrote, "that it might not be an undesirable mode of testing the question of the right of a State to withdraw from the Union." But no arresting officer called.

During these last days, while his physician kept him quiet as many hours of the day as he could, Mr. Davis received visitors who came to discuss the fate of the South: Captain Raphael Semmes of the U.S. Navy, ex-Senator Chestnut of South Carolina, Clement C. Clay, and ex-Secretary of War Floyd. Mrs. Davis writes that after callers left, when they were alone, it was painful to see the depression that enveloped her husband. The hearts of both of them, she says, were " 'exceedingly sorrowful even unto death'—we felt blood in the air." And yet Davis still did not give up hope that the moderation of President Buchanan would temper any violent action on the part of the anti-Southern legislators. "If they will only give me time," he said, "all is not lost."

In leaving Washington, Jefferson Davis was personally giving up much. No Senator was more distinguished, more respected. None could claim to have done more for his country. None held more gloriously that combined record of statesmanship and conspicuous service on the battlefield. Though temporarily depleted, at fifty-two he was still at his prime. Varina, too, was making a great sacrifice. She had come to Washington as a bride of nineteen, and three of her children had been born there. Though she was only thirty-four, no grand dame with wealth had a more secure and honored place in the social affairs of the capital. And she took a certain pleasure in limelight, which meant so little to her husband. Now she was returning to a remote plantation, miles from all society except that of her septuagenarian brother-in-law and his wife; and while the immediate respite was devoutly desired, a prolonged isolation was not to her taste. Resentment against the South's enemies stirred within her. According to her biographer Eron Rowland, Mrs. Davis told friends in Natchez that in those last days in Washington she felt that changes were taking place in her nature—a kind of "drying up process of hope and fraternity going on in her whole being."

Shortly before Jefferson Davis set out for Mississippi and the mist-enshrouded future, he received a letter from Governor Pickens in answer to his last one cautioning prudence and patience.[1]

". . . I am deeply obliged to you for your wise suggestions as to the forts in our harbor. The truth is that I have not been prepared to take Sumter. It is a very strong fortress, and in the most commanding position. . . . The movement of Anderson from Moultrie so suddenly and under the circumstances of the case, plunged me right into the highest and most scientific branches of modern warfare, and also the most expensive. I found great difficulty in repairing and altering Moultrie. . . . Of course, I would desire to do nothing to prejudice our cause with our sister states of the South. . . .

[1] As far as the author has ascertained, this letter in the New York Public Library is the last extant one Jefferson Davis received in the capital. It is dated January 23, 1861.

"What we want is, as soon as the states can meet at Montgomery, Alabama, for them to elect immediately a Commander-in-Chief for the States and assess the States their quota in army and men and money. . . . Allow me to say that I think you are the proper man to be selected at this juncture, and I hope it will be done unanimously. . . . We must have all the organization and form of a government in full operation before the 4th of March, and if anything can save the peace of this country it will be this.

"As to who may be selected to fill the highest civil offices, it is not of so much consequence at present, only that they should be high-toned gentlemen of exemplary honesty and firmness of character with full and thorough statesmanship and no demagoguism. We must start one government free from the vulgar influences that have debauched and demoralized the government at Washington. . . .

"The formation of a new union is full of great and momentous issues. I trust wisdom and patriotism will prevail."

Davis, who had lived so long close to the very heart of national affairs, could indeed appreciate the line: "The formation of a new Union is full of great and momentous issues." Though he was in sore need of an extended period of quiescence and repose, he had offered his services to his state, and the convention of the Republic of Mississippi had made him head of its so-called "army." He would give his best to ready the state for defense, though he prayed there would be no necessity for battle.

When their train pulled out of the Washington station, the Davises took a last memory-stirring look at the city's silhouette with the Capitol's almost completed dome. When Secretary of War, Jefferson Davis had been the chief motivating force in the construction of that dome and the extension of the Capitol. The annual reports of the progress and expenditures by his chief engineer, written in careful script, were a memento in Varina's luggage.[2]

[2] In the summer of 1953, the author examined these reports which are in the possession of Jefferson Hayes-Davis of Colorado Springs.

Their route to Jackson, Mississippi, lay through southwestern Virginia, eastern Tennessee, and northern Alabama. At important and unimportant stops men anxious as to the future boarded the train to ask Jefferson Davis what was going to happen. Some citizens expressed the belief that the sober thought and better feeling of the Northern people would compel their Republican representatives to give guarantees to the South before a confederacy of seceded states was formed. A majority, however, believed that the separation would be final and that the North would not attempt coercion and invasion. There was little in the way of assurance Jefferson Davis could give them, for to him "the course which events were likely to take was shrouded in the greatest uncertainty." He had to tell the people that, while he believed secession was a right and properly the peaceable remedy, he did not believe the North would let them break away peaceably. He found few to agree with him; his apprehension that a war might be forced upon the seceded states was not well received. At many of the stations public clamoring forced Jefferson Davis to make a speech. He endeavored to impress upon the citizens the gravity of the present crisis and to prepare their minds for a probable war.

Under the strain of a series of brief speeches, Davis became so obviously exhausted that the conductor was concerned. The rest of the way, as soon as the ex-Senator began "My friends and fellow citizens"—the conductor would yank the cord, blow off steam, and the train would pull out immediately, leaving the crowd with only a flashing picture of the man and the haunting sound of his melodious voice.

At Chattanooga, where the family stopped for the night, a drunken pro-Union man attempted to keep Mr. Davis from speaking to a crowd that assembled at the hotel, but he was hustled away. When the train reached the Mississippi border the next day, admirers began boarding it at every station, and soon the coaches became crammed with self-appointed escorts. At the Jackson station the governor, together with numerous state officers and four newly created brigadier generals, welcomed Jefferson Davis. He was therewith presented with his commission as major general, head of the armed forces of Mississippi. The commission bore the date of January 25, 1861. Despite the stirring enthusiasm in the Mississippi air, to Davis it was only too obvious that the South was prepared for defense in nothing except the morale of her people.

As Governor Pettus and General Davis conferred on the needs of armament, the former named 75,000 stands of arms as a sufficient figure. The ex-Secretary of War replied with grave emphasis that the limit of arms purchased should be only the ability to pay. "We shall need all and more, I fear, than we can get."

"General," Pettus said—and it might have been the voice of 95 per cent of the South—"you overrate the risk."

General Davis shook his head. "I only wish I did."

# CHAPTER XXIV

# THE MAN AND THE HOUR MEET

THE REST and recuperation Jefferson Davis so desperately needed were denied him. During the days in Jackson, politicians, businessmen, newly created brigadier generals, came and went. Because he feared a war, Davis urged strictest economy of consumer goods and the immediate creation of small factories to supply domestic needs when, or if, Northern products would no longer be available. With his wide military experience he saw, as few men could, the pitiable lack of preparedness. The state had to start from scratch in arranging its defenses. Not even an establishment for the repair of arms existed in Mississippi, and nothing like a cannon factory stood in the whole domain of the Lower South. "Had the Southern states," as Davis later wrote, "possessed arsenals and collected in them the requisite supplies of arms and ammunition, such preparations would not only have placed them more nearly on an equality with the North in the beginning of the war, but might, perhaps, have been the best conservator of peace."

Though he was realistic with his callers, Davis presented an air of confidence and concealed as well as he could both his exhaustion and his unhappiness. Alone with his wife he could not pretend that he was not careworn. Insomnia still plagued his nights. But he had not given up all hope of a pacific solution. He told his wife that even though the admittance of controversial Kansas as a non-slave state on January 29 had added gall to the

## THE MAN AND THE HOUR MEET 399

South's resentment "a simple guarantee of the South's equal rights would bring the seceded states back into the Union tomorrow."

At the end of a wearing week of interviews and conferences the Davises left for Brierfield, where Varina and the children were to settle in the plantation home. The General prepared to put in order his business and planting affairs against an indefinite absence while he formed an army. As they approached Brierfield, he foresaw the end of slavery coming years sooner than he had expected. "In any case," he said to his wife, "I think our slave property will be eventually lost."

The return to the plantation and the welcome of loyal servants cheered the heavy hearts of the master and mistress and gave the children boundless joy. In the enfoldment of a devoted Negro's love is an ineffable comfort that cannot possibly be conceived of by one who has not experienced it. To Marse Jeff and Miss Varina the overflowing measure of affection was healing to the nerve-jangling anguish of the recent months in Washington. Brother Joseph, now seventy-six, helped to rally the spirits of his younger brother, who still loved him like a father. Joseph, less conservative than Jefferson, rejoiced that the Southern states had exercised their constitutional rights to secede. In his remoteness he had kept up with every political move for a decade; he had no doubt that the South's action was the only solution, and he looked forward to the establishment of a wonderful new nation.

As Jefferson Davis walked among the whitewashed cabins of the quarters with their neat garden patches, visited the artisans in the shops, and attended the Reverend Damos's services for the colored people, he was more convinced than ever that the intimate contact which Negroes enjoyed with Southern gentry had an elevating effect upon them, and that in giving them Christianity, the South had been "a greater practical missionary than all the Society missionaries of the world." In surveying various aspects of a plantation routine, which were to him manifestations of a special grace, he was nevertheless aware of the taxing responsibility of owning and caring for slaves.

He went about his acres among his people, smiling, but troubled, and without that spontaneous joy the daily life of the plantation had heretofore inspired. In his sensitized consciousness he could not shake off a prescience that the state of things on the plantation would not be the same for long. He felt a compelling compassion for the Negroes who somehow might be suddenly bereft of security and that comforting assurance that in sickness or old age the master would provide. How long, he wondered, would the bonds of mutual affection between the Southern white man and the black man endure? And what would be the inheritance of his own children?

After a few days Mr. Davis called the more dependable Negroes to warn them that serious trouble might lie ahead. He told them he trusted them to defend their mistress and the children during his absence. He enjoined them to take good care of the old slaves whose workdays were past. He consulted with rheumatic old Uncle Bob, who had been his plantation preacher, as to his special needs. Providing comfortable rocking chairs in which Bob and his wife Rhinah might sit out their twilight years, he also bought measures of red flannel and a stack of extra blankets to keep them warm.[1]

Relaxing in the gentle air and ordered peace of Brierfield, the General lent Varina a hand with her prized flower garden, where violets and daffodils and camellias were already in bloom. While he was savoring the imponderable satisfactions of country life, a momentous convention was being held in Montgomery, Alabama. Elected delegates from the first six seceded states, who had gathered on February 4, were now establishing a new nation. Destiny was about to point a significant finger at Jefferson Davis, even though he had taken precaution to have his name not presented for any civil office in the new government. Both he and Varina welcomed the thought that he was to be in command of armed

---

[1] In her *Memoir* Mrs. Davis writes that when Federal soldiers sacked the plantation in 1863, they appropriated the old Negro's best furniture and blankets, and when he remonstrated in dismay, they accused him of stealing them. It was Bob's first contact with this new kind of "white folks."

forces rather than in public administration. His wife, as well as he, believed that his special genius lay in the military. If war came he could best serve his state as a soldier. He felt he lacked the equipment of the practical politician. She knew he was both too sensitive and too high-toned for political scheming.

One afternoon—February 10—while Jefferson was helping Varina prune rose bushes and lay by cuttings to extend the rose garden, a messenger arrived in hot haste with a telegram from Vicksburg, eighteen miles away by road. Putting down his shears, he opened the envelope and read the message. Such a stricken expression came over his countenance that his wife thought some personal calamity had befallen the family. After a painful silence, he told her he had been chosen President of the Confederacy.[2]

Dismayed as Varina was, her heart involuntarily swelled with pride: her husband and her children's father was President of the Confederate States; she, its First Lady. Joseph, who vicariously through Jefferson had lived day by day in the great world of affairs, was elated. His faith and his early tutelage had been fully justified and fully rewarded.

Next morning the emergency plantation bell brought all the Negroes to the house. The master told his people the news, made them an affectionate farewell speech, and in turn received spon-

[2] In the Davis family papers there are other versions besides Varina's of the receipt of the news. Joseph's granddaughter Lise Hamer says that Jefferson Davis was ill when "a committee," accompanied by her grandfather and grandmother, arrived at Brierfield with the message and that Mrs. Joseph Davis went to his room and "notified" him, at which he rose, and cried out, "O God, spare me this responsibility."

Major Lee S. Daniel, who was the young manager of the telegraph office in Vicksburg in 1861, was quoted in the Victoria (Texas) *Advocate* of June 2, 1905, thus: "Fully realizing the importance of the dispatch, I employed a discreet messenger with horse with instructions to speed the distance, deliver the document, await reply and return without loss of time, as I would hold the office open for the transmission of a reply. He did his duty well, as a little after midnight he handed me the important reply, also a little personal note of thanks for prompt action. The reply of acceptance was flashed through to the waiting assembly at Montgomery by one o'clock A.M. The information was immediately given to the Vicksburg *Whig*, the most prominent of Mississippi's press, and created wide-spread excitement and rejoicing that our good and great fellow citizen, Jefferson Davis, had been placed at the helm, 'the right man in the right place.'"

taneous oaths of loyalty and devotion. Then he began to pack. He would send for the family when he had found a suitable house. He started alone for the Confederate capital.

But the President-elect almost missed the boat. The most convenient route to Vicksburg was the thirty-five-mile winding way by the river. As the landing near the Davis plantations could accommodate only small boats, Mr. Davis set out in a rowboat to meet the *Natchez* at a landing three miles below his place. Isaiah Montgomery, the colored youth, was at the oars. They had gone only a short distance when they heard Captain Leathers, a longtime friend, blow for the lower landing. Mr. Davis knew they could not possibly cover the distance in time. So he directed Isaiah to head for an island in the middle of the river, where they might meet the *Natchez*. Tom Leathers was expecting his distinguished passenger, and when he did not find him at the proper landing, he was looking out for him all along the river. At last he spied the President-elect signaling from the rowboat. The Captain blew his whistle in welcoming response and steamed over to pick him up. When he disappeared over the rail onto the deck, it was the last time Isaiah ever saw the master of Brierfield.

Each of the seceded states had sent to the Montgomery convention the same number of delegates as they had had members in the United States Congress. For the most part the chosen delegates were men known for their caution and conservatism—men who up to the last minute had opposed secession and worked for compromise. Paradoxically those sent by their respective states to bring to birth a new nation were men who had generally regarded secession as injudicious. William Yancey, the famous secessionist orator, although a delegate of the Alabama convention, had not been elected to the general convention. The chief fiery revolutionist among the lot was South Carolina's Robert Barnwell Rhett, Jr., and perhaps the next most ardent secessionist was Robert Toombs of Georgia. After meeting with the Confederate convention for a month, Alexander H. Stephens, ex-Congressman and the only important Southern friend Lincoln had, could write: "Upon the whole, this congress, taken all in all, is the ablest, soberest, most intelligent and conservative body I was ever in. . . ." Howell Cobb of Georgia, who had been Buchanan's Secretary of Treasury, was selected presiding officer. All questions were to be decided by a vote of the states, and each state, regardless of the size of its delegation, was entitled to one vote.

On February 8, after the Texas delegation had arrived, a provisional constitution was adopted. With the Constitution of the United States as the basis for the temporary one, certain changes, emendations, and innovations were made, chief among which was one absolutely prohibiting foreign slave trade "except in the case of states and territories within the United States." At the insistence of Thomas R. R. Cobb the blessings of Almighty God were invoked in the new preamble, whereas in the Federal Constitution divinity had been ignored. Immediately after the temporary constitution had been adopted a committee was set to preparing a permanent document. The twelve amendments to the original United States Constitution were to be worked into the text of the new one.

The following day, Saturday, the names of Howell, Cobb, Toombs, and Stephens, all Georgians, were suggested for the presidency. Then, as the noted Northern historian James Ford Rhodes writes: "After a short consideration of the merits and failings of each man proposed, the selection of the ablest statesman of the South fitly issued to meet the conditions confronting the new government." Jefferson Davis was unanimously elected provisional President of the Confederacy.

Speculations as to the wisdom of that choice have not ceased since the second year of the Civil War. As late as February 9, 1954, on the ninety-third anniversary of Mr. Davis's election, a King Features syndicated column by Clark Kinnaird posed the much-belabored question: Would the outcome of the Civil War have been different if Davis had been left in an army command and "some abler statesman had been chosen President of the C.S.A."? Rhodes had given the answer in 1895: There was no abler statesman in the South. None of Jefferson Davis's critics, not even the most vicious, has ever been able to offer with any conviction a putative candidate whose weighed qualities equaled those of the man selected. His immediate contemporaries overwhelmingly gave the palm to him.

In his biography of Jefferson Davis written in 1868, only three years after the bitter defeat of the Confederacy, Virginia's Frank H. Alfriend stated unequivocally: "Of the public conviction as to his preeminent fitness, there could not be a question. His character, his abilities, his military education and experience, had long been recognized throughout the Union, and his exalted reputation was a source of just pride to the South. No Southern statesman presented so admirable a combination of purity, dignity, firmness, devotion, and skill—qualities for which there is an inexorable demand in revolutionary periods." Ex-Congressman Duncan Kenner testified: "We, the Louisiana delegates, without hesitation, and unanimously, after a very short session, decided in favor of Mr. Davis. No other name was mentioned. The claims of no one else were considered, or even alluded to." And W. Porcher Miles of Virginia, who became a member of the Provisional Congress of 1861, said: "I think there was no question that Mr. Davis was the choice of the whole people of the South."

It is true that the dynamic Robert Toombs had expected the position and even announced his willingness to accept. If Toombs had possessed Davis's military record and if he had avoided getting tipsy at a dinner party the night before the election, he might possibly have been the choice for president. At least one man, his Georgia colleague and ardent admirer, Alexander H. Stephens, believed that he was the most eminently suited for the office. The impressive Toombs had a high reputation as a debater and he was a shrewd businessman. But as Alfriend judged his mind and disposition, he was "strong and impassioned, but desultory, vehement and blustering . . . arrogant and intolerant, a destructive and inveterate agitator."

Brilliant, aristocratic Robert Barnwell Rhett, the most intense of the revolutionaries, had also coveted the presidency and felt he deserved it, since for twenty years he had been the leading apostle of secession. Though he had a few supporters among the passionate fire-eaters, because of his uncompromising radicalism he was hardly considered for the position. Many people, however, were saying that perhaps Rhett with his "sardonic insight" had been right when he urged secession in 1850. If the South had withdrawn from the Union then, the establishment of the Confederacy would have succeeded without serious difficulty. In the decade following, the North had grown vastly stronger; manufactories had increased enormously, and the population was greatly augmented by European immigration.

Rhett was not at all pleased with Davis, who was far too temperate for him. He declared sourly in his paper, the Charleston *Mercury:* "Jefferson Davis will exert all his powers to reunite the Confederacy to the Empire." Rhett never forgave Jefferson Davis for being chosen instead of himself. Nor could the expansive, leonine Robert Toombs swallow his own disappointment.

For the Vice-President the convention unanimously chose wizened little Alexander H. Stephens with his precocious-child face and brilliant intellect. For the two top positions the Confederacy had selected recognized conservatives: Jefferson Davis, the reluctant secessionist, who had urged delay; Alexander H. Stephens, who had opposed secession until the very hour Georgia outvoted him. These two men had only one other thing in common besides their conservatism: they did not believe the North would let the seceded states escape armed coercion.

From Vicksburg Mr. Davis first went to Jackson, where he spent the night. Next day he called at the governor's mansion, and there, on executive office stationery, under the date of February 12, 1861, he wrote out his formal resignation as major general of the army of Mississippi. While waiting in the railway station, he was sought and found by Mississippi's Chief Justice William L. Sharkey, who desired to know if the reports were true that Mr. Davis really believed there would be war. The Judge was shocked to learn that the President-elect supposed a war *could* result from "the peaceable withdrawal of a sovereign state."

Because there was no railway to cover the miles between Meridian, Mississippi, and Montgomery, Alabama, Mr. Davis had to travel a circuitous route northeast to Chattanooga, Tennessee, thence southeast to Atlanta, Georgia, and back southwest to Montgomery. According to press reports his journey was "one continuous ovation." The President-elect had to present himself to the crowds gathered at the stations to receive plaudits. At night torches flared and bonfires blazed in his honor. While such enthusiasm was heartening, he should have been allowed to sleep or to prepare his inaugural address. There were no sleeping cars in those days, but in his coach a bed had been set up for him, where he reclined fully dressed so that he could respond to the clamorings at the stations all through the night. Altogether Jefferson Davis made twenty-five short speeches in his progress to the capital. Such an ordeal was enough to wreck a man of iron constitution, but Mr. Davis endured the strain remarkably well.

In the Northern press these speeches were falsely represented as breathing defiance against the North, inciting his hearers to war. While he did disillusion those who felt sure there would be no war, his tone was extremely measured.

About eighty miles from his destination two committees of reception from the Confederate capital boarded the train to welcome him formally. It was nearly ten o'clock at night when the President-elect's train pulled into Montgomery as artillery salutes announced his approach. A mass of local citizens and important figures from all the seceded states were at the station to greet him. When he appeared, he was hailed with tremendous cheering. In returning thanks, he said—as if in answer to Rhett's criticism—the time for compromise had passed, self-government should be maintained at all cost, "no reconstruction could now be entertained." As chief of the reception committee William Yancey escorted him to the Exchange Hotel, followed by the enthusiastic throng.

After a half-hour, in response to insistent calls, Yancey led

Jefferson Davis to the hotel balcony to present him to the excited crowd dotted with ladies in billowy hoop skirts and beribboned bonnets. In his public introduction the golden-tongued Yancey uttered the words that became famous: "The man and the hour have met."

When the applause had subsided, fatigued as he was by three days' travel and hoarse from twenty-five speeches, Mr. Davis spoke his gratitude. He addressed his hearers as "Fellow Citizens and Brethren of the Confederate States of America—men of one flesh, one bone, one interest, one purpose, and of identity of domestic institutions." Humbly he confessed: "I come with diffidence and distrust to discharge the great duties devolved on me by the kindness and confidence of the Congress of the Confederate States. I will devote to the duties of the high office to which I have been called all that I have of heart, of head, and of hand. . . . We have henceforth, I trust, a prospect of living together in peace. . . . It may be, however, that our career will be ushered in, in the midst of storm. . . . If war should come . . . we shall show . . . that Southern valor still shines as brightly as in the days of '76."

That he had not given up hope that his command might yet be in the military he implied in his last sentence: "If, in the progress of events . . . necessity shall require that I shall enter the ranks as a soldier, I hope you will welcome me there." Then with a heart-warming, if weary, smile he bid them good night. His speech had lasted no more than two minutes, but when he vanished his hearers felt they had chosen "a born leader of men who could attract love and secure trust."

At last when he was in his darkened room, alone with his thoughts, he must have heard the re-echoing of Yancey's words: "The man and the hour have met." It was his custom to say a prayer before he retired, and on this night of February 16, 1861, he had never felt more need of divine guidance.

# CHAPTER XXV

## "IF WE SUCCEED"

———•◦•———

THE MORNING of Monday, February 18, 1861, was as fine a day for the birth of a nation as the heavens could provide. The sun shone full in a cloudless sky, making the atmosphere balmy and invigorating; more like a rare June day in Maine than one which the calendar claimed for February. Ladies had no apprehension in risking their best garden-party costumes, and some got out silken parasols to shade their complexions. By ten o'clock a crowd, white and black, had gathered on the sidewalks of Dexter Avenue, which led from the public fountain and the Exchange Hotel up to the white-domed Capitol crowning the hill at the top of the thoroughfare. Tennant Lomax, one of Montgomery's leading citizens, had lent his handsome new carriage to take the President-elect to his inauguration. Today, this elegant equipage, lined with white and yellow silk hangings, was drawn by four white horses.

Just before the stroke of noon, when Arnold's Band and the First Alabama Regiment were already in line, Jefferson Davis and Alexander Stephens took their seats in the carriage, along with the Reverend Basil Manly and an army officer, who sat facing them. As the President's carriage swung into position, Herman Arnold led his musicians up the avenue in a tune that had never been played anywhere before by a band, for he had orchestrated it himself only a week before. It was a minstrel piece called "I Wish I Was in Dixie's Land" just published the preceding June as sheet music arranged for pianoforte. It proved to be stirring, as well as catchy. The soldiers marched briskly; the horses pricked up their ears, lifted their feet proudly, and held their heads high. The music helped to excite the crowd to rousing cheers. But no one dreamed then that "Dixie" was to become the Southern "Marseillaise."[1]

As Mr. Davis's carriage passed, the crowd cheered lustily and fell in behind the procession in its slow progress up the gently rising street. The "important" people were already assembled on the green-sod terraces of the Capitol to witness the ceremony. Within the building, members of the Confederate Congress sat waiting to greet their leader. When the carriage halted, Robert Barnwell Rhett received Mr. Davis, gave him his arm in the grand manner, and escorted him to the congressional chamber. Dwarfish Alexander Stephens walked on the other side of the President-elect. As Allen Tate observed, "Had Davis known it, he was at that moment between the upper and nether millstone." For this chief begetter of secession and this "mite of a man" who had opposed it came to be bitter enemies of the Chief Executive and sought to mangle his authority, and in the end effectively helped to wreck the Confederacy.

In presenting the President-elect, Rhett announced courteously but with laconic formality, "Gentlemen of the Congress, allow me to present to you the Honorable Jefferson Davis, who in obedience to your choice has come to assume the important trust you have confided to his care."

After making a brief speech of greeting, Mr. Davis was escorted

[1] Few in the crowd had ever heard "Dixie," though it had been sung in Bryant's Traveling Minstrel Show since 1859, when, purportedly, Dan Emmett, one of the minstrels, had composed it hurriedly for an opening "walk around" during a New York engagement. As Arnold, a naturalized German musician who had married a Montgomery girl, searched for something new and exciting to play for the inauguration, his wife suggested, "Why don't you play that minstrel piece about Dixie's Land? It's lively and catchy and would make a good band number." So Arnold had hurriedly orchestrated the score and rehearsed his band vigorously in a room of the Capitol provided for the purpose. Now for the first time a band played "Dixie," composed by Dan Emmett, a showman from Ohio. As the Baltimore *Sun* declared, even if written by the son of an Abolitionist, "Dixie" is essentially a plantation song supposedly sung by slaves.

back outside to a stage arranged on the front portico between the towering white pillars of the western façade. The members of the Congress filed out to seats set up on the top terrace facing the speaker's stand. As the clock struck one, Jefferson Davis rose and stood before a table on which lay a wreath of red, white, and blue flowers cradling a Bible. Howell Cobb administered the simple oath of office. The President delivered his inaugural address. Its tone was tempered and calm. The natural music of his voice charmed his hearers.

"Our present political position," the President affirmed, "has been achieved in a manner unprecedented in the history of nations. It illustrates the American idea that governments rest on the consent of the governed, and that it is the right of all those to whom we would sell, and from whom we would buy, that there should be the fewest practicable restrictions upon the interchange of these commodities. . . .

"There can be, however, but little rivalry between ours and any manufacturing or navigating community, such as the Northeastern States of the American Union. It must follow, therefore, that mutual interests will invite to goodwill and kind offices on both parts."

Then, with an expression in which pain and resolution mingled, he spoke out over the heads of the crowd. "If, however, passion or lust of dominion should cloud the judgment or inflame the ambition of those States, we must prepare to meet the emergency and maintain, by the final arbitrament of the sword, the position which we have assumed among the nations of the earth.

"We have entered upon the career of independence, and it must be inflexibly pursued. . . . As a necessity, not a choice, we have resorted to the remedy of separation, and henceforth our energies must be directed to the conduct of our own affairs, and the perpetuity of the Confederacy which we have formed. If a just perception of mutual interest shall permit us peaceably to pursue our separate political career, my most earnest desire will have been fulfilled. But if this be denied to us, and the integrity of our territory and jurisdiction be assailed, it will but remain for us with firm resolve to appeal to arms and invoke the blessing of Providence on a just cause. . . ."

He warned the incoming Washington administration that war would be a policy so detrimental to the civilized world, including the Northern states, that he did not see how it could be dictated by even "the strongest desire to inflict injury upon us." But if the North *should* make war, he emphasized the terrible responsibility that would rest upon it. "The suffering of millions will bear testimony to the folly and wickedness of our aggressors."

As he drew to his conclusion, he humbly asked the people of the Confederacy to bear with him in the responsibilities he faced. "Experience in public stations . . . has taught me that toil and care and disappointment are the price of official elevation. You will see many errors to forgive, many deficiencies to tolerate; but you shall not find in me either want of zeal or fidelity to the cause that is to me the highest in hope, and of most enduring affection. . . ."

As his glance swept the throng from left to right, a heart-lifting smile lighted his countenance. "It is joyous in the midst of perilous times to look around upon a people united in heart, where one purpose of high resolve animates and actuates the whole; where the sacrifices to be made are not weighed in the balance against honor and right and liberty and equality. . . ." Then he ended his brief address with an invocation to divinity: "Reverently let us invoke the God of our fathers to guide and protect us in our efforts to perpetuate the principles which by His blessing they were able to vindicate, establish, and transmit to their posterity. With the continuance of His favor ever gratefully acknowledged, we may hopefully look forward to success, to peace, and to prosperity."

Like a gigantic spotlight the sun of half-past one fell full upon Jefferson Davis, illuminating the thin chiseled features, the gray-gold hair, the blue-gray eyes. He stood there like some handsome ascetic, congenial to sacrificial fastings, dedicated to a righteous cause, and, for this particular moment, blessed with a special grace. Before the South, as well as this immediate audience, he stood, a leader to inspire confidence, admiration, and a certain devotion. It was the high hour of his career, and Varina was not there to share in it.

The men on the portico surged about him to grasp his hand. To attract his attention, Mrs. Kilpatrick, the beautiful wife of the onetime Alabama Senator, in an oddly democratic gesture, poked him in the back with her parasol. Arnold's Band again struck up "Dixie," a tumultuous shout arose, and ladies began tossing flowers at their President. The ceremony of birthing a nation was over.

The inaugural address made a most favorable impression throughout the South, even with the hot-blooded Rhett and other impetuous Charleston newspapermen. Hesitant Virginia was pleased both with the tone and the sentiments, and now inclined more definitely toward the new government with which she had so much in common, socially and economically. Alexander Stephens, who resented Mr. Davis, said the speech clearly showed "that these states had quit the Union only to preserve, for themselves, at least, the principles of the Constitution," and that "there was no purpose, wish, design or intention on the part of them or Mr. Davis to make war . . . commit aggression, or do wrong to those states . . . which remained in the old Union." Richmond's Frank Alfriend, editor of the *Southern Literary Messenger*, deemed the address "unquestionably of the highest order of state papers," and "a model of composition." "Its statement of the position of the South," he said, "the grievances which have led to the assumption of that position, her hopes, aspirations, and purposes, has never been surpassed in power and perspicuity by any similar document." For all that Alfriend's hyperbole was not justified, the world in general regarded it as a very good speech. The London *Times* honored it by printing the text in full. Many commentators were pleased to note that the President had astutely made no reference whatever to slavery.[2]

[2] In comparing the inaugural address of Jefferson Davis with that of Abraham Lincoln three weeks later, let it be recalled that Mr. Lincoln had almost four months in which to ponder and prepare his address in the seclusion of an up-

"As an exposition of the causes leading to secession," Landon Knight, Mr. Davis's Ohio biographer, regards the speech as "a masterpiece." He says, "It is impossible to read it today [1904] without feeling that in every sentence it breathed a prayer for peace." But "considering it as the first official advice to a new nation beset with stupendous problems," he is critical. Since the President outlined no policies and offered no suggestions on the question of revenue, Knight is inclined to believe that he still hoped for some readjustment that would unite the severed Union. He is doubtless right in assuming that Jefferson Davis refrained from a more vigorous attitude so that "compromise would not be placed completely beyond the pale of possibility."

With thoroughgoing optimism, however, most Southerners expected the new nation to continue for unreckoned centuries. While Jefferson Davis inspired confidence and lifted hearts from Charleston to Austin, he himself was painfully aware of the dangers that lay ahead. In his first letter to his wife, written on the Wednesday following his inauguration, he barely hints at the immensity of his problems.

"I have been so crowded and pressed that the first wish to write to you has been thus long deferred.

"I was inaugurated on Monday, having reached here on Saturday night. The audience was large and brilliant. Upon my weary heart was showered smiles, plaudits, and flowers; but, beyond them I saw troubles and thorns innumerable.

"We are without machinery, without means, and threatened by a powerful opposition; but I do not despond, and will not shrink from the task imposed upon me. . . ."

Jefferson Davis's task was something to stagger the imagination of a statesman of any historic period. He was called upon to administer a brand-new nation, now in the mere process of formation, and at the same time prepare a defenseless country, without navy, army, or proper materials to withstand a likely invasion.

stairs room in downtown Springfield. Jefferson Davis had to snatch what odd moments he could from four surpassingly strenuous days.

To defy the power of Great Britain across an ocean in 1776 when ships were propelled by whimsical winds was far less daring than to challenge powerful next-door Northern states with a thousand miles of unfortified marching boundary. Besides, there were more than three thousand miles of coastline to defend, while rivers that emptied into the sea reached into the heartland of the Southeastern and Gulf states. And navigable streams rising in midwestern territory and flowing into the Mississippi could bring enemy craft straight through the Confederacy. In all the South there was no ship-building plant.

The railroad system of the South was scant indeed compared with that of the North, and that little in operation was dependent on the North for supplies to keep it running. By numerous estimates the North's booming factory power was a hundredfold greater than that of the South. While Northern machinery was complete for the production of the manifold materials of war, that of the South was close to zero. Below the Potomac the only iron mill that could cast a cannon was the small Tredegar works at Richmond.

George Washington had assumed his presidential duties when the new nation was at peace. Abraham Lincoln was inheriting a government which had enjoyed established order for fourscore years and which possessed merchant fleet, navy, army, arsenals, manufactories for every human need, four times the white population of the South, and a recognized authority of power about the globe.

Everything in the Confederacy seemed to depend on the inspiration and genius of Jefferson Davis: to guide the government, establish a foreign policy, create an army. It was incumbent upon him to foresee difficulties and meet them, or the new nation might soon crumble.

Some of the Confederate women in Montgomery were aware of the awesome obstacles facing the President. Mrs. Chestnut wrote in her diary: "We have to meet tremendous odds by pluck, activity, zeal, dash, endurance of the toughest military instinct." She was apprehensive, too, over political intrigue, "as rife as in

Washington." "Everybody who comes here wants an office, and the many who, of course, are disappointed raise a cry of corruption against the few who are successful. . . . I thought we had left all that in Washington. Nobody is willing to be out of sight, and all will take office." In the midst of pressing state business Jefferson Davis was plagued by office seekers.

On February 21, the day after he wrote his wife, President Davis followed the advice of Washington in his Farewell Address: "to place ourselves upon a respectable defensive." Like that great revolutionary patriot, Davis believed that preparedness would best protect peace. He had to act expeditiously, since the Republican administration, which he regarded ominously, would be installed in less than a fortnight. He sent Major Huse to Europe to purchase ships and available arms and to make contracts for the manufacture and delivery of armaments at future dates. General Raines he put in charge of establishing a manufactory for making gunpowder. General Josias Gorgas, a Pennsylvanian who had married a daughter of Governor Gayle of Alabama and had chosen the side of the South, was appointed Chief of Ordnance.

The President commissioned his friend Raphael Semmes, who had resigned a captaincy in the Federal navy, to go North to buy guns and hire workmen who could handle machinery. Though Davis's instructions were precise as well as general, Semmes was to use his own discretion in every case.[3] He also asked Semmes to secure any vessels which could be made serviceable.

The Confederacy was without a warship, because the resigning Southern naval commanders had honorably taken their charges and surrendered them in Northern ports. The Confederate States were doubly bereft by losing not only their share of the navy they had helped to build, but by having the whole force of it ready to be employed in assailing the South. Had the officers believed that the guns of the vessels they commanded would be used to blast Southern harbors, many would doubtless have steered them into Southern ports instead of handing them over to an enemy.

[3] The President was careful to state that all contracts should be sent to the Secretary of War and be formally approved by him.

The day before Davis's arrival in Montgomery, the Confederate Congress had passed a resolution that a commission of three persons be appointed by the President and sent to the Government of the United States to negotiate friendly relations and settle all questions of disagreement. This move accorded with Davis's desire that matters of dispute might be settled "around a conference table with honor and dignity to both sides." On February 25 the President named the three men he had chosen as commissioners accredited to discuss terms of peace with Mr. Lincoln as soon as possible after his inauguration. The political color of the commissioners revealed the President's eagerness to harmonize the various elements in the Confederacy. Martin J. Crawford was a State Rights Democrat from Georgia; Judge A. B. Roman of Louisiana, a diehard Whig; and Alabama's John Forsyth, an ardent Douglas Democrat. Forsyth, a high-toned newspaper editor of Mobile, Alabama, had been minister to Mexico under Pierce and Buchanan; Roman was an ex-governor of Louisiana; and Crawford had served with distinction in the United States Congress. In Davis's words these "three discreet, well-informed, and distinguished citizens" were all regarded as conservatives, and two had directly opposed secession.

The same day the peace commissioners were named and confirmed, the President got the Confederate Congress to declare and establish "free navigation of the Mississippi River without any duty or hinderance except light-money, pilotage, and other like customary charges." This prompt measure was to reassure businessmen of the West who feared their commerce on the Mississippi would be restricted.

While the President and the Confederate Congress were preparing peaceful overtures in Montgomery, a last desperate effort to save the Union was being made in Washington. On the initiative of Virginia a commission had met on February 4 with ex-President Tyler as chairman. "The Peace Convention," as it was called, represented twenty-one states, fourteen Northern nonslaveholding states and eight Southern slaveholding states. Mr. Davis had keenly noted every scrap of information that came to him about its activities. Near the end of the month a plan of settlement was finally adopted with amendments deemed essential to end contention. Though it offered less to Southern interests it was very much like the Crittenden plan, which had still not been acted upon by Congress. But the peace plan failed to get the nod from President-elect Lincoln and was defeated by one vote.[4] In the bitter opinion of Jefferson Davis, "the arrogance of a sectional majority, inflated by its recent triumph, was too powerful to be allayed by the appeals of patriotism or the counsels of wisdom. The plan of the Peace Congress was treated with contempt."

As March 4 drew nearer, Jefferson Davis reflected that the direct issue of peace or war might be up to one man to decide, and that man, of course, was the enigmatical figure who had been born not far from his own Kentucky birthplace. Davis kept before him in his mind a statement Abraham Lincoln had made on January 12, 1848, during his only term in Congress. "Any people anywhere . . . have the right to rise up, and shake off the existing government, and form a new one that suits them better. . . . This is a most valuable, a sacred right—a right which we hope and believe is to liberate the world. Any portion of such people that can, may revolutionize, and make their own, of so much of the territory as they inhabit." When he was in power would Lincoln abide by his expressed convictions? Since he had kept the Republican leaders from agreeing to Crittenden's compromise measure in December, and had seen their negative votes bring on secession, what would his inaugural address reveal? Would Lincoln's own remembrance of his widely quoted statement of 1848 deter him from sending hostile ships into Confederate territory to reinforce Sumter? If an overt incident did occur, Davis devoutly believed that the question for history to decide would be not which side fired the first shot, but which offered the first show of aggression, which first indicated the purpose of hostility.

The Confederate President felt at a loss how to gauge the in-

[4] Finally, on March 3, the very day before Lincoln's inauguration, the old Crittenden Compromise was at last voted upon in the Senate, and it, too, failed to be adopted by a single vote.

coming Union President, who was certainly no open book. He knew virtually nothing about Mr. Lincoln personally and he could form no clear opinion from the Northern press, much of which was extremely uncomplimentary. He had not been helped in reaching a conclusion by reading what Gordon Bennett had to say in an editorial in the New York *Herald* of February 19, 1861, the day following his own inauguration. After declaring it quite evident that Lincoln "has not sufficient mental calibre for the discharge of the duties he has undertaken," the editorial went on to contrast the character of the two rival presidents.

"The other President, Mr. Davis, has been received with the greatest enthusiasm during his journey from Mississippi to Montgomery, Ala. He made five and twenty speeches en route, but we do not hear that he told any stories, cracked any jokes, asked the advice of young women about his whiskers, or discussed political platforms. His speeches are rather highly flavored with the odor of villainous salpetre, and he evidently believes that civil war is inevitable.[5] But we must recollect that Mr. Davis is a soldier, a graduate of West Point, a hero of the Mexican War and a statesman of military turn of mind. Mr. Lincoln was a splitter of rails, a distiller of whisky, a storyteller and a joke maker. He afterwards became a stump orator, and used his early experiences as his literary capital. Now we have the rails abandoned, the whisky still stopped, but the scent of both hangs about the manner and the matter of his speeches. For the future, the Northern President should profit by the example of his Southern rival, who does not attempt to tell the Southern people that the crisis is nothing, that nobody is hurt, (on the contrary he acknowledges that the revolution hurts both North and South) but declares that the South is ready to meet any hardship rather than to abandon its principles. Mr. Lincoln must look this state of things in the face. It cannot be turned off with a joke; and when next he opens his mouth we trust he will not put his foot in it. If Mr. Lincoln aspires to be

---

[5] Only at Opelika, the last stop before Montgomery, did Davis utter threats against the North if Federal troops attempted armed invasion.

the second Washington of this great Confederacy let him come out emphatically in his inauguration in favor of the Crittenden resolutions as amendments to the Constitution; let him call an extra session of the new Congress and in his first message boldly reiterate this plan and its submission at once to the people through the States; let him appoint his Cabinet but not dispose of another office in his gift till this great and overwhelming question is settled."

The troubled Confederate President took some comfort in recalling Horace Greeley's strong anticoercive editorials in the New York *Tribune*, the foremost Republican daily. Mr. Greeley had made statements that Davis himself might have written: "Five millions of people can never be subdued while fighting around their own hearth-stones" (November 30); "the South has as good a right to secede from the Union as the Colonies had to secede from Great Britain" (December 17). On February 23, 1861, just five days after Davis's inauguration, Greeley had written: "If the Cotton States wish to form an independent nation, they have a clear moral right to do so." How much weight would the words of this "moulder of Republican opinion" carry with the untried Abraham Lincoln?

Davis had other cuttings from Northern papers to give him a modicum of hope. The editor of the Albany *Argus* expected that Mr. Lincoln "would quietly allow the function of the Federal Government within the seceded states' limits to be suspended." "Any other course would be madness," he warned, "as it would at once enlist all the Southern States in the controversy and plunge the whole country into a civil war. . . . As a matter of policy and wisdom, therefore, independent of the question of right, we should deem resort to force most disastrous."

The Bangor (Maine) *Union* had spoken out resolutely: "If the Republican party refuses to go the full length of the Crittenden amendment—which is the very least the South can or ought to take—then, here in Maine, not a Democrat will be found who will raise his arm against his brethren in the South." But even more than the Eastern advocates of peace did Detroit's *Free Press* encourage Southerners by declaring: "If troops shall be raised in the North to march against the people of the South, a fire in the rear will be opened against such troops, which will either stop their march altogether or wonderfully accelerate it."

Happily, observers in Washington insisted that in the new regime Seward would be in high ascendancy, and, for all his barking, Davis knew that Seward was universally regarded as "a friend of peace." An editorial in the New York *Tribune* of February 4 had commented on the amazing fact that "Senator Seward in his speech of Thursday last [January 31] declares his readiness to renounce Republican principles for the sake of the Union." Though from personal experience Davis felt that Seward could be trusted only so far, he believed, like everyone else, that his one-time friend would never favor warlike aggression. Davis might have been still more optimistic if he had known then that two days before his inauguration, his old enemy, General-in-Chief Winfield Scott, had proposed to Mr. Seward in a private letter "to let the wayward sisters go in peace."

In the meantime the President had been ruminating over the choice of his Cabinet. He felt that for the sake of unity, all factions should have consideration, and, as far as possible, all should be represented. As it turned out, when Davis followed his own inclination his choices proved excellent. When he heeded the advice of prominent politicos he did less well. Davis, who is often condemned for obstinacy, was, on the contrary, perhaps too considerate of the desires and opinions of others in selecting his secretaries. In only one case did he offer a post to an old friend —that of Postmaster General to Henry T. Ellett, a prominent Mississippi lawyer. But Ellett declined the position, and Howell Cobb forestalled the offer to himself of any portfolio.

During the period from February 21 to March 5 nominations for the various Cabinet posts were sent to the Congress. "I was governed by considerations of the public welfare only," Davis later wrote. In the end not a single member of the Cabinet bore him the relation of close personal friendship and indeed with two of them he had had no previous acquaintance. Since South Carolina and Georgia were the most important states, the two top positions were more or less earmarked for them. Davis had hoped to make his rival Robert Toombs Secretary of Treasury, a post for which his knowledge of economics and his business ability made him eminently suitable. But when South Carolina's Robert Barnwell declined the portfolio of State, he shifted Toombs to that most important place. With some show of reluctance Toombs, brilliant but blustering, often unpredictable and unstable, accepted his high office and entered it with a huge chip on his shoulder because he had not been made President.

Barnwell urged his South Carolina friend C. G. Memminger for the Treasury, though that gentleman had stoutly opposed Barnwell's own kinsman, R. B. Rhett, and the other flaming secessionists. Memminger was a highly respected banker, who had been born in the German Duchy of Württemberg, brought to Charleston an infant in arms, and soon orphaned. From a Charleston orphanage he had risen by sheer ability to an eminent position in the aristocratic city. An able, conservative financier, his appointment gave very general satisfaction—at the time. Thomas R. R. Cobb considered him "shrewd as a Yankee." Even the Charleston *Mercury*, Rhett's paper, conceded that there were few men in the South possessed of greater business capacity than Memminger, who had "great intellect, initiative, and experience."

When Alabama's William Yancey declined the minor post of Attorney General, he urged the President to make Leroy Pope Walker of Huntsville Secretary of War. Davis had wanted Braxton Bragg, who had helped save the day at Buena Vista, to head the War Department, or as second choice, Clement C. Clay. But Clay joined Yancey in pressing the appointment of his fellow townsman Walker. Fearing he had lost Rhett's influence by giving posts to his enemies Toombs and Memminger, and needing Yancey's good will, the President made Walker Secretary of War. An able enough lawyer, Walker's chief assets for the post, according to William Russell of the London *Times*, were his "ardent devotion to the cause and confidence to the last degree of its speedy success." Walker, eager secessionist, did not expect war. Indeed, when he had canvassed Alabama advising withdrawal from the Union he had declared that with his pocket handkerchief he would wipe up all the blood spilled because of secession.

The three remaining choices were Davis's own, and these three men, who remained in his Cabinet until the dissolution of the Confederacy, were the better half. Florida's Stephen R. Mallory he appointed Secretary of Navy; John Henninger Reagan of Texas, Postmaster General; Louisiana's Judah P. Benjamin, Attorney General. Though Mallory, who had been born the son of a Connecticut shipbuilder, lacked personal popularity because he had been a strong Union man, he had served as chairman of the Committee on Naval Affairs in the United States Senate, and was an excellent choice for Secretary of Navy. The big rugged Texan, Reagan, whom Davis had known in Congress, proved not only honest and industrious as Postmaster, but singularly successful in that he provided a postal service that had no annual deficit. Benjamin, born of English-Jewish parents in the West Indies, a Catholic convert and married into a prominent French family, was a brilliant man, with an ingratiating manner and a perpetual smile. Though a decidedly controversial figure, partly because he was a Jew, the President had implicit faith in Benjamin, who came to be known as "the brains of the Confederacy," and who remained Davis's best adviser and most loyal friend.

On February 27 the President named the three commissioners to Europe: William L. Yancey, Pierre Adolphe Rost, and A. Dudley Mann. Of the three, Mann, a personal friend of Davis, was the only one seasoned by experience for diplomacy abroad. A cultivated Virginia gentleman, he had served as American minister to Switzerland and in various diplomatic posts in Germany.

In the pressure of making these all-important appointments in the first ten days of his administration while attending to a mass of other pressing business, Mr. Davis must have longed for more time in which to consider and weigh the respective abilities of the various men for the assigned positions. Although in future decades he was to be criticized for many of his appointments, he had the satisfaction of knowing that they were currently well received.

If Jefferson Davis questioned his own qualifications for his difficult job, he had only to read the papers to be assured that he was generally regarded as larger in stature than any other living Southerner. This high opinion was as widespread in the North as the South. As Rhodes wrote: "One voice went up from all the States that Davis should be chosen." The North, as Senator Seward told William Russell, correspondent of the London *Times*, considered Davis as the only man in the South with the abilities to make secession successful.[6]

In February of 1861, this "virtuous and resolute man" was generally believed to have as few flaws in his character as anyone in the North American continent. These few were really extremely minor. Because of his own abilities in numerous fields, it was sometimes hard for him to delegate authority to lesser men, and so he might spend too much time on details. Because he lacked thick skin, if unjustly criticized, he would bother to explain himself. Perhaps he was too loyal to old friends after they had proved disappointing. He had little aptitude for high finance. Though some were immediately urging a military despotism as the best solution for survival—"anything," as Mrs. Chestnut observed, "to prevent the triumph of the Yankees"—democracy was too ingrained in Davis's very soul for him to be a dictator. It was not in his nature to act the part of the political serpent; he must always be the kingly lion. But his humility in accepting the position thrust upon him was sincere and deep. "He approached the task of creating a nation," Mrs. Davis says, "with many humble petitions to Almighty God for guidance and support." Though he had affiliated with no orthodox faith, Jefferson Davis had an abiding faith in the Lord's will. He read his Bible for inspiration; a favorite verse was, "Tarry thou the Lord's pleasure, be strong and he will comfort thy heart."

Despite his realistic awareness of the potential damage the

---

[6] Russell himself after visiting the South was to write to Sumner that "the Confederates believe in no other man except Davis."

North might do the Confederacy, Davis by no means looked upon himself as the leader of a forlorn hope, as Breckinridge had about his own presidential nomination in 1860. In a sense Davis considered the outlook promising. Here was a chance to put into operation his creative ideas, unhampered by Northern political vetoes, with which his forward-looking objectives had been met in the past. He could forge ahead in building up a Southern Republic and make the region more self-sufficient. Money saved from protective tariff duties that enriched the East could be utilized in improving Southern schools. As to geographic expansion he believed Virginia, Tennessee, North Carolina, and Arkansas would soon join the Confederacy, with which they had common heritage, and so in time would farther-off Maryland, Missouri, Kentucky, and even Delaware, which were also slave states. The Confederacy might try to purchase Cuba from Spain, expand in Central America, secure a right of way on the Isthmus of Panama, build railways, open up an export-import trade with South America. Davis fully expected Britain and France to recognize the Confederacy as soon as it got into smooth working order. Although slavery would be hard for the English to accept—though it did not bother their consciences in Turkey or numerous other parts of the world where they had profitable trade relations—raw cotton was essential to their economy, and the upper classes were on the side of the South. France would inevitably follow Britain. With the recognition of two great powers, the North would hardly dare to make aggression.

But whatever hope he had for the new nation's future, Davis knew full well, as he said, that the course which events were likely to take "was shrouded with the greatest uncertainty."

In the afternoon of the last day in February, the President went to the boat landing to meet his wife and children, who had come by way of the Alabama River from Mobile. The steamboat had arrived too late for Varina to witness the ceremony at which the new Confederate flag was raised. But Mr. Davis pointed it out, waving in the breeze: a standard with one broad white bar and two red ones and a blue union containing seven white stars. The honor of hoisting the new flag had gone to Letitia Tyler, the ex-President's granddaughter, whose father, Colonel Robert Tyler, had recently moved to Alabama. Jefferson Davis had been averse to relinquishing the flag under which he had fought and bled. He had insisted that, if the unhappy exigency arose, a different battle flag would be distinction enough. But the Confederate Congress had overruled him. Now he told Varina that when the new flag had gone up, though cannon roared, the crowd showed no great enthusiasm. Someone suggested the reason was that "gentlemen are apt to be quiet" and that this had been a "thoughtful crowd," for the so-called popular element was busy with its spring plowing. The new flag did not thrill Varina any more than it did her husband, for the attachment of them both to the Stars and Stripes was strong.

Though she tried to conceal the fact from him, his wife had come in a depressed mood. It had been hard for her to close up Brierfield, to say good-by to their Negroes. En route to Montgomery she had stopped for a day and night at her father's house in New Orleans. His ineffectualness and her mother's valiant efforts at makeshift grieved her to the heart, for she was a dutiful and very loving daughter. When Captain Dreux and his company came to serenade the Confederacy's First Lady, bringing with them several immense bouquets of violets, Varina had been so overcome with emotion that she could not reply to the Captain's charming speech or respond to the cheers of the valorous boys in uniform. The purple color of the violets seemed to her portentous of mourning.[7] As Varina approached Montgomery on the river she felt little elation that at thirty-four she was stepping into such a high and historic position. Though she had no fear about measuring up to her role, she arrived at the Confederate capital with melancholy apprehension.

Because the executive mansion, which had been selected, was not yet in readiness, Mr. Davis took his family to a suite in the

[7] Captain Dreux was the first to be killed on the Peninsula near Yorktown.

Exchange Hotel, where "hampers of blossoms" had been sent to welcome the President's lady. When they were alone, Varina studied her husband's face solicitously. She had heard that a few disgruntled persons who had not secured offices were beginning to mutter criticisms. He smiled away her concern. "If we succeed," he said, "we shall hear nothing of these malcontents." Then he added prophetically, "If we do not, then I shall be held accountable by friends as well as foes. I will do my best, and God will give me strength to bear whatever comes." But he did not see himself in a tragic role. He had no conception that he was to be the hero in another version of the ultimate tragedy, which is that of a good and great man destroyed.

*Acknowledgments*
*Sources and Notes on Sources*
*Index*

## ACKNOWLEDGMENTS

FOR incomparable assistance in the way of unpublished material I am indebted most deeply to Jefferson Hayes-Davis of Colorado Springs, grandson of Jefferson Davis, who permitted me to be the first person to see and make use of five boxes of intimate family papers and who has given me exclusive rights to the documents until this work is completed.

To Mrs. Gerald Bennett, born Varina Margaret Webb, eldest great-granddaughter of Jefferson Davis, I am grateful for a variety of material and especially for having the photographic reproductions made of the portrait on the jacket, which belongs to her brother Joel Webb; the portrait of Joseph Davis by Raphael Lamar West and the Saunders' miniature of Jefferson Davis, both possessed by Jefferson Hayes-Davis; and the picture of her great-grandmother Varina, owned by herself.

My very special thanks to Ruth Hayes-Davis for her housewifely indulgence in allowing me to turn her sunparlor into my workshop and for helping me decipher difficult handwriting; to Joel Webb, great-grandson, for use of scrapbooks, inherited from his grandmother Margaret Davis Hayes, with pertinent newspaper clippings and informal family photographs; to Lucy Hayes Young, only living granddaughter of Jefferson Davis, dynamic septuagenarian sheep rancher in southwestern Colorado, for an invitation to visit at her ranch, one hundred miles from the nearest bus stop, and particularly for kind offers of assistance with material for Volume II. To the various direct descendants of Jefferson Davis in Colorado I am indebted for hospitality and friendship, as well as for the quantity of new material put at my disposal.

Of the numerous collateral relatives who have given me generous co-operation I am indebted above all others to Anna Farrar Goldsborough of Newark, New York. This perceptive great-grandniece of Jefferson Davis and kinswoman of Mrs. Davis, from her own store of personal memories, her mother's and father's earlier remembrances, and inherited letters, wrote me some 120 pages on the Davises and individual family characteristics. Mrs. Goldsborough was only a little girl of eight in New Orleans when her "Uncle Jeff" died, but her memories of him are "deep," and she saw much of her "Aunt Varina" in the seventeen years following.

Next, I am most indebted to Mary Lucy O'Kelley of Pass Christian, Mississippi, great-grandniece of Jefferson Davis and great-granddaughter of Joseph Davis, for entrusting to me a copy of her mother's journal. Later at her home I took down copious notes from her graphic remembrances and from Davis letters.

To Mrs. Ralph Wood of Biloxi, Mississippi, great-grandniece of Jefferson Davis, I am indebted for valuable contacts in securing unpublished material, and to her sister-in-law, Mrs. Stamps Farrar of New Orleans, for family letters. To Albert Ganier of Nashville, Tennessee, great-grandnephew of Jefferson Davis, former president of the Tennessee Academy of Science, I am obligated for the fruits of his labor on Davis genealogy and for dozens of pages of answers to my inquiries. To Lucinda Ballard Dietz, the stage costume designer, great-great-grandniece of Jefferson Davis, and her husband, Howard Dietz, playwright and librettist, I am indebted for a week-end visit at their Long Island home, where I read letters from Jefferson Davis to his sister Lucinda, whose portrait hangs over the library mantel.

Heading the list of nonrelatives I am perhaps most obligated to Professor John A. Kelly of the German Department of Haverford College, Haverford, Pennsylvania, for the loan of letters from Sarah Knox Taylor Davis and several members of the Zachary Taylor family on her marriage to Jefferson Davis, and particularly for an unpublished manuscript article by Charles Anderson, brother of Major Robert Anderson of Fort Sumter, which gives the most vivid, authentic impression of Jefferson Davis as a young man I have found anywhere. Professor Kelly inherited these documents from Trist Wood, great-grandson of Zachary Taylor.

To Jessie Palfrey Leake, great-granddaughter of General Josias Gorgas, I am deeply obligated for a large collection of original Jefferson Davis letters.

To the late dean of Southern biographers, Douglas Southall Freeman, I am extremely grateful for stimulating conversations, sage advice, hospitality, and encouragement.

To Virginius Dabney, editor of the Richmond *Times-Dispatch,* I am indebted for introductions and hospitality while doing research in Richmond, and for the gift of some out-of-print books, and to Douglas, his wife, for driving me to the various points of interest connected with Mr. Davis in Richmond.

To Thomas J. Rountree, instructor in English at Troy State Teachers College, I am grateful for indispensable assistance with research in New York, New Orleans, Montgomery, Aberdeen, and at Beauvoir, and for reading the first half of the manuscript in various drafts; and to Robert Knight Moffett for research assistance, for copying scores of letters from microfilm, and for reading and shrewdly criticizing two drafts of the last half of the manuscript.

To Dr. Johnstone Parr, professor of English, University of Alabama, I cannot express sufficient thanks for his painstaking preparation of an exhaustive bibliography of all magazine articles concerning Jefferson Davis as listed in *Pooles' Index, Nineteenth Century Readers' Guide, Readers' Guide,* and *International Index.*

To Dr. Charles Summersell, head of the History Department, I am uncommonly indebted for a critical reading of the 661-page typescript; to Dr. Frank Owsley, professor of Southern History, author of the authoritative *State Rights in the Confederacy* and *King Cotton Diplomacy*, for helpful suggestions; to the historian Dr. A. B. Moore, dean of the Graduate School, for the loan of books and other kindnesses; and to Dr. James McMillan, director of the University of Alabama Press, for critical advice.

To Margaret Coit, Pulitzer Prize-winning biographer of John C. Calhoun, I am grateful for her remarkable generosity in offering the research notes she had taken on a proposed biography of Jefferson Davis, which she abandoned for other work.

To Dr. Emmett Kilpatrick, head of the Department of English at Troy State Teachers College, lifelong student of Jefferson Davis, who wrote his doctor's dissertation at the Sorbonne on *Le Département Exécutif des Etats Confédérés d'Amérique*, I am grateful for a three days' consultation as his house guest and for his enthusiastic interest.

I am indebted to Walton Linsey of Fairview, Kentucky, for valuable information about the Jefferson Davis birthplace and for old items from the Todd County *Times;* to John S. Tilley of Montgomery, Alabama, author of *Mr. Lincoln Takes Command*, and Thomas M. Galey of Owensboro, Kentucky, Lincoln enthusiast and collector, for special items of research; to Dallas Irvine, chief archivist of War Records Branch, National Archives and Records Service, Washington, D. C., and his assistant Richard G. Wood for official information about Jefferson Davis's army service.

To Rucker Agee, past president of the Alabama Historical Society, I am grateful for consultations, the loan of rare books, and inspiring encouragement; and to Dr. Thomas W. Martin, chairman of the board of the Alabama Power Company, for furnishing me with a facsimile of the original song "Dixie" as published by Firth, Pond & Co., New York, June 21, 1860, and for photostats of old newspaper articles on the history of "Dixie." My thanks to Preston Haskel for a manuscript copy of Colonel John C. Haskel's stirring *Memoirs* of the war.

Among those who lent me Davis letters I am indebted to Anna Garber Webb of Demopolis, Alabama; Elizabeth Garth of Columbus, Mississippi; Frances Tillotson of Tuscaloosa, Alabama; E. F. McCrossin, Jr., of Leonia, New Jersey.

To Paul North Rice, chief of Reference Department, and to other members of the staff of the New York Public Library I am deeply grateful for most generous and expert help; to Lucille Peacock, librarian of the Evans Memorial Library of Aberdeen, Mississippi, for gracious and tireless assistance; to Dora S. Pool of the Confederate Memorial Hall, New Orleans, for arranging for me to work with priceless letters and documents in the vaults of the museum, and for her extraordinary goodness in opening the museum for me on a holiday; to Dr. William Stanley Hoole, librarian of the University of Alabama, and three members of the library staff for three years of enthusiastic co-operation: Mrs. Cade Verner of the Rare Books Collection, Vivien M. Lawson of the Reference Library, and Mildren S. Coley, circulation librarian.

For courteous responses to my queries, my warm thanks to David C. Mearnes, chief of Manuscript Division, Library of Congress, and to Dr. C. P. Powell for arranging pertinent manuscripts most conveniently for my work.

Over a period of three and a half years I am indebted for various kinds of help to Ruth Rowell, regent of the First White House of the Confederacy, and her capable assistants Janie Troy and Eltrym Chalker. I express special gratitude to Marguerite M. Murphy, director of the Jefferson Davis Shrine at Beauvoir, and to her co-worker Salome Brady. I am grateful also to: India Thomas, regent, and Eleanor Brockenbrough of the Confederate Museum in Richmond; Marie Bankhead Owen, retiring director, and Peter Brannon, director of the Alabama Department of Archives and History, Montgomery; Charlotte Capers of the Mississippi Department of Archives and History, Jackson; Eva Davis, director of the Confederate Museum, Vicksburg.

For leading me to an obscure collection of Jefferson Davis material in Charleston, South Carolina, and having copies made of revealing letters from Mrs. Davis now in the possession of Mrs. Arthur B. Young, I am especially indebted to Mrs. I'On L.

Rhett, great-granddaughter-in-law of the controversial figure Robert Barnwell Rhett. For hospitality, contacts, suggestions about research material in Charleston I am grateful to: Josephine Pinckney, the novelist; Herbert Ravenel Sass, historian; Thomas Waring, editor of the Charleston *Courier-Journal;* my long-time friends, William and Wilhelmina Johnston of No. 1 South Battery.

To Frances and Eugene Pennebaker of New Orleans I am indeed grateful for old books and for an introduction to Mrs. William Fayssoux, who knew the Davises as a child on an estate neighboring Beauvoir. I am indebted to Mr. and Mrs. F. G. Strachan for receiving me at their beautiful home where Jefferson Davis died; to Rudolph Weinmann, attorney, for helpful contacts in obtaining material; to Carleton King for the diary of his aunt, the New Orleans memorialist Grace King.

To the Honorable S. B. Laub, ex-mayor of Natchez, Mississippi, I am deeply indebted for research in legal documents: especially for a copy of Joseph Davis's will and maps and abstracts of the Hurricane and Brierfield estates. To Mrs. William Wall, owner of The Briers, Varina Howell Davis's birthplace, I am indebted for information on the history of the house. I thank R. Lee Parker, Jr., of Natchez, and Edwin L. Brunini, attorney of Vicksburg, for legal research; Frank E. Everett, Jr., lawyer and student of the Jefferson Davis period, for a memorable drive through Warren County, Mississippi; the Reverend William Christian, president of All Saints Episcopal College, Vicksburg; Miss Louise Randolph Johnson and her brother Joseph Johnson, owners of Rosemont Plantation, Jefferson Davis's childhood home, for hospitality and valuable information; John Lewis, editor of the Woodville *Republican,* Mississippi's oldest newspaper, for research assistance and copies of old letters and editorials from files of the Vicksburg *Herald;* Albert M. Daniel of St. Francisville, Louisiana, for his special courtesy in driving me to the grave of Sarah Knox Taylor Davis on the Locust Grove Plantation, which he rents and farms.

To three young teachers and writers, former students of mine, David Strode Akens, M.A. in History, James Daniels, M.A. in

English, and Yewell Lybrand, I am indebted for discriminating research in old newspapers and periodicals.

I express gratitude to Hermione Embry, genealogical reference librarian of the Tennessee State Library and Archives, Nashville, and the late Sallie W. Shore of the Virginia Historical Society, Richmond, and to James W. Patton, director of Southern Historical Collection, who furnished microfilm copies of an excellent collection of Jefferson Davis letters in the University of North Carolina Library.

For doing rush, overtime jobs of typing I want to thank Patricia Dillon of Colorado Springs and Hazel Chambers of Delray Beach, Florida.

My special gratitude goes to the editorial staff of my publishers, Harcourt, Brace.

To the late Albert Spalding, violinist and author, and Mary Pyle Spalding, I am indebted for separate critical comments on early chapters, and for hospitality in the summers of 1952 and 1954, when I wrote parts of this biography at their home in Great Barrington, Massachusetts.

Coming to the place of emphasis, I express overflowing gratitude to Naboth Hedin, former director of the American-Swedish News Exchange, who read and commented on the manuscript at various stages of composition and offered valuable suggestions.

I want to express my profound gratitude to the late Marielou Armstrong Cory, my mother-in-law, who spent half a century in helping to memorialize Jefferson Davis. Though the writing of this biography was not begun until a fortnight after her death, because I feel in a certain measure that her ardent interest in Mr. Davis inspired it, I am dedicating this volume to her in loving memory.

And now, as always, but this time more than ever, I am grateful to my wife, Thérèse. Without her incalculable and her imponderable help, her loving patience and constant inspiration, I could hardly have finished this volume in twice the number of years the work has taken.

# SOURCES AND NOTES ON SOURCES

FEELING that an abundance of footnotes on the printed page of a biography interrupts the rhythm of the reading, I have deleted virtually all except those concerning especially controversial points and a few that add some pertinent information not precisely warranted in the text. However, I have made considerable use of "internal documentation," often giving the authority directly in the text. For the most part, where this procedure has been employed, I have refrained from repeating it in the list of sources.

In helping me to discern and portray the real Jefferson Davis, six sources have been of transcending value: (1) the hitherto unpublished personal letters and papers of Jefferson Davis owned by his grandson Jefferson Hayes-Davis; (2) testimonies and family reminiscences of descendants and collateral relatives, and manuscript letters in their possession; (3) the two-volume, 1,638-page *Jefferson Davis, A Memoir* by His Wife; (4) Dunbar Rowland's monumental ten-volume *Jefferson Davis: Constitutionalist*, a collection of all Davis letters and speeches that had come to light by 1923, including letters from a host of correspondents for over half a century; (5) Walter L. Fleming's published monographs on special phases of Mr. Davis's life, together with his collection of notes, letters, documents in the New York Public Library; (6) early chapters of Jefferson Davis's *Rise and Fall of the Confederate Government* and of his *Short History of the Con-*

*federate States,* as well as his own brief biography in *Belford's Magazine,* January, 1890. Dunbar Rowland, Dr. Fleming, and Mrs. Davis are three outstanding authorities whose work on Jefferson Davis is indispensable.

The other dozen biographies of Jefferson Davis, besides that of his wife, range from the intensely partisan one of Frank H. Alfriend (1868) to the malicious one by Edward Albert Pollard (1869). A sound and tempered biography is that of Dr. William E. Dodd (1907). The latest, longest, and perhaps most comprehensive is *Jefferson Davis: The Unreal and the Real,* by Robert McElroy, professor of American History at Oxford University. Two of the most perceptive and understanding lives are those by General Morris Schaff of Massachusetts and Landon Knight of Ohio. A miscellany of interesting Davis material may be found in *Life and Reminiscences of Jefferson Davis by Distinguished Men of His Time* (1890) and *The Davis Memorial Volume* (672 pages) edited by J. Wm. Jones (1890). While repetitious in the extreme, Eron Rowland's two-volume study, *Varina Howell, Wife of Jefferson Davis* (1931) has some good information not to be found elsewhere.

Listed in the order of their publication are the biographies of Jefferson Davis, all of which I have consulted. Frank H. Alfriend, *The Life of Jefferson Davis* (1868); Edward A. Pollard, *Life of Jefferson Davis* (1869); A. C. Bancroft (editor), *The Life and Death of Jefferson Davis* (1889); *Jefferson Davis, Ex-President of the Confederate States of America, A Memoir,* by His Wife (1890); Landon Knight, *The Real Jefferson Davis* (1904); William E. Dodd, *Jefferson Davis* (1907); Armistead Churchill Gordon, *Jefferson Davis* (1918); Morris Schaff, *Jefferson Davis, His Life and Personality* (1922); H. J. Eckenrode, *Jefferson Davis, President of the South* (1923); Allen Tate, *Jefferson Davis: His Rise and Fall* (1929); Elizabeth Cutting, *Jefferson Davis: Political Soldier* (1930); Robert Watson Winston, *High Stakes and Hair Trigger: The Life of Jefferson Davis* (1930); Robert McElroy, *Jefferson Davis: The Real and the Unreal* (1937).

In the last quarter-century only one biography of Jefferson Davis has appeared: Dr. McElroy's two-volume work in 1937.

Of books on the period preceding the war, two are outstanding among many first-rate ones: Professor Avery O. Craven, *The Coming of the Civil War* and Professor Allan Nevins, *The Emergence of Lincoln*. The works of these two distinguished scholars and writers are particularly interesting because of their sometimes sharply divergent views. Also excellent are the early chapters of E. Merton Coulter's *The Confederate States of America, 1861-1865*, and the introductory 258 pages of J. G. Randall's *The Civil War and Reconstruction*.

Horace Greeley's *The American Conflict*, Charles and Mary Beard's *The Rise of American Civilization*, and Edward Channing's authoritative *A History of the United States* (Vol. 6, *The War for Southern Independence*) are required reading, as well as the works of the important historians James Ford Rhodes and Ulrich B. Phillips. Rembert W. Patrick's *Jefferson Davis and His Cabinet* is a judicious work of inestimable value. Frank Owsley's compact *State Rights in the Confederacy* is generally considered the best in its field.

In my opinion the most interesting works on great democrats of earlier times are Dumas Malone's many-volumed *Thomas Jefferson*, and Arthur Schlesinger, Jr.'s *The Age of Jackson*.

Among general books on the South of special value which I have consulted are W. J. Cash, *The Mind of the South* (1941); Francis Butler Simkins, *The South Old and New*, revised edition (1947); Walter Prescott Webb, *Divided We Stand* (1927); Stark Young's well-chosen anthology *Southern Treasury of Life and Literature* (1937).

For Mississippi opinions on local politics and the milieu of Joseph and Jefferson Davis, see Reuben Davis, *Recollections of Mississippi and Mississippians* (1890); James D. Lynch, *The Bench and Bar of Mississippi* (1876); Robert Lowry (and W. H. McCardle), *A History of Mississippi* (1896); J. F. H. Claiborne, *History of Mississippi* (1880); J. G. Baldwin, *Flush Times in Alabama and Mississippi* (1853).

To get a perspective on public figures with whom Jefferson Davis came in significant contact, I have made a study of numerous biographies. For instance, I read four of President Franklin Pierce, including those by Nathaniel Hawthorne and D. W. Bartlett written for the campaign of 1852. The fullest and best life of Pierce is that by Professor Roy F. Nichols (1931). By all odds the most thorough, best-proportioned biography of Zachary Taylor, Jefferson Davis's first father-in-law, is that of Holman Hamilton in two volumes: *Zachary Taylor: Soldier of the Republic* (1941) and *Zachary Taylor: Soldier in the White House* (1951).

To give me insight into the character of Abraham Lincoln, I have read the monumental work of Nicolay and Hay, the clear-visioned, unfinished biography of Albert J. Beveridge, the elevated yet earthy one of Carl Sandburg, and those of Lord Charnwood, Edgar Lee Masters, William H. Herndon, James Garfield Randall, and Benjamin P. Thomas.

Among biographies of other significant men of the period the following in particular proved helpful: Margaret Coit, *John C. Calhoun* (1950); Douglas Southall Freeman, *R. E. Lee* (1934); William Preston Johnston, *The Life of General Albert Sidney Johnston* (1878); George Fort Milton, *The Eve of Conflict: Stephen A. Douglas, and the Needless War* (1934); John Witherspoon Dubose, *The Life and Times of William Lowndes Yancey* (1892); Ulrich Bonnell Phillips, *The Life of Robert Toombs* (1913); Oswald Garrison Villard, *John Brown, 1800-1859: A Biography Fifty Years After* (1910); Robert Penn Warren, *John Brown: The Making of a Martyr* (1930); Carl Schurz, *Life of Henry Clay* (1888); Lloyd P. Stryker, *Andrew Johnson* (1929), and George Fort Milton, *The Age of Hate: Andrew Johnson and the Radicals* (1930); Frederic Bancroft, *The Life of William H. Seward* (1900); Philip G. Auchampaugh, *James Buchanan and His Cabinet on the Eve of Secession* (1929); Robert Douthat Meade, *Judah P. Benjamin: Confederate Statesman* (1943); Rudolph von Abele, *Alexander H. Stephens: A Biography* (1946).

Newspaper files which I have consulted include: New York's *Tribune, Herald,* and *Times;* Washington's *National Intelligencer* and *Union;* Charleston's *Mercury* and *Daily Courier;* New Orleans' *Picayune, Daily Delta, Times-Democrat,* and *Bee;* Richmond's *Dispatch, Sentinel, Examiner,* and *Inquirer;* Montgomery's *Advertiser* and *Daily Mail;* Vicksburg's *Sentinel* and *Whig;* Jackson's *Mississippian* and *Southron;* Natchez *Free Trader;* Woodville *Republican;* Memphis *Daily Appeal.*

I have made use of the *Southern Historical Society Papers,* Richmond, *New-York Historical Society Collections, Transactions of the Illinois State Historical Society and Journal,* the *Georgia Historical Quarterly,* the *Mississippi Valley Historical Review, Mississippi Historical Society Papers, Kentucky Historical Society Papers,* and the files of *The Confederate Veteran Magazine* and *Southern Bivouac.*

## CHAPTER I

"Autobiography of Jefferson Davis," *Belford's Magazine,* January, 1890, dated Beauvoir, Miss., November, 1889 (the month before he died)

*Jefferson Davis, A Memoir* by His Wife

Nannie Davis Smith, "Reminiscences of Jefferson Davis," *The Confederate Veteran,* May, 1930

Manuscript article by Nannie Davis Smith, McElroy collection of Davis material, New York Public Library

William H. Whitsitt, *Genealogy of Jefferson Davis and of Samuel Davies,* 1910

Recorder's Office, New Castle County, Delaware, Deed Record Q., Vol. I

*Records of the Welsh Tract Baptist Meeting,* Wilmington, 1904

Lengthy letter from Walton Linsey of Fairview, Kentucky, in the author's possession

Creed T. Davis's investigations of the Davis family (Copy in Jefferson Davis Shrine, Beauvoir, Mississippi)

Private letter of Jefferson Davis to Jerome S. Ridley on February 3,

1875, concerning his family's settling first in Kentucky and then in Mississippi

*Southern Historical Society Papers*, Vol. XXXVI

The democratic Jefferson Davis cared so little about genealogy—indeed he thought it un-American to be interested in ancestry—that in his brief autobiography in *Belford's Magazine*, he mistakenly wrote that his paternal grandfather had been born in Wales. Dr. William Whitsitt, president of the Southern Baptist Theological Seminary, spent several years in investigations and produced in 1910 the little book called *Genealogy of Jefferson Davis and of Samuel Davies*. While there are errors, and little that is absolutely conclusive, the book is valuable for the amount of research done. In legal documents, the brothers John and David Davis both appear as turners and as yeomen, and in one David is called "gentleman."

Doubtless because the Davises look so aristocratic, investigators have been determined to search for a fountainhead of blue blood. In the New York Public Library among the McElroy papers on Davis may be seen the theory of the Kentish aristocratic heritage. Major Harry A. Davis's careful work *The Davis Family (Davies and David) in Wales and America* gives Evan Davis as born in Merion Township, near Philadelphia in 1702, and descended from Evan, "one of three brothers who came to America in the early part of the eighteenth century."

A third investigation, by Creed T. Davis of Virginia, reveals that a patent was issued to one Evan Davis for 512 acres of land in Lancaster County, Virginia, dated between the years 1652 and 1655. Five more grants were made to this Evan in Rappahannock County between 1655 and 1695. These Rappahannock acres, which totaled 4,335, were given to Evan Davis, who owned a sailing vessel, for "the transportation of persons to dwell in the colony." He brought the colonists in five groups of eight to eighteen. This "much-landed" Evan, who retired before the close of the seventeenth century, is believed by Creed Davis to be "the progenitor of Jefferson Davis." In further evidence of his theory, he found that nine patents for more than 2,000 acres of land in adjoining counties were issued "about the same time in names of Thomas, John and Henry Emory—the family name of Jefferson Davis's paternal grandmother who was born Lydia Emory."

In the May, 1930, issue of *The Confederate Veteran*, Miss Nannie

Davis Smith, Jefferson Davis's favorite grandniece and his last secretary, gives the Davis Family Chart with Captain Dolan Davis from Kent as the progenitor, with Dolan's grandparents, William and Elizabeth Jordan Davis, both born in Wales. The crest of Dolan Davis with a lion's head emerging from a ducal crown suggests that the family had served the king. After Jefferson Davis's death, his widow was presented with a framed copy of the heraldic emblem. It now hangs in the drawing room of the eldest grandson, Jefferson Hayes-Davis in Colorado Springs.

Since the name of Davis is anything but unusual, in Wales about as common as Jones, it seems unlikely that the forebears of Jefferson Davis will ever be assuredly identified.

Of Samuel Davis's six sons, only Samuel, Jr., was survived by a male descendant to perpetuate the name. But 141 adult relatives of Jefferson Davis were living in 1930, and today the roll is considerably larger.

## CHAPTER II

*Jefferson Davis, A Memoir* by His Wife
*Audubon's America*, edited by Donald Culross Peattie
Walter L. Fleming, *The Religious Life of Jefferson Davis* (monograph)
Herman de Bachellé Seebold, *Old Louisiana Plantation Homes and Family Trees*, Vol. I
Reuben Davis, *Recollections of Mississippi and Mississippians*
James D. Lynch, *The Bench and Bar of Mississippi*
Margaret Newman Wagers, *The Education of a Gentleman*
Lexington *Reporter*, March 7, 1825
"Jefferson Davis at the University," *The Transylvanian*, June, 1907

The revealing letter from Samuel Davis, which first appeared in Whitsitt's *Genealogy of Jefferson Davis*, was presented to the library of Richmond in February, 1909, by S. S. P. Patterson, who procured it from Byron A. Nevins of Albany, N. Y.

SOURCES AND NOTES ON SOURCES 443

## CHAPTER III

Appleton's *Cyclopaedia of American Biography*
*Official Register of the United States Military Academy*
*American State Papers, Military Affairs*
Albert E. Church, *Personal Reminiscences of the Military Academy from 1824 to 1831*
Samuel P. Heintzelman, *Diary*
F. H. Smith, *West Point Fifty Years Ago*
W. Cullom, *Biographical Register of United States Military Academy Graduates*
Walter L. Fleming, "Jefferson Davis at West Point" (monograph), *Southern Historical Society Papers*
*Jefferson Davis, A Memoir* by His Wife
William Preston Johnston, *The Life of General Albert Sidney Johnston*
Douglas Southall Freeman, *R. E. Lee*
Morris Schaff, *Jefferson Davis: His Life and Personality*

## CHAPTERS IV AND V

Since the material for the two chapters on Jefferson Davis's years as a soldier on the Northwest frontier overlap, the sources are listed together.

The best authority for this period is *Jefferson Davis, A Memoir* by His Wife, for she sets down the stories her husband intended to use in the autobiography he had begun the year of his death.

Charles Aldrich, *Jefferson Davis and Black Hawk*, *Midland Monthly* (Des Moines), Vol. V (Aldrich visited Jefferson Davis to obtain material for this article.)
Milo M. Quaife, "The Northwestern Career of Jefferson Davis," *Illinois State Historical Society Journal*, Vol. 16 (July, 1923)
James Hall, *Sketches of the West*
James Handasyd Perkins, *Annals of the West*
Mrs. J. H. Kinzie, *Wau Bun* (written from her own frontier experiences)

William Preston Johnston, *The Life of General Albert Sidney Johnston*
Quotations from Black Hawk are taken from *Life of Ma-ka-tai-me-she-kia-kiak or Black Hawk, Dictated by Himself*
See *Niles Weekly Register* XLIII for Colonel Taylor's speech to the Winnebagos
Perry A. Armstrong, *The Sauks and the Black Hawk War*
Governor John Reynolds, *My Own Times*
Frank A. Stevens, *The Black Hawk War* (While sometimes inaccurate as to dates, Frank A. Stevens, who grew up at Dixon's Ferry, Illinois, steeped in its history and legend, has provided a lively account of the time.)
Reuben Gold Twaithe, *The Black Hawk War* (monograph)
Davis McBride, "Capture of Black Hawk," *Wisconsin Historical Collections*, Vol. V (romanticized and sentimental)
Cyrenus Cole, *I Am a Man: The Indian Black Hawk* (published on the hundredth anniversary of the warrior's death, 1938)
F. B. Heitmann, *Historical Register of the United States Army from September 29, 1789 to September 29, 1889*

## CHAPTER VI

For interesting details on Jefferson Davis's courtship of Sarah Knox Taylor see feature article in New York *Times*, October 20, 1906, by her sister Mary Elizabeth Taylor Dandridge.

An unpublished article by Charles Anderson furnished the most illuminating material of this chapter. It forms a part of the Trist Wood Collection of Taylor papers, inherited by Professor John A. Kelly of Haverford College.

Walter L. Fleming, *The First Marriage of Jefferson Davis* (monograph)
Frank Stevens in *The Black Hawk War* describes the Wisconsin spring and summer of 1833
Manuscript articles in Evans Memorial Library, Aberdeen, Mississippi
Ganoe, *History of the United States Army*
Holman Hamilton, *Zachary Taylor: Soldier of the Republic*

## CHAPTER VII

Letters and photostatic copies in Zachary Taylor Collection, Library of Congress, Washington, D. C.
Taylor family letters in Trist Wood Collection and Charles Anderson's manuscript article
Trist Wood, "Jefferson Davis's First Marriage," New Orleans *Daily Picayune*, August 28, 1910
Walter L. Fleming, *The First Marriage of Jefferson Davis* (monograph)
Holman Hamilton, *Zachary Taylor: Soldier of the Republic*
*Jefferson Davis, A Memoir* by His Wife
James Lynch, *The Bench and Bar in Mississippi*

## CHAPTER VIII

Much of the material for this chapter came from Mrs. Mary Lucy O'Kelley, Joseph Davis's great-granddaughter, Pass Christian, Mississippi.

The letter from William van Bentheysen, April 18, 1838, heretofore unpublished, makes it clear that Jefferson Davis was in Washington in the spring of 1838. Mrs. Davis mistakenly puts this visit in 1836.

Testimony of Isaiah Montgomery, onetime Davis slave, Boston *Transcript*, 1907
Personal letters owned by Jefferson Hayes-Davis and Mrs. Mary Lucy O'Kelley
Manuscript letters, University of North Carolina Library
Files of Vicksburg *Sentinel*, 1843, 1844, 1845
H. J. Eckenrode, *Jefferson Davis: President of the South* (particularly good on the repudiation, as is A. E. Pollard, who exonerates Davis completely and blames the slanders on falsifications of Robert J. Walker)
Reuben Davis, *Recollections of Mississippi and Mississippians*
J. G. Baldwin, *Flush Times in Alabama and Mississippi*

## CHAPTER IX

Love letters to Varina Howell in the possession of Jefferson Hayes-Davis, Colorado Springs
Plantation records in library of Jefferson Davis Shrine, Beauvoir, Mississippi
Letters in Manuscript Division, Library of Congress
Letters quoted in Dunbar Rowland, *Jefferson Davis: Constitutionalist*
Eron Rowland, *Varina Howell, Wife of Jefferson Davis*, Vol. I
*Jefferson Davis, A Memoir* by His Wife
Special information about The Briers comes from the present owner, Mrs. William W. Wall
Records of Episcopal Church, Woodville, Mississippi
Personal communication by family members, particularly Anna Farrar Goldsborough and Mary Lucy O'Kelley, great-grandnieces of Jefferson Davis

At Rosemont in Woodville the author was given a copy of Jane Davis's will by Miss Louise R. Johnson, present owner of the place. The will, dated May 20, 1839, may be found in Will Book No. 2, Chancery Clerk's Office, Woodville, Mississippi. It was recorded and probated on February 12, 1846.

## CHAPTER X

For descriptions of Washington at mid-century see four books in particular: Marian Gouverneur, *As I Remember*; Rufus Wilson, *Washington the Capital City*; Samuel Clagett Busey, *Personal Reminiscences and Recollections*; Wilhelmus Bryan, *History of the National Capital*.

For illuminating comments of Jefferson Davis's loyalty to the Union, see *Congressional Globe*, Twenty-ninth Congress, First Session, March 16, 1846.

William E. Dodd, *Jefferson Davis*
Marquis James, *Sam Houston*
Margaret Coit, *John C. Calhoun*

*National Intelligencer*
Unpublished Davis letters in possession of Anna Farrar Goldsborough

## CHAPTERS XI AND XII

Zachary Taylor's letters, Manuscript Division, Library of Congress
Davis letters quoted in full in Dunbar Rowland, *Jefferson Davis: Constitutionalist*
Justin H. Smith, *The War with Mexico*
J. Fred Rippy, *United States and Mexico*
Hudson Strode, *Timeless Mexico*
Manuscript article of Charles Anderson
Holman Hamilton, *Zachary Taylor: Soldier of the Republic*
Robert McElroy, *Jefferson Davis: The Real and the Unreal*
William E. Dodd, *Jefferson Davis*
*Jefferson Davis, A Memoir* by His Wife
William Preston Johnston, *The Life of General Albert Sidney Johnston*
Natchez *Weekly Courier*
Lawsuit of Davis *vs.* Bomar, recorded in full in 55 *Mississippi Reports*, April Term, 1878, beginning at page 671
*Journal of Mississippi History* (July, 1947)

To the author the most interesting document concerning Jefferson Davis's soldiering is the lengthy report of the Battle of Buena Vista the wounded Colonel Davis wrote on long strips of brown paper, now in Confederate Memorial Hall, New Orleans.

## CHAPTER XIII

For a full account of the slaves and property of Zachary Taylor see Holman Hamilton, *Zachary Taylor: Soldier in the White House.*

*Congressional Globe,* Thirtieth Congress, First Session
E. G. Bourne's article in *American Historical Review,* April, 1900
Zachary Taylor's letters, Manuscript Division, Library of Congress
Revealing letters of Varina Davis, quoted in part or in full, heretofore

unpublished, in possession of Jefferson Hayes-Davis, Colorado Springs
Ulrich Bonnell Phillips, *The Life of Robert Toombs*
*National Intelligencer*
New York *Sun*
Douglas Southall Freeman, *R. E. Lee*
*Jefferson Davis, A Memoir* by His Wife
Hudson Strode, *The Pageant of Cuba*
Unpublished letters in possession of Mary Lucy O'Kelley, Pass Christian, Mississippi

## CHAPTER XIV

*Congressional Globe*, Thirty-first Congress, First Session
William E. Dodd, *Jefferson Davis*
Holman Hamilton, *Zachary Taylor: Soldier in the White House*
Morris Schaff, *Jefferson Davis: His Life and Personality*
Frederika Bremer, *Homes in the New World*
Charles Anderson, manuscript article
Dunbar Rowland, *Jefferson Davis: Constitutionalist*
Frank H. Alfriend, *The Life of Jefferson Davis*, for more of the scenes between Henry Clay and Jefferson Davis
Margaret Coit, *John C. Calhoun*, for graphic details of the old statesman's last days of illness and despair
*Jefferson Davis, A Memoir* by His Wife

## CHAPTER XV

*Congressional Globe*, Thirty-first Congress, First Session
Mississippi *Free Trader*
Letters in New York Public Library
Walter L. Fleming, *The Negroes and the Negro Problem* (monograph)
*Jefferson Davis, A Memoir* by His Wife
Robert W. Winston, *High Stakes and Hair Trigger*, for details of Foote's campaign for governor
Nathaniel Hawthorne, *Franklin Pierce*
Lawsuit of Davis vs. Bomar in 55 *Mississippi Reports*

## CHAPTERS XVI, XVII, XVIII

Roy Franklin Nichols, *Franklin Pierce: Young Hickory of the Granite Hills*
James Ford Rhodes, *History of the United States,* Vol. 1
Reports of Secretary of War to Thirty-third Congress, First and Second Sessions, *Congressional Globe*
Richardson, *Messages and Papers of the Presidents,* Vol. V
Jefferson Davis's letters to Franklin Pierce, Library of Congress
Franklin Pierce's letters to Jefferson Davis, Library of Congress
*Congressional Globe,* Thirty-first Congress, First Session
Mrs. Clay, *A Belle of the Fifties*
*New-York Historical Society Collections*
*Jefferson Davis, A Memoir* by His Wife
Jefferson Davis, *The Rise and Fall of the Confederate Government*
Dunbar Rowland, *Jefferson Davis: Constitutionalist*
Walter L. Fleming, *Jefferson Davis's Camel Experiment* (monograph)
Oswald Garrison Villard, *John Brown: A Biography Fifty Years After*
Robert Penn Warren, *John Brown: The Making of a Martyr*
Allan Nevins, *The Emergence of Lincoln* (one of the most lucid discussions of the Dred Scott suit)
Sidney Webster, *Franklin Pierce and His Administration*
Mrs. Holloway, *Ladies of the White House,* for the life of Mrs. Franklin Pierce

For detailed discussion of the Gadsden Purchase see Nichols, *Franklin Pierce* and a recent excellent article in *Arizona Highways* by Samuel A. Siciliano, November, 1953.

## CHAPTERS XIX AND XX

James Buchanan, Manuscript Collection, Historical Society of Pennsylvania
James Buchanan, *Mr. Buchanan's Administration on the Eve of the Rebellion*
William M. Gwin, *Memoirs,* University of California

450   SOURCES AND NOTES ON SOURCES

John Bassett Moore, *James Buchanan, Works*
Mrs. Chapman Coleman, *John J. Crittenden*
Catherine Drinker Bowen, *Yankee from Olympus*
*Congressional Globe*, Thirty-fourth Congress
Frederic Bancroft, *The Life of William A. Seward*
Mrs. Roger A. Pryor, *Reminiscences of Peace and War*
Mary Boykin Chestnut, *A Diary from Dixie*
Mrs. Clay, *A Belle of the Fifties*
Mrs. Hezekiah Sturges, "Recollections of Jefferson Davis," *Register of Kentucky History*, May, 1912
William Schomberg Robert Kerr, 8th Marquess of Lothian, *The Confederate Secession*
Robert Douthat Meade, *Judah P. Benjamin: Confederate Statesman*
Letters of Jefferson Davis, Library of Congress
Dunbar Rowland, *Jefferson Davis: Constitutionalist*

The heretofore unpublished letters of Varina Davis and those of Jefferson Davis to his father-in-law are in possession of Jefferson Hayes-Davis, Colorado Springs.

## CHAPTER XXI

Oswald Garrison Villard, *John Brown: A Biography Fifty Years After*
Robert Penn Warren, *John Brown: The Making of a Martyr*
Albert Bushnell Hart, *Salmon P. Chase*
Douglas Southall Freeman, *R. E. Lee*
*Congressional Globe*, Thirty-sixth Congress
James Ford Rhodes, *History of the United States*, Vol. II
*Trinity College Historical Papers*, 1899
Hinton Rowan Helper, *The Impending Crisis in the South: How to Meet It*
A. C. Bancroft, *The Life and Death of Jefferson Davis*
Jefferson Davis, *Rise and Fall of the Confederate Government*
Frank H. Alfriend, *The Life of Jefferson Davis*
B. F. Butler's letters favoring Jefferson Davis's candidacy in 1860, Library of Congress
Carl Sandburg, *Abraham Lincoln*
*Transactions of the Illinois State Historical Society*

Letters otherwise unidentified in text may be found in Dunbar Rowland, *Jefferson Davis: Constitutionalist,* Vol. IV

## CHAPTER XXII

J. B. Randall, *The Civil War and Reconstruction*
J. B. Randall, *Abraham Lincoln*
Charles Francis Adams, *An Autobiography*
William E. Dodd, *Statesmen of the Old South*
Mary Boykin Chestnut, *A Diary from Dixie*
Correspondence between Davis and Pickens, Library of Congress
Philip G. Auchampaugh, *James Buchanan and His Cabinet on the Eve of Secession*
*Parallel Source Problems in American History,* edited by McLaughlin, Dodd, Jernegan, and Scott
James Ford Rhodes, *History of the United States,* Vol. III
George T. Curtis, *The Life of James Buchanan*
J. B. Richardson, *Messages and Papers of the President*
Letters to and from Jefferson Davis not otherwise specified, in Dunbar Rowland, *Jefferson Davis: Constitutionalist*
Abraham Lincoln, *Works*
Mrs. Roger A. Pryor, *Reminiscences of Peace and War*
Benjamin P. Thomas, *Abraham Lincoln*
*Jefferson Davis, A Memoir* by His Wife
*Congressional Globe,* Thirty-sixth Congress
New York *Tribune* and *Herald;* Charleston *Mercury*
W. A. Burk, "The Secession of South Carolina," *The Confederate Veteran,* January, 1890

## CHAPTER XXIII

*Congressional Globe,* Thirty-sixth Congress
Davis letters, Manuscript Division, Library of Congress
Davis letters reprinted in Dunbar Rowland, *Jefferson Davis: Constitutionalist*
*Official Records,* Series I, Vol. I

Jefferson Davis, *Rise and Fall of the Confederate Government*
*American Historical Review*, Vol. I
*South Atlantic Quarterly*, Vol. II
Allen Tate, *Jefferson Davis: His Rise and Fall*, for account of the farewell speech in the Senate
Pickens letters, New York Public Library

Mrs. Davis in her *Memoir* gives the most vivid account of Mr. Davis's last days in Washington.

## CHAPTERS XXIV AND XXV

Letters of Thomas Cobb, *Southern Historical Association*, June and August, 1907
Jefferson Davis, *Rise and Fall of the Confederate Government*
John Witherspoon Dubose, *The Life and Times of William Lowndes Yancey*
Charleston *Mercury*, February 19, 1861, for full report of Mr. Davis's journey to and arrival at the capital. All the nation's papers carried the story at length.
J. B. Richardson, *Messages and Papers of the Confederacy*
Burton Hendrix, *Statesmen of the Lost Cause*
Rembert W. Patrick, *Jefferson Davis and His Cabinet*
*Jefferson Davis, A Memoir* by His Wife
Elizabeth Mitchell Hamer, *Journal*, in possession of Mrs. Mary Lucy O'Kelley, Pass Christian, Mississippi
New York *Herald*, February 19, 1861; New York *Tribune*, November 30, December 17, 1860, and February 23, 1861
Files of Montgomery *Advertiser* and *Daily Mail*, February, 1861
Mary Boykin Chestnut, *A Diary from Dixie*
Robert Douthat Meade, *Judah P. Benjamin: Confederate Statesman*

# INDEX

Abercrombie, Lt. John J., 59-60
Abolitionists, 269, 284, 312, 314-15, 365, 377
Act of Repudiation, 123
Adams, James H., 375
Adams, John Quincy, 150, 151, 194
*Aetna*, steamship, 16, 17, 18
Agassiz, Louis, 279
Agua Nueva, Mexico, 176, 177
*Alabama*, U.S.S., 161
Albany *Argus*, 419
Aldrich, Charles, 71
Alfriend, Frank H., 404, 412
Allen, William, 107, 115, 120, 121, 133, 148, 150
*Ambassador*, steamboat, 135
Ampudia, General Pedro de, 164, 166, 167-68, 169, 179
Anderson, Charles, 83, 98, 223
Anderson, Richard Clough, 83 fn.
Anderson, Robert, 39, 66, 69 fn., 75 fn., 375-76, 379
Angier, Father, 14, 15
Arista, General Mariano, 155
Arnold, Herman, 408
Ashe, Reverend Mr., 98
Astor, John Jacob, 54
Atchinson, David Rice, 264, 265
Atkinson, Henry, 51, 67, 69, 72, 75, 76, 77, 84, 85
Atkinson, Mary, 84
Atlanta, Ga., 406
Audubon, John James, 16, 17, 20
Augusta, Ga., 4

Bache, Alexander Dallas, 36-37, 154, 304, 308
Bache, Eliza, 325
*Baltimore*, steamboat, 222
Bangor, Maine, 308
Bangor (Me.) *Union*, 419
Barnwell, Robert W., 375, 421
Bartlett, William H. C., 37, 45
Bates, Edward, 353
Bayard, James A., 305
Bayou Sara, La., 94, 104, 137

Beardstown, Ill., 66
Beer, Thomas, 361
Bell, John, 356, 358, 360
Benét, Stephen, 339
Benjamin, Judah P., 305, 306, 422
Bennett, Gerald, Jr., 137 fn.
Bennett, Gordon, 418
Bennett, Varina Webb, 137 fn.
Benton, Thomas H., 107, 147, 220, 228
Bérard, Claudius, 34
Bishop, Reverend Mr., 23
Black Hawk, 63-77
*Black Hawk War, The*, 65, 77
*Black Warrior* affair, 270, 271, 298
Blaine, James G., 346
Blair, Francis Preston, 229
Blanchard, Albert, 39
Bliss, William W. S., 178, 209, 228, 229, 255
Bodisco, Alexandre de, 148
Boston, Mass., 306, 309-11, 355
Boston *Morning Post*, 310, 355
Bouligny, John E., 370
Bowdoin College, 243, 309
Bowen, Catherine Drinker, 297, 355
Boyle, Lucy J., 233 fn.
Bradford, David, 26, 86-87, 131
Bradford, Gamaliel, 147
Bradford, Jefferson Davis, 87 fn.
Bradford, Mary Jane, 125, 127, 142, 157, 255
Bradford, Major, 179
Bragg, Braxton, 179, 198, 421
Breckenridge, John C., 264, 285, 357, 358, 360, 424
Breckenridge, Robert J., 31
Bremer, Frederika, 222, 225-26, 227
Brodhead, Richard, 255
*Brooklyn*, U.S.S., 379
Brooks, Preston, 283-84
Brown, A. G., 190-91, 234, 237
Brown, John, 282-83, 336-39
Browning, Elizabeth Barrett, 79, 257
Brunswick, Maine, 307
Buchanan, James, 148, 210, 253, 267, 270, 283, 285, 293, 299, 313, 316,

453

## INDEX

328, 330, 337, 339, 363, 364-65, 371, 375-76, 377, 379, 380, 393
Buena Vista, battle, 175-86
Bull, Ole, 320
Burk, W. A., 372-73
Burr, Aaron, 127
Burr, Keziah, 127
Burt, Armistead, 195
Butler, Benjamin F., 227, 283, 310, 351

Cairo, Ill., 17, 100
Calhoun, John C., 27, 81, 121, 133, 141-42, 147-49, 150, 151, 192, 194, 198-99, 214, 219-22, 252, 313
California gold rush of 1849, 216
Camel military transport, 276-77
Cameron, Simon, 353
Campbell, James, 249, 278
Campbell, Lewis, 322
Capon Springs, Va., 268
Cass, Lewis, 152, 200, 283
Castle Pinckney, 376
Chaeter, chief of Winnebagos, 74
Chalfont, Thérèse, 317, 318
Charleston *Mercury*, 362, 373, 405
Charles Town, Va., 338, 339
Chase, Salmon P., 336-37, 338-39, 353, 374
Chattanooga, Tenn., 396, 406
Chestnut, James, 363
Chestnut, Mrs. James, 317, 361, 376, 414-15, 423
Choctaw Indians, 12, 358
Church, Albert E., 35, 43
Clay, Clement C., 303, 345, 363, 389, 393, 421
Clay, Mrs. Clement, 259, 317, 320-21
Clay, Henry, 24, 134, 152, 194, 200-01, 216, 218, 223-25, 228, 229, 233
Clay, Henry, Jr., 24, 39, 182, 185, 224, 272
Clay, Theodore W., 31
Clay Compromise, *see* Compromise of 1850
Cobb, Howell, 403, 410, 420
Cobb, Thomas R. R., 403, 421
Cocke, Stephen, 190, 192-93, 201, 286
Coe, F. W., 46 fn.
Coit, Margaret, 148
Cole, Cyrenus, 73
Comanche Indians, 57
Compromise of 1850, 218-19, 220, 223, 229, 231, 234, 242, 266
Comte, John le, 279
Confederate States of America, 398-426

*Congressional Globe*, 231
*Congressional Record*, 380
Cook, Jennie Strahan, 5
Corpus Christi, Texas, 154
Craven, Dr. John J., 114
Crawford, Martin J., 416
Crawford, Thomas, 319
Crimean War, 274
Crittenden, John J., 107, 115, 206, 369, 374, 378
Crittenden, T. L., 170, 175, 184-85
Crittenden Compromise, 374, 378, 417 fn.
Cruikshank, George, 39
Cuba, 210-11, 234, 270-71, 299
Cushing, Caleb, 249, 250, 310, 356
Cushman, Charlotte, 320
Cutts, Adèle, 264, 317, 318

Dallas, George, 154, 219
Daniel, Lee S., 401 fn.
Daniels, Jonathan, 222 fn.
Davies, Samuel, 4
Davis, Amanda, 7, 26 fn., 131, 139, 173
Davis, Anna, 5, 6, 7, 9, 20, 104, 105, 173, 233
Davis, Benjamin, 6, 9, 20, 105
Davis, Caroline, 51
Davis, Charles, 33
Davis, David, 4, 354
Davis, Dolan, 4
Davis, Ellen M., 140
Davis, Evan, 4-5
Davis, Florida, 51, 86, 117, 125
Davis, Hugh, 108 fn., 140
Davis, Isaac, 5, 6, 9, 19, 30, 50, 94
Davis, Jane Cook, 3, 5, 6, 7-8, 9, 10, 12, 16, 19-20, 29 fn., 40, 107, 108, 138, 140, 333-35
Davis, Jane L., 140
Davis, Jefferson Finis, birth, 3; ancestry, 4-5; appointment to Senate, 189-93; battle of Buena Vista, 175-86; Black Hawk War, 63-77; children, 242, 273, 292, 295, 328, 330; court-martial, 89-92; education, 11-31; election to Congress, 140-41; farewell to Washington, 384-97; first love, 78-92; inaugural address, 410-12; marriages, 95-99, 136-37; Mexican War, 161-93; military experience in North, 50-62; planter, 106-24, 236-44; political defeat, 234-36; policies, 133-34; President of the Confederacy, 401-26; Representative from Mississippi, 145-60; Secretary of War, 245-95; Senator

# INDEX

Davis, Jefferson Finis (Cont.)
from Mississippi, 194-234, 286, 296-383; West Point training, 32-49
Davis, Jefferson, Jr., 295, 298, 306, 309, 326
Davis, John, 4
Davis, Sir Jonathan, 4
Davis, Joseph Emory, 3, 5, 9, 11, 19, 22, 25, 27, 30, 32, 39-40, 50, 61, 71, 93-94, 99-100, 101-02, 106, 109-12, 113, 118, 120, 124, 125, 128, 135, 139, 143, 161, 185, 187, 189, 191, 197, 201, 213, 238, 324, 327, 330, 335, 399, 401
Davis, Joseph Evan, 330, 347
Davis, Lucinda, 7, 9, 51, 107, 158-60, 174
Davis, Margaret Howell, 272 fn., 273, 286-87, 306, 307
Davis, Mary, 7, 11, 28, 29 fn., 51 fn., 118, 136, 137
Davis, Matilda, 7, 86
Davis, Nathanael, 4
Davis, Reuben, 110, 368
Davis, Robert, 29
Davis, Samuel Emory, 3-4, 5-7, 8, 9, 10, 11, 20, 21-22, 25-27, 28, 29-30, 113, 132
Davis, Samuel Emory, Jr., 6, 9, 30, 242, 255, 257, 263, 268
Davis, Susannah, 28, 50
Davis, Varina Anne Howell, 5, 24, 40, 47, 58 fn., 111, 119, 125-44, 146-47, 148, 150, 152, 153, 154, 158, 171-74, 186, 189, 190, 191, 195, 196, 207-08, 209, 211, 225-26, 235, 238, 240, 242, 246, 248, 255-56, 257, 258, 268, 271, 277-78, 279, 292-93, 297-98, 302, 303, 317, 318, 319, 321, 324, 328-29, 330, 351, 388, 390, 393, 394, 399, 401, 423, 424-26
Davis, Varina Ann, 233 fn.
Davis vs. Bowmar, 173
De Hart, Robinson, 17
Delafield, R., 274
Detroit *Free Press*, 420
Dickerson, J. D., 348
Dixon, John, 65, 66
Dixon, Thomas, 124, 265
Dixon's Ferry, Ill., 65, 66, 68, 69.
Dodd, William, 40, 43, 56, 109, 113, 140, 148, 170, 184, 252, 351, 374, 393
Dodge, Henry, 82, 154
Douglas, Stephen A., 263-68, 269, 294, 296, 300-01, 315, 317, 340, 348-53, 355, 356, 360, 369, 378

Drayton, Thomas, 39, 47
Dred Scott decision, 291-92, 296-97, 299, 350, 370
Dreux, Captain, 425
Dubuque, Iowa, 59-60, 183
Dubuque *Herald*, 183

Eckenrode, Dr., 256, 370
Edwards, Ann Taylor, 96
Eliot, George, 320
Ellett, Henry T., 420
Elliott, Thomas, 79
Emerson, John, 291
Emerson, Ralph Waldo, 339
Emmett, Dan, 409 fn.
Eustis, Abram, 182
Evans, Mary Ann, 320
Evansville, Ind., 17
Everett, Edward, 271, 310, 356

Faneuil Hall, Boston, 310-11
Featherston, W. S., 234
Ficklin, Joseph, 23-24, 30
Fillmore, Millard, 209, 229
Fitzpatrick, Benjamin, 357, 389
Fleming, Dr. Walter H., 43
Floyd, John B., 277 fn., 376, 377, 393
Foote, Henry S., 219-20, 227, 233, 234, 235, 236-37, 287, 322-23
Forbes, Colonel, 341
Forsyth, John, 416
Fort Armstrong, 63, 67
Fort Crawford, 52-54, 57, 58, 63, 74, 83
Fort Gibson, 89
Fort Mins massacre, 9, 12
Fort Moultrie, 81, 375
Fort Snelling, 79
Fort Sumter, 39, 375, 376, 377, 379, 382
Fort Winnebago, 54-57
Fortress Monroe, 259
Franklin, Benjamin, 36
Freeman, Douglas Southall, 212
Freeman, Dr. W. L., 38, 46 fn.
Frémont, John, 285
Fugitive Slave Law, 221, 269

Gadsden, James, 262
Gadsden Purchase, 262-63
Galena, Ill., 64-65, 76
Garrison, William Lloyd, 269
Goldsborough, Anna Farrar, 160 fn.
Gordon, George H., 241
Gorgas, Josias, 415
Grant, Ulysses S., 164, 169
Greeley, Horace, 228, 301, 353, 369, 419

## INDEX

Green, Bishop, 138 fn.
Green, Charles, 16
Green, Jim, 161
Greene, Nathanael, 5
Gregg, Maxey, 372
Gridley's hotel, West Point, 32
Guion, Walter, 43
Guthrie, James, 249, 252
Gwin, William M., 318

Hale, John P., 217
Hamer, Lise Mitchell, 101 fn., 189-90, 213, 330, 335, 401 fn.
Hamilton, Holman, 205
Hardie, Colonel, 303
Harney, W. S., 56
Harpe, Micajah, 17
Harpers Ferry, Va., 337-38
Harrison, William Henry, 63, 205
Hart, Albert Bushnell, 336
Havana, Cuba, 106-07
Havens, Benny, 40-41
Hawthorne, Nathaniel, 243, 304
Hayes, Dr., 302
Hayes-Davis, Jefferson, 28 fn., 71 fn., 108 fn., 130 fn., 287 fn., 395 fn.
Haynes, M. D., 349
Henderson, General James P., 167
Henderson, Ky., 17
Henry, General James D., 73
Henry, Professor, 279
Hetzel, Mrs., 293, 327
Heyward, Shepherd, 337
Higginson, Thomas H., 269
Hinds, Howell, 12
Hinds, Major, 12
*History of the United States Army*, 89
*History of the War Department*, 261
Hitchcock, Ethan Allen, 32, 33, 41, 43
Holley, Horace, 23, 31
Holt, Joseph, 377
Hopkinsville, Ky., 3
Houston, Samuel, 147, 384
Howe, S. G., 336, 338
Howell, Becket, 196, 249, 255, 334
Howell, "Jeffy D," 286, 302
Howell, Joseph Davis, 139, 161
Howell, Margaret, 196, 232, 255, 271
Howell, Richard, 127
Howell, William Burr, 39-40, 125, 139, 196-97, 248-49
Hunter, R. M. T., 264, 369, 375
Huse, Caleb, 415

Indians, 12, 17, 18, 53, 54, 55-56, 57, 63-77, 273
Indian Territory, 83

Ingersoll, Charles Jared, 151, 154, 261
Irving, Washington, 319

Jackson, Andrew, 13-14, 19, 64, 81, 82, 83 fn., 183, 262
Jackson, Andrew, Jr., 13
Jackson, Mich., 284
Jackson, Miss., 297, 396, 398, 405
Jackson, Rachel, 13-14
Jackson, Thomas Jonathan, 38 fn.
Jefferson, Thomas, 3, 113, 195, 391
Jefferson Barracks, Mo., 48, 50-52, 75, 76, 77, 83
Jefferson College, 21
Jesup, Thomas, 74, 94
Johnson, Andrew, 156-57
Johnson, Herschel V., 357
Johnson, Louise R., 140 fn.
Johnston, Albert Sidney, 24-25, 30, 36, 37, 38, 44, 45, 46, 51, 52, 57 fn., 66, 67, 69, 75 fn., 77, 163, 168-69, 212, 274
Johnston, Joseph Eggleston, 37-38, 43
Johnston, Josias Stoddard, 25
Johnston, William Preston, 36, 37, 57
Jones, George Wallace, 24, 54, 60, 107, 109, 115, 116, 117, 120, 152, 386
Jones, Jacob, 348

Kansas-Nebraska Act, 263, 264-68, 269, 282, 285, 297
Kansas statehood, 299-300
Kansas Territory, 281-83
Kearney, Stephen W., 85
Keitt, Lawrence, 371
Kellogg, William, 368
Kelly, John A., 83 fn., 87 fn., 223 fn.
Kempe, Margaret, 39
Kempe, Margaret Louisa, 132, 137
Kenner, Duncan, 404
*Kentucky Reporter*, 31
Keokuk, chief of the Sacs, 64
King, William Rufus, 241-42
Kinnaird, Clark, 403
Kinsley, Lt., 47
Knight, Landon, 413

Lane, Harriet, 316
Lane, Joseph, 357
Lassere, Emile, 42
Lawrence, Kansas, 282
Leathers, Tom, 402
Le Claire, Antoine, 76 fn.
Lecompton, Kansas, 299
Lee, Custis, 273
Lee, Lighthorse Harry, 37

## INDEX 457

Lee, Robert Edward, 37-38, 43, 44, 45, 46, 175, 198, 209, 211, 212, 260, 272-73, 274, 338, 339
Lexington, Ky., 22
Lexington (Ky.) *Monitor*, 24
Lincoln, Abraham, 16, 66, 67-68, 69-70, 114, 209, 313, 353-56, 360, 361-62, 367-68, 373, 374, 378, 414, 416, 417-18, 419
Lind, Jenny, 320
Linn, Lewis, 107, 115, 116, 120
Lomax, Tennant, 408
London *Times*, 412, 421, 423
Longfellow, Henry W., 243
López, General Narcisco, 211, 234
Lothian, Lord, 316, 357, 359, 362
Louisville, Mo., 95, 97
Lyons, Richard B. P., Lord, 325, 326

Madison, Dolly, 264, 316, 317
*Magnolia*, steamboat, 125
Magruder, John B., 39
Mallory, Stephen R., 389, 422
Manly, Basil, 408
Mann, A. Dudley, 319, 422
Marcy, William, 154, 249, 251-52, 262, 266, 270, 281
Marshall, John, 113
Mason, James Maury, 264
Mason, John Y., 270
Mason, Major, 90-92
Mason, Samuel, 17
Matson, Nehemiah, 62
McAllister, James, 21
McClelland, George B., 249, 261, 274, 275-76
McClung, Alexander K., 165
McComb, Alexander, 42
McElroy, Dr. Robert, 165
McGruggy, Mrs., 143
McIlvaine, Charles, 43-44
McRee, Samuel and Mrs., 80, 95
McWillie, William, 195, 234
Meade, Robert Douthat, 306 fn.
Means, Abby, 257
Memminger, C. G., 421
*Memories of Shaukena*, 62
Memphis, Tenn., 18, 100
Meredith, William, 229
Mexican War, 154-55, 161-93
Mexico City, Mexico, 171, 175, 192
Miles, W. Porcher, 404
Mississippi City, Miss., 297-98
Mississippi *Free Trader*, 205, 231
Mississippi Rifles, 157, 179, 184, 185, 186

Missouri Compromise, 198, 219, 265, 296
Mitchell, Charles, 51 fn., 118
Mitchell, Hugh, 213
Mitchell, Joseph, 213, 330, 335
Mobile, Ala., 255
Monroe, James, 27, 83 fn.
Monterey, battle, 164-71
Montgomery, Ala., 400, 402, 406-26
Montgomery, Benjamin Thornton, 112, 113, 335
Montgomery, Isaiah, 113, 402
Montgomery, John, 112-13
Montgomery, Thornton, 113
Mordecai, A., 274
Morse, Samuel, 153
Murphy, E. V., 344

Napier, Lord and Lady, 302-03, 316, 318-19, 326
Nashville, Tenn., 13, 230
Natchez, Miss., 12, 18-19, 111, 141, 186
*Natchez*, steamboat, 402
Natchez *Weekly Courier*, 187
*National Intelligencer*, 209
Negro slavery, 112-15, 203-05, 216, 217-18, 297, 311, 315, 344
Nevins, Allan, 292 fn.
New Madrid, Mo., 18
New Orleans, La., 138, 186, 255, 373
New Orleans *Picayune*, 180, 186
New Orleans *Times Democrat*, 124
*New View of Society, A*, 112
New York, N. Y., 32, 107, 254, 311-12
New York *Herald*, 257, 263, 337, 418
New York *Tribune*, 228, 301, 331, 369, 377, 419, 420
New York *World*, 145
Nichols, Dr. Roy F., 250, 257
Noble, Sidney, 367
*North American Review*, 272
Northrop, L. B., 39
Nullification theory, 81-82

Oakland, Md., 330
O'Conor, Charles, 279
O'Kelley, Mary Lucy, 51 fn., 101 fn., 213 fn.
One-eyed Decori, chief of Winnebagos, 74, 75
*On the Constitution*, 44
Orr, James L., 375
Osage Indians, 18
Ostend Manifesto, 270
Otis, Mrs. Harrison Grey, 309-10
Owen, Robert, 39, 112

Page, David, 137
Palmyra, Miss., 18
Parker, Theodore, 336
Patrick, Professor, 79
Patterson, J. D., 76 fn.
Patti, Adelina, 320
Payne, George E., 258
Peace commissioners, 416
Peale, Rembrandt, 51 fn.
Pemberton, James, 50, 58, 86, 89, 102, 106, 111, 118, 120, 129, 141, 161, 173, 239
Perkins, Judge, 132, 201
Perry, Matthew C., 278
*Personal Reminiscences of the Military Academy from 1824 to 1831*, 35
Peters, Judge, 24
Pettus, Governor J. J., 363, 397
Philadelphia, Pa., 4, 25, 252, 253
Phillips, Philip, 264
Phillips, Wendell, 269, 338, 355, 361
Pickens, Francis W., 384, 385, 394
Pickett School, Cincinnati, 79
Pierce, Bennie, 246-47, 257
Pierce, Franklin, 107, 115, 241, 242, 243-44, 245-48, 249-51, 258-59, 262, 263, 278-79, 280, 281, 285, 287, 293-94, 304, 321, 346-48, 386, 387
Pierce, Franklin, Jr., 247
Pierce, Jane, 247, 256-57, 268, 273, 276, 304, 319
Poe, Edgar Allan, 272
Poinsett, Joel, 115
Polk, James Knox, 134, 135, 144, 154, 155, 157, 170, 176, 187, 188, 192-93, 197, 210
Polk, Leonidas, 36, 38, 44, 138
Pope, Pendleton, 97, 98
Portland, Maine, 306-07, 308-09
Posey, Carnot, 241
Powder Point, Texas, 277
Prairie du Chien, Wis., 52-54, 83
Prentiss, Seargent S., 110, 122, 123, 134, 186
Prescott, William, 215
Preston, Henrietta, 52
Princeton, N. J., 252
Pryor, Mrs. Roger, 250, 317, 318, 371
Pugh, George, 317

Quitman, John Anthony, 102, 164, 165, 198, 233-34

Railways, 70-71, 261, 262, 291, 323-24, 414
Raines, Gabriel, 39, 415

Randall, J. G., 360, 378
Rankin, Congressman, 27
Rawle, Judge William, 44
Reagan, John Henninger, 422
*Recollections of Jefferson Davis*, 319
*Recollections of Mississippi*, 110
Red Bird, 57 fn.
Reed, W. B., 31
Reeder, Andrew H., 281
Regulators, 7
Resistance Movement, 230
Reynolds, John, 64, 67
Rhett, Robert Barnwell, 198, 230, 362, 402, 404-05, 409, 421
Rhodes, James Ford, 403, 423
Richmond *Dispatch*, 270
Riley, Bennett, 52, 163
*Rise and Fall of the Confederate Government*, 345, 358
Roberts, Robert N., 143-44
Robinson, Mrs. Magill, 99 fn.
Roman, A. B., 416
Roosevelt, Franklin D., 121
Roosevelt, Theodore, 124, 261 fn., 287
Rost, Pierre Adolphe, 422
Rowland, Eron, 394
Russell, Lord John, 287
Russell, William, 421, 423

Sac Indians, 64
St. Mary's Parish, La., 8
St. Thomas Academy, 14-16
Sandburg, Carl, 68 fn., 306 fn., 354, 388
Sanford, John F. A., 292
Santa Anna, Antonio López de, 176-79, 181, 183, 262
Sartige, Count de, 275
Savannah, Ga., 4
Sayre, Robert, 255
Schaff, Morris, 48, 218, 311
Schurz, Carl, 252
Scott, Winfield, 65, 75, 124, 157, 163, 171, 175, 176, 198, 200, 201, 228, 229, 244, 260, 275, 287-90, 379, 420
Secession, 230, 360-83, 384
Semmes, Raphael, 393, 415
Seward, William, 210, 221, 293, 303-04, 312, 313, 315, 320-21, 340, 353, 355, 374, 378, 384, 420, 423
Sharkey, William L., 230, 405
Shaw, John A., 21
Sherman, Thomas, 179
*Short History of the Confederate States of America*, 380

## INDEX

*Slavery As It Is, the Testimony of a Thousand Witnesses*, 241
Smith, Caleb, 261 fn.
Smith, Gerrit, 336, 338
Smith, Justin H., 165
Smith, Luther, 20, 105
Smith, Margaret Mackall, 61
Smith, Thomas, 62, 80
Soulé, Pierre, 270, 271
*Southern Literary Messenger*, 412
Speight, Jesse, 152, 189
Springfield, Ill., 313
Springfield, Ky., 12
Stamps, Isaac Davis, 108 fn.
Stamps, William, 30 fn., 108
Stanton, H. T., 95
*Star of the West*, 379, 386
Stephens, Alexander H., 350, 402, 404, 405, 408, 409, 412
Stevens, Frank, 65, 66
Stewart, George, 113
Stillman, Isaiah, 68-69, 74
Stowe, Harriet Beecher, 240-41, 307, 309
Strakoch, Maurice, 320
Street, General Joseph M., 75
Street, Mary, 80-81
Strode, James M., 64-65, 66
Stuart, J. E. B., 338
Sturges, Mrs. Hezekiah, 319
Sumner, Charles, 283-84
Sumner, Edwin, 303

Taney, Roger B., 296, 297
Tate, Allen, 23, 409
Taylor, Ann, 79, 94, 97, 104, 228
Taylor, Betty, 79, 81, 209-10, 227, 228
Taylor, Fall, 96
Taylor, Hancock, 97, 98
Taylor, John Gibson, 95
Taylor, Joseph, 97, 228
Taylor, Margaret, 227, 228, 229
Taylor, Mary, 255
Taylor, Nicholas, 97
Taylor, Richard, 61, 79, 81, 95
Taylor, Sara Knox, 78-92, 94-105, 106, 136, 137, 138
Taylor, Zachary, 61-62, 65, 67, 68, 70, 73, 74, 75, 78, 79, 80, 81, 83, 94, 95-96, 98, 136, 154, 155, 156, 157, 162, 163, 164, 167, 169, 170, 171, 176, 177, 178, 179, 181-82, 183, 184, 189, 191-92, 194, 196, 198, 199-200, 201-02, 204-05, 206, 209, 223, 227-29, 287
Thayer, Sylvanus, 34

Thomas, Benjamin P., 373
Thompson, Jacob, 234
Throckmorton, Captain, 73
Toombs, Robert, 195, 216, 285, 369, 402, 404, 405, 421
Transylvania University, 16, 22-31, 54
Trenton, N. J., 252, 253
Trumbull, Lyman, 340, 341, 382
Tucker, Beverly, 221
Tucson, Ariz., 263
Twaite, Reuben, 77
*Twenty Years in Congress*, 346
Tyler, John, 151, 152-53, 416
Tyler, Letitia, 425
Tyler, Robert, 425

*Uncle Tom's Cabin*, 240, 307
United States Military Academy, 27, 32-49, 260
University of Virginia, 27
Ursuline College, New Orleans, 51

Van Bentheysen, Elizabeth, 50-51, 101, 103, 120, 139, 159, 186, 187, 189, 330
Van Bentheysen, Mary, 335
Van Bentheysen, William, 116-17, 130
Van Buren, Martin, 115, 133, 134
Vera Cruz, Mexico, 171, 175
*Vesuvius*, steamship, 16
Vicksburg, Miss., 18, 141-42, 157, 187, 297, 405
*Vicksburg Sentinel*, 122, 155
Villard, Oswald Garrison, 282, 283
Vincennes, Ind., 78
*Volcano*, steamship, 16

Walker, Leroy Pope, 421-22
Walker, Robert J., 123-24
Walker, Robert H., 154
Walker, William, 298
Wall, Mrs. William, 132 fn.
War of 1812, 9, 61, 63, 262
War for Independence, 4
*Warrior*, steamboat, 72, 73
*War with Mexico, The*, 165
Washburne, Elihu B., 373
Washington, D. C., 107, 115-17, 144, 145-57, 192-93
Washington, Ga., 4
Washington, George, 195, 257
Washington, Lewis, 337
Washington, Miss., 20
Wayne, H. C., 276, 277
Weatherford, Chief, 9
Webster, Daniel, 151-52, 194, 199, 201, 220, 225, 226, 227, 228, 233

Weed, Thurlow, 354, 374
Weeks, Levi, 132
West, Raphael, 109
West Feliciana Parish, La., 20, 61, 104
Wheeling, W. Va., 143
Whistler, James McNeil, 272
Whitman, Walt, 195
Wigfall, Louis Trezevant, 322, 377
Williams, Daniel, 3
Williams, Isaac, 3
Williams, Lydia Emory, 4-5
Willis, Spillman, 87
Wilmington, Del., 252, 253
Wilmot, David, 197
Wilmot Proviso, 192, 193, 197-98, 214, 223, 378
Wilson, Father, 15
Wilson, George, 59, 80-81
Wilson, Posey S., 79 fn.
Wilson, Henry, 340
Winchester, George, 125, 127, 129, 144, 187
*Winnebago*, steamship, 75
Winnebago Indians, 74
Winston, Robert, 183
Winthrop, Robert C., 310
Wise, Henry A., 338
Wood, Robert, 79, 97, 171, 189, 192, 200, 228
Wood, Sara Knox, 210
Wood, Trist, 83 fn., 96, 223 fn.
Woodville, Miss., 8, 21, 66, 138, 140
Woodville *Republican*, 231
Wool, General John E., 177, 183, 198
Worth, William J., 34, 46, 166, 167, 180, 198, 211
Wright, Crafts J., 48

Yancey, William, 230, 314, 350, 402, 406-07, 421, 422